Therapies for School Behavior Problems

A Handbook of Practical Interventions

Howard L. Millman

Charles E. Schaefer

Jeffrey J. Cohen

THERAPIES FOR SCHOOL BEHAVIOR PROBLEMS

Jossey-Bass Publishers

San Francisco • London • 1986

THERAPIES FOR SCHOOL BEHAVIOR PROBLEMS
A Handbook of Practical Interventions
by Howard L. Millman, Charles E. Schaefer, and Jeffrey J. Cohen

Copyright © 1980 by: Jossey-Bass Inc., Publishers
433 California Street
San Francisco, California 94104
&
Jossey-Bass Limited
28 Banner Street
London EC1Y 8QE

Library of Congress Cataloging in Publication Data

Millman, Howard L
    Therapies for school behavior problems.

    Bibliographies and indexes.
    1. School discipline. 2. Problem children.
3. Students—Psychology. I. Schaefer, Charles E.,
joint author. II. Cohen, Jeffrey J., joint author.
III. Title.
LB3012.M54   371.93   80-8318
ISBN 0-87589-483-6

Manufactured in the United States of America

JACKET DESIGN BY WILLI BAUM

FIRST EDITION
        First printing: November 1980
        Second printing: May 1981
        Third printing: December 1982
        Fourth printing: July 1983
        Fifth printing: May 1985
        Sixth printing: September 1986

Code 8040

The Jossey-Bass
Social and Behavioral Science Series

GUIDEBOOKS FOR THERAPEUTIC PRACTICE
Charles E. Schaefer and Howard L. Millman
Consulting Editors

Therapies for School Behavior Problems
Howard L. Millman, Charles E. Schaefer,
and Jeffrey J. Cohen
1980

Therapies for Psychosomatic Disorders in Children
Charles E. Schaefer, Howard L. Millman,
and Gary F. Levine
1979

*Therapies for Children: A Handbook of Effective
Treatments for Problem Behaviors*
Charles E. Schaefer and Howard L. Millman
1977

Therapies for Adolescents: Current Treatments
for Problem Behaviors
Michael D. Stein and J. Kent Davis
1982

Group Therapies for Children and Youth:
Principles and Practices of Group Treatment
Charles E. Schaefer, Lynnette Johnson,
and Jeffrey N. Wherry
1982

Therapies for Adults:
Depressive, Anxiety, and Personality Disorders
Howard L. Millman, Jack F. Huber,
and Dean R. Diggins
1982

Family Therapy Techniques for Problem Behaviors
of Children and Teenagers
Charles E. Schaefer, James M. Briesmeister,
and Maureen E. Fitton
1984

Therapeutic Practice in Behavioral Medicine:
A Selective Guide to Assessment, Treatment,
Clinical Issues, and Therapies for Specific Disorders
David I. Mostofsky and Ralph L. Piedmont
1985

Preface

Among the major tasks of childhood are learning and socializing in school, and problems faced by children arise very frequently in the educational process. Weaknesses within the educational system can cause problems in the child or exaggerate already existing ones. This book attempts to provide a variety of methods to reduce these problems and to enhance the psychological, social, and cognitive development of children in schools. The recent literature sets forth a large number of diverse techniques specifically applicable to school settings. But this knowledge explosion has made it difficult for professionals working with children to keep abreast of useful information. Hence, our sourcebook provides convenient access to a wide array of practical and effective approaches.

The subject index enables the reader to locate a variety of interventions designed for a specific problem area. To make the information available to the reader in the most clear and concise form, we use the method of digesting the most relevant and practical articles. In making these detailed abstracts of articles from all relevant fields, we clarified and simplified technical material whenever possible. Our goal was to make the methods usable by the wide range of professionals who work with children. The digests focus on practical, specific "how to" information. Readers should study the original articles to fully understand the theoretical and research base for the method described and to avoid any tendency to apply the technique mechanically. The exact reference for the article is listed at the end of each digest. The number of digests in each section is based on how many high-quality interventions were available in the literature. In areas with a large number of effective strategies, we selected those that best represented different approaches.

The book is directed to those who have the responsibility for dealing with problems that arise in the educational process from preschool through high school. These professionals include school psychologists, guidance counselors, social workers, psychiatrists, teachers, special educational personnel, and administrators. Schools are increasingly required to set educational and behavioral goals for children and to include specific methods for attaining these goals within a specified time. In particular, school psychologists are often required not only to diagnose problems but to outline practical intervention procedures. For example, Public Law 94-142 states that all handicapped persons must receive an education geared to their special needs. The required "individual education plan" must include a description of the methods needed to attain stated goals. This book can therefore be used as a source of specific methods for coping with behavior problems that interfere with learning and general adjustment to school. Moreover, parental awareness and use of the many methods presented would greatly enhance the coordination of efforts to help children.

We are grateful to the authors, who gave permission for their articles to be digested, as well as to Phyllis Saccone, who assisted in coordinating, assembling, and typing the manuscript.

August 1980

Howard L. Millman
Dobbs Ferry, New York

Charles E. Schaefer
Dobbs Ferry, New York

Jeffrey J. Cohen
Ardsley, New York

Contents

Preface   *ix*

The Authors   *xxv*

**Introduction: Recognizing and Dealing with
School Behavior Problems**   1

Chapter 1: Classroom Management Problems   9

Dishonest Behavior   *12*

Reducing Stealing in Second Graders—*E. B. Switzer,
T. E. Deal, and J. S. Bailey*

Increasing Admissions of Cheating—*A. S. Winston*
Controlling Stealing Through a Group Contingency—
    R. B. Brooks and D. L. Snow
Overcorrection to Eliminate Theft in a Retarded
    Population—*N. H. Azrin and M. D. Wesolowski*
Additional Readings

Truancy   24

Contingency Contracting for Truants—*B. D. Brooks*
Home Contacts to Improve School Attendance—
    D. W. Sheats and G. E. Dunkleberger
Reinforcing School Attendance in Elementary
    Students—*R. M. Barber and J. R. Kagey*
A Community-Based Program to Reduce High
    School Absenteeism—*C. Grala and C. McCauley*
Additional Readings

Cursing   39

Managing Children's Profanity in the Classroom—
    R. B. Bloom
Controlling Obscene Gestures Through Group
    Contingencies—*S. I. Sulzbacher and J. E. Houser*
Reinforcing Low Rates of Obscene Behavior—
    M. H. Epstein, A. C. Repp, and D. Cullinan
Effective Punishment for Obscene Language—
    B. B. Lahey, M. P. McNees, and M. C. McNees
Additional Readings

Classroom Disturbance   48

Classroom Disturbance: Boisterous or Rowdy Behavior   49

The Daily Report Card System—*E. H. Dougherty
    and A. Dougherty*
Three Punishment Strategies for Boisterous
    Behavior—*R. Swanson*
Positive Practice to Reduce Disruptive Behavior—
    N. H. Azrin and M. A. Powers
Additional Readings

Classroom Disturbance: Noncompliance   60

A Humanistic Approach to Discipline—*T. E. Bratter*

Modifying Disruptive Behavior by Using Delayed
  Consequences—*B. H. Salzberg, B. L. Hopkins,
  A. J. Wheeler, and L. Taylor*
Self-Directed Time-Outs to Control Behavior—
  G. A. Pease and V. O. Tyler, Jr.
Additional Readings

Classroom Disturbance: Playing the Class Clown   71

  A Combined Approach to Behavior and Academic
    Problems—*A. Chan, A. Chiu, and D. J. Mueller*
  The Effectiveness of Soft Reprimands—*K. D. O'Leary,
    K. F. Kaufman, R. E. Kass, and R. S. Drabman*
  Modifying Disruptive Behavior with Systematic
    Attention—*E. H. Zimmerman and J. Zimmerman*
  Additional Readings

Classroom Disturbance: Temper Tantrums   80

  Reducing Temper Tantrums in an Elementary
    Classroom—*C. S. Carlson, C. R. Arnold,
    W. C. Becker, and C. H. Madsen*
  Integrating Psychodynamic and Reinforcement
    Strategies to Reduce Disruptiveness—*F. M.
    Culbertson*
  Additional Readings

Classroom Disturbance: Annoying or Bothering Others   87

  I-Messages in the Classroom—*R. F. Peterson,
    S. E. Loveless, T. J. Knapp, B. W. Loveless,
    S. M. Basta, and S. Anderson*
  Reducing Disruptions by Increasing Academic
    Performance—*T. Ayllon and M. D. Roberts*
  Teaching Self-Control to a Disruptive Student—
    R. Epstein and C. M. Goss
  Additional Readings

*Classroom Disturbance: Out-of-Seat (Off-Task)
Behavior*   96

  Grandma's Rule for Classroom Management—*R. J.
    Cowen, F. H. Jones, and A. S. Bellack*
  A DRL Schedule to Reduce Out-of-Seat Behavior—
    S. M. Dietz and A. C. Repp

Goal Setting and Self-Monitoring in the Classroom—
G. Sagotsky, C. J. Patterson, and M. R. Lepper
Additional Readings

Destructive Behavior   *107*

Negative Reinforcement to Control Disruptive
Behavior—*T. H. Wasserman*
Group and Individual Response-Cost Strategies—
S. Axelrod
The Good Behavior Game with Unruly Students—
M. R. Johnson, P. F. Turner, and E. A. Konarski
Reinforcing Improved Behavior with a DRL
Schedule—*S. M. Deitz, D. J. Slack, E. B.
Schwarzmueller, A. P. Wilander, T. J. Weatherly,
and G. Hilliard*
Additional Readings

Chapter 2: Immature Behaviors   **119**

Hyperactivity   *121*

Self-Instruction for Overactivity—*P. H. Bornstein
and R. P. Quevillon*
Relaxation and Exercise for Hyperactivity—*S. A.
Klein and J. L. Deffenbacher*
Behavioral Treatment of Hyperkinesis—*K. D. O'Leary,
W. E. Pelham, A. Rosenbaum, and G. H. Price*
Behavioral Intervention with Hyperactive Children—
H. T. Prout
Hyperactivity and Artificial Food Colors—*T. L. Rose*
Covert Positive Reinforcement in Treating
Hyperactivity—*E. A. Workman and D. J. Dickinson*
Environmental Stimulation—*S. S. Zentall*
Additional Readings

Distractible and Inattentive Behavior   *142*

Teacher Attention to Increase Student Attention—
*M. Broden, C. Bruce, M. A. Mitchell, V. Carter,
and R. V. Hall*
Increasing Attention with a "Workclock"—*V. T.
Devine and J. R. Tomlinson*

Teaching Learning Skills to Disturbed, Delinquent
Children—*S. Minuchin, P. Chamberlain, and
P. Graubard*
Group Counseling for Inattentiveness—*R. D.
Myrick and F. D. Kelly*
Classroom Management Techniques for Increasing
Attention—*J. T. Simmons and B. H. Wasik*
An Ecological Approach to Disruptive Classroom
Behavior—*S. M. Swap*
Positive Reinforcement for Conditioning Attention—
H. M. Walker and N. K. Buckley
Contingency Management for Increasing Attention—
A. E. Woolfolk and R. L. Woolfolk
Additional Readings

Impulsiveness   165

Modifying Impulsive Tempo—*D. Cullinan, M. H.
Epstein, and L. Silver*
Improving Efficiency in Impulsive Children—
*G. Digate, M. H. Epstein, D. Cullinan, and
H. N. Switzky*
Cognitive Training to Reduce Impulsiveness—
*V. I. Douglass, P. Parry, P. Marton, and
C. Garson*
Reinstatement for Increased Self-Control—
D. H. Karpowitz
Modifying Impulsiveness in the Classroom—
H. Margolis, G. G. Brannigan, and M. A. Poston
Self-Directed Verbal Commands for Hyperactive
Impulsive Behavior—*H. Palkes, M. Stewart, and
B. Kahana*
Improving Impulse Control Through Fantasy
Training—*E. Saltz, D. Dixon, and J. Johnson*
Additional Readings

Messy and Sloppy Behavior   187

Anti-Litter Procedures—*R. L. Burgess, R. N. Clark,
and J. C. Hendee*
Modifying Preschoolers' Bathroom Behavior—
M. J. Taylor and T. R. Kratochwill
Additional Readings

Daydreaming   *194*

Reinforcing Improved Classroom Behavior—
R. N. Alexander and C. H. Apfel
Using a Student to Modify Behavior—P. R. Surratt,
R. E. Ulrich, and R. P. Hawkins
Additional Readings

Procrastination and Dawdling   *199*

Behavior Consultation for Increasing Assignment
Completion—H. Farber and G. R. Mayer
Modifying Lethargic Behavior—A. J. La Pray and
J. Chipman
Intrinsic Reinforcers for Assignment Completion—
T. F. McLaughlin and J. Malaby
Additional Readings

Poor Coordination   *208*

Motor-Sensory Training with Music—
S. de Vincentis and L. Johnson
Treating Perceptual-Motor Disorders—B. B. Lahey,
M. K. Busemeyer, C. O'Hara, and V. E. Beggs
Kinetic Family Drawings—L. M. Raskin and
G. Pitcher-Baker
Additional Readings

Crying   *218*

Reducing Crying by Social Reinforcement—B. M.
Hart, K. E. Allen, J. S. Buell, F. R. Harris, and
M. M. Wolf
Overcorrection of Crying and Hitting—T. H.
Ollendick and J. L. Matson
Time-Outs for Crying—S. K. Teel
Additional Reading

Chapter 3: Insecure Behaviors   **225**

Anxiety and Tension   *228*

Self-Control Training—S. D. Brown
A Rational-Emotive Program in the School—
R. Digiuseppe and H. Kassinove

Contents

The School Psychologist's Role with Anxious
Children—*G. T. Doyal and R. J. Friedman*

Reducing Test Anxiety by Psychodrama and
Systematic Desensitization—*D. A. Kipper and
D. Giladi*

Using the Classroom for Desensitization—*R. J.
Kravetz and S. R. Forness*

Meditation for Reducing Test Anxiety—*W. Linden*

Desensitizing Anxiety to Improve Reading—*S. D.
Muller and C. H. Madsen, Jr.*

Relaxation Through Yoga—*G. Seiler and
K. Renshaw*

Psychogenic Illness in the Schools—*V. M. Thompson*

Additional Readings

Phobias   *255*

Rehabilitating School-Phobic Adolescents—
C. J. G. Cretekos

Natural Consequences and a Makeup Period for
Eliminating School Phobia—*D. M. Doleys and
S. C. Williams*

Paraprofessional Treatment of School Phobia—
A. LeUnes and S. Siemsglusz

An Overview of School Phobias—*J. E. McDonald
and G. Sheperd*

Implosive Therapy for a Bodily Injury Phobia—
T. H. Ollendick and G. E. Gruen

Desensitizing School Fears—*H. T. Prout and
J. R. Harvey*

Automated Direct Deconditioning of a Phobia—
P. A. Wish, J. E. Hasazi, and A. R. Jurgela

Additional Readings

Compulsive-Perfectionistic Behavior   *276*

Behavioral Treatment of Childhood Neurosis—
T. Ayllon, S. W. Garber, and M. G. Allison

Using a Relationship with the Teacher to Increase
Socially Appropriate Behavior—*G. G. Brannigan
and R. Reimondi*

Sensory Extinction of Compulsiveness—*A. Rincover,
C. D. Newsom, and E. G. Carr*

Additional Readings

Poor Self-Esteem   *285*

Success Counseling to Build Self-Concept—*K. R. Washington*

Self-Concept Change Through Art Counseling— *K. White and R. Allen*

Teaching Self-Concept to Preadolescents—*J. L. Schulman, R. C. Ford, and P. Busk*

Reinforcing Positive Self-Esteem in Elementary School Children—*N. Hauserman, J. S. Miller, and F. T. Bond*

Attribution and Self-Concept Improvement— *R. L. Miller, P. Brickman, and D. Bolen*

Self-Esteem and an Alternative School— *M. Strathe and V. Hash*

Additional Readings

Gender Disturbance   *302*

Modifying Self-Role Behaviors and Attitudes— *R. D. Myrick*

Treating Gender-Identity Problems in a Young Boy—*G. A. Rekers, O. I. Lovaas, and B. Low*

Additional Readings

Depression   *309*

Childhood Depression and the School Psychologist— *R. J. Friedman and G. T. Doyal*

Cognitive-Behavioral Therapy for Depression—*A. J. Rush, M. Khatami, and A. T. Beck*

Additional Readings

Elective Mutism   *316*

Guidelines for Managing Elective Mutism— *R. Friedman and N. Karagan*

Classroom Treatment of Elective Mutism—*R. W. Colligan, R. C. Colligan, and M. K. Dilliard*

Additional Readings

Chapter 4: Habit Disorders   **325**

Poor Academic Performance

A Home-School Reinforcement Program to Improve Academic Performance—*R. J. Karraker*

Goal Setting to Enhance Learning—*D. C. Gardner and P. L. Gardner*
Self-Management of Academic Performance—*L. L. Humphrey, P. Karoly, and D. S. Kirschenbaum*
Encouraging Achievement Through Positive Grading Practices—*R. A. Brown and J. Epstein*
Reality Therapy and Underachievement—*H. Margolis, C. Muhlfelder, and G. Brannigan*
The Principal's Influence on Academic Performance—*R. E. Copeland, R. E. Brown, and R. V. Hall*
Behavior Modification in an Open Classroom—*D. Ascare and S. Axelrod*
The Helper Therapy Principle—*J. A. Durlak*
Self-Recording Study Rate—*M. Broden, R. V. Hall, and B. Mitts*
Additional Readings

Enuresis-Encopresis 355

Treatment of Soiling in a Resource Room Setting—*T. W. George, J. Coleman, and P. Williams*
Behavioral Treatment of Encopresis—*E. A. Scott*
Additional Readings

Masturbation 364

Reducing Excessive Masturbation at Home and School—*L. N. Ferguson and G. A. Rekers*
Punishing Public Masturbation—*J. W. Cook, K. Altman, J. Shaw, and M. Blaylock*
Overcorrection to Eliminate Masturbation—*J. K. Luiselli, C. S. Helfen, B. W. Pemberton, and J. Reisman*
Additional Reading

Thumb-Sucking/Nail-Biting 372

Controlling Thumb-Sucking Through Social Reinforcement—*E. A. Skiba, L. E. Pettigrew, and S. E. Alden*
A Group Contingency to Eliminate Thumb-Sucking—*J. A. Ross and B. A. Levine*
Habit Reversal Training to Eliminate Nail-Biting—*R. G. Nunn and N. H. Azrin*

Cue-Controlled Relaxation for Nail-Biting—
B. A. Barrios
Additional Readings

Speech Disorders   *383*

Reinforcing Verbal Fluency in Stutterers—*W. H.
Manning, P. A. Trutna, and C. K. Shaw*
Shaping Audible Speech in a Special Education
Student—*T. Evans, L. Pierce, R. York, and
L. Brown*
A Time-Out Procedure for Young Stutterers—
R. R. Martin, P. Kuhl, and S. Haroldson
Additional Readings

Substance Abuse   *396*

Drug Prevention in Elementary Schools—*O. W.
Sadler and N. R. Dillard*
Drug Education for High School Students—*J. D.
Swishĕr, R. W. Warner, Jr., and E. L. Herr*
Relaxation Training and Drug Abuse—*B. W.
Bergland and A. H. Chal*
Smoking Prevention Programs for High School
Students—*J. S. Greenberg and Z. Deputat*
Additional Readings

Sexual Behavior   *408*

Pregnancy Prevention for Adolescents—*S. P.
Schinke and L. D. Gilchrist*
A Cognitive-Behavioral Approach to Pregnancy
Prevention—*S. P. Schinke, L. D. Gilchrist, and
R. W. Small*
Values Clarification in Venereal Disease Prevention
Programs—*D. Breckon and D. Sweeney*
Sex Information Through Peer-Group Contacts—
M. A. Carrera
Additional Readings

Chapter 5: Disturbed Peer Relationships   **421**

Aggression   *424*

Psychosituational Classroom Intervention (PCI)—
*J. I. Bardon, V. C. Bennett, P. K. Bruchez, and
R. A. Sanderson*

Contents

Developing Self-Control in Aggressive Children—
*B. W. Camp, G. E. Blom, F. Hebert, and W. J.
van Doorninck*

Decreasing Aggression in Kindergarten Children—
T. Grieger, J. M. Kauffman, and R. M. Grieger

Effective Use of Punishment in the Classroom—
*R. V. Hall, S. Axelrod, M. Foundopoulos,
J. Shellman, R. A. Campbell, and S. S. Cranston*

What to Do About Aggression—*J. Hendrick*

Classical Conditioning and Childhood Aggression—
T. S. Parish, J. Maly, and A. M. Shirazi

Direct Intervention for Classroom Aggression—
G. R. Patterson, J. A. Cobb, and R. S. Ray

A Time-Out Procedure in a Public School—
R. E. Webster

Additional Readings

Prejudice   *449*

Modification of Racial Prejudice in White
Children—*P. A. Katz and S. R. Zalk*

Changing the Racial Attitudes of Children—
T. S. Parish and R. S. Fleetwood

Integrating the Desegregated Classroom—
R. E. Slavin

Effects of Cooperative Interethnic Contact—
R. H. Weigel, P. L. Wiser, and S. W. Cook

Additional Readings

Shyness and Withdrawal   *459*

Effects of Social Reinforcement on a Withdrawn
Preschooler—*K. E. Allen, B. M. Hart, J. S. Buell,
F. R. Harris, and M. M. Wolf*

Social Skills Training for Unassertive Children—
M. R. Bornstein, A. S. Bellack, and M. Hersen

Modifying Social Withdrawal in Preschoolers—
W. Evers-Pasquale and M. Sherman

Use of Teacher Prompts and Attention to Increase
a Child's Social Interaction—*E. M. Goetz, C. L.
Thomson, and B. C. Etzel*

Increasing Cooperative Play of a Preschool Child—
*B. M. Hart, N. J. Reynolds, D. M. Baer, E. R.
Brawley, and F. R. Harris*

The Teacher and the Withdrawn Child—*O. G.*
Johnson
Promoting Cooperation in Preschoolers—*R. G.*
Slaby and C. G. Crowly
Additional Readings

Social Isolation   477

Treating Extreme Social Withdrawal in Nursery
School Children—*H. J. Kandel, T. Ayllon, and*
M. S. Rosenbaum
Effect of Peer Interaction on the Withdrawn
Behavior of Preschoolers—*P. S. Strain, R. E.*
Shores, and M. A. Timm
Additional Reading

Chapter 6: Disturbed Relationships with Teachers   483

Disrespect and Defiance   485

Special Classes for Disruptive Children—*T. W. Allen*
Student Behavior in Alternate Schools—*D. L. Duke*
and C. Perry
Family Psychotherapy for a Disruptive Boy—*S. Kaplan*
Transactional Analysis for Classroom Management—
K. J. Kravas and C. H. Kravas
Treatment of Aggression in a Sixteen-Year-Old Male—
J. P. McCullough, G. M. Huntsinger, and W. R. Nay
Additional Reading

Inhibition   500

Reinforcing Student Participation in Class
Discussions—*R. E. Hosford*
Testing a Severely Inhibited Child—*E. G. Tava*
Helping a Child Speak Up in Class—*B. B. Varenhorst*

Overdependency   505

Effects of Teacher Social Reinforcement—*F. R.*
Harris, M. M. Wolf, and D. M. Baer
Intensive Therapeutic Programs for Prepubertal
Children—*M. West, M. Carlin, B. Baserman, and*
M. Milstein

Author Index   509

Subject Index   518

The Authors

Howard L. Millman is the director of Psychological and Educational Services of Westchester, which provides an integrated approach to learning, behavioral, and psychological problems. For the past eleven years, he has been the director of the Department of Psychological Services and Research at The Children's Village, a residential treatment center in Dobbs Ferry, New York. Millman received the Ph.D. degree in clinical psychology from Adelphi University and completed a clinical psychology internship at the Neuropsychiatric Institute at the University of California at Los Angeles. For several years, he was the chief psychologist at the Middlesex County Mental Health Clinic in New Jersey. He has taught and supervised doctoral psychology students at Rutgers—the State University and at the City College of New York. Currently, he is a member of the Division of Psychotherapy of the American Psychological Association and the Council for Exceptional Children.

Millman has published numerous articles in professional journals concerning learning disabilities, psychotherapy, and program evaluation. He is the coauthor of *Therapies for Psychosomatic Disorders in Children* (with C. E. Schaefer and G. F. Levine, 1979), *Therapies for Children* (with C. E. Schaefer, 1977), and *Goals and Behavior in Psychotherapy and Counseling* (with J. T. Huber, 1972).

Charles E. Schaefer has been a supervising psychologist at The Children's Village for the past ten years. He also maintains a private practice for children and their families. He received his Ph.D. degree in clinical psychology from Fordham University, where he conducted postdoctoral research on the identification and development of creative thinking in children and adolescents.

Schaefer is the author or coauthor of eight books about child therapy, parenting, and creativity: *Therapies for Psychosomatic Disorders in Children* (1979), *How to Influence Children: A Handbook of Practical Parenting Skills* (1978), *Therapies for Children* (1977), *Therapeutic Use of Child's Play* (1976), *Developing Creativity in Children* (1973), *Becoming Somebody: Creative Activities for Preschool and Primary Grade Children* (1973), and *Young Voices: An Anthology of Poetry by Children* (1971). He is also the author of numerous psychological tests and articles in professional journals.

Schaefer's current professional interests center on the identification and development of effective child management techniques for the prevention and reduction of behavior problems in youth. His affiliations include fellow in the American Orthopsychiatric Association and member of the American Psychological Association, American Educational Research Association, and Psychologists in Private Practice.

Jeffrey J. Cohen is a school psychologist in the Ardsley Union Free School District in New York, where, among other projects, he has designed and implemented educational and therapeutic programs for learning disabled preadolescents. As a result of this work, he has developed a deep interest in the psychological and emotional problems of learning impaired students. He also supervises doctoral interns in school psychological practice. He received his Ph.D. degree in school psychology from Hofstra University in 1971.

From 1969 to 1975, Cohen taught undergraduate courses at Hofstra University. Since 1975 he has been an adjunct faculty member at Mercy College in Dobbs Ferry, New York, teaching primarily on the graduate level. He currently has several articles forthcoming on cross-sex friendships in children; he plans to continue research in this area. Cohen is a member of the Division of School Psychology of the American Psychological Association and the National Association of School Psychologists.

To closer interdisciplinary collaboration
among mental health professionals, teachers,
and school administrators

Therapies for
School Behavior
Problems

A Handbook
of Practical Interventions

Introduction: Recognizing and Dealing with School Behavior Problems

A recent study found that 23 to 31 percent of children in elementary schools were judged by their teachers to have behavior problems (Rubin and Balow, 1978). Also noteworthy is the finding that self-esteem of children steadily *decreases* from grades 3 to 11. In a recent national survey (Foundation for Child Development, 1978), schoolwork was found to be a source of anxiety, shame, frustration, and unhappiness for a majority of children aged seven through eleven. Approximately two thirds worry about tests and feel ashamed of making mistakes. Almost half feel angry when they have trouble learning new material.

1

In the past decade, there has been increasing concern about the behaviors that children act out in schools (particularly in middle and high schools). Teachers frequently complain that they spend more time trying to control students than teaching them. Administrators are concerned about problems ranging from chronic truancy to assaults on teachers. Students express fear of walking in school corridors and of losing property. Drug use and gang activities in schools have made recent newspaper headlines. Teachers and parents are very concerned about the frequent lack of respect for authority and the apparent lack of discipline in schools. Thus, the goal of our book is to highlight ways to prevent and solve this broad spectrum of behavior problems.

Unfortunately, there is no unanimity in grouping or even in describing problem behaviors. We have somewhat arbitrarily grouped problem behaviors into six broad categories: Classroom Management Problems, Immature Behaviors, Insecure Behaviors, Habit Disorders, Disturbed Peer Relationships, and Disturbed Relationships with Teachers. Each of these is treated in a separate chapter.

Teachers as Change Agents

Recent legislation (Public Law 94-142) mandates a mainstreaming process in which handicapped children are to be educated in the least restrictive environment possible. This development places increased demands upon teachers' management and therapeutic skills. Frequently, however, teachers avoid dealing intensively with the problems of their students. Their rationale is that they are not trained therapists or that they are too busy to deal even with one or two disturbed children. In fact, however, teachers are forced to spend a great deal of time contending with behavior problems that interfere with teaching and academic learning in the classroom. Since teachers are often poorly trained to cope with behavior problems, it is not unusual for their methods to be ineffective, negative, and even physically abusive at times. Rather than helping to improve classroom problems, such discipline methods may actually exaggerate them.

Teachers as change agents are a potentially powerful but largely untapped force. Rather than referring a child to a mental health clinic or independent professional, teachers can learn to deal more effectively with problem behaviors as they occur in the classroom. Positive change can be achieved by teachers with the help of recent advances in effective strategies. Often the first to detect a child's behavior problems, a teacher is in a unique position to alter that behavior immediately in the natural environment of the classroom.

Teachers are also facing more active parent involvement. Parents not only want to know how their child is doing in school, but they also seek advice from, and sometimes offer assistance to, teachers. But there is often a lack of rapport between parent and teacher that must be overcome if constructive communication is to occur. Recognizing the importance of parent-teacher interactions, many authors (Kroth and Simpson, 1977; Losen and Diament, 1978; Rutherford, 1979) have presented strategies for increasing cooperative efforts between teachers and parents, such as parent-teacher conferences that result in specific plans of action agreed upon by all parties.

At present, the most widely used therapeutic approaches in the classroom are based upon learning theory and are popularly called behavior modification. Teachers alter antecedents (elements that come before or cause a problem) and/or consequences in order to change behavior. Point systems in the classroom have been effective in changing social and academic behaviors in all kinds of children. Other widely used techniques that are described in this book include values clarification, life-space interviewing, role playing, and discussion groups.

If behavior problems were prevented or identified early enough in school, untold effort and anguish could be avoided. The school is in a uniquely influential position to promote adjustment and mental health. Budget limitations notwithstanding, legislators show interest in programs that provide for early identification of problems in schools. When problems are found too late, a pattern has already been set, and secondary consequences can be very negative (Cowen, 1971). The label "maladjusted" sets up negative expectations and self-fulfilling prophecies. Early school experiences set the tone for determining later adaptations. Removal of a child from school makes an adequate adjustment upon return more difficult. Cowen recommends early identification of problems and modification of the school environment to facilitate adaptation by children. What is most important here is the strengthening of teacher management skills. The methods described in our book, along with aid from consultants when necessary, can greatly enhance teacher effectiveness. Many outstanding methods developed in clinical research studies have been, or could be, carried out by teachers. These methods are often not inordinately time consuming, and with adequate preparation most teachers can become proficient in their use. Escalation of problems can be prevented when intervention is immediate and decisive.

Human Ecology

Ecology is the scientific study of the totality or pattern of relationships between individuals and their environment. Rather than simply talking about a disturbed child, we refer to a disturbed ecological system. The school system itself may cause or contribute to the development of behavior disorders. Kauffman (1977) notes that school personnel may be insensitive to children's individuality and that there may be little tolerance for children who are "different," as well as a lack of flexibility in approaches to them. The inappropriate expectations of many teachers regarding "dumb," "bad," or "crazy" children are well documented. A frequent complaint of children is that instruction is irrelevant to their interests and that they are taught nonfunctional skills. Many teachers are unable to be relatively consistent, and many do not provide a predictable structure. In a similar vein, reinforcement contingencies are often inappropriate; that is, teachers inadvertently reinforce (pay attention to) inappropriate behavior and do not reinforce desirable behavior. And there has been increasing recognition that a negative tone set by a principal can exacerbate behavior problems.

Redl (1956), moreover, has pointed out that many school behavior problems result from problems in group structure rather than from individual difficulties. Frequently, there is dissatisfaction with subject matter, and assignments are considered too difficult or too easy. Interpersonal relations are often poor, and the result is tension and the forming of cliques. The grouping process may be too heterogeneous or homogeneous to provide for balanced, positive peer interaction. The group climate may foster punitiveness, hostility, and competition. Finally, there may be organizational mistakes such as autocratic leadership, a lack of security, inconsistencies, and standards that are too high or too low.

Problems in group structure are also discussed by Warner and Hansen (1970). They point out that school goals often have no meaning to students, who feel that school is irrelevant to their present or future lives. Unless students conform, they are not considered to be worthwhile. Warner and Hansen state that school environments should be modified for these disenchanted students and alternative types of education provided. Opportunities for self-expression should be greatly increased. A useful overview regarding important aspects of classroom social climate is provided by Manderscheid, Koenig, and Silbergeld (1977): (1) affect set (emotional climate) is the student's perception of the classroom environment, especially his or her sense of freedom; (2) personal development is the process of the individual's perception of attaining personal goals; (3) system maintenance is a climate of perceived stability of day-to-day functioning; and (4) the perceived quality of interpersonal relations is a key factor in determining a positive or negative atmosphere.

Having briefly reviewed ecological concerns, we turn to some possible methods for improving classroom and school climate. The powerful effect of interpersonal relations has often been neglected in designing classroom groupings (Thelen, 1967). Teachers and pupils tend to be mismatched in terms of their personalities and preferences. Studies have been conducted in which teachers rated the different student characteristics that they included in their personal definitions of "teachability." Classes chosen and taught according to this selection process showed greater group cohesion and were more manageable and work oriented than control groups. Additionally, they were more attentive, less distractible, and received higher grades. Most striking were the different characteristics selected. Some teachers want to be very personally involved with students, while others prefer to have students who are deeply interested in the subject matter. Some teachers want a class that moves quickly through material, while others want a friendly, but not very work-oriented, group. A selection process by teachers could avoid blatant personality clashes and could allow some students to be with the teachers best for them.

In terms of group interaction, Boocock (1966) suggests that schools often do not use peer influence constructively. A given student's behavior is greatly influenced by peers, whose attitudes are often at variance with the learning and achievement goals of the schools. In a number of studies, older students have been effectively used to tutor or counsel younger pupils. Moreover, academic games and team projects designed to enhance peer relations and promote positive attitudes toward learning have proved effective.

Positive or negative feelings directly influence academic learning as well as attitudes and behavior. In a recent study (Masters, Barden, and Ford, 1979) positive feelings were shown to enhance learning while negative feelings dramatically retarded learning. Children were taught to use their imagination to think of something that made them happy or sad. This use of thought to induce an emotional state is called affect induction and is similar to rational-emotive approaches in which thought is used to correct negative emotions brought on by illogical thinking. Positive affect increased children's interest in learning, while negative feelings decreased positive arousal for learning. Emotional states clearly influence adaptive learning (including nonintellectual social learning). Attention to tasks and striving for success are also increased when children feel happy. Strikingly, positive emotional states enhance the effectiveness of social reinforcers (especially feedback regarding performance). Therefore, praise or rewards from a teacher are more effective when children feel relatively happy. Conversely, negative emotional states directly interfere with learning. Attention is diverted from tasks to the self, and there is little incentive for mastery.

All those involved in education should find a recent book about group processes in the school (Schmuck and Schmuck,

1975) extremely useful. It defines group interaction at different organizational levels and offers practical techniques for influencing group processes in positive ways. This book pulls together the various concerns expressed above in that it covers classroom climate, expectations (self-fulfilling prophecies), leadership (roles of teacher and students in influencing the group), attraction (patterns of liking and friendship), norms, communication, cohesiveness, and sequential stages of group development. On an organizational level, according to Schmuck and Schmuck, there should be joint decision making among administrators, teachers, parents, and students in influencing school management. Increased collaboration can lead to clarification of educational issues, reduced conflicts, and discovery of new resources. Such organizational problem solving is often neglected (Runkel and others, 1979), and there is often a vicious cycle of organizational difficulties and overwhelmed, ineffective reactions. It is in a cooperative spirit that schools should address and try to solve organizational problems that contribute to the behavior problems of students.

References

Boocock, S. S. "Toward a Sociology of Learning: Peer-Group Effects on Student Performance." *Sociology of Education,* 1966, *39,* 26-32.

Cowen, E. L. "Coping with School Adaptation Problems." *Psychology in The Schools,* 1971, *8,* 322-329.

Foundation for Child Development. "National Survey of Children." New York: Foundation for Child Development, 1978.

Kauffman, J. M. "Characteristics of Children's Behavior Disorders." Columbus, Ohio: Merrill, 1977.

Kroth, R. L. and Simpson, R. L. "Parent Conferences as a Teaching Strategy." Denver: Love, 1977.

Losen, S. M. and Diament, B. "Parent Conferences in the Schools." Boston: Allyn & Bacon, 1978.

Manderscheid, R. W., Koenig, G. R., and Silbergeld, S. "Dimensions of Classroom Psychosocial Environment." *American Journal of Community Psychology,* 1977, *5,* 299-306.

Masters, J. C., Barden, R. C., and Ford, M. E. "Affective States,

Expressive Behavior, and Learning in Children." *Journal of Personality and Social Psychology,* 1979, *37,* 380-389.

Redl, F. "What Most Frequently Goes Wrong in School Groups." In F. Redl and G. Sheviakov (Eds.), *Discipline for Today's Children and Youth.* Washington, D.C.: National Education Association, 1956.

Rubin, R. A., and Balow, B. "Prevalence of Teacher-Identified Behavior Problems." *Exceptional Children,* 1978, *45,* 102-111.

Runkel, P. J., and others. "Transforming the School's Capacity for Problem Solving." Eugene, Ore.: Center for Educational Policy and Management, 1979.

Rutherford, R. B. *Teachers and Parents: A Guide to Interaction and Cooperation.* Boston: Allyn & Bacon, 1979.

Schmuck, R. A., and Schmuck, P. A. *Group Processes in the Classroom.* Dubuque, Iowa: Brown, 1975.

Thelen, H. A. *Classroom Grouping for Teachability.* New York: Wiley, 1967.

Warner, R. W., and Hansen, J. C. "Alienated Youth: A Counselor's Task." *Personnel and Guidance Journal,* 1970, *48,* 443-448.

1 Classroom Management Problems

In the 1979 Gallup poll of public attitudes toward education, discipline was seen as the most significant problem facing the public schools. People are increasingly concerned about the apparent lack of control teachers have over students in their classes—a concern reflected in the call for corporal punishment in the schools. Truancy and vandalism rates among students have increased, as have reports of physical assaults on teachers. When teachers talk of "burnout," they are referring to the stress associated with day-to-day threats to their classroom control and to their physical safety.

Numerous reasons have been advanced for the increase in disruptive student behaviors. Blame has been focused on the

9

school itself for its laxity in enforcing regulations for proper conduct. Some writers fault the school for creating an atmosphere that stifles creativity, rewards conformity, and breeds alienation and mistrust. Others look to the "do your own thing" philosophy of the sixties as having resulted in a self-centered generation of students in the seventies and a loss of community and group spirit. They view the past decade as a period in which personal needs were considered all-important and in which any behavior was justified to satisfy selfish desires. Still others regard the breakdown of the family unit and the loss of family stability as a major factor in increased disruptiveness. Divorce, remarriage, and single parenthood have been seen as disrupting the traditional family bonds and thus making it more difficult to teach children responsible behavior. Finally, economic issues have been implicated in the problem. The stress felt by families struggling to "make ends meet" has been seen as aggravating feelings of uncertainty about the future. For some students, this insecurity may have found expression in classroom disruptiveness. Whatever the reasons for this, it is clear that indiscriminate punishment, moralizing, lecturing, threats, suspension, and expulsion have had little positive effect on school behavior disturbances.

More has been written about controlling disruptive behavior in the classroom than about any other school behavior problem. This emphasis clearly reflects the concerns of teachers, parents, and the public. The results of many studies have identified specific strategies that teachers can use to control classroom behavior. Furthermore, with the array of techniques available, the matching of a particular technique to a particular problem has become an important element of program planning. The selection of certain strategies may depend on such issues as the seriousness or danger of the behavior, its frequency, its effect on academic progress, ethical considerations, parental cooperation, the number of target students, the classroom environment, teacher skill and cooperation, administrative support, and the availability of time and space.

Once these issues have been examined, the practitioner can choose among group or individual contingencies, teacher controlled or student-controlled strategies, reward or punishment approaches, natural classroom reinforcers or artificial ones, time-outs, response-cost procedures, home-school programs, praise/ignore techniques, I-messages, rule setting, and other interventions. In short, the variety and sophistication of available programs make careful planning and judgment a necessity. For example, if a group contingency is selected, it is important to determine whether each child is capable of displaying the desired behavior. If not, the continuous social pressure on the less able child may be harmful. Two points are crucial. First, it is advisable to begin with the least intrusive strategies and move to more powerful ones only as the situation demands it. Second, when techniques are applied systematically, they should allow the teacher to do more teaching and praising and less reprimanding and punishing.

In this chapter, the section on Classroom Disturbance has been further divided into six subsections. This was done for the convenience of the reader and to make the point that disruptiveness can be displayed in various ways. However, it is important to note that the techniques described under a particular subsection are often applicable to other subsections. Furthermore, the target behaviors in many of the articles overlap with one another; in real life, behavior is not neatly categorized. The reader should keep in mind that the overall intent was to select the widest variety of techniques for a given section.

A final point should be made. Studies have shown that reducing inappropriate behavior in the classroom does not necessarily affect behavior at home. The same finding is true in reverse. Each setting has its own unique characteristics, and there is no reason to expect that improvement in one location will automatically carry over to the other. Interventions must be specifically designed to promote generalization of gains over time and space.

Dishonest Behavior

Dishonesty covers the three areas of lying, stealing, and cheating. Research on dishonesty has not been prolific because of the difficulty in observing and recording these behaviors. Lying may occur as an innocent form of imaginative wish fulfillment or as a more serious disturbance in moral development. It may also reflect fear of failure, fear of a punitive, insensitive parent, or a disturbed capacity to distinguish reality from fantasy. Stealing may result from a momentary lack of judgment or from misdirected peer influence. It may also represent hostility toward parents, an attempt to win attention (or love), or a plea for assistance with a problem. Cheating too may symbolize fear of failure, an attempt to defy authority, or, if done to get caught, a call for help.

Reducing Stealing in Second Graders

AUTHORS: E. Beth Switzer, Terrence E. Deal, and Jon S. Bailey

PRECIS: Using group reward and punishment to control the theft of classroom items

INTRODUCTION: Stealing is difficult to control because the guilty student often remains unknown. Teachers will typically punish an entire class for a missing item or lecture on the value of honesty. Threats are also used but are rarely effective in preventing thefts. In this case, the school psychologist was asked to intervene to stop stealing episodes in several second-grade classes. Teachers complained that items such as pencils, toys, and money were being stolen daily from students and teachers. The psychologist developed a group contingency strategy in which rewards and punishments were given for the behavior of the entire class.

METHOD: Each day throughout the treatment, items such as nickels, erasers, magic-markers, gum, and pens were placed around each classroom at various natural locations. Observers recorded the number of items stolen or returned during a ninety-minute period each morning. After pretreatment stealing rates had been recorded for a number of weeks, teachers in two classes gave an anti-stealing lecture in the morning, once every five days. The teacher told the class that if they wanted to be good boys and girls (and she knew they did), they should remember not to take things that didn't belong to them, not to make up stories, and not to cheat from another student's paper. After about two weeks, a group contingency was introduced, and a third class, which did not receive an anti-stealing lecture was included. Each day the teacher announced that if nothing was missing during the morning, the students would have ten minutes of free time after their snack. After the morning period, the students were praised and were reminded that they would have free time if no stealing had occurred. If something was missing, the teacher acknowledged the theft and told the class, "I am going to leave the room; if you return _____ by putting it on my desk, then you will be able to talk during your snack as usual. If _____ is not returned, then you will have to sit quietly while you eat your snack and lay your hands on your desks when you have finished." She then left the room for a few minutes and delivered the appropriate consequence upon returning.

The lecture on dishonesty had no effect on either class, while the group contingency immediately reduced stealing in all three classes. It was noted that no hostile or negative comments were passed among students during this phase and that no undue pressure was placed on any student, as is sometimes anticipated when group contingencies are introduced. Interestingly, there was also a reduction in the stealing of items not placed by the psychologist.

COMMENTARY: While the group contingency was successful without increasing social pressure on any student, the authors urge caution if this procedure is used with older children. Peer pressure increases in intensity as adolescence approaches, and steps might be needed to reduce the possibility of hostile behavior toward a suspected thief. For example, in this study, few children returned stolen items, and the "return" procedure seemed to have little effect on the results. Removing this step (which requires a public action) might reduce the scapegoating of a particular student, while maintaining the group contingency effect. While the authors recognize the difficulty in designing treatments for unknown students, this paper demonstrates the feasibility of controlling stealing in younger students through a behavioral strategy.

SOURCE: Switzer, E. B., Deal, T. E., and Bailey, J. S. "The Reduction of Stealing in Second Graders Using a Group Contingency." *Journal of Applied Behavior Analysis*, 1977, *10*, 267-272.

Increasing Admissions of Cheating

AUTHOR: Andrew S. Winston

PRECIS: Assessing the effect of praise and punishment on cheating and admission of cheating

INTRODUCTION: Children who admit to cheating may be rewarded for truthfulness, punished for their admission, or both. They may also try to avoid punishment by denying cheating; they may, however, be punished anyway if the adult thinks that cheating occurred. In this paper, the author examined the effects of adult praise and punishment on the cheating behaviors of three elementary school boys aged ten to twelve. The boys occasionally cheated in class, denied their cheating, and were observed to cheat in the early sessions of this study.

METHOD: The study was performed in class during the regular math period. Three twenty-minute sessions were conducted each week. The child sat in a corner of the classroom and was presented with twenty math problems taken from his math workbook. Each problem was displayed individually as a multiple-choice question in an apparatus that allowed an observer to monitor correct answers, as well as cheating behavior. At the first session, the child was shown how to use the apparatus and was cautioned against cheating (the apparatus was designed to make cheating easy). Two points were awarded for each right answer as part of the regular classroom token reinforcement program. When each session began, the rule against cheating was repeated, and the child was left to work alone. After each problem, the experimenter checked the answer and gave a response according to the experimental condition listed below. In addition, on half the problems the child was asked in a nonthreatening manner if he had cheated.

Each child was exposed to all the following conditions:

1. Cheating Baseline—in session one, the child was not asked about cheating. He received points for correct answers and continued with the next problem.

2. No Consequence—the child was asked if he had cheated

but received no consequence for admitting that he had. He continued to receive points for correct answers.

3. Praise Only—if the child admitted cheating, he was praised for being helpful and received his tokens for correct answers.

4. Praise + Extra Points—praise for admitting cheating was accompanied by two bonus points in addition to the points for correct answers.

5. Praise + Punishment—praise was given for admitting cheating, but the child was told that he could not earn points for his correct answer because he had cheated.

Throughout the treatments no consequences were imposed if the child denied cheating; he always received two points if his answer was correct. After the procedure ended, results showed that admissions of cheating increased when bonus points were given for telling the truth. However, actual cheating also increased in two of the three boys. On several problems during the bonus condition, two students said they had cheated even when they had not. Praise alone did not increase admissions of cheating but did raise cheating levels in two students. When punishment was combined with praise, admissions of cheating were reduced to near zero, but cheating itself increased to its highest level in all three boys.

COMMENTARY: The author demonstrates that children more willingly admit to their cheating if rewarded for their admission and not punished for their cheating behavior. However, actual cheating may depend on other factors. First, if the child feels he is being monitored, he may be less likely to cheat and more likely to admit cheating even if punished for it. By confessing, he tries to avoid greater punishment for denying his act. However, the children in this study believed that they were not being monitored. Therefore, when punished for their admission of guilt, they did not reduce their cheating behavior but simply stopped admitting to it. Second, there is the factor of task difficulty. If students feel able to succeed in their schoolwork, they will probably not risk cheating. If the work is extremely difficult, cheating and denial of cheating may be viewed as the only ways to succeed. Teachers are thus advised to (1) openly monitor situations in which cheating may occur; (2) arrange conditions so that cheating is difficult and therefore risky; (3) provide reasonable chances for students to succeed; and (4) think twice before punishing a student who admits to suspected, but not confirmed, cheating.

SOURCE: Winston, A. S. "Experimental Analysis of Admission of Cheating: An Exploratory Study." *Psychological Record,* 1978, *28,* 517-523.

Controlling Stealing
Through a Group Contingency

AUTHORS: Robert B. Brooks and David L. Snow

PRECIS: Reduction of stealing by rewarding and punishing an entire class for one student's behavior

INTRODUCTION: The authors describe two case studies in which behavior modification techniques were used to alter classroom behavior. In one case, a ten-year-old Mexican-American student named Jim was referred for stealing. He would disappear when students were involved in activities outside the classroom, and he was suspected of stealing during these times. His behavior was supported by the attention he received from students when reprimanded and by the fact that he traded the stolen items for things that he wanted from other students. His academic performance was low, and his teacher found his behavior difficult to control.

GROUP CONTINGENCY: With Jim present, the teacher explained his behavior to his classmates and told them that they could help him change. Jim would receive one point each time he completed a designated amount of assigned work, remained in class for each forty-five-minute period, or stayed with the group when it left the class for an activity. When he had earned ten points, the entire class would be given fifteen minutes of free time to play a game or have recess. However, each time Jim did not complete his work, left class, or left the group, the whole class would lose one minute from its next desired activity. In private, Jim was also told that he would receive ten cents for each ten points he earned.

During the first week of this contingency, Jim earned free time for his class each day and was given much peer support for his appropriate behavior. Stealing incidents stopped, assigned work was completed, and Jim no longer disappeared from the group. The teacher terminated the program after one week. These improvements were maintained for the remainder of the school year, and Jim seemed more motivated to participate in school activities.

COMMENTARY: The group contingency was easily applied in this situation. A group reward for desired behavior was combined with a group response-cost procedure when the student acted inappropriately. When stealing occurs in school, it is often difficult to know who the culprits are. However, group reinforcement approaches have been used even when the teacher was unable to identify the thief. In these cases the reward or punishment was dependent on the behavior of the entire class rather than on that of one student. Group contingencies are flexible; consequences can be delivered for the behavior of one child, small groups, or whole classes. In addition, this treatment allows the student(s) to receive attention and support for positive rather than negative behaviors, thus adding to its power as a behavior modifier.

SOURCE: Brooks, R. B., and Snow, D. L. "Two Case Illustrations of the Use of Behavior Modification Techniques in the School Setting." *Behavior Therapy*, 1972, *3*, 100-103.

Overcorrection to Eliminate Theft
in a Retarded Population

AUTHORS: N. H. Azrin and M. D. Wesolowski

PRECIS: Reducing stealing by requiring the thief to return more than was stolen

INTRODUCTION: Programs to reduce stealing are often hindered by the difficulty in identifying the thief. However, stealing may be easier to control with severely retarded persons because of the ease of detection. This paper reports the use of overcorrection; that is, the offender is required to return items in addition to those that were stolen.

OVERCORRECTION: Stealing had occurred at serious levels in a residential ward for severely retarded men and women. The incidents, which were obvious and easily observed, consisted of residents' grabbing snacks from neighbors while they were seated together during between-meal commissary periods. For the first five days, treatment involved correcting the theft by interrupting the act and guiding the thief's hands while instructing him or her to return the item. Starting on day six, the overcorrection procedure was implemented. The thief was reprimanded and assisted in returning the item. He or she was then instructed or helped to obtain an identical item from the display area and place it in the victim's hands. While the simple correction procedure maintained stealing at about twenty episodes per day, overcorrection totally eliminated thefts by the fourth day. This compares with a 57 percent reduction in stealing when time-out from meals was used in another study (E. S. Barton, D. Guess, E. Garcia, and D. M. Baer, "Improvement of Retardates' Mealtime Behaviors by Time-Out Procedures Using Multiple Baseline Techniques," *Journal of Applied Behavior Analysis,* 1970, *3,* 77-84).

COMMENTARY: The authors cite several reasons for the success of overcorrection: (1) the stolen item was returned, and this undid the positive reinforcement associated with its possession; (2) the effort required to obtain an additional item was negatively reinforcing; (3) the loss of time from commissary activity necessitated by overcorrection represented a time-out from positive reinforcement; and (4) the practice involved in returning items to the victim was positive and reeducative. Overcorrection is thus one of the various techniques that comprise the so-called positive practice approach. The authors add that these four factors also apply to nonretarded persons and should therefore make overcorrection effective in many situations. Of course, higher functioning students may cleverly conceal their acts of theft and thus make it difficult to apply the technique as consistently as with a retarded population. However, this article has the virtue of describing a relatively nonaversive punishment that has the added effect of rewarding the victim. It might be useful to apply this technique· with younger students, who are more likely than older children to be detected when stealing.

SOURCE: Azrin, N. H., and Wesolowski, M. D. "Theft Reversal: An Overcorrection Procedure for Eliminating Stealing by Retarded Persons." *Journal of Applied Behavior Analysis,* 1974, *7,* 577-581.

Additional Readings

Flowers, J. V. "Behavior Modification of Cheating in an Elementary School Student: A Brief Note." *Behavior Therapy,* 1972, *3,* 311-312.

To control her cheating, a sixth-grade student was rewarded for accurate self-assessment of work. She graded her own daily assignments on Monday through Thursday and was tested (while closely proctored) in each subject on Friday. She received an A if her test score was less than five points below her average daily assignment grades, a B if within five to ten points, a C if ten to twenty points below, and a D if more than twenty points below. She charted her daily scores, and her teacher entered her Friday mark in red on her chart. Over five weeks her inflated self-assessed daily scores gradually decreased until they closely matched the teacher-scored tests. Reports of cheating dropped to zero, and this level was maintained after treatment ended. Her grades simultaneously improved.

Kehl, D. G. "Moonshine, Flummadiddle, and Flots: Teaching About Doublespeak in the Primary Grades." *Language Arts,* 1976, *53*(8), 899-901.

The author discusses methods and materials in literature for teaching children about "doublespeak" (lying). Children can learn about the problems associated with lying through such excellent reading materials as Evelyn Ness' *Sam, Bangs, and Moonshine* (New York: Holt, Rinehart and Winston, 1966). This story (for kindergarten through third-grade students) also teaches the difference between "bad Moonshine" (lying) and "good Moonshine" (myths, fables, legends, and poetry). Kehl suggests activities adapted for older children based on this story. "Lie poems," an activity developed by Kenneth Koch in *Wishes, Lies, and Dreams: Teaching Children to Write Poetry* (New York: Chelsea House, 1970, pp. 19 and 198), is cited as an additional method to heighten awareness about "good Moonshine" and the beauty of art. Books for grades 4 to 6 and 5 to 7 are also suggested.

Monohan, J., and O'Leary, K. D. "Effects of Self-Instruction on Rule-Breaking Behavior." *Psychological Reports,* 1971, *29,* 1059-1066.

Children in kindergarten and first grade engaged in a task designed to make it easy for them to cheat. They were to press a telegraph key only when certain shapes were projected on a screen, and they were told they would receive rewards for these "correct" presses. In reality, they could press when any shape was presented and still be rewarded. In experiment one, they were instructed to verbalize to themselves the "proper" pressing behavior before responding. For one group, a nine-second delay between self-instruction and response was programmed into the apparatus. For another, a one-second delay was required. While both self-instructional groups cheated less than a no-instruction control group (1 percent versus 26 percent) the different delay times did not produce different cheating rates. In addition, less cheating occurred on trials in which children instructed themselves correctly. In a second experiment, the number of self-instructional training trials was varied. One group was trained to a criterion of eight consecutive correct trials and a second group to sixteen. A control group had no training. A timer, preset to the length of the experiment, was also placed before each child. The child could cheat by resetting the timer when the experimenter was out of the room. No significant differences in cheating occurred among the three groups, although significantly more control-group children reset the timer to give them more time than did the children in the sixteen-trial group. Self-instructions can inhibit rule-breaking behavior, but the delay times in the first study did not have a differential effect. The behavior with the timer indicates that self-instructions may generalize and reduce rule-breaking behavior not directly trained. The overall absence of cheating in a sizable minority of the children suggests that children who do not cheat when given the chance may already be in the habit of using covert self-instructions.

Smith, A. H., Jr. "Encountering the Family System in School-Related Behavior Problems." *Psychology in the Schools,* 1978, *15*(3), 379-386.

This article argues for inclusion of the family system in evaluation and treatment by the school psychologist. Many problems, such as stealing, are outgrowths of family dynamics. The child may be acting out family-related needs or problems and may be subtly reinforced by family members in maintaining the behavior. The school psychologist can apply Gestalt techniques to sensitize the family to their individual needs and encourage their interactions as differentiated individuals. Such techniques aim for direct contact among family members in a "here-and-now" framework, along with heightened awareness of the verbal and nonverbal behaviors that reveal their interacting needs. An example is given of a boy who steals in order to satisfy needs submerged within the disturbed family system. In a family session, the needs of his mother were made explicit as she revealed her personal despair over having to discipline her son without his father's help. Her focus on her son as a criminal was redirected to her marital relationship, and a true issue within the family was thus confronted. Once individual needs have been redefined, the son may have less reason to misbehave. He may then be better able to benefit from school. The role of the school psychologist is crucial to this process.

Warren, S. "The Truth About Children's Lies." *Education Digest*, 1977, *42*, 51-53.

The author cautions against reacting with anger and punishment to lying. Adults can help children overcome the need to lie by helping them confront the reasons for lying. Lying may cover feelings of insecurity and inadequacy or fears of punishment and rejection. Children may lie to make themselves feel important or to appear more valued by peers and adults. Lying also provides excitement or wish fulfillment. From birth, children are often discouraged from expressing feelings honestly. In this context, lying is not totally unacceptable. To prevent lying, it is crucial to encourage honesty in the expression of feelings as well as of facts. By giving children the chance to be responsible, listening to them, accepting their failures, and helping them correct problems, we remove the reasons for lying.

Truancy

Truancy is often associated with poor school performance and low grades. Not only do grades suffer because of the truant's poor attendance record, but the truant may remain absent from school because of a felt inability to succeed. In any event, truancy removes the student from school and makes learning impossible. Truancy may result from a combination of factors, including alienation from school life and its values, family conflicts, emotional disturbance, and peer pressure. It is distinguished from school phobia in that the school phobic experiences an intense yet undefinable fear of attending school. The phobic child will often remain at home, using somatic complaints or fear of harm at school as reasons for doing so. When in school, however, this child may be quite happy and academically successful. But the truant child does poorly in school, tends to dislike it, and may well spend his time away from home when cutting school without his parents' knowledge.

Contingency Contracting for Truants

AUTHOR: B. David Brooks

PRECIS: A contract among the student, counselor, and parent to repay school attendance with specified rewards

INTRODUCTION: The author presents two case studies to illustrate the use of contingency contracting with truant high school students. He notes that this behavior management technique deals directly with behavior and does not require an examination of underlying conflicts or problems.

Mary A.: Mary was a fifteen-year-old high school sophomore who was absent from school up to 40 percent of the time. When she did attend, she usually cut most of her classes. Despite school counseling, home punishments, and warnings of suspension, Mary continued to be truant. Her mother had restricted her to the house, had hit her with a belt, and had threatened to remove her from school.

Recognizing the ineffectiveness of these procedures, the school counselor met with Mary and her mother to describe contingency contracting and to develop a contract for attendance. After they had discussed the reinforcers that would motivate Mary to attend, the following contract was drawn up and signed by all three participants:

NAME: Mary A.
PROBLEM: Excessive period and full-day truancy.
BACKGROUND: Mary has missed as much as four days of school each week during the first quarter. She has been continually counseled, and her mother has (1) restricted her for long periods of time (Mary is now on restriction), (2) "blistered her with a belt," and (3) threatened to remove Mary from school. Mary continued to be truant.
BEHAVIORAL IMPLEMENTATION: Mary will do the following in exchange for the rewards stated below: (1) Mary will attend every class she is scheduled into. (2) Mary will have her teacher initial an attendance card at the end of each period. (3) Mary will

turn in the attendance card at the end of each school day. (4) Mary will record on a chart in the counseling office the number of classes she attended. (5) Mary will attend a group rap session once a week.

REWARD SCHEDULE: Successful completion of the implementation will be rewarded in the following manner:

Week One: Mary will be taken off restriction for four (4) hours Friday night (time specified by mother).

Week Two: Mary will be taken off restriction for four (4) hours Friday night (time specified by mother) and six (6) hours Saturday (time specified by mother).

Week Three: All restrictions for Friday and Saturday will be removed.

Following the third week, a conference will be held during which a determination will be made as to a new reinforcement schedule.

SIGNATURE AND AGREEMENT STATEMENTS: I agree to follow the contract and dispense the rewards according to the provisions stated above.

_____

Mrs. A.

I agree to follow the provisions of this contract (1 through 5).

_____

Mary A.

I agree to monitor this contract and to make a written or verbal progress report to Mary and her mother at the end of each week.

_____

Counselor

Each participant followed the agreement, and six weeks later contracting was terminated since Mary was attending classes regularly. She reported a better attitude toward school and a desire to plan for future schooling. Her mother was pleased with Mary's progress and was developing a more positive attitude toward her.

Bill C.: Bill, a sixteen-year-old junior, had been a good student with no problems until his parents separated the previous year. He began missing school, writing his own excuses, and deceiving his mother by leaving home in the morning and arriving back in the afternoon as though he had attended classes. When he came to school, he would attend homeroom, be recorded as present, then miss the entire day. His mother refused to accept the fact that he had become a truant until the counselor met with her and Bill to draw up a contract. Bill agreed to fulfill behavior requirements similar to Mary's in the case above, and he was rewarded with ten cents for each class attended. He was to save this money for a trip to Disneyland on New Year's Eve. Mrs. C., Bill, and the counselor signed the contract. Three weeks after the contract began, Bill was still attending every class. A daily attendance card that each teacher had to sign was reduced to a Friday-only arrangement, and the need for monetary reward was terminated by mutual agreement.

COMMENTARY: Negative behaviors such as truancy are usually punished in the hope that they will disappear. Contracting takes the opposite approach by rewarding positive behaviors to undo the maladaptive pattern. The author notes that the student is treated as an equal in the process and dealt with as a mature participant who has the major responsibility for change. Contracts should be reviewed continuously and renegotiated, if necessary, to ensure that the rewards remain appropriate. The counselor, psychologist, teacher, or administrator initiating the contract should be familiar with behavioral principles, so that problems with a contract can be analyzed and solved. Requiring only a minimal amount of time to draw up, a contract nevertheless has potentially powerful effects.

SOURCE: Brooks, B. D. "Contingency Contracts with Truants," *Personnel and Guidance Journal,* 1974, *52*(5), 316-320.

Home Contacts to Improve School Attendance

AUTHORS: Daniel W. Sheats and Gary E. Dunkleberger

PRECIS: Comparing phone calls from a principal and a secretary to the home as methods of reducing chronic absenteeism

INTRODUCTION: When principals praise truant students for improved attendance, absentee rates consistently decline. Principals can also achieve the same effect by telephoning parents to request that they reinforce school attendance at home. However, principals may not always have the time to initiate home contacts and may wish to delegate the responsibility to other staff. The authors investigated whether telephone calls from a school secretary would be as effective as those from a principal.

METHOD: Elementary school students who had been absent more than fifteen school days during the previous year were selected as targets for home calls. The principal sent the parents of each student a letter at the beginning of the new school year in which he indicated that the school would attempt to improve their child's attendance rate. The relationship between a good attendance record and school success was stressed in all home contacts throughout the year.

Half the parents were called by the principal and half by a school secretary; both used the same schedule. At the third absence, the importance of regular attendance was emphasized to the parent; if possible, the child's improved attendance was praised. After the sixth absence, the child's absentee record was reviewed, and the parent was urged to help the child improve that record. Upon the ninth absence, the school expressed concern about the days missed and offered medical assistance. At the twelfth absence the parent was told that the student had been out more days than 90 percent of the other children. Health services were reoffered, and the importance of regular attendance was again stressed. At the fifteenth absence, the parent was informed that absenteeism was definitely affecting the child's progress in school.

The principal and secretary used prepared scripts to prevent variations in their phone calls, and messages became more serious as the number of absences increased. Results showed that both principal and secretary home contacts significantly reduced absenteeism. Furthermore, both treatments were equally successful, reducing nonattendance by about one third.

COMMENTARY: School-initiated home contacts are an effective means of increasing the attendance of chronically absent students. The principal does not have to make the calls but can delegate this task to other staff members without reducing the power of the technique. Although parents would probably assume that the secretary is calling on behalf of the principal, the secretary should make that point explicit. The authors also point out that communication to the home remained serious in tone but was generally positive. While critical statements to the parent may have a different effect from positive ones, it is likely that most schools would prefer to have encouraging, rather than unpleasant, contacts with the home.

SOURCE: Sheats, D. W., and Dunkleberger, G. E. "A Determination of the Principal's Effect in School-Initiated Home Contacts Concerning Attendance of Elementary School Students." *Journal of Educational Research*, 1979, 72(6), 310-312.

Reinforcing School Attendance in Elementary Students

AUTHORS: Robert M. Barber and J. Robert Kagey

PRECIS: Rewarding improved attendance with a party and reduced work assignments

INTRODUCTION: When students are chronically truant, they are deprived of the academic and social stimulation provided by school. This problem tends to be more acute in rural settings, in minority groups, and in families with low incomes, unemployed parents, and/or little schooling. The authors indicate the need for low-cost interventions that can utilize existing school staff to motivate better attendance. They describe a behavioral program implemented in an elementary school with a history of high absenteeism. Children in grades 1, 2, and 3 were allowed to attend all or part of a monthly party, depending on their attendance record for the month. For perfect attendance the child earned the full one-hour party time and access to four "fun-rooms," which included movies, puppet shows, dancing, games, and art. Forty-five minutes of party time and two fun-rooms were earned if the child was absent for only one day. If two days were missed, thirty minutes of the party and one fun-room were available, while three absences earned only fifteen minutes of the party and no fun-room. For more than three absences students were assigned school work in another room and missed the party entirely. Children who attended a portion of the party spent their initial time in the workroom.

METHOD: Throughout December, teachers explained the program to their students; parents were notified by letter. The first party was held just after Christmas vacation in January to let all children experience the reinforcer. Then the program was explained once more, with emphasis placed on the importance of good attendance. Starting in January, attendance records were publicly posted on charts in each classroom. Children were given a star for each day of attendance and were required to be in school for at least half the day to earn a star. Principal-validated illnesses were not counted against the child.

Parties were held on the first Wednesday of each month from February through May. Teachers tallied attendance records and completed a slip that indicated earned party time and the number of fun-rooms allowed for each child. These were handed to the children along with work assignments just before the party. Teachers also described the fun-rooms, reviewed rules for good party behavior, and reminded children that poor conduct or lost slips would result in a return to the workroom.

Children doing assignments were then taken to the workroom while those with perfect attendance records went to the party, where they received a free drink and could buy candy. Ten minutes later they chose and attended their first fun-room, rotating to a new fun-room every fifteen minutes. During the second fun-room, children who had earned forty-five party minutes were allowed to join the party, receive a drink, and buy candy. These children then chose their first fun-room while perfect attenders selected their third. As the third fun-room began, two-day absentees joined the party and, after fifteen minutes, attended the final fun-room. The children who had missed three days of school were allowed to attend the remaining fifteen minutes of the party but could not visit a fun-room. The school bell signaled each change of room and also the time when children in the workroom could begin the party. Teachers and parents supervised all activities and checked slips before a child could enter a fun-room. After the May party, children still received stars for attendance, but no further parties were held.

Before the program was instituted (September through November), attendance in the school was lower than the average attendance for the same months during the previous four years. In December, when the program was first described, the children became excited about the party, and attendance improved slightly over the four preceding Decembers. Significant improvement occurred during the four months of contingent party attendance. During April, attendance was increased by 275 days for the total school population, placing this school ahead of nine other elementary schools in the county. After the May party, when the parties ended but the use of stars continued, attendance rates returned to slightly above previous May rates.

COMMENTARY: The authors note two practical advantages of the program. First, it does not require teachers to have extensive knowledge of behavioral principles. In an initial two-hour meeting with the teachers, the authors briefly described the effects of reinforcers on behavior. They spent the remaining time detailing the program and providing teachers with written instructions. Another advantage is the additional money that schools can realize from state funding, which is often based on district attendance figures. Programs that cost school systems nothing but have the potential to increase income are important tools for the school mental health specialist.

SOURCE: Barber, R. M., and Kagey, J. R. "Modification of School Attendance for an Elementary Population." *Journal of Applied Behavior Analysis*, 1977, *10*, 41-48.

A Community-Based Program
to Reduce High School Absenteeism

AUTHORS: Christopher Grala and Clark McCauley

PRECIS: Using appeals and supportive guidance to increase attendance in chronic high school truants

INTRODUCTION: The authors compared the effects of threats, encouragement, and supportive instructions on the school attendance of truant male adolescents. The teen-agers regularly visited the local community center (where Grala was a volunteer staff assistant) in a low-income, ghettolike, urban neighborhood. Their school attendance was usually less than fifty percent.

METHOD: None of the thirty-two students in the study was informed of the experiment. One member of the center staff, who had been raised in a ghetto area and was a former gang member, asked each student whether he intended to go to school on a regular basis and then applied one of four different treatments:
    Threat Appeal-Supportive Instruction. This treatment emphasized the destructive life of a dropout. Unemployment, criminal and violent behavior, alcoholism, drugs, and the horrors of prison were all portrayed as consequences of truancy. The counselor discussed friends of his whose lives had been ruined by leaving school. Each teen-ager was also told that if he did not return to school in two weeks, he would not be allowed

to use the center during the school day. The counselor then offered to escort the student to school, talk to school personnel about his problems, obtain a tutor to assist him with school-work, and make the center available for homework after school.

Threat Appeal. For these students, counseling support was not offered. The same descriptions of the dropout's life were given, but the students were told to "shape up," get back to school, and talk to a school counselor on their own.

Optimistic Appeal-Supportive Instruction. The supportive guidance provided to the first group was given here, along with advice on such benefits of attending school as increased income potential, work opportunities, and feelings of personal security and self-worth. Vague references to the life of a dropout were made, but the counselor focused his appeal on the advantages that he had gained from school. He asked the students to try attending school again.

Optimistic Appeal. No counseling was given to these students. They were encouraged to attend school regularly, and the benefits of doing so were discussed as they were with the other "optimistic appeal" group.

Immediately following the treatments, each student was again asked if he intended to return to school. Actual attendance for each group was then followed weekly for four weeks. Of the students who did not intend to return when initially asked, 70 percent changed their intention after the threat appeal, while only 9 percent (one student) changed after the optimistic appeal. When actual attendance was examined, it was found that 63 percent of the students receiving supportive instruction had attended school every day after one week, compared with 13 percent of the groups receiving no instruction. Without support, neither threat nor optimistic appeal was successful; with support, both were effective. While daily attendance for all groups declined over the four-week follow-up, more students in the two supportive instruction group continued to attend daily than in the nonsupport groups. In addition, almost all "support" students came for daily tutoring at the center.

COMMENTARY: These results provide meaningful information for counselors and school psychologists working with chronic truants. First, emphasizing negative consequences may alter the student's stated intentions when encouragement fails, but it will probably not lead to improved attendance unless support is provided and the student is actively guided in returning to school. Second, active involvement by the counselor in providing support services will be more successful if the benefits of attending rather than the consequences of dropping out are stressed. Third, one application of the treatment may not have enough influence to maintain a student's attendance after a few weeks. Continued counseling to support and reinforce attendance will be crucial. Perhaps a behavioral intervention to reinforce attendance on a regular basis might help maintain treatment effects. Fourth, developing liaisons with community agencies may allow schools to reach out to students who are traditionally unresponsive to school-based services and mistrust the school's intentions. Finally, this study set daily attendance as the criterion for success. In other settings it may be more realistic to begin with a less stringent standard and gradually work toward this goal.

SOURCE: Grala, C., and McCauley, C. "Counseling Truants Back to School." *Journal of Counseling Psychology,* 1976, *23*(2), 166-169.

Additional Readings

Demsch, B., and Garth, J. "A Multidisciplinary Approach to Truancy." *Psychology in the Schools,* 1970, *7,* 194-197.

Project IMPACT (a program for the improvement of attendance and the curtailment of truancy) operates in the Chicago public elementary schools to reduce truancy. It offers special classes for students who have been truants. A district committee composed of a district superintendent, a principal, a social worker, a psychologist, a nurse, an attendance officer, and others selects boys for enrollment in the IMPACT program after careful evaluation of referrals from district schools. The

committee is also responsible for operation of the program and
for ongoing follow-up of participating students. At case conferences a recommendation may be made for placement in an IM-
PACT class. These classes provide the core of the treatment.
The curriculum, schedule, and activities are designed to offer a
meaningful yet corrective experience for the child. A warm,
supportive, experienced teacher who understands the problems
associated with truancy works to maintain a positive relationship with the students. The class operates with recognition of
the relationship between emotional and social factors and academic achievement (see also B. Demsch and J. Garth, "Truancy
Prevention: A First Step in Curtailing Delinquency Proneness,"
Federal Probation, 1968, pp. 31-37). The success of the program is shown by the fact that of thirty-six students who have
completed the program, twenty-nine are now in regular schools,
two are employed, and three are attending vocational schools.

Fo, W. S. O., and O'Donnell, C. R. "The Buddy System: Rela-
    tionship and Contingency Conditions in a Community Inter-
    vention Program for Youth with Nonprofessionals as Behav-
    ior Change Agents." *Journal of Consulting and Clinical
    Psychology,* 1974, *42*(2), 163-169.

In this family court program, community people ("Buddies") worked with professional consultants to establish relationships with problem adolescents. The primary goal was to
increase school attendance. Paid volunteers ranging in age from
seventeen to sixty-five served as Buddies. They were trained in
techniques of contingency behavior management and were
taught how to develop relationships that would foster behavior
change. Pay was based on the points that they earned for meeting their role requirements. They were to meet weekly with
assigned youths, establish a trusting relationship (including involvement in social and recreational activities), identify, monitor, and intervene in problem behaviors, and act as advocates.
The consultant's roles—training and supervision of Buddies, designing behavioral strategies, collecting data, troubleshooting
and monitoring Buddy points for pay—were also specified.

Youth were assigned to Buddies under one of four conditions:

1. Relationship—Buddies were told to establish a noncontingent positive relationship as the most effective behavior change approach.

2. Social Approval—a positive relationship contingent upon desired behavior was stressed as the most effective approach.

3. Social and Material Reinforcement—in addition to the instructions for condition two, the ten-dollar monthly allotment given to each youngster was to be spent contingent upon acceptable behavior.

4. Control—youth were referred to the program but not assigned to Buddies.

After six weeks of these conditions, all groups except the control group were switched to social and material reinforcement for six additional weeks. Results for the first six weeks showed substantial truancy reductions under conditions two and three. Condition one showed very slight changes. When all groups were switched, the initial Relationship group showed a significant truancy decrease, while the group in condition three showed an even greater decrease. The authors stress the importance of a trusting relationship between the Buddy and the student even though the relationship condition produced no change by itself. Consideration was also given to the inclusion of parents and teachers as natural mediators trained by Buddies.

Moos, R. H., and Moos, B. S. "Classroom Social Climate and Student Absences and Grades." *Journal of Educational Psychology*, 1978, 70(2), 263-269.

Adolescent student absenteeism was found to be related to classroom social climate in several ways: (1) absences tended to be higher in classes with stricter grading practices; (2) higher absences were found in classes that students perceived as very competitive and teacher controlled; and (3) more absence occurred in classes that teachers saw as low in teacher support. In classes with high absence rates, students tended to feel that they watched the clock more, had to be careful about comments, were under clear and set rules, and got into trouble more quickly. They enjoyed these classes less than other ones, were unable to discuss topics not related to the class, felt that these classes were difficult to pass, and viewed the teachers as strict. The authors note that the relationship between classroom climate and absenteeism is complex and requires further study. For example, the high rate of absence in competitive classes suggests the need for more supports to meet the needs of students who do poorly and therefore may not attend class regularly. Assessment of social climates in such classes can provide the information necessary to reduce student absenteeism.

Nagle, R. J., Gresham, F. M., and Johnson, G. "Truancy Intervention Among Secondary Special Education Students." *School Psychology Digest,* 1979, *9*(4), 464-468.

This study combined group counseling and contingency contracting to reduce absenteeism in ninth and tenth graders attending a resource room. Two groups of students for whom previous token programs had not been effective participated in counseling twice per week for four weeks. Values clarification, vocational goals, and the importance of attendance were presented in a nondirective framework. In the fifth week both groups began a four-week behavioral contract in which five consecutive days of attendance earned a fast-food gift certificate. One group also continued to receive counseling while the other did not. After treatment both groups had significantly increased their attendance rates and maintained them throughout both phases of treatment. No differences in improvement rate were noted between these groups, although both showed significant improvement over a no-treatment control group. It appears that a behavioral contract can maintain the effectiveness of group counseling. The importance of group treatment and peer support for low-achieving, alienated adolescents was stressed.

Needels, M., and Stallings, J. "Classroom Processes Related to Absence Rate." Paper presented at the annual meeting of the American Educational Research Association, Washington, D.C., March 31, 1975.

The authors found that at grades 1 and 3, there were fewer absences in classrooms in which children engaged in independent learning activities, questioned the teacher and received responses, obtained individualized instruction, and received positive feelings from teachers. Higher absentee rates occurred when children worked in larger groups, received critical feedback, and passively accepted information from adults. These and other variables suggest a relationship between classroom process and absenteeism.

Neel, R. A., and De Bruler, L. "The Effects of Self-Management of School Attendance by Problem Adolescents." *Adolescence*, 1979, *14*(53), 175-184.

Seventh, eighth, and ninth graders with learning problems attended an alternative school. They were also considered to be high risks for dropping out. A self-management program was developed in which students were required to get to class on time and complete assignments in order to be allowed to attend school. They were responsible for meeting these criteria in any way they chose and received help when they requested it. However, they would not be admitted into school unless they met these standards. Over the seventy-two days of this program, the number of students attending class significantly improved, and more classwork was completed. It appears that when appropriate contingencies are arranged, students will attend class even though academic performance is consistently required. Constant program changes or the introduction of "entertainment" activities to promote attendance is not necessarily required.

◎◎◎◎◎◎◎◎◎◎◎◎◎◎◎◎◎◎◎◎◎◎◎◎◎◎

Cursing

Children may curse in moments of excitement, pleasure, anger, frustration, and/or fear. In these instances the adult may decide to ignore the isolated occurrence, respond to the message behind the curse, or discuss it later with the child. When cursing occurs regularly or is used to annoy or taunt others, interventions are available to undue the pattern. It is important for adults to respond to the inappropriateness of the behavior and not to get caught up by the emotional intensity it can generate. Moralizing or lecturing to the child on "proper" language is usually ineffective.

◎◎◎◎◎◎◎◎◎◎◎◎◎◎◎◎◎◎◎◎◎◎◎◎◎

Managing Children's Profanity
in the Classroom

AUTHOR: Robert B. Bloom

PRECIS: Responding effectively to children's cursing by recognizing its underlying message

INTRODUCTION: The author discusses the power of profanity and the tension created in adults when they hear children use obscene words. Anxiety may result from the power of curse words to evoke sexual imagery or from the embarrassment that follows their use. The listener may feel as guilty as the speaker simply for having heard the words. These factors provoke punishment of the child and interfere with a therapeutic approach to the problem. If the adult feels assaulted by the child's words, he or she will usually ignore the meaning behind their use and respond negatively to the profanity itself.

In the professional literature, cursing is often associated with severe mental disorder. In reality, swearing may be a message signaling fear or anger. It may also be an habitual response triggered by states of excitement. Psychologists and psychiatrists often miss the message of profanity by attributing it to emotional disturbance, and they thus add little to an understanding of its significance.

INCIDENTS: Bloom discusses six incidents in which children made obscene statements and invites the reader to develop a response to each situation. Several incidents, such as the one involving Ron, occurred in the classroom. This fourteen-year-old entered the author's classroom, grinned, and said hello. Bloom responded in kind and indicated to Ron that his assignment was at his desk. "I ain't got no book," said Ron. The teacher then gave him one. "I ain't got no paper," said Ron, a bit less happily. The teacher gave him paper, and the exchange was repeated with a pencil. At this, Ron slammed his books on his desk. "Shit!" was his response. He looked for the expected anger from Bloom but got only a smile. He then settled down to work. In this incident, Ron tried an obscenity for its shock value. It was his last effort to provoke the teacher and disrupt the class. It failed because the teacher recognized its intent and did not give Ron what he wanted.

Ten-year-old Tommy's obscenity surfaced for different reasons. During math work, the word *shit* rang out, as books crashed to the floor and a dish was knocked over. Tommy became tense, and the class looked to the teacher for a response. The teacher interpreted Tommy's outburst as a response to frustration and felt no need to lecture him on proper language. She sat down next to him, acknowledged that the math might be hard for him, and offered help. At another time she could suggest to Tommy other ways to handle his anger. The immediate need was to reduce his tension.

Carol, a third grader, stated out loud, "Teacher, I gotta piss," five minutes after the class was asked to use the bathroom. Further questioning established that Carol's choice of words represented a language deficiency. "Gotta piss" was her naive equivalent of "use the bathroom." In this case a simple instruction that "use the bathroom" was a better way to express her need ended the incident.

COMMENTARY: There are other reasons besides these why children curse. Peer pressure and cultural models are two not cited in these examples. But whatever the reason, adults can respond meaningfully if they free themselves from the magical power of obscenity, analyze its meaning, and respond to the feeling or need that underlies it.

SOURCE: Bloom, R. B. "Therapeutic Management of Children's Profanity." *Behavioral Disorders*, 1977, 2(4), 205-211.

Controlling Obscene Gestures
Through Group Contingencies

AUTHORS: Stephen I. Sulzbacher and Joyce E. Houser

PRECIS: Using withdrawal of group free time to reduce the occurrence of the "naughty finger"

INTRODUCTION: The authors applied a group contingency to control display of the "naughty finger" and the verbal references associated with it. The action involved extending the middle finger from a raised clenched fist.

GROUP CONTINGENCY: The procedure was employed in a class of educable retarded students aged six to ten. After recording pretreatment behavior for nine days, the teacher mounted ten cards, numbered one through ten, in the front of the room on a desk calendar bracket. She instructed the class that at the end of each day there would be a ten-minute recess. However, each time she saw a finger gesture or heard a reference to one, she would flip a card and one minute of recess would be lost. This strategy, which lasted eighteen days, resulted in an immediate and dramatic decline in the behaviors. After the contingency was removed, profanity gradually rose to near pretreatment levels.

COMMENTARY: The authors note several factors that may have contributed to reducing use of the naughty finger. First, there was a personal reward available to each student. Second, since peer comments about the gesture may have reinforced its occurrence, eliminating those comments removed a source of reward, thus reducing use of the gesture. Third, under the group contingency there was increased peer pressure not to use the naughty finger. However, maintaining treatment gains was a problem, and the addition of other strategies may be necessary to produce a carry-over of improvement. Perhaps treatment did not last long enough, or perhaps it should have been augmented by a positive contingency. Efforts to promote long-term effects are crucial to the acceptance of these approaches. Nevertheless, the technique was easy to implement, minimally disruptive to class routine, inexpensive, yet quite powerful. A group contingency is especially useful when the target behavior is displayed by an entire class. However, when a single student is disruptive, an individual contingency is often recommended as the treatment of choice.

SOURCE: Sulzbacher, S. I., and Houser, J. E. "A Tactic to Eliminate Disruptive Behaviors in the Classroom: Group Contingent Consequences." *American Journal of Mental Deficiency*, 1968, *1*, 182-187.

Reinforcing Low Rates of Obscene Behavior

AUTHORS: Michael H. Epstein, Alan C. Repp, and Douglas Cullinan

PRECIS: Rewarding students for low rates of obscenity over a specified time interval

INTRODUCTION: The *differential reinforcement of low rates of responding* (DRL) is a positive alternative to punishment and other aversive interventions that attempt to reduce inappropriate behaviors. The authors describe the use of a DRL schedule to modify obscene language in a special education class composed of children aged six to nine.

DRL: The classroom was run on a token reinforcement system that rewarded academic achievement and appropriate social behavior. On the first day of treatment the children were told of their unacceptable language. It was explained that twenty bonus tokens could be earned by students who kept their daily obscene statements below a predesignated level. Tokens could be used to purchase items such as toy cars or privileges such as extra free time. For the first twelve days the limit was set at three obscene statements per day. It was later reduced to two statements per day for a five-day period, then to one per day for eight days, and finally to zero for fifteen days (this last phase is known as the *differential reinforcement of other behavior* or DRO schedule).

With each new phase the rules were clearly specified. Praise was given for previous reductions in the level of profanity. Over the forty-day program, obscene language decreased with each phase until it reached zero for all six target students during the final five days of the DRO schedule.

COMMENTARY: As the authors indicate, DRL schedules are effective with a variety of school populations. They can be applied to individuals, small groups, or whole classes and used for a wide range of target behaviors. A major advantage is that they reward reduction of inappropriate behavior rather than punish its continued occurrence. Most importantly, students tend to view this intervention as fair because it allows for a gradual cessation of the target behavior instead of forcing immediate and total compliance.

SOURCE: Epstein, M. H., Repp, A. C., and Cullinan, D. "Decreasing 'Obscene' Language of Behaviorally Disordered Children Through the Use of a DRL Schedule." *Psychology in the Schools*, 1978, *15*(3), 419-423.

Effective Punishment for Obscene Language

AUTHORS: Benjamin B. Lahey, M. Patrick McNees, and Margaret C. McNees

PRECIS: Using a time-out procedure to reduce obscenities

INTRODUCTION: Lahey and his colleagues utilized "instructed repetition" (also called "massed practive" or "negative practice") and time-outs to reduce obscene language in a ten-year-old educable retarded student. These obscenities were usually accompanied by stuttering and various facial twitches, which together are sometimes referred to as "verbal tics" or as Tourette's Syndrome. The authors note that no such diagnosis had been confirmed in this boy.

PROCEDURE: Pretreatment rates of obscene speech were obtained for four days before instructed repetition began. Then, for eight days, the teacher took the boy to a separate room four times daily and conducted fifteen-minute sessions in which he had to repeat rapidly his most frequently used obscene word. He was not allowed to rest and was firmly ordered to continue using the word if he stopped. This procedure was disliked by both teacher and student. Furthermore, complaints about his behavior increased during the treatment period. Instructed repetition was therefore replaced by a time-out contingency for fourteen days. It was explained to the boy that he would immediately be placed in the time-out room by his teacher after an obscene remark. The time-out room was an empty, four-by-ten-foot, well-lit room connected to the classroom. In earlier sessions the teacher escorted the boy to the room, but later he went by himself when instructed. He stayed at least five minutes and until he had been quiet for one minute. The room was locked when the boy was inside. Following the time-out phase, a brief no-treatment period was instituted; this was followed by reintroduction of the time-out for eight days.

Before treatment began, the student averaged more than two obscene comments per minute. Instructed repetition reduced this rate by about one half. However, because of its negative side effects and the continuing frequency of the behavior, time-out was substituted. By the fourth day of the second time-out phase, obscenities were close to zero, with no negative side effects. Furthermore, teachers reported that the student's obscene comments were quiet enough to be rarely understandable. Two weeks later, low levels of obscene language were still being maintained. Interestingly, about one month after the treatment, the time-out room was used for another purpose for an hour a day. During this hour only, the boy's obscenities returned to their original rate. The authors did not speculate on the possible reasons for this pattern.

COMMENTARY: The boy's parents were pleased that their son could now control his behavior in public places and for days at a time. The effects had apparently generalized to nonclassroom situations. However, the school practitioner cannot assume that progress in school will be automatically matched by improvement outside. While parents may try a procedure at home when they hear of its successful effect in school, it is best to plan the parents' treatment role with them or structure the school intervention to increase the chances for carry-over. The authors also point out that instructed repetition should not necessarily be rejected as a treatment strategy, even though several problems with it emerged in this study. More research is needed to assess its utility.

SOURCE: Lahey, B. B., McNees, M. P., and McNees, M. C. "Control of an Obscene 'Verbal Tic' Through Time-Out in an Elementary School Classroom." *Journal of Applied Behavior Analysis*, 1973, *6*, 101-104.

Additional Readings

Josephs, E. "Helping Billy Control His Temper." *Educational Technology Monograph*, 1968, *1*(2), 9-10.

Billy's temper outbursts frequently included profanity, and he was suspended from school for cursing a teacher. When he returned, he was instructed that if he had more than twenty-five outbursts per day, he would be placed in a corner at a small desk and would be ignored by everyone. He requested that the limit be set at five. This was done, and he exceeded this criterion only twice. When he stayed under five outbursts for the day, he received a treat or a privilege, such as being allowed to help the teacher or being given an extended recess. His behavior was much improved, and peers noticed the change.

Kubany, E. S., Weiss, L. E., and Sloggett, B. B. "The Good Behavior Clock: A Reinforcement/Time-Out Procedure for Reducing Disruptive Classroom Behavior." *Journal of Behavior
Therapy and Experimental Psychiatry,* 1971, *2,* 173-179.

According to his teacher, Henry enjoyed swearing and
being destructive. In class, a large fifteen-minute timer was
adapted as "Henry's clock" and placed on a desk in the front of
the room. It was kept running as long as Henry was quiet and in
his seat. For every two minutes of appropriate behavior, he
earned treats that were shared with the class at the end of the
day. After fifteen minutes of good behavior he was awarded a
star on his "good behavior chart," also displayed in front of the
room. At one point in the program a time-out procedure was
imposed that left Henry alone in the room to clean up the results of a tantrum. At another point he began to receive his
candy in regular rotation with classmates instead of receiving it
first each time. During the first intervention phase (approximately thirty days), Henry's disruptiveness decreased from 88
percent to 17 percent of the observation intervals. A further decrease to 13 percent occurred during a second intervention
phase following a no-treatment period. This second intervention
included a class party for a filled good behavior chart and a
morning point system for prosocial academic behaviors. Lateness to class was also reduced.

Mosier, D., and Vaal, J. J., Jr. "The Manipulation of One Child's
Behavior by Another Child in a School Adjustment Classroom." *School Applications of Learning Theory,* 1970, *2,*
25-27.

An eleven-year-old boy directed name-calling at a classmate. The classmate was instructed to ignore the boy and walk
away if he called him a name ("Keify"). If the boy spoke to
him without using the name, he was to thank him or express his
satisfaction. After four days, name-calling stopped completely.
The authors indicate that name-calling was eliminated because
the attention it received was withdrawn. They also note the
power of children to control each other's behavior.

Classroom Disturbance

Classroom disturbance has been divided into the following six subsections: (1) boisterous or rowdy behavior; (2) noncompliance; (3) playing the class clown; (4) temper tantrums; (5) annoying or bothering others; and (6) out-of-seat (off-task) behavior. These behaviors are most characteristic of disruptive children in the classroom and often occur in combination with one another (see H. M. Walker, The Acting-Out Child: Coping with Classroom Disruption, *Boston: Allyn & Bacon, 1979). Disruptive children are the most frequent targets of classroom interventions because of the effect that these children have on classroom routine. The reader should note that the articles are arranged in the order of the subsections listed above. However, there is considerable overlap of behavior problems among the articles, and techniques are often applicable across categories.*

Classroom Disturbance:
Boisterous or Rowdy Behavior

This child is quick to talk out without permission, to talk loudly, or to call out while the teacher is speaking. Since the initial response by the teacher often has little effect, the result is repeated student-teacher exchanges. These may further disrupt the operation of the classroom.

The Daily Report Card System

AUTHORS: Edward H. Dougherty and Anne Dougherty

PRECIS: Using simple daily reports to parents to reduce talking out and improve homework completion

INTRODUCTION: The authors describe a system in which appropriate school behavior is reported to the parents and rewarded at home. It is an inexpensive technique that requires no special training and appeals to teachers who are reluctant to modify their class routines for special programs. It can be used to monitor a variety of behaviors and offers reinforcers from the home that may not be available in school. Furthermore, the program can be tailored to the behavior problems of individual youngsters yet still be operated for many students simultaneously.

DAILY REPORT CARD: The teacher of students aged eight to eleven identified talking out and incomplete homework as two problems. Talk-outs included such behaviors as talking to others, answering questions without permission, and yelling. One week before the program was implemented, letters went home that outlined the reporting system. Its goals were described as increasing communication among the home, the school, and the student through daily feedback on behavior and performance. Students were instructed to give the cards to their parents each evening and to make sure they were rated by their teachers in all appropriate areas. If a card was lost, all ratings would be considered "poor." Students were also encouraged to discuss their ratings with their teachers, to question their marks if they disagreed, and to discuss ways to improve their performance. Teacher responsibilities were also outlined in the letter. They were to rate the children in the designated areas, sign their names, and, if necessary, explain the reasons for the grade. Parents were directed to read the report card each evening, compliment their child for good ratings, and then constructively address the areas needing improvement. Parents were also urged to save the cards so that future school-related discussions would be more meaningful.

On the first day of the system, cards were taped to each student's desk. They were divided into the three areas of behavior, schoolwork, and homework. Students were told that they would receive a score of four on their daily report card if their homework had been completed and was all correct. A three would be given for all homework completed and mostly correct, a two for completed homework mostly incorrect, and a one for incomplete work. After twelve days, ratings for talking out were added to the system. Students earned a score of four for no talk-outs, a three for one talk-out, a two for two talk-outs, and a one for more than two. Talk-out ratings were made after each one-hour period. After day thirty-four, reports were taken home on Friday only, although daily scoring continued.

Under the system, the percentage of children not completing homework dropped from 35 to 17, and remained just under this rate for the entire treatment. The change to weekly reports did not weaken the effect. When feedback on talk-outs began, incidents were quickly reduced from an average of thirteen and one half per hour to about two per hour. After eleven days the rate dropped to near zero and remained there during the weekly reports.

COMMENTARY: School-home management programs have several important advantages. First, by allowing parents to actively monitor their child's academic progress, and they provide valuable feedback to parents. This consistent involvement by parents is a novelty for many children, the resulting attention may itself promote change. Second, the procedure allows for positive contact between home and school. Schools typically send reports home when grades are low and behavior is bad. Students might be less anxious about parent-teacher communication if these contacts also included reports of achievements. Third, this technique can enhance parental support of the teacher's efforts and project the teacher as a professional working in the interest of the student. Conflicts between parents and teachers often occur when teachers fail to notify parents of potential problems. Daily or weekly reporting systems are a quick, simple, and efficient way to spot problems and enlist the parent's aid in addressing them.

SOURCE: Dougherty, E. H., and Dougherty, A. "The Daily Report Card: A Simplified and Flexible Package for Classroom Behavior Management." *Psychology in the Schools*, 1977, *14*(2), 191-195.

Three Punishment Strategies for Boisterous Behavior

AUTHOR: Lee Swanson

PRECIS: Using variations of punishment with individuals and small groups to reduce disruptive behavior in a resource room

INTRODUCTION: The author indicates that academic progress depends on the children's displaying appropriate preacademic behaviors. When these behaviors are not mastered, the student is difficult to teach and often becomes disruptive. Under such conditions, strategies that provide praise for appropriate behavior but ignore negative conduct are not always effective. Sometimes punishments need to be applied to reduce an undesirable behavior and allow learning to take place. The author investigated three punishment contingencies with students whose behavior was seriously interfering with their learning and with others' work. A praise/ignore program had proved unsuccessful in each case.

CASE ONE: Keith was a sixteen-year-old high school sophomore who attended a learning disabilities class each day for math instruction. His verbal disruptions affected learning in the entire class. Typical behaviors included calling out, screaming, blowing, coughing, whistling, singing, belching, and cursing. After pretreatment behaviors had been recorded for ten sessions, the teacher changed her praise/ignore strategy. Keith was told that each noise or talk-out during class would cost him two minutes from his lunch period and that he would have to spend this time with the teacher in individual tutoring. He would not be allowed to eat his lunch during this time nor would other students be allowed to enter the classroom. After eight sessions the teacher returned to the praise/ignore procedure for ten sessions. Then the punishment condition was reestablished for eight days. After the program ended, checkups were conducted three times over the next twenty-five days. Before treatment Keith's talk-outs averaged about eighteen per thirty-minute session. By the end of the second punishment condition, talk-outs had been reduced to about four per session. Follow-up rates stabilized at about eight and one half per session.

CASE TWO: Eleven-year-old Tim was retained in fourth grade because of a reading disability. He had been attending the school's resource room since the second grade, but his calling out, noise making, tapping, and out-of-seat behavior made him difficult to teach. A token system that rewarded Tim for appropriate behavior was only moderately successful in curtailing his disruptiveness. After pretreatment rates had been obtained for talking out, out-of-seat behavior, and noise making, the token procedure was modified. Tim began the reading class by receiving ten tokens and had one removed by the teacher for each instance of talking out. Remaining tokens could be used to purchase time in a desired classroom activity. Removal of tokens for out-of-seat behavior and noise making was introduced on days fourteen and seventeen, respectively. During this procedure talking out was reduced by about two thirds, while out-of-seat behavior declined to about one sixth of its pretreatment rate. Noise making also decreased to about one third of its original level.

CASE THREE: Four students aged fourteen to sixteen worked in a resource room and were constantly talking out, cursing, leaving their seats, and bothering others. Group rates were recorded for these students for nine days. On day ten, each of the four students started class with twenty tokens. It was explained that if any one of them disturbed others in the class, each would lose a token. Contingencies for each of the other three behaviors were begun at later sessions. As in case two, the tokens that each student retained could be used to choose various enjoyable activities. During this treatment, disturbing others and leaving seats decreased by one half, talk-outs by about two thirds, and cursing by more than 80 percent.

COMMENTARY: Cases one and two are examples of individual response-cost procedures. For Keith, misconduct cost him lunch time, while Tim lost tokens. In case three, a response cost was implemented as a group contingency, so that each student's behavior had consequences for the entire group. The author does not advocate the indiscriminate use of punishment. Nor does he suggest that praise/ignore strategies be eliminated. Used appropriately, however, punishment can be an effective tool to reduce disruptive behaviors that severely interfere with the teaching process and are not responsive to reward-based interventions. Proper use of punishment can also reduce inappropriate behavior to the point where praise/ignore strategies become more effective. Most programs attempt to combine positive with negative procedures to inhibit disruptiveness and encourage appropriate behaviors. Many articles describing punishment procedures stress the need for a combined approach and usually emphasize the positive outcomes that result from appropriately applied punishments.

SOURCE: Swanson, L. "Removal of Positive Reinforcement to Alter Learning Disabled Adolescents' Preacademic Problems." *Psychology in the Schools,* 1979, *16*(2), 286-292.

Positive Practice to Reduce Disruptive Behavior

AUTHORS: N. H. Azrin and M. A. Powers

PRECIS: Controlling talk-outs and out-of-seat behavior by having students rehearse proper procedure

INTRODUCTION: Positive practice involves the practice of appropriate behavior to improve conduct. It thus differs from classroom strategies in which students are threatened, reprimanded, or actively punished. The authors compared positive practice with traditional punishments to assess its effectiveness.

METHODS: Six boys aged seven to eleven attending a special summer class were identified as frequently talking out or leaving their seats. In the first phase of the study, students were exposed to a *warnings, reminders, and reinforcement* condition. Before each class the students were informed that talking or leaving their seats without permission was prohibited. If a youngster misbehaved, the teacher called his name and repeated the rules in a clear, short statement. Throughout all phases of the study the teacher also praised students regularly for appropriate studying behavior.

After three days, loss of a ten-minute recess was added to the first condition. If a child failed to ask permission to talk or leave his seat, he had to sit quietly during recess and was given nothing to do. Four days later *delayed positive practice* was introduced. The same rules as in the previous condition were described at the start of each class, and recess was denied to misbehaving students. However, during recess the student had to perform the following positive practice exercises: (1) the child repeated the rules upon request by the teacher; (2) he practiced raising his hand, waiting for teacher recognition, and asking permission to talk or get up; (3) the teacher remarked on the appropriateness of this behavior and had the child practice again; and (4) several practice trials were repeated. If the student hesitated or performed incorrectly, he was instructed to start over. Practice lasted for five minutes unless there were more than two students. In that case, the ten minutes were divided among the students present. When he had completed the exercises, the student was allowed to return to recess.

After twelve days of delayed practice, *immediate positive practice* was initiated for six days. The practice sequence was the same, except that one trial was held in class at the moment of the rule infraction. Practice was then continued for five minutes during recess. Finally, a fading procedure was included in which immediate practice was reduced until only the rule had to be repeated. In recess, practice time was halved each day if the student broke the rule no more than two times the previous day. If not, the five-minute practice period was maintained.

When warnings and reminders alone were given, disruptions remained high—an average of twenty-nine per day. Loss of recess reduced them by about 60 percent, but delayed and immediate positive practice further lowered them by 95 and 98 percent, respectively. Checkups during the following school year showed maintenance of appropriate behavior after the teachers had been instructed in positive practice.

COMMENTARY: The authors indicate that positive practice is useful with children who have severe behavior problems. The students showed little resistance to the procedure, and any reluctance quickly disappeared when instructions were repeated. A desire to return to recess also motivated students to complete the task. The procedure takes only a few seconds of class time (none if practice is delayed) and can be done in a reeducative, rather than a purely punitive, spirit. However, in some instances, the reeducative character of the technique may be diminished. For example, it is questionable whether immediate practice should be the treatment of choice with preadolescents or adolescents. Public practice for this population might well create embarrassment and negative side effects. Delayed practice may be more appropriate for older students.

SOURCE: Azrin, N. H., and Powers, M. A. "Eliminating Classroom Disturbances of Emotionally Disturbed Children by Positive Practice Procedures." *Behavior Therapy*, 1975, *6*, 525-534.

Additional Readings

Blackwood, R. O. "The Operant Conditioning of Verbally Mediated Self-Control in the Classroom." *Journal of School Psychology*, 1970, *8*(4), 251-258.

Verbal self-statements can have a powerful mediating effect on subsequent behavior. When a child is tempted to misbehave, overt or covert self-verbalizations regarding the consequences will strongly affect whether misbehavior actually occurs. If students can learn to control these mediating comments, misconduct may be reduced. In this study eighth- and ninth-grade students were given verbal mediation training to reduce talking out and other inappropriate behaviors in class. Youngsters were required to copy a "mediation essay" if they misbehaved in class. The essay reviewed the nature of the wrongdoing, the reason for its inappropriateness, the negative consequences of its occurrence, the appropriate behavior that should be displayed, and why acceptable behavior is necessary. A control group received an essay on the steam engine to copy if its members acted up. Failure to copy essays met with increased punishments (including detention), while compliance was praised or resulted in release from detention. If misbehavior continued, increasingly strong mediation tasks were required; for example, writing the essay from memory or acting out correct and incorrect behaviors. Results showed a significant decrease in disruptive behavior in the mediation group compared to the control group. Establishing operant control over verbal behavior thus has an effect on disruptive classroom behavior.

Ellery, M. D., Blampied, N. M., and Black, W. A. M. "Reduction of Disruptive Behavior in the Classroom: Group and Individual Reinforcement Contingencies Compared." *New Zealand Journal of Educational Studies*, 1975, *10*, 59-65.

Controlling inappropriate talk-outs with eight-to-ten year-olds. During thirty minutes of daily individual math, rules for appropriate talking were displayed on the blackboard, and the token system was explained. For the first phase of this study each student was individually rewarded with a token for every five minutes of obedience to the rules. Five tokens earned the child a backup reinforcer selected from a list of preferred items.

In the group contingency phase, no child earned backup rewards unless all children earned five tokens. Results indicated that group and individual contingencies were equally effective in suppressing the disruptive behaviors. When a small number of children are disruptive, an individual contingency may be the preferred strategy. However, under group contingencies, cooperative behaviors such as peer prompting and peer tutoring have been observed. The decision to use one or the other approach or both of them should depend on student and classroom variables.

Jones, F. H., and Eimers, R. C. "Role Playing to Train Elementary Teachers to Use a Classroom Management 'Skill Package.'" *Journal of Applied Behavior Analysis*, 1975, *8*, 421-433.

The training of third-grade teachers to use a skill package of behavior management techniques in the classroom is described. The purpose was to control talking and out-of-seat behavior and to increase academic performance of students. The teachers were trained by means of role playing in six to seven sessions. In contrived classroom lessons, participants role played a teacher, a "good" student, and a "bad" student, while the skill package was explained and modeled by the trainer. Each teacher received feedback during their role playing from the trainer and other participants. Training focused on limit-setting skills, prompting, and reinforcing on-task behavior. Identification of, and responses to disruptiveness were practiced, including circulating around the classroom, the use of verbal and facial messages, quickness of response, establishing physical proximity to the target student, time-outs, and proper sequencing of disapproving and approving feedback. Teachers rehearsed how to prompt the participation of shy or unmotivated students and how to structure periods of transition between lessons. Verbal and physical praise for on-task behavior during seatwork was role played. Responding to students without interrupting praise and limit setting for others was also practiced. During the training process, the classes of the trainees experienced a reduction in talking to neighbors, inappropriate talk, and out-of-seat behaviors. The number of correctly completed math problems also increased significantly.

Lovitt, T. C., Lovitt, A. O., Eaton, M. D., and Kirkwood, M. "The Deceleration of Inappropriate Comments by a Natural Consequence." *Journal of School Psychology,* 1973, *11*(2), 148-154.

Ivan, a nine-year-old special education student, was treated for inappropriate comments relating to bathroom or sexual themes. A peer whom Ivan liked (Curtis) was recruited as a "manager." He was instructed that whenever Ivan made an inappropriate statement, he should approach Ivan and tell him that he doesn't like him when he says ———. He was then to move away from Ivan until his talk became more acceptable. At certain times, Ivan had the opportunity to undo a remark and win back his friend. For example, Ivan's teacher would prompt him to make appropriate statements. If Ivan complied, Curtis would return to Ivan's desk. After sixty treatment days the frequency of Ivan's inappropriate comments was reduced to zero, and this level was maintained during the following school year. During and after treatment Curtis received much praise and many requests for his services from other classes. Peer managers are powerful behavior modifiers because of the importance of peer approval for many children. In addition, they may remove the burden of managing the treatment from the teacher, while at the same time learning more about behavior and its causes.

Classroom Disturbance:
Noncompliance

The noncompliant child frequently ignores or disobeys classroom rules, refuses to comply with requests or directions from the teacher, or talks back to the teacher. Such refusals are particularly disturbing to teachers who gauge their own effectiveness by their ability to maintain classroom control. While most children disobey now and then, noncompliant students display a consistent pattern of oppositional attitudes and behaviors.

A Humanistic Approach to Discipline

AUTHOR: Thomas Edward Bratter

PRECIS: Discipline as a process to encourage responsibility rather than as an aversive punishment

INTRODUCTION: The author criticizes the educational system for its inability to provide a meaningful education for students. Motivated by an intense need to control disruptiveness, schools have become like prisons, emphasizing control, compliance, and the threat of punishment. Students are not encouraged to think or be creative and, as a result, have become alienated, unmotivated, and unresponsive. They are no longer willing to comply with adult standards and often drop out to embrace opposing value systems. According to the author, a key factor in student noncompliance has been the disciplinary methods of schools. Instead of emphasizing punishment alone, those who administer discipline should also try to teach a sense of responsibility, so that the student can develop self-discipline and begin to move toward desired goals. If schools would abandon their obsessive stress on conformity, students might feel freer to explore alternate solutions to problems in an atmosphere of constructive disagreement. In this environment, students would feel more valued and worthwhile, and disruptiveness and noncompliance would be reduced.

There are times when traditional disciplinary procedures are necessary for certain students. The author outlines nine steps in a responsibility-oriented process that includes, but does not focus on, punishment:

1. In the early stages of problems, punishments or warnings are premature. The teacher should handle early difficulties by attempting to find interesting and meaningful activities for the student and by demonstrating friendliness and a spirit of caring. This approach often defuses potentially serious resistance.

2. A conference with the student should be held to explore his or her topics of interest and to suggest better use of time. This can be done when the student is reacting more posi-

tively in class than usual. The teacher might suggest alternatives to disruptive behavior or discuss goals for the year (or the more distant future). The tone of the conference should be nonjudgmental and nonthreatening.

3. If problems persist, the teacher should direct the student to evaluate the negative effects of his actions and should make suggestions for more responsible behavior.

4. If these steps are not successful, brief class discussions might help—discussions in which classmates suggest ways to aid the student to behave more productively (It is not uncommon to hear students warn a classmate that his behavior could get him in trouble. Such comments might be constructively utilized in a classroom discussion.) The student should be informed of this step in advance.

5. If these efforts are also fruitless, a referral to a trustworthy person outside class can be made. The ensuing conference should be cordial but should inform the student very directly of the decreasing tolerance for his behavior. Plans for change should then be discussed.

6. The person in charge of discipline should also see the student, set and clarify behavioral limits, and draw up a contract that outlines the changes the student will make. The student must sign the contract, and copies should be given to the student and teacher. The student should then be informed of possible parental involvement.

7. If parents have been notified and there is still no improvement in behavior, the student may be suspended for a specified number of days. Parents should be asked to see that the youngster remains at home and does assigned work.

8. After the student returns to school, a conference should be held with the student, teacher, and school disciplinarian. The student should be asked what he is prepared to do to return to class. A new behavior contract should be drawn up and signed. Expulsion should be discussed as the next step, and the student should be reminded that the outcome is his choice.

9. The final step would be expulsion and the development of alternate educational plans. One possibility would be part-time attendance at school, with the option to attend full time if behavior improves.

COMMENTARY: When disciplinary measures are planned with reason and not imposed in anger (or as retaliation), they are more likely to achieve their goal of purposeful behavior change. The author's step-by-step approach offers the student the chance to plan for change and yet communicates the increasing seriousness of the situation. While a school may adapt the plan to its own needs, the concept of sequencing the disciplinary process is important in that it teaches the student responsibility for his own behavior. It also allows other students to recognize the personal control they have over their own actions. As the author states, if schools are willing to abandon authoritarian punishment, they can develop discipline procedures that educate students to their responsibility for what they do.

SOURCE: Bratter, T. E. "From Discipline to Responsibility Training: A Humanistic Orientation for the School." *Psychology in the Schools*, 1977, *14*(1), 45-54.

===

Modifying Disruptive Behavior
by Using Delayed Consequences

AUTHORS: Bernard H. Salzberg, B. L. Hopkins, Andrew J. Wheeler, and Linda Taylor

PRECIS: Controlling noncompliance with contingencies delayed for as long as thirty minutes

INTRODUCTION: Most behavior management programs stress the importance of reinforcing target behaviors immediately after they occur. However, the realities of school life often result in delays between the behavior and its consequences. This paper investigated the effects of delayed consequences on disruptive kindergarten behavior.

METHOD: The children were required to remain seated at their tables during fifteen minutes of their lunch period. During one-minute observation intervals, observers recorded the frequency with which students failed to comply with the rule. Children were marked as noncompliant if they made physical contact with other children (hitting, hugging, playing patty-cake, or other behaviors), were out of their seats or sitting improperly, or played with objects on the table. After lunch the teacher returned with her class to their room and delivered the appropriate contingency. However, for the final thirty days of the fifty-day treatment period, the teacher was not immediately available to meet her class. When this happened, the students were kept in the cafeteria or allowed to play for as long as thirty minutes. This constituted the delayed contingency.

Upon returning to the class, the teacher carried out one of several procedures. For the first eight sessions, each child was allowed to play after returning from the lunchroom. No feedback was given to the children about disruptive lunchroom behavior. During sessions nine to thirteen, each child received feedback but was allowed to play regardless of how disruptive he or she was during lunch. In sessions fourteen to thirty, the child could not play after lunch unless he or she had behaved during at least four one-minute observation periods. If the child did not meet this criterion, he or she was required to lie down on his or her mat for the fifteen-minute play period. For sessions thirty-one to forty, the children were divided into two groups. Group one contained children who had responded well to the contingency in sessions fourteen to thirty. In group two were children who had not improved during these sessions. For group one, the criterion for play was raised from four to ten good-behavior intervals. The criterion for group two remained at four but also included teacher demonstration and description of the disruptive behavior. Sessions forty-one to forty-seven returned to the no-feedback and no-reward condition. In the last three sessions, students were rewarded for ten or more *disruptive* observation intervals.

When the play contingency was applied, the children who were later included in group one quickly reduced their disruptive behavior in the cafeteria. For group two, teacher demonstration was necessary to significantly reduce their misconduct.

Children who responded well to the four-interval condition did not show any further significant improvement when the criterion for reward was raised to ten intervals. In addition, these children did not return to high rates of disruptiveness when feedback and rewards were terminated, while group two immediately did so. When rewards were given for disruption, both groups increased their misconduct.

COMMENTARY: Delayed contingencies effectively reduced noncompliance, although some students required teacher demonstration of the prohibited behaviors. If a teacher can delay rewards or punishments or both until more convenient times, she will be able to utilize behavior management strategies without interrupting class routine. It may then also be possible to select more powerful contingencies that would not be available during academic time (for example, giving free time or allowing the child to help the teacher). However, it is unclear how long rewards can be delayed before they lose their power to regulate behavior. These results also suggest that token systems may not always be necessary to sustain the power of later rewards. In some situations a knowledge of future consequences might be enough to control behaviors. In addition, feedback alone was not shown to be a potent change agent. It must be augmented by some systematic consequence, even if a delayed one.

SOURCE: Salzberg, B. H., Hopkins, B. L., Wheeler, A. J., and Taylor, L. "Reduction of Kindergarten Children's Disruptive Behavior with Delayed Feedback and Delayed Contingent Access to Play." *Journal of School Psychology*, 1974, *12*(1), 24-30.

Self-Directed Time-Outs to Control Behavior

AUTHORS: Gary Allen Pease and Vernon O. Tyler, Jr.

PRECIS: Comparing teacher- and student-determined time-out durations to reduce disruptiveness

INTRODUCTION: When students misbehave, teachers will sometimes prevent them from continuing the activity and send them to a secluded area in the schoolroom. This time-out procedure has been shown to be an effective management tool when applied consistently. In some programs, a time-out room is established with a monitor to supervise students in the room. The authors examined whether students could manage their own time-outs without the need for teacher intervention.

TIME-OUT: Fifteen students aged seven to fourteen displayed a variety of disruptive behaviors, including refusal to work, arguing or talking back, and getting into the teacher's desk or files without permission. Each student participated in all five phases of the study; each phase lasted ten days. In phase one, students were observed for their disruptiveness under an ongoing five-minute time-out procedure directed by the teacher. For phase two, time-outs were ended, and teachers simply told the student that he was misbehaving. Phase three reinstated the teacher-directed five-minute time-outs. In phase four, students were sent to the time-out area by the teacher but determined for themselves the length of time they remained there. During phase five, the teacher determined the time-out duration but used the times that each student had chosen for himself or herself during phase four.

After the final phase, results showed that self-imposed durations were as effective as teacher-determined ones. Students chose durations similar to those chosen by the teacher, although their decisions may have been influenced by prior experience with the five-minute time-out.

COMMENTARY: While self-management seems as successful as teacher-managed durations, it is unclear what students would impose on themselves without earlier time-out experience. Therefore, it might be helpful in using this strategy to begin with a teacher-directed approach (to establish the process) and then move to a self-determined procedure. Self-management programs seem to give students the chance to regulate their own behavior and thus fulfill an assumed goal of the educational experience. They free the teacher from the burden of constant supervision and can be used by younger elementary school students as well as by older students.

SOURCE: Pease, G. A., and Tyler, V. O., Jr. "Self-Regulation of Time-Out Duration in the Modification of Disruptive Classroom Behavior." *Psychology in the Schools,* 1979, *16*(1), 101-105.

Additional Readings

Gumaer, J., and Myrick, R. D. "Behavioral Group Counseling with Disruptive Children." *The School Counselor,* 1974, *21*(4), 313-317.

This study combined client-centered and behavior modification techniques in counseling sessions for noncompliant, talking-out elementary students. During the eight sessions, the counselor set clear rules for behavior, charted the progress of three student-identified misbehaviors, and rewarded the absence of these target behaviors during the sessions with M&M's and praise. Group discussions focused on punishments that the students had received, the effects of their misconduct on others, and events that trigger disruptiveness. Discussion skills became increasingly sophisticated during these sessions; by the final meeting, students reported greater self-understanding and improved relationships with peers. Teachers were kept informed as the group progressed and were advised to apply basic management techniques in the classroom, such as praise and ignoring. Disruptive behavior in the group declined to almost zero, while teacher reports indicated transfer of improved behavior outside the sessions. Since unruly behavior resurfaced ten weeks later, the authors suggest an ongoing reinforcement contingency to maintain treatment gains.

Karpowitz, D. H. "Reinstatement as a Method to Increase the Effectiveness of Discipline in the School or Home." *Journal of School Psychology*, 1977, *15*(3), 230-238.

First-grade boys were placed in a tempting situation. They were individually escorted to a room with toys in it to play a game, and they received marbles as a reward for their participation. Once in the room, they were told to look through a boring book until the experimenter returned to play with them. When she returned and found they had played with the toys, she disciplined them in one of three ways. First, using "verbal reinstatement," she described the transgression in detail, employing eye contact and gestures in outlining each step. Second, for "verbal and behavioral reinstatement," she detailed the same misconduct but also walked the child through each step as she talked. The child had to repeat which toys he had played with. Third, under "minimal reinstatement," she indicated that toys had been used, without discussing or rehearsing specifics. In addition to these methods, one half of the boys in each condition had to return one marble (delayed discipline). Following these interventions, the game was played for five minutes, and the child was then returned to the room with the toys. He was told to look through the boring book again, and the time that elapsed before he went back to the toys was measured. It was found that delayed discipline was more effective in inhibiting a return to the toys than no discipline and that reinstatement plus discipline was more effective than discipline alone. However, verbal and behavioral reinstatement was no more effective than verbal reinstatement. The behavioral component did not enhance the effect. Finally, in the no-discipline groups, minimal reinstatement was as effective as the more elaborate reinstatements. These findings suggest that discipline may be augmented by verbal rehearsal of the rule-breaking sequence. Behavioral rehearsal may be unnecessary.

Schumaker, J. B., Hovell, M. F., and Sherman, J. A. "An Analysis of Daily Report Cards and Parent-Managed Privileges in the Improvement of Adolescents' Classroom Performance." *Journal of Applied Behavior Analysis*, 1977, *10,* 449-464.

In the first experiment, the parents of three noncompliant seventh-grade boys received daily reports of behavior and academic performance. Reports noted whether rules were followed, whether classwork was satisfactory, the degree of teacher satisfaction, and grades for assignments. Parents were instructed in setting up a point system, praising the child, and providing privileges for progress. Daily reporting substantially increased rule following, academic performance, and teacher satisfaction. Grade point averages also increased. In the second experiment, the parents of one of two other students were instructed to praise improved reports but to give no privileges. Removing contingent privileges did not lessen the improvement in rule-following behavior but did cause a decline in classroom academic performance after an initial improvement. In a final experiment, counselors implemented the daily program without consultation, using a manual developed by the authors· (*Managing Behavior: A Home-Based School Achievement System,* Lawrence, Kan.: H&H Enterprises, 1977). This provides detailed instructions for program presentation to the family and teachers, as well as for the establishment of grading criteria and privileges, point exchanges, and program monitoring. Counselors successfully applied the program with two students, thus demonstrating its practicality and effectiveness. A fading system has also been developed to maintain progress after reporting ends.

Struble, J. B. "The Application of Positive Social Reinforcement to the Behaviors of Getting Ready to Work." *School Applications of Learning Theory*, 1971, *1,* 34-39.

A fourth-grade class showed considerable delay in getting ready for classwork upon returning from an outside activity. They did not comply with instructions on the board that outlined work assignments. To modify this behavior, the teacher told class members that they would be timed on how long they took to get ready to work. Immediate praise was given to students who demonstrated quick readiness. The teacher informed students of their times; and, because the students compared their times and monitored their progress, there was mutual reinforcement and encouragement. In sessions ten to sixteen, children were praised for being ready in less than two minutes. This was dropped to seventy seconds at session seventeen. At session twenty-one the class agreed to add quietness to "ready-to-work" behavior. The total procedure resulted in a stabilized "ready time" of one minute.

Classroom Disturbance: Playing the Class Clown

The class clown is a student who inappropriately or disruptively seeks peer and/or teacher attention. Sometimes the intent is to provoke laughter from others. While some clowns are well liked, others are disliked intensely because they play jokes at the expense of other students. More research is needed to understand the child who solicits attention in this way.

A Combined Approach to Behavior
and Academic Problems

AUTHORS: Adrian Chan, Ada Chiu, and Donald J. Mueller

PRECIS: Using tutoring, counseling, and teacher consultation to modify attention-seeking behavior

INTRODUCTION: The authors combined social reinforcement and a remedial reading program based on reinforcement principles to modify classroom failure and disruption in an eleven-year-old student. Charley enjoyed the laughter and attention he received from classmates for his misconduct. He would often leave his seat, walk around the room, turn on his radio, and beat rhythms with his hands and feet. His reading performance was quite poor, and he was usually inattentive or asleep during reading class. His teacher was unable to control his antics.

INTERVENTION: Three procedures were employed to improve Charley's reading skills, encourage more positive attitudes toward school, and increase the teacher's control over his behavior.

Remedial Reading Instruction. Instruction was carried out by a "therapeutic educator." During each session Charley was told to read a passage from a book of his choice to encourage his participation in the lesson. After informal testing for comprehension, he practiced on the "controlled reader" program (S. E. Taylor, and H. Frankenpohl, *Controlled Reading Machine,* New York: Educational Developmental Laboratories, 1959). Vocabulary words were presented on a filmstrip; this was followed by ten minutes of speed reading and a comprehension exercise. Then Charley indicated the pages that he had read in his home assignment of the previous day. His comprehension on this reading was tested and a new homework assignment given.

For the first six sessions Charley received a piece of gum for completing all comprehension exercises and for every five pages read at home. In sessions six to twelve, the home criterion was raised to ten pages, and comprehension exercises required five or fewer wrong answers. Beginning with session thirteen, praise was substituted for gum, but this change was not successful. Charley was then given the choice of earning gum or bringing a friend to the reading sessions. He chose the friend. This step was designed to strengthen social reinforcement through competition and public praise and to further reduce Charley's early unease at being singled out for help. He and his friend worked together for the final eight sessions and were aware of each other's progress.

Counseling. The therapeutic educator provided a nondirective, supportive, and reinforcing atmosphere in which Charley was encouraged to discuss his feelings about himself and school. After some initial resistance, he freely vented feelings of anger, frustration, and dissatisfaction with his school experience.

Classroom Modification. Suggestions were made to Charley's teacher about the use of praise and attention to encourage performance and appropriate behavior.

Charley's performance in the reading sessions, as well as his motivation to read, improved significantly during the program, especially when his friend was in class with him. In his regular class his behavior changed dramatically. He participated enthusiastically, attended to his work, and became a class leader. He learned to enjoy reading both in school and at home. Incidents of clowning decreased markedly, and the teacher felt more able to handle his occasional flare-ups. Four months later, improvement was still being maintained.

COMMENTARY: Students who misbehave to gain attention from the teacher and peers can be helped when attention is made contingent on positive behavior. Charley's improvement through this strategy carried over to class, where he was also recognized for appropriate behavior. This paper highlights the importance of skill building through a combination of remedial education, counseling for emotional support, and consultation to increase teacher sensitivity and management skills. When necessary, the psychologist and other remedial specialists should team together to coordinate their services for the most effective intervention. Federal and state laws are increasingly emphasizing this multidisciplinary approach for serving students with behavior and academic problems. Thus, coordinated efforts are not simply advisable but are often mandated.

SOURCE: Chan, A., Chiu, A., and Mueller, D. J. "An Integrated Approach to the Modification of Classroom Failure and Disruption: A Case Study." *Journal of School Psychology*, 1970, *8*(2), 114-121.

The Effectiveness of Soft Reprimands

AUTHORS: K. Daniel O'Leary, Kenneth F. Kaufman, Ruth E. Kass, and Ronald S. Drabman

PRECIS: Comparing the effects of loud and soft reprimands to reduce attention-getting and other behaviors

INTRODUCTION: Soft reprimands for misbehavior offer several practical advantages. They do not call as much attention to the child as loud reprimands and thus limit peer reinforcement for negative behavior. Furthermore, they offer a more active alternative for the teacher who has tried unsuccessfully to ignore inappropriate behavior. In this paper the authors compare reprimand intensities for their ability to control disruptiveness.

INTERVENTIONS: A second-grade child rarely attended to work but instead giggled and talked out loud. According to his teacher, he enjoyed having classmates laugh at him and behaved this way to gain their attention. After observers recorded pretreatment behavior rates, the teacher was asked to continue her usual approach to handling disruptiveness. This phase was called the *loud reprimand condition* because most of the responses made by the teacher were loud ones. For the *soft reprimand condition,* the teacher was instructed to reprimand at her usual frequency but to speak so that only the target child could hear her. She was also asked to reprimand all children softly, not just the target child.

After two alternations of loud and soft reprimand conditions, results showed that disruptive behaviors were about half as frequent under soft reprimands. However, the authors noted that loud reprimands were dispensed more frequently than soft ones. The resulting increased attention for loud versus soft reprimands may have affected the results more strongly than the intensity of the reprimands. For a second study teachers were asked to equalize the number of loud and soft reprimands as much as possible. Results showed that soft reprimands more effectively reduced disruptive behavior even when they were equal in number with.louder comments.

COMMENTARY: Soft reprimands may not be effective with all disruptive children. Furthermore, some teachers seem to find it difficult to use this strategy simply because they feel that it may not be effective. For others, the teacher's moving closer to the child in order to deliver soft reprimands may be seen as disruptive to the lesson. However, with children who misbehave to gain attention, using fewer soft than loud reprimands successfully reduced undesirable behavior by removing the attention that loud comments attract. The authors view soft reprimands as a technique that is most successful when combined with other management approaches in a well-planned academic program.

SOURCE: O'Leary, K. D., Kaufman, K. F., Kass, R. E., and Drabman, R. S. "The Effects of Loud and Soft Reprimands on the Behavior of Disruptive Students." *Exceptional Children,* 1970, *37,* 145-155.

Modifying Disruptive Behavior
with Systematic Attention

AUTHORS: Elaine H. Zimmerman and Joseph Zimmerman

PRECIS: Modifying attention-getting behavior through systematically praising and ignoring it

INTRODUCTION: The authors report two case studies of eleven-year-old boys who attended class in an inpatient residential treatment center. Their inappropriate behaviors seemed designed to catch the attention of adults and peers and may have been maintained by such focus.

CASE I: The first subject was afforded a great deal of attention during spelling lessons. Only after much assistance, cueing, and encouragement would the boy verbalize the correct spelling when called upon. In addition, he would wrinkle and throw away clean sheets of paper, laughing when the teacher and students noticed him.

For the intervention the teacher instructed the boy to go to the blackboard after he had turned in a barely legible spelling test. She informed him that he would have a quiz and that he was to correctly spell words on the board as she read them. She read the first word and then completely ignored him as he misspelled it numerous times while looking over at her. After ten minutes he spelled the word correctly; the teacher responded positively and read the second word. With each of the ten words, the time required for a correct response decreased as did the number of inappropriate responses. When the test was finished, the teacher gave him an A and praised him. They then engaged in an enjoyable activity together. In all further interactions, social attention was given only when appropriate classroom behavior was displayed. Other behaviors were ignored. After one month the boy's attention-getting misbehavior had been almost completely eliminated, and he was working more efficiently.

CASE II: This youngster displayed tantrums, spoke baby talk, and made frequent erroneous comments. On occasion he screamed and threw tantrums on the floor in the front of the classroom, causing a crowd to gather around him. During treatment he was put at his desk in the classroom and completely ignored by the teacher as he kicked and screamed. After a few moments the boy looked at the teacher, who told him she was ready to work when he was. After another few minutes he indicated his readiness. The teacher then smiled, went to his desk, and with a positive comment began to work with the boy. During a period of several weeks, the teacher ignored his tantrums. When they ended, the teacher involved him in an enjoyable activity, remained near him, and talked with him. Tantrums disappeared during these weeks. The other inappropriate behaviors also declined and almost completely ceased when attention was withheld at their occurrence. The boy was also rewarded intermittently for attentiveness in class with smiles, a question he could easily answer, and so forth. His talk became more appropriate, and his work in school improved.

COMMENTARY: When undesirable behaviors are maintained by the attention they receive, they can be modified by redirecting attention to follow positive rather than inappropriate actions. Such strategies eliminate the rewarding value of the misconduct and instead attach rewards to productive behaviors. These interventions are practical and efficient for use with emotionally disturbed children, as well as with problem students in regular classroom settings.

SOURCE: Zimmerman, E. H., and Zimmerman, J. "The Alteration of Behavior in a Special Classroom Situation." *Journal of the Experimental Analysis of Behavior,* 1962, *5,* 59-60.

Additional Readings

Damico, S., and Purkey, W. "The Class Clown Phenomenon Among Middle School Students." Paper presented at annual meeting of American Educational Research Association, San Francisco, April, 1976.

This paper, which notes the lack of information about the class clown phenomenon despite its common occurrence, examined the characteristics of class clowns through student and teacher questionnaires. Clowns tend to be male, and super clowns (those with twenty-five or more peer nominations as clowns) tend to be the oldest child or an only child. Teachers generally see clowns as unruly, attention seeking, and possessed of strong leadership qualities. They are not seen as different in academic self-concept or as kinder or more cheerful than other students. On a sociometric measure, more clowns were listed as being liked by almost everyone than as having good ideas or being good to work with on class projects. Two types of clowns emerged from the data. One was popular, creative, and well liked, while the other was an isolate. Isolate clowns are alone because they often use others to cause laughter (for example, teasing, dumping a girl from her chair, or popping a bag near someone's ear). These differences require further study. Because of the importance of humor in social systems, the study of class clowns may add to an understanding of the role of humor in the educational process.

Madsen, C. H., Jr., Becker, W. C., and Thomas, D. R. "Rules, Praise, and Ignoring: Elements of Elementary Classroom Control." *Journal of Applied Behavior Analysis,* 1968, *1,* 139-150.

A teacher systematically applied rules, praise, and ignoring to modify classroom behavior, with a focus on one second grader. Cliff acted "silly," was uninterested in school, and often tried to attract the attention of neighboring girls with pranks. After observers had rated the behaviors of teacher and child, the teacher was instructed to specify to the class five or six explicit rules of conduct and to post them in an obvious place. Rules were to be stated in positive terms (what *should* be done rather than what was forbidden) and were to be reviewed and rehearsed throughout the day. After a few weeks, instructions were given to the teacher to ignore inappropriate behavior in addition to specifying classroom rules. It was pointed out that if a teacher criticizes negative behavior, the attention given may strengthen rather than weaken it. Examples of behaviors to be ignored were given. Finally, praise was added; it was to be delivered in the form of attention, smiles, and positive comments. Behaviors to be praised included following rules, concentrating on work assignments, and prosocial actions. Results showed that rules alone had no effect on inappropriate classroom behavior, while ignoring plus rules achieved erratic results. In fact, Cliff's behavior worsened during this phase. But adding praise to rules and ignoring appreciably reduced misconduct. Cliff worked harder to get the teacher's attention and became less interested in gaining peer attention. He markedly improved his arithmetic skills.

Maletzky, B. M. "Behavior Recording as Treatment: A Brief Note." *Behavior Therapy,* 1974, *5,* 107-111.

Five cases are reported in which the simple self-counting of undesirable behavior modified the maladaptive pattern. Clients wore a wrist counter and pushed a button on it each time the unwanted behavior occurred. After totaling frequencies at the end of the day, they charted the results on a graph to keep a running account of progress. In one case a nine-year-old boy agreed to wear the counter to modify disruptive class behavior. He would raise and wave his hand furiously when the teacher asked a question even if he did not know the answer. Over a four-week treatment period, his hand waving declined. After a brief no-treatment phase, it diminished to zero during a second four-week treatment. Six months later, gains were being maintained without further use of the counter. The authors indicate the occasional need for gradual fading through less frequent wearings of the counter. In addition, some clients reported increased awareness of the absence of the unwanted behavior or the presence of new behaviors.

Classroom Disturbance:
Temper Tantrums

Tantrums are violent episodes of anger accompanied by loss of control, screaming, kicking, or cursing. Often viewed as attention-getting devices, tantrums usually occur in a social context. Tantrums are most commonly displayed by young children; the social pressures of adolescence and adulthood tend to suppress such overt expressions of feeling.

Reducing Temper Tantrums
in an Elementary Classroom

AUTHORS: Constance S. Carlson, Carole R. Arnold, Wesley C. Becker, and Charles H. Madsen

PRECIS: Using reward, punishment, and loss of attention to control classroom temper tantrums

INTRODUCTION: The authors describe the case of an eight-year-old girl with severe temper tantrums in school and at home. In treating her, they combined punishment, loss of attention, and reinforcement for nontantrum behavior.

CASE STUDY: One of five children, Diane was of average intelligence. Two of her sisters had suffered from sickle-cell anemia; one had died, leaving her parents in debt because of high medical bills. Her mother reported that Diane engaged in frequent tantrums at home to which the mother gave total attention. In school Diane had tantrums as often as three times a week. When tantrums occurred, she would be taken to the office, where school personnel provided a great deal of attention. During one episode Diane ran amuck in class, cursing wildly, throwing chairs, and attacking other children.

INTERVENTION: The authors established the following procedures in consultation with the teacher:
    1. Punishment—Diane was told that the teacher aide would hold her down in her chair if she misbehaved. Diane disliked physical contact, so for her this procedure was aversive.
    2. Loss of Attention—this step was designed to eliminate peer attention. Diane was seated in the back of the room, and the other children were told that they would receive candy if they did not turn around to watch her tantrum. Treats were distributed as the explanation was given and also intermittently during the day to prevent students from encouraging tantrums to get candy.
    3. Reinforcement—Diane earned a star on the board for each half day of tantrum-free behavior. After she earned four

consecutive stars, a little class party would be held during which Diane could pass out treats. Since she was a fearful, timid girl who was disliked by her peers, this reward was planned to increase her acceptance in class.

Diane threw a tantrum once on the first day of the program, but she was well-behaved the rest of the week and earned the class party. There were five tantrums the second week. During these, the teacher aide held her down while the teacher passed out treats to the students who did not pay any attention to the tantrums. There were no tantrums the next week, and Diane began to interact more with other girls. During the fourth week, as a problem brewed, the teacher reminded her that she had three stars and could not come into the building if she misbehaved. Diane stood near the building and then lingered by the classroom. She was ignored by the class. A little while later she was invited in. She cried and apologized, demonstrating that the class had become a positive place for her. No tantrums occurred the last month of school. However, they returned the following year in a new school and became worse when the principal and teacher chose not to use the procedure described above.

COMMENTARY: Temper tantrums are believed to be maintained by the attention they receive. To counteract this effect, time-out procedures are often used. The child is isolated in a separate room or area of the classroom for a specified period of time or until the tantrum ends. When space is not available, alternate procedures such as those described here may be used. In Diane's case, there are several reasons why improvements may not have carried over to the following year. For example, the behavior of the personnel at her new school may have again rewarded her for throwing tantrums. It may also be that the original treatment period was not long enough to sustain the positive effects. Nevertheless, it is clear that punishment, loss of attention, and reinforcement successfully reduced her tantrums when time-out procedures were not practical.

SOURCE: Carlson, C. S., Arnold, C. R., Becker, W. C., and Madsen, C. H. "The Elimination of Tantrum Behavior in a Child in an Elementary Classroom." *Behavior Research and Therapy*, 1968, *6*, 117-119.

Integrating Psychodynamic and Reinforcement
Strategies to Reduce Disruptiveness

AUTHOR: Frances M. Culbertson

PRECIS: Combining behavior modification and psychodynamic treatments to modify inappropriate classroom behavior

INTRODUCTION: Although behavior modification techniques can reduce specific problem behaviors in relatively short periods of time, the author argues that they do not take into account the underlying feelings of the child. The youngster also needs a warm, nonjudgmental, sympathetic adult who will allow and acknowledge expressions of anger, fear, hate, or other feelings that arise during treatment. She advocates a combined approach in which reinforcement is used to teach appropriate behavior and a therapeutic relationship is developed with a caring, supportive, affectively oriented therapist.

METHOD: Six kindergarten children were referred for group therapy. Their class behaviors included temper tantrums, teacher dependence, and aggressiveness. Three of the children were from homes with no father. Every Friday the children came to a special room called "our room," where a fifteen-minute group therapy session was conducted. During these sessions both behavioral and affective strategies were employed. The therapist worked to develop a close, personal rapport with the children. They were able to vent feelings about home and school while the therapist stressed her care and concern for them. The therapist also visited the students in class, at play, and at home to emphasize her interest in their well-being. Other school and community personnel (for example, firemen and policemen) attended sessions in which their roles as helpers and protectors were explained. Children were taught how to contact these people if necessary. During group sessions a behavioral strategy was also used in which the children earned candy for sitting in their seats, listening to others, and taking turns talking. These behaviors had been previously identified by the teacher as desirable classroom behaviors. The reinforcement schedule for dispensing candy was determined on the basis of behavior during the previous session.

After six weeks the teacher reported improvement in all six children. They displayed the reinforced therapy behaviors in class and were proud to announce how the therapist was "helping us learn to go to school." The group sessions were continued through the school year. Figure drawings completed at the beginning and end of the school year and scored according to a modified Harris "draw-a-person" procedure indicated that there had been personal growth in the therapy group as compared to a no-therapy group. The following year, the first-grade teacher reported continued positive behavior and attitudes among the children. Two years later, only one of the children was having academic problems.

COMMENTARY: In this study the author combined two interventions usually considered incompatible. Interestingly, she implemented the reinforcements in the therapy sessions rather than directly in the classroom. Thus, it was necessary for behavior change to generalize from the sessions to the classroom. A combined program in which the reinforcers were earned *in the classroom* for appropriate classroom behavior might have yielded even more powerful results. However, when in-class strategies are not practical, it is useful to know that behavior changes occurring in this type of school therapy program will carry over to other school settings.

SOURCE: Culbertson, F. M. "An Effective Low-Cost Approach to the Treatment of Disruptive Schoolchildren." *Psychology in the Schools,* 1974, *11*(2), 183-187.

Additional Readings

Greenberg, D. J., and O'Donnell, W. J. "A Note on the Effects of Group and Individual Contingencies upon Deviant Classroom Behavior." *Journal of Child Psychology and Psychiatry,* 1972, *13,* 55-58.

A combined individual and group contingency was used to modify the tantrums of a six-year-old first grader. When he threw a tantrum in class, Mike was requested to stand in an adjoining cloakroom until the tantrum stopped. For each ninety minutes of tantrum-free behavior, he and the entire class received a small piece of candy and verbal praise. Over twelve weeks, tantrums decreased from six per day to one or two per week. However, as the treatment progressed, the teacher stopped the group reward, while continuing the individual time-out. This caused a deterioration in Mike's schoolwork and peer relations, both of which had improved under the group contingency. The authors stressed the importance of the group strategy in generalizing improvement to these two behaviors. Group contingencies are powerful when a child is amenable to peer influence.

Schneider, M. R. "Turtle Technique in the Classroom." *Teaching Exceptional Children,* 1974, *7,* 22-24.

A technique to help young children manage the frustrations that lead to aggression and tantrums was described. The technique involves learning the so-called turtle position, relaxation training, and instruction in problem solving. It is introduced with a story about a turtle who didn't want to go to school or listen to his teacher. Every day he would get mad, even though he tried to stay calm and keep out of trouble. Then he met a wise old turtle who told him to hide in his shell whenever he was angry. There he could rest until the angry feeling went away. He tried it in school the next day and liked how he felt. It was warm and comfortable in his shell. When he came out, his teacher was happy with his behavior, and everyone admired him. He used his secret for the whole year and received a wonderful report card. After hearing the story, the class practiced the technique. When the teacher said the cue word *turtle,* the children pulled their arms and legs in close to their bodies

and rested their chins on their chests. They were also instructed
to apply the technique while imagining frustrating situations,
and they were rewarded with stars for good performances. The
children were subsequently trained in relaxation, learning to
tense and relax various muscles of the body. After experiencing
feelings of relaxation, they practiced relaxation techniques in
the turtle position. They tensed, counted to ten, then relaxed,
letting the calm feeling remain as they slowly resumed working.
Gradually they were encouraged to cue themselves with the
word *turtle,* receiving stars and backup rewards for doing so. In
addition, daily problem-solving sessions were held to teach them
alternative behaviors to aggression and tantrums. The turtle
technique is an effective tool and can be used in regular classroom settings.

Classroom Disturbance: Annoying or Bothering Others

Some children roam about the classroom, hitting others, touching or grabbing their possessions, or generally interfering with others' work through their comments or actions. While such behavior is difficult to handle in the classroom, it may pose even greater problems in the lunchroom or on the playground, where supervision may be laxer and physical aggression between students more likely.

I-Messages in the Classroom

AUTHORS: Robert F. Peterson, Stephen E. Loveless, Terry J. Knapp, Ben W. Loveless, Samuel M. Basta, and Steven Anderson

PRECIS: Using I-messages instead of reprimands or disapproval to reduce disruptive behavior and increase studying

INTRODUCTION: You-messages and I-messages are two kinds of verbal comments that teachers can deliver when students misbehave. A you-message is typically delivered as a reprimand, command, or disapproving statement. In contrast, I-messages do not tell the child how to behave, nor do they judge his or her action. They simply describe the inappropriate behavior, state the teacher's feelings about it, and indicate why the behavior is considered disruptive. The teacher might say, for example, "Johnny, when you yell across the room, I feel frustrated because I can't concentrate on this lesson." In this paper the authors investigated the effect of I-messages on disruptions and studying. Previous research had indicated their effectiveness in reducing classroom misconduct.

STUDY ONE: Four disruptive fifth graders were observed in class for forty-minute sessions. Out-of-seat behaviors, talking out, studying, and unauthorized contact with peers were recorded. The teacher was instructed to conduct class in her usual way for about fifteen sessions. Then she was told to begin using I-messages in response to disruptions. Prior to the study teachers received training in the delivery of these statements. The training included (1) a discussion of the three components of the I-message; (2) an I-message form to memorize that read: "[Name of student], when you _____ , I feel _____ , because _____ ;" (3) a demonstration of I-message delivery; and (4) using role-playing to practice I-message delivery. After the I-messages had been used in class for a number of sessions, the teacher returned to her usual method of responding to disruptions.

The use of I-messages reduced disruptiveness to less than half its pretreatment rate for each of the target students. Furthermore, studying rates increased by almost 25 percent. However, during the I-message phase, the rate of non-I-responses by teachers was also lower. Thus, it was possible that results were due to this reduction rather than to the I-messages themselves. The second study tested this issue.

STUDY TWO: Eight disruptive sixth graders were exposed to the same procedures as in the first study, except that after each session teachers were given feedback on their rate of I-messages and non-I-responses. The goal was to maintain the non-I verbalizations of teachers at a constant rate from pretreatment to treatment phases. Results showed that six of the eight students reduced their disruptive behavior, and four modified study rates. The frequency of non-I-responses remained unchanged across conditions.

COMMENTARY: The authors note several problems in the use of I-messages. First, once they were stopped, disruptiveness increased and studying behavior decreased. If the teacher does not adopt I-messages as part of her regular teaching style, their effectiveness seems to be short-lived. Further research may help to determine how their effects may be generalized to situations in which they are not used. Perhaps if I-messages were initially paired with other behavioral contingencies (such as time-outs or group consequences), they might take on added power. Second, as demonstrated in this article, I-messages may not be effective for all children, and the integration of other strategies with I-messages may help in reaching more resistant students.

On the positive side, this technique requires no special equipment and only minimal training. Since I-messages can be delivered to every student in the class, a target student need not feel singled out for special treatment. The authors also speculate on why this approach is effective. The description of personal feelings by the teacher or the novelty of the method of communication may be major factors. Also, children's awareness of their negative behavior may increase through these messages, and the knowledge that their behavior is interrupting a valued class activity may then alter their conduct.

SOURCE: Peterson, R. F., Loveless, S. E., Knapp, T. J., Loveless, B. W., Basta, S. M., and Anderson, S. "The Effects of

Teacher Use of I-Messages on Student Disruptive and Study Behavior." *Psychological Record,* 1979, *29,* 187-199.

Reducing Disruptions by Increasing Academic Performance

AUTHORS: Teodoro Ayllon and Michael D. Roberts

PRECIS: Reinforcing academic achievement through a token economy as a way of modifying misbehavior

INTRODUCTION: The authors treated disruptiveness in the classroom by rewarding academic performance rather than focusing on the behavior itself. Other research has found that reducing inappropriate behavior does not necessarily lead to increased achievement. Therefore, with academic performance as the priority target, it may be possible to affect both performance and misconduct simultaneously.

METHOD: Five students were selected as the most problematic fifth graders in a school. Their disruptive and academic behaviors were recorded during randomly selected ten-second intervals over daily fifteen-minute reading sessions. Disruptiveness included interfering with the studying of other students, out-of-seat behavior, and inappropriate talking out. Academic performance was measured by the percentage of correct answers given during daily reading workbook assignments.

A token economy was established in the classroom to improve performance. Students earned points for meeting specified performance standards and could trade them for daily or weekly backup rewards, such as extra free time, use of a game room, seeing a movie, or writing a letter home to parents. Performance criteria and the cost of various backup rewards were publicly posted. Each day the child received an index card that listed the number of points earned the previous day, along with a listing of available reinforcers. The child either presented the card to obtain the reward or saved the points to spend later.

The reinforcement period was in effect for sixteen sessions. Students earned two points for scores of 80 to 99 percent on their reading assignments and five points for a perfect score. Under these conditions reading accuracy rose from the 45-percent range to about 70 percent, while disruptiveness dropped from the same initial percentage to about 15 percent. During the last few sessions, misbehavior declined to approximately 9 percent. When the token system was terminated for fifteen sessions, reading performance declined, and disruptiveness returned to a 40-percent rate. The system having been reinstated for six additional sessions, reading improved to an 85-percent accuracy rate while disruptive behavior dropped to 5 percent.

COMMENTARY: The important finding of this study is that consistent teaching methods backed up by appropriate recognition will reduce disruptive behaviors. This strategy differs from interventions that stress the need to eliminate misconduct *before* learning can take place. When rewards for achievement are the focus, both behavior and performance improve. The authors note that these students were at or above grade level. For students who have poor achievement histories or who are extremely disruptive, it may be necessary to focus directly on disruptive behavior first, so that classroom order can be established. Only then can academic responding be reinforced. Despite this limitation, the authors indicate that teachers have available a growing variety of methods for reducing misbehavior: (1) they can structure classroom procedures and establish exact time requirements; (2) they can directly attack disruptions through reinforcement strategies and later apply other procedures to increase academic functioning; and (3) they can reduce misconduct by reinforcing academic behavior alone. A variety of additional techniques have since been introduced.

SOURCE: Ayllon, T., and Roberts, M. D. "Eliminating Discipline Problems by Strengthening Academic Performance." *Journal of Applied Behavior Analysis,* 1974, 7, 71-76.

Teaching Self-Control to a Disruptive Student

AUTHORS: Robert Epstein and Claire M. Goss

PRECIS: Teaching a fifth grader to self-evaluate his behavior for points and backup rewards

INTRODUCTION: The authors discuss the need for management techniques that produce long-term behavior improvements. With many behavior modification strategies, altered behaviors return to pretreatment levels when the intervention is ended. In this paper a self-control procedure was taught to an elementary school boy in an effort to promote more lasting treatment effects. Previous research has demonstrated the potential of self-control programs to maintain progress beyond the treatment period.

METHOD: A self-control process was taught to Ike, a fifth grader who frequently annoyed others, completed little work, and roamed around the room. The teacher had difficulty controlling his behavior and agreed to cooperate (although quite passively) in a procedure designed by the school psychologist.

A seven-phase procedure was implemented that ensured the effectiveness of the reinforcers, trained the student in self-evaluation, allowed him to maintain it beyond the treatment period, and required little teacher supervision:

1. Baseline—for eight days Ike's on-task, in-seat, and talking-out behaviors were monitored as he engaged in class activities. Observations throughout all phases of the study were conducted during several half-hour intervals each day.

2. Contingent Reinforcement—Ike was told that he would earn points for quiet, in-seat behavior and academic performance—points that could be traded for backup rewards. This phase ran eight days.

3. Noncontingent Reinforcement—for four days, Ike earned thirty points per day regardless of his behavior. The teacher told him that his behavior had been good and that she hoped he would continue to behave properly.

4. Contingent Reinforcement—phase two was repeated for five days.

5. Social Reinforcement—Ike's class was told that he would receive points for good behavior. If he earned twenty-five points each day for several days, the whole class would be allowed extra recess time. This phase lasted four days.

6. Self-Evaluation Matching—for three days Ike could receive three bonus points for guessing within one point his number of earned points during each half-hour interval.

7. Postexperimental Conditions—after accurate self-evaluation had been established in phase six, Ike received a booklet in which he gave himself from one to ten points each morning and afternoon. He then brought the ratings to his teacher. If she agreed with his ratings, his points doubled. The daily point totals were then posted by him in front of the classroom on a scale resembling a thermometer. When he reached one hundred points, he earned game time. At two hundred points he earned more game time, and the class received extra recess.

During phases one to four, contingent reinforcement effectively reduced talk-outs and increased in-seat behavior. Data for on-task behavior were incomplete because of monitoring problems. Phases five (social reinforcement) and six (self-evaluation matching) maintained appropriate behaviors. During self-evaluation matching, Ike learned to evaluate his behavior quite accurately. When Ike himself managed his behavior during phase seven, talk-outs rose somewhat, in-seat behavior remained strong, and on-task behavior dropped slightly. Ike stuck faithfully to the self-control procedure. A six-week follow-up showed that improvements were being maintained.

COMMENTARY: Ike was successfully taught to control his behavior on his own, and gains were maintained for more than two months after phase seven, that is, to the end of the school year. In numerous instances (and for many reasons), teachers may choose not to play an active role in behavior management strategies implemented in their classrooms. Under these circumstances the school psychologist can design self-control procedures that can be taught to youngsters and may result in long-term improvements with minimal teacher involvement.

SOURCE: Epstein, R., and Goss, C. M. "Case Study: A Self-Control Procedure for the Maintenance of Nondisruptive

Behavior in an Elementary School Child." *Behavior Therapy*, 1978, *9*, 109-117.

Additional Readings

Allen, J. I. "Jogging Can Modify Disruptive Behaviors." *Teaching Exceptional Children*, 1980, *12*, 66-70.

First through sixth graders with behavioral and learning disorders participated in daily fifteen-minute jogging sessions. The activity was designed to promote fitness, reduce stress, and increase self-concept. After morning attendance was taken, the students and teacher went outside, warmed up with stretching exercises, and jogged for five to ten minutes. Students could choose to walk or run as long as they maintained continuous movement. They could jog alone, with a friend, or with the teacher. Afterwards, a "cool down" period allowed students and teacher to relax together before the school day resumed. Awards were given when students passed intervals of ten, twenty-five, and fifty miles, regardless of how long it took them. They were urged to improve themselves and set personal goals, while competition with others was deemphasized. Effort rather than ability was recognized, and students often supported one another through praise and encouragement. Over six weeks the effects of jogging were assessed on such behaviors as bothering or hitting others, name-calling, talking out of turn, and noncompliance. Jogging for ten minutes reduced disruptive behavior by 50 percent with maximum benefits occurring in the first hour after the exercise.

Fairchild, T. N. "Home-School Token Economies: Bridging the Communication Gap." *Psychology in the Schools*, 1976, *13*(4), 463-467.

In a case study a kindergartener was reinforced at home for earning five good-behavior tickets in school. To earn a ticket he had to avoid interrupting other students, listen in class, and stay in his seat. He was awarded one ticket for each successful period. Under this token system, disruptive behavior was substantially reduced. The author notes several advantages of home-school strategies, including improved communication and parental involvement, more continuous reinforcement and feed-back for the child, a recognition by the child of home-school consistency, and reduced management time by the teacher. Reinforcement for learning is not "bribery" but a legitimate form of extrinsic motivation. Success of home-school programs requires identification of specific target behaviors, conferences with parents, and mutual agreement on the reinforcements.

Jones, F. H., and Miller, W. H. "The Effective Use of Negative Attention for Reducing Group Disruption in Special Elementary School Classrooms." *Psychological Record*, 1974, *24*, 435-448.

Using the classroom techniques of two effective teachers, two less effective teachers were trained in behavior management. Observers recorded student interruptions of classmates, talking to neighbors without permission, and nonverbal disruptions. Teacher responses to misconduct were also recorded. The less effective teachers were found to give negative attention only when disruptiveness reached high levels. Effective teachers responded quickly and mildly to prevent high-intensity misconduct. The two less successful teachers were then trained in (1) identifying potentially disruptive behavior; (2) developing brief comments and gestures in response; (3) placing themselves in close proximity to the student and clearly directing their attention to the student; (4) responding quickly to short-circuit the incident; (5) using disapproving expressions and vocal tones; (6) delivering positive attention for appropriate behavior in another student immediately following negative attention to an offender; (7) prompting and reinforcing the offender as soon as possible after reinforcing a good student; and (8) using time-outs for highly disturbing behaviors. Role playing was used to train effective responses. The result was that disruptive student behaviors and the frequency with which teachers ignored such behavior both decreased. While training did not increase the frequency of negative attention delivered by the teachers, it seemed to influence the manner in which it was given. Training may have taught a more consistent and better-timed use of negative attention. It also may have encouraged behaviors that made the negative attention more effective when used.

Classroom Disturbance:
Out-of-Seat (Off-Task) Behavior

Some children pay erratic attention to work and are frequently away from their desks. While these children may leave their seats to bother others or to defy classroom rules, off-task behavior may also involve daydreaming, looking out the window, or attempts to avoid work through frequent trips to the bathroom or the pencil sharpener.

Grandma's Rule for Classroom Management

AUTHORS: Richard J. Cowen, Frederic H. Jones, and Alan S. Bellack

PRECIS: Enabling students to earn free time for appropriate behavior and performance

INTRODUCTION: Packaged classroom management programs have been developed for disruptive student behaviors. Many emphasize a low-keyed but decisive teacher response to misconduct. But quick, directive action is sometimes difficult to initiate; this is true, for example, when the teacher is supervising a small group of students while others are working independently at their desks. To remedy this deficiency, the authors compared two techniques based on a strategy known as "Grandma's Rule." This rule requires students to do productive classwork for a predetermined amount of time before engaging in desired activities. In this study the method of recording behavior, was varied between the teacher's use of a stopwatch and classroom display of a large stop clock. The stop clock provided continuous feedback to students on their accumulated work time, while the stopwatch was held by the teacher, who supplied periodic feedback. These methods were tested on elementary students aged six to nine in five classrooms. Each class reported high rates of misbehavior during assigned independent work while the teacher conducted a small reading group. Out-of-seat behaviors, talking, and off-task behaviors were targeted for change; these behaviors were observed for one and one-half hours each morning throughout the study.

GRANDMA'S RULE: The teachers were instructed in the concept of Grandma's Rule and then role played disruptive classroom incidents to practice managing behavior with the stopwatch. On the first day of the program students were instructed in the new format. For the thirty-minute reading period each day, those not reading with the teacher would have to complete fifteen minutes of good work at their desks. Good work rules were reviewed with the students. Once they had met this fifteen-minute criterion, members of the class would be entitled to a preferred activity for the rest of the period. They were informed that the teacher would keep track of their good work with a stopwatch and would stop it when disruptive behavior occurred. Each day, just before the reading period, the activity would be chosen by the class from a "reinforcement menu" consisting of such games as tag and musical chairs.

At the start of each daily reading period, the teacher announced that the stopwatch was running. When a behavior rule was broken, the teacher called out the name(s) of the misbehaving student(s), stated the appropriate behavior, and held up the stopwatch, while reminding the offender(s) that the watch would remain stopped until proper behavior was resumed. As soon as the students were again working well, the watch was publicly restarted. Reading class ended when the students had completed their fifteen minutes of good work. The teacher then stated how much free time was available.

For the stop clock condition, a nine-inch commercially manufactured darkroom clock was used; a red light indicated when it was running. An on-off extension switch allowed the teacher to control it from her reading group. Teachers were instructed in its use through role playing. It was then introduced to the children in the same manner as the stopwatch had been, except that they could now see how much good work time was left to accomplish. When reading class began, the teacher placed the clock in full view and set it for fifteen minutes. Using the on-off switch, she followed the stopwatch procedure for announcing disruptions. After fifteen minutes of good work, a buzzer sounded and free time was given.

Each condition was implemented for about two weeks in each of the five classrooms. After the stop clock condition had been in effect, the stopwatch was reinstated for a few additional weeks.

Both procedures produced substantial decreases in all three target behaviors. Out-of-seat behavior was reduced by as much as 42 percent, talking up to 65 percent, and off-task behavior up to 66 percent. Teachers gave significantly more reminders to disruptive students during both phases of the study than before the interventions began. This matched their reported feelings of greater control over the class. Not only were the teachers attending more to disruption, but their responses had a greater influence on student behavior. In short, they had become better behavior managers. Students also felt positive about the program. Some asked that it be reinstated, while others had worked beyond the required fifteen minutes when it was in effect.

COMMENTARY: Continuous public feedback from the stop clock did not enhance the effectiveness of "Grandma's Rule." Free time, appropriate teacher feedback, and peer pressure through the group contingency seemed to be the main components that affected change. However, students and teachers both felt the clock to be more effective than the stopwatch. The authors indicate that continuous public feedback and impressive machinery give the appearance of greater influence on behavior than they in fact have, since personal perceptions did not affect actual behavior. Teachers also indicated that the strategy allowed them to teach more and shout less. They felt that their students were better behaved and more motivated than they had been previously. By fostering such positive attitudes, these programs enhance the classroom atmosphere and contribute to a more productive learning experience.

SOURCE: Cowen, R. J., Jones, F. H., and Bellack, A. S. "Grandma's Rule with Group Contingencies—A Cost-Efficient Means of Classroom Management." *Behavior Modification*, 1979, *3*(3), 397-418.

A DRL Schedule to Reduce Out-of-Seat Behavior

AUTHORS: Samuel M. Deitz and Alan C. Repp

PRECIS: Using gold stars to reinforce low response rates in a sixth-grade girl

INTRODUCTION: Differential reinforcement of low rates of responding (DRL) rewards the child for making less than a specified number of undesirable responses within a given time period. The authors applied the technique to students in regular elementary classes. In one case a sixth grader was constantly leaving her seat to talk to other students, engage in unassigned activities, or leave the room. After ten sessions in which her behavior was recorded, the procedure was explained to her. If she left her seat no more than two times during the forty-five-minute period, she would receive a star in the teacher's notebook. She was informed at the end of each period whether she had earned a star but was never told of her status during the period. Treatment initially lasted for six sessions, was terminated for five sessions, and then reinstated for five more sessions.

During the first DRL condition, out-of-seat behavior was reduced from approximately six occurrences during pretreatment periods to less than one. The girl earned a star each day of the treatment. When the intervention was terminated, the negative behavior returned to its previous rate but dropped back to less than one incident per period when the DRL schedule was reinstated.

COMMENTARY: It was not necessary for the girl to exchange stars for backup rewards in order to reduce her out-of-seat behavior. This reduces the cost of the procedure and makes it an attractive option for schools. However, the authors suggest caution in setting the behavior criterion for reinforcement. This study selected a frequency of two responses per session because of the initially low level of misconduct. If pretreatment disruptiveness is high, the authors suggest a less rigid criterion, so that success is attainable from the start. The criterion can then be changed gradually to achieve an appropriate level of desired behavior.

SOURCE: Deitz, S. M., and Repp, A. C. "Differentially Reinforcing Low Rates of Misbehavior with Normal Elementary School Children." *Journal of Applied Behavior Analysis,* 1974, 7, 622.

Goal Setting and Self-Monitoring
in the Classroom

AUTHORS: Gerald Sagotsky, Charlotte J. Patterson, and Mark R. Lepper

PRECIS: Comparing effects of goal-setting and self-monitoring procedures on off-task behavior and academic performance

INTRODUCTION: The authors note that when individuals are encouraged to monitor their own behavior, the behavior being monitored is often modified without any other imposed contingency. This "therapeutic" effect of self-monitoring is sometimes attributed to a process of self-evaluation in which the person compares her behavior with a predetermined goal and provides herself feedback on progress toward the goal. Implicit in this process is the act of goal setting itself. In this study, fifth- and sixth-grade students were introduced to both goal-setting and self-monitoring procedures to assess their effect on specified target behaviors.

METHOD: The students worked on individualized math units, progressing to the next unit as they reached a criterion level of accuracy. During this time, on-task and off-task behaviors were observed daily for two minutes for each student. After a four-week pretreatment observation period, the treatment phase began. The children were individually told that they would receive daily green sheets with their math units. They were to write their names, the date, and the page and problem numbers at which they ended the math period.

Children in the *goal-setting condition* were further told to decide how much they could do during the period and to record these goals on their green sheets. They were also told to mark their goals on their math units, so that they could see how close they were to their goals as they worked. At the end of the period they marked on their sheets the page and problem numbers they had reached and compared them with their self-determined goals.

Children in the *self-monitoring condition* received a grid

with twelve boxes. They were instructed to note from time to time during the math period whether they were working appropriately. If so, they were to place a plus sign in one of the boxes; if not, a minus sign was to be written in.

Children in the *goal-setting and self-monitoring condition* received both sets of instructions. They recorded daily goals and monitored themselves during the math period.

A *control group* of children received no instructions other than to record on the green sheets the point at which they ended the math period.

The self-monitoring procedure effectively increased on-task study behavior and the rate of progress in the math program. The goal-setting procedure had no effect on either behavior or performance, nor did it add to the power of the self-monitoring procedure in the combined condition. In addition, students in the goal-setting condition failed to use the procedure more often than self-monitoring students did.

COMMENTARY: In assessing the effectiveness of the self-monitoring procedure, the authors note that the recording of positive and negative behaviors created a self-evaluative component and also generated an increased awareness of off-task instances. Both these factors contributed to its success. As for the other procedure, the math program may not have been conducive to a goal-setting strategy, and more training in goal setting may have been necessary. (In other research, goal setting has proved successful in modifying behavior.) Self-monitoring programs are practical and inexpensive techniques that intrude minimally into classroom routine. They may also be included as components of more extensive behavior change programs.

SOURCE: Sagotsky, G., Patterson, C. J., and Lepper, M. R. "Training Children's Self-Control: A Field Experiment in Self-Monitoring and Goal Setting in the Classroom." *Journal of Experimental Child Psychology*, 1978, *25*, 242-253.

Additional Readings

Carnine, D. W. "Effects of Two Teacher Presentation Rates on Off-Task Behavior, Answering Correctly, and Participation." *Journal of Applied Behavior Analysis*, 1976, *9*, 199-206.

Teacher presentation rates were varied for two students who were frequently off-task during small-group reading instruction. In using the Level 1 Distar Program, the teacher was first instructed to present material at a slow rate. (This is a highly structured reading program in which component reading skills are taught first, then combined into more complex skills. Teacher instructions are also very specific.) The teacher was to count to five after each student response before presenting the next reading task. She was also to deliver contingent praise for correct answers or attending behaviors as soon as possible after hearing a tone that was sounded every ninety seconds. For the fast-rate presentation, she was to move to the next task immediately after the student's response. Fast rates were substantially more successful in reducing off-task behavior than slow rates. In addition, student responses were quicker and more accurate during the fast rates. Presentation rate is another technique that can supplement more extensive management strategies. However, too quick a rate can be as detrimental as too slow a rate.

Darch, C. B., and Thorpe, H. W. "The Principal Game: A Group-Consequence Procedure to Increase Classroom On-Task Behavior." *Psychology in the Schools*, 1977, *14*(3), 341-347.

Fourth graders displayed significant off-task behavior, so the class was divided into five teams (by rows). A timer sounded six times during the period; if each student on a team was working, the team received a point. Five points won, and all teams could win. No point was earned if one team member was not working. The principal entered the room after class, had the winning team(s) stand, and praised their performance. After ten sessions of this game a no-treatment phase was established for three days. Then the point system was reinstated except that students worked to earn their own points and praise from the principal. There were no teams. The Principal Game immediately increased on-task behavior from 26 percent to an average of 86 percent. Individual praise increased on-task behavior to an average of 75 percent. The principal is an effective reinforcer, and his power can be enhanced by a group contingency. Individual reward is effective but was less powerful than the group strategy in this instance.

Hay, W. M., Hay, L. R., and Nelson, R. O. "Direct and Collateral Changes in On-Task and Academic Behavior Resulting from On-Task Versus Academic Contingencies." *Behavior Therapy*, 1977, *8*, 431-441.

Boys in the second, fourth, and fifth grades were identified as exhibiting off-task behavior. They were assigned thirty minutes of work at their seats each day while observers recorded on-task behavior, academic accuracy, and rate of performance. During the *on-task contingency*, the teacher placed a star on the student's "good work" card (distributed at the beginning of the thirty-minute period) and delivered verbal praise five times during each session for on-task behavior. For the *academic contingency*, the teacher examined the student's work five times during the period. If she found a correct answer, she praised it with a comment and a star on the "good work" card. If no answers were correct, no comments were made. When on-task behavior was rewarded, only on-task behavior improved. When academic performance was reinforced, both performance and on-task behavior were improved. These students were not severely disruptive and possessed the appropriate "academic repertoires" before the study began. For students with severe problems, a separate strategy for each behavior may be required.

Hegerle, D. R., Kesecker, M. P., and Couch, J. V. "A Behavior Game for the Reduction of Inappropriate Classroom Behaviors." *School Psychology Digest*, 1979, *8*(3), 339-343.

The authors described a version of the Good Behavior Game to reduce out-of-seat and talking-out behaviors. Students in one class formed two teams that competed in following classroom rules. These included remaining seated, remaining quiet, and raising one's hand for permission to talk or move about. Records were kept and winners posted. Both teams could win by receiving less than a prespecified number of bad behavior points—a number that was reduced as the game progressed. Backup reinforcers for winning teams included candy, extra recess, and/or a party. By the fifth week, out-of-seat behavior and talking out were reduced by 80 to 90 percent. Both teams won every day. The procedure combines peer pressure, group competition, group and individual contingencies, and social reinforcement.

Iwata, B. A., and Bailey, J. S. "Reward Versus Cost Token Systems: An Analysis of the Effects on Students and Teacher." *Journal of Applied Behavior Analysis,* 1974, *7,* 567-576.

Elementary students were observed for off-task behavior and rule violations. For the study each student received either an empty cup or one with ten tokens in it. Students with empty cups (reward group) received a token at predetermined intervals for following rules, while those who began with tokens (cost group) lost one at the same intervals for breaking rules. If six tokens were in the cup by the end of class, the student earned a snack or a special bonus on "surprise" days. The criterion was raised to eight tokens on day six. After a brief no-treatment phase, the token system was reversed, so that by the end of the study all students had been exposed to both reward and cost conditions. In a final phase, students chose which condition they preferred. Results indicated that both reward and cost systems were equally effective in decreasing target behaviors and in increasing academic output. Performance accuracy remained unchanged. No adverse side effects occurred during the cost condition, and student choices reflected no consistent preference for either condition.

Page, D. P., and Edwards, R. P. "Behavior Change Strategies for Reducing Disruptive Classroom Behavior." *Psychology in the Schools,* 1978, *15*(3), 413-418.

Group contingencies controlled off-task and disruptive behaviors of sixth to eighth graders. During a forty-five-minute class, they worked on thirty-minute assignments with fifteen minutes left for free time. If 80 percent of the work was correct, students received a star on a name chart. Under an *independent group contingency,* students earning a star were awarded the free time while those who did not continued working. During the *interdependent group contingency,* all students had to earn the star for any one of them to receive free time. Both strategies were equally effective in reducing target behaviors. Rewarding academic performance reduced disruptive behavior and also improved output.

Wolf, M. M., Hanley, E. L., King, L. A., Lachowicz, J., and Giles, D. K. "The Timer-Game: A Variable-Interval Contingency for the Management of Out-of-Seat Behavior." *Exceptional Children,* 1970, *37,* 113-117.

A kitchen timer was set to ring at varying intervals from zero to forty minutes. Every student in a third- and fourth-grade remedial classroom who was seated when the timer rang earned five points as part of a token reinforcement system already in operation. Over six sessions out-of-seat behavior dropped by about 88 percent. For one student who did not respond additional strategies were introduced. First, she began the sessions with fifty points posted on the wall in ten-number intervals from ten to fifty. Each time that she was out of her seat when the timer rang she lost ten points, which were crossed off the wall chart. Second, after several days her remaining points were shared equally with four neighboring students. These contingencies quickly lowered her out-of-seat behavior.

Destructive Behavior

This section concerns children who destroy, misuse, or abuse others' possessions. Such actions may be done deliberately, in anger, or in a moment of frustration. School vandalism is a different type of destructive behavior; it may represent alienation or be an act of rebellion against the authoritarian system that outlaws such behavior. The reader is referred to the earlier sections on Classroom Disturbance and Cursing, as these behaviors are sometimes accompanied by destructive acting out.

Negative Reinforcement to Control
Disruptive Behavior

AUTHOR: Theodore H. Wasserman

PRECIS: Helping a disruptive youngster avoid returning to a residential setting

INTRODUCTION: The author discusses the feasibility of using negative reinforcement as a treatment procedure when positive reinforcers are unavailable or cannot be used. When negative reinforcement is in effect, the child performs the desired behavior to terminate or avoid an aversive consequence rather than to receive a rewarding consequence. The author describes the use of negative reinforcement in the case of a twelve-year-old boy with destructive and other disruptive behaviors.

CASE STUDY: The boy was enrolled in a day-treatment program that included residence in a community group home and attendance in the day-treatment school. He had been placed in a residential program three years before by his mother, who refused to have him back. Instead of telling her son that she did not want him to come home, she blamed various agencies for delaying his return to her. Thus, he did not accept the real reason when told it by his counselor. In the day-treatment program he destroyed property, refused to wash or do work, made animal noises, and demanded to return home. He was unresponsive to a token reinforcement system that rewarded positive behavior, would not modify his behavior in individual behavior therapy, and repeated his intention not to work until he could go home. Since he would respond only to an unattainable positive reinforcer, an alternate treatment strategy was developed and discussed with him:

1. His behavior would no longer be tolerated.
2. His mother was not able to take him home, and it was not known when she would be ready to do so. Every effort would be made to return him to his home, but no promises could be made because of his mother's behavior.

3. If he continued his destructive behavior, he would be returned to the upstate residential placement from which he had come, thus making it more difficult for him to see his mother.

The staff prepared the referral material required to place him back in residential treatment, and he was told that each day his teacher and group-home parent would record whether or not he had displayed four target behaviors: (1) ripping up school papers and drawing on desks; (2) not completing all schoolwork; (3) grunting or snorting; and (4) not washing before coming to school. If, by the end of the week, he had engaged in more than 25 percent of these behaviors, a page of the residential referral materials would be sent for processing. If he met the criterion for acceptable behavior, standards would be raised until he was behaving correctly 90 percent of the time. The boy was also helped to accept his mother's rejection of him. Attempts were made to set up weekend home visits and to arrange weekly meetings between him and his mother to discuss the issue of his going home.

After a brief no-treatment period, the total procedure was reinstated. Over a period of approximately two months, negative behavior decreased markedly while acceptable behavior increased. The plan was to maintain the program until the issue with his mother could be settled.

COMMENTARY: As the author suggests, once positive behaviors are established, it is desirable to encourage them with a positive reinforcing contingency, if one can be found. Positive treatments are usually preferred to negative strategies, and in most cases children will readily identify rewards they wish to achieve. However, in situations in which the behaviors are destructive (or perhaps dangerous) and/or positive contingencies cannot be found, the use of negative reinforcers may have to be considered. In the case presented here, continued negative behavior would have led to the boy's return to a residential psychiatric treatment facility. The professional must weigh the use of negative reinforcers against the consequences of ongoing destructive behavior. For example, in public school special education classes, teachers might find it necessary to employ aversive consequences or punishment on occasion to control behavior and thus enable students to remain in a mainstream setting. A technique with aversive components must always be considered in relationship to its potential benefit. When such procedures are being considered, the parents of the student should be informed of the process and why it might be implemented.

SOURCE: Wasserman, T. H. "Negative Reinforcement to Alter Disruptive Behavior of an Adolescent in a Day-Treatment Setting." *Journal of Behavior Therapy and Experimental Psychiatry*, 1977, *8*, 315-317.

Group and Individual Response-Cost Strategies

AUTHOR: Saul Axelrod

PRECIS: Using response-cost strategies to punish individual students and whole classes

INTRODUCTION: The author compared the effectiveness of an individual versus a group response-cost procedure to reduce destructive and other disruptive behaviors in eight- and nine-year-old educable retarded students. In this group contingency, students were punished for their own behaviors and for the behaviors of the entire class. When the actions of any one student determine consequences for the total group, social pressure is created on all students to behave appropriately.

METHOD: Among other behaviors, all students in the two target classes destroyed other students' property, knocked books off desks, grabbed others' work or belongings, and threw objects. For phase one of the study, teachers handled disruptiveness in their usual manner while observers recorded the frequency of these behaviors. When the group contingency was started, the teacher listed the numbers zero to twenty-five in decreasing order on the blackboard. For each disruptive incident the highest number was crossed off, and the offending child's name was placed next to it. After the one-hour period, each child received the number of tokens indicated by the highest remaining number. The teacher called students two at a time to receive their tokens, which could be exchanged for candy and toys. For the individual contingency each child's name was written on the board with the numbers zero to twenty-five in decreasing order listed below each name. If the child misbehaved, only his or her highest number was crossed off. At the end of the period each student received the number of tokens that he had individually earned.

In the two classes exposed to both individual and group response-cost contingencies, disruptive incidents were reduced by 88 percent in one class and by 94 percent in the other. Both contingencies were equally effective in achieving a significant decrease in misconduct.

COMMENTARY: Because group and individual response-cost procedures appear to be equally successful, the decision to use one or the other should be based on other factors. Thus, recording negative behaviors is easier in a group contingency because only one set of numbers is needed. In larger classes, tracking individual misconduct can become difficult. Moreover, all students receive the same number of tokens under a group contingency, making distribution easier, and rewards are also easier to manage in the group condition because all students receive the same amount. However, undue social pressure among students may create problems in a group contingency. Threats, gestures, or other actions may force students to behave but may adversely affect academic performance and personal relationships. In addition, some teachers may object to a group contingency because it may unfairly penalize or reward certain students. The author concludes that because of its convenience and practicality, the group contingency should be tried first but should be discontinued if negative academic or social side effects develop.

SOURCE: Axelrod, S. "Comparison of Individual and Group Contingencies in Two Special Classes." *Behavior Therapy,* 1973, *4,* 83-90.

The Good Behavior Game with Unruly Students

AUTHORS: Moses R. Johnson, Paul F. Turner, and Edward A. Konarski

PRECIS: Reducing disruptiveness by rewarding student teams for appropriate behavior

INTRODUCTION: The authors introduced the Good Behavior Game into third- and fourth-grade "transitional" classes composed of destructive, unmotivated, and disruptive students. Students were divided into teams and were rewarded individually and in groups for appropriate behavior. The game involved the entire class and made use of natural classroom reinforcers. Only minimal changes in classroom procedures were required, and the teacher did not need special training or additional personnel.

GOOD BEHAVIOR GAME: Before the game began, college students observed and recorded appropriate behaviors, disruptive behaviors, and teacher responses. On the sixth morning the teacher in each class divided the class into teams and announced that they were going to play a game. The rules, posted in the front of the class, were reviewed every day for the first two weeks. They required students to work on their assignments at their seats and prohibited talking out without permission, throwing objects, and fighting. The best-behaved children were chosen by the teacher as team captains. The teacher explained that if a member of the team broke a rule, she would give that team a mark on the blackboard. At the end of the game the team captain or another well-behaved student would count the team's marks, and the team with the fewest marks would win. In the ten-minute reward period the winning team members would receive their reward; this might be fruits and candy and/ or special privileges such as early lunch or being first in line for recess. Members of the losing team would have to continue working at their desks. If the game ended in a tie, both teams would be declared winners and receive rewards.

After a brief question-and-answer period, students chose a name for their teams, and the game was played daily for fifteen to twenty minutes. After about two weeks, the winning team was required to have less than ten marks to receive its reward. Disruptive behavior decreased immediately after the game began from almost 100 percent of the observation intervals to between 8 and 15 percent. This decrease was maintained throughout the treatment period, which lasted an average of twenty-five to thirty sessions. Teacher attention to disruptive behavior declined just as dramatically; by the end of the study teachers were attending to appropriate behaviors and generally ignoring misconduct. However, about seven weeks after the game ended, improvements were not being maintained.

COMMENTARY: The Good Behavior Game shows how classroom structure can be altered to change behavior without interrupting the regular learning routine. Rules can also be changed depending on the target behaviors selected. The authors point out that this approach frees the teacher to teach and praise rather than to punish. However, marks must be recorded faithfully, promised rewards must be given, and losing teams must be denied reinforcement. Without consistency, the chances of carry-over after treatment may be greatly reduced. The authors note the lack of such carry-over as a problem in their study and indicate the need for further research on long-term maintenance of effects. They suggest that the power of teacher attention to control behavior may be increased by pairing it with reinforcers during the game. Then, when the game is over, consistent teacher attention by itself may be used to maintain improvements.

SOURCE: Johnson, M. R., Turner, P. F., and Konarski, E. A. "The 'Good Behavior Game': A Systematic Replication in Two Unruly Transitional Classrooms." *Education and Treatment of Children,* 1978, *1*(3), 25-33.

Reinforcing Improved Behavior
with a DRL Schedule

AUTHORS: Samuel M. Deitz, Daniel J. Slack, E. Beth Schwarzmueller, Ann P. Wilander, Thomas J. Weatherly, and Geraldine
Hilliard

PRECIS: Rewarding increased intervals of appropriate behavior
with playtime

INTRODUCTION: Legal and ethical concerns about the use of
punishment in the classroom have led to the development of
techniques that reward reduced misbehavior. Differential reinforcement of low rates of behavior (DRL) is a positive reinforcement schedule that rewards low rates of disruptiveness. In
this paper the authors applied one type of DRL procedure with
a seven-year-old student whose behavior was difficult to control. He would roll on the floor, pound on the furniture, throw,
drop, or destroy objects, and stand on chairs and desks.

DRL SCHEDULE: On the first day of the procedure disruptive
behavior was defined for the boy, and he was reminded of this
definition daily throughout the study. Then he was given a
piece of paper divided into fifteen blocks. For each two minutes
in which he displayed one or no disruptive behaviors, a star rep-
resenting one minute of playground time was placed in a block.
If he engaged in two or more misbehaviors, the two-minute
interval was immediately restarted, delaying award of the star.
No star was awarded unless he completed a trouble-free two-
minute interval.

During each thirty-minute daily session, it was possible for
the student to earn fifteen minutes of playtime. While he knew
this, he was not aware of the two-minute interval length or of
the time represented by each star (the two-minute duration was
determined by an analysis of pretreatment behavior). Beginning
with session nine, the interval for good behavior was increased
to three minutes and the value of the star to one and one-half
minutes. After five more sessions all schedules were ended for
five sessions. They were then reinstated with a three-minute
interval for a final five sessions.

Before treatment, the boy averaged about nineteen inappropriate behaviors per session. When two-minute DRL schedules were begun, the rate dropped to five. When the interval was lengthened to three minutes, a further drop to just under two occurred. The period of no-treatment raised the rate to almost nine misbehaviors per session, but it dropped again to just over one per session when the three-minute DRL schedule was reestablished.

COMMENTARY: The teacher reported no emotional side effects during the DRL intervention, as is sometimes observed with punishment strategies. However, the authors note that the procedure required extra assistance in the classroom to time, observe, and reinforce the student. Thus, it may initially require a teacher aide, a psychologist, or a counselor to implement the procedure. Even then, however, some teachers may find it difficult to teach and to implement a DRL at the same time. For others, research suggests that these procedures can be implemented without additional help. After some initial adjustments, DRL schedules have been effectively managed by classroom teachers alone. The outcome seems to rest with the individual teacher.

SOURCE: Deitz, S. M., Slack, D. J., Schwarzmueller, E. B., Wilander, A. P., Weatherly, T. J., and Hilliard, G. "Reducing Inappropriate Behavior in Special Classrooms by Reinforcing Average Interresponse Times: Interval DRL." *Behavior Therapy,* 1978, *9,* 37-46.

Additional Readings

Gershman, L. "Eliminating A Fire-Setting Compulsion Through Contingency Management." In J. D. Krumboltz and C. E. Thoresen (Eds.), *Counseling Methods*. New York: Holt, Rinehart and Winston, 1976, 206-213.

A mother was taught to control fire setting in her eight-year-old son through behavior management. The therapist assigned readings and exercises to familiarize the mother with behavioral techniques. They then developed a contingency-contracting program for completing homework. Task cards were prepared that listed assignments or review work. The points that were received for completed work earned daily and weekly backup rewards and accompanying praise. A chart was kept that listed the agreement between mother and son about points and rewards, and it also displayed his progress. This was hung on his bedroom door. The next step was controlling the use of matches. Matchbooks were placed around the house with varying numbers of matches in them (zero to fifteen). Each time her son brought the matches to her that he had found, he received five cents and verbal and physical praise (a hug or kiss). After the tenth day the reward was varied between one and ten cents. Beginning on day twenty, money was not always given. When this behavior had become stable, the program to stop the boy from striking matches was started. At dinner he was handed a book of matches and told to strike as many as he wished. For every match not lit, he received a penny and also praise for the matches that remained. This was continued until he did not want to light any matches even though encouraged to do so. By the eighteenth night he had lit no matches for four consecutive nights. Reduction in fire setting followed rapidly. Follow-ups for two years showed maintenance of effects.

Meisels, L. "The Disturbing Child and Social Competence in the Classroom: Implications for Child Care Workers." *Child Care Quarterly,* 1975, *4*(4), 231-240.

The author describes the Walker School in Needham, Massachusetts, for destructive and/or abusive boys aged seven to twelve. The goal of this residential program is to help youngsters recognize the ineffectiveness of their behaviors and develop alternative modes of socially competent interaction. Classrooms are designed to minimize extraneous stimulation. Children work in individual cubicles to increase on-task behavior, using them less as social controls develop. A quiet room is available to control tantrums; students can also use it if they want a setting more private than cubicles. Teaching the use of privacy is stressed as one means of giving children social competence. Teaching is also directed toward the student's learning competencies, with planning based on thorough assessment of his abilities. Learning contracts are developed with the child as a way to promote feelings of self-worth. Resource teachers develop programs for learning-disabled students, intervene in crisis situations, and organize self-discovery experiences. Students are never forced to participate in lessons but are led to develop alternatives for classroom work as another aspect of competent behavior. Contingency management of behavior stresses reward rather than punishment. Behavior and academic contracts are developed on an individual and school-wide basis. Through the kind of programming that contingency management provides, students develop alternatives to destructive behavior and build their academic and social competencies.

Steele, M. "Enrolling Community Support." *Journal of Research and Development in Education,* 1978, *11*(2), 84-93.

The potential importance of school-based community education programs as a deterrent to student violence and vandalism is discussed. These programs must have active participation by community residents and students in order to develop appropriate adult and youth education and recreation activities. If adults and students are encouraged to participate in the development and implementation of community education projects, the alienation and powerlessness that lead to vandalism and violence may be reduced. Examples of rural and urban community education programs that decreased vandalism are cited. In addition, when school-community facilities are designed with active adult and student involvement, destructive acts seem less likely to occur. The core of the community education concept is inclusion of students and the creation of facilities and programs that reflect their input and expressed needs.

2

Immature Behaviors

Immaturity literally means the lack of complete growth or development. Since children are still in the process of formation, they are, of course, expected to develop further. Therefore, immaturity must be viewed according to some standard expectation. Immature children are below the norm in some way, whether this norm is defined by parents' or teachers' subjective judgment or by some objective criteria. Their behavior is inappropriate for their age and appears similar to the behavior of younger children. We use the concept of immaturity as a category for specific behaviors because it is important to avoid using a global label of immaturity when describing children. Calling children immature or babyish often leads to a general expecta-

tion of inadequate behavior. Normal children often develop un-
evenly and act age appropriately in some ways but not in
others. Also, behavior is "situation specific" in that children
may act one way under certain conditions and situations and a
different way in other contexts. Under stress, children often
regress to a behavior typical of themselves when much younger.
When the stress is removed, their customary behavior returns.

The specific behaviors covered in this chapter are hyperactivity, distractibility, impulsiveness, messiness and sloppiness,
daydreaming, procrastination and dawdling, poor coordination,
and crying. It should be noted that hyperactivity, distractibility,
and impulsiveness are very often viewed as learning disabilities,
developmental learning disorders, or hyperkinetic reactions.
Most evidence points to a central nervous system dysfunction as
the cause of these inhibitory control problems. Strikingly, brain
dysfunction may also underlie messiness, dawdling, and poor
coordination. There may be a lag in the development of brain
structures that causes certain forms of behavioral immaturity.
Roughly 5 to 10 percent of children demonstrate serious problems in one or more of these behaviors. However, incidence
totally depends upon the criteria used to measure intensity and/
or frequency of a given behavior. All children show some of
these behaviors at some point in time in some situations.

Mature or age-appropriate behavior may be defined as the
opposite or absence of impulsiveness, daydreaming, and so
forth. The teacher's task is to promote maturation, since academic learning is directly related to the relative absence of immature behaviors. The methods most frequently used to promote more age-appropriate behavior include modeling, point
systems to earn privileges, positive reinforcement (especially
praise), positive self-verbalizations by children, and training in
specific skills.

Hyperactivity

Hyperactivity is excessive movement caused by physiological factors (for example, a dysfunction in the central nervous system may prevent normal self-control), or psychological ones (especially anxiety). Whatever the cause of their problem, hyperactive children can learn to be less active and more purposeful. Psychotropic drugs, especially stimulants, have long been successfully used to reduce hyperactivity in the classroom. There has been much concern about the possibly indiscriminant use or overuse of such drugs, and the vast majority of professionals working with hyperactive children agree that nondrug methods should be tried first. Even when drugs are deemed appropriate, other methods should be used concurrently. Most studies estimate that 5 to 10 percent of schoolchildren are hyperactive and that approximately 40 percent of the children referred to mental health clinics are hyperactive. One recent study had parents, teachers, and physicians identify hyperactive elementary school children among 5,000 students. Approximately 5 percent were hyperactive as defined by at least one group, but only one percent were considered hyperactive by all three groups (N. M. Lambert, J. Sandoval, and D. Sassone, "Prevalence of Hyperactivity in Elementary School Children as a Function of Social System Definers," American Journal of Orthopsychiatry, 1978, 48, 446-463). *The maximum prevalence rate of hyperactivity was 13 percent, with a ratio of boys to girls of about seven to one. Many methods have reportedly been effective in reducing hyperactivity, including modeling, self-verbalization, relaxation training, positive reinforcement, biofeedback, environmental manipulation, dietary management, drugs (especially stimulants), and increased stimulation.*

121

Self-Instruction for Overactivity

AUTHORS: Philip H. Bornstein and Randal P. Quevillon

PRECIS: Increasing on-task behavior of three preschool boys by modeling and self-verbalization

INTRODUCTION: Hyperactive behavior has been reduced by aversive stimulation, response cost, time-outs, group contingencies, and contingency management. However, some methods fail to alter such behavior in a significant percentage of children, and durability and generalization of improvement are often not achieved. Self-control training (through verbal mediation) and programming for generalization are discussed as possible solutions. The authors note that self-produced verbalizations have effectively eliminated lunchroom disruptions and reduced the breaking of rules.

METHOD: Three four-year-old boys had problems such as general overactivity, not following directions, short attention spans, and distractibility. The goal was to measure the possible increase in on-task behavior (attentive, silent, performing assigned tasks). Off-task behavior included doing unassigned activities, moving around the room, playing, shouting, fighting, or leaving the room. Two judges observed the children for thirty-minute periods, twice per day.

  Self-instruction sessions lasted for two hours. The adult first performed a task while speaking aloud. The child then did the task while the adult gave instructions. In the next step the adult whispered, and the child again performed the task. Next, the adult only moved his lips, and the child first did the task while whispering and then while only moving his lips. Finally, the child did the task while instructing himself only by thinking about the instructions. The adult modeled questions ("What does the teacher want me to do?"), answers that used cognitive rehearsal ("Oh, that's right, I'm supposed to copy that picture"), self-instruction ("OK, first I draw a line"), and self-reinforcement ("I really did that one well"). The adult frequently made an error on purpose and then immediately corrected it. Only at the beginning did the adult create incentive by giving M&M's while the child used self-praise. Throughout training, children spoke as if the teacher were asking them to do the tasks ("Mrs. B. wants me to draw that picture. . . . How can I do that?").

The children were told to watch what the adult did and listen to what he said. Candy was used to reinforce attention, but the amount given was quickly reduced. If children did not carry out the correct behavior, the adult again modeled appropriate behavior while speaking aloud. Many different tasks, increasing in difficulty, were used. These included copying lines and figures, making designs with blocks, and conceptual grouping. Test reliability was excellent, and there was control for expectancy effects. Baseline on-task behavior ranged from 10 to 14 percent. After the two-hour training session, a dramatic increase was seen (70 to 82 percent in on-task behavior). Gains were being maintained twenty-two weeks after the study and transferred to the classroom.

COMMENTARY: The authors discuss the need for more research to determine which are the active ingredients that promote change and lead to durability and generalization of the method employed. This program used instruction, self-instruction, verbal modeling, prompts, reinforcement, and fading, and this package significantly improved the behavior of overly active preschoolers. The procedures used are readily adaptable by teachers for children of any age. There is clear evidence that one block of training (massed practice) is a particularly feasible approach. Teachers may therefore be encouraged to set aside one two-hour period with a hyperactive child who is not attending to tasks. An obstacle with many teachers is that one or two sessions with children is often seen as "only a drop in the bucket." This study demonstrates that even a small amount of time may produce significant results. Mental health personnel can serve the valuable function of consulting with teachers and providing them with advice as to the best strategies to use with a particular child.

SOURCE: Bornstein, P. H., and Quevillon, R. P. "The Effects

of a Self-Instructional Package on Overactive Preschool Boys." *Journal of Applied Behavior Analysis*, 1976, *9*, 179-188.

Relaxation and Exercise for Hyperactivity

AUTHORS: Stephen A. Klein and Jerry L. Deffenbacher

PRECIS: Reducing tension and, improving cognitive perfor-mance in hyperactive and impulsive third graders

INTRODUCTION: Task orientation has been improved in dis-tractible, inattentive, impulsive, and overactive children. But the authors point out that there has been little research into the direct modification of heightened activity or tension in hyper-active children. Relaxation training should lead to reduced ten-sion and greater calmness in hyperactive children. Progressive relaxation has been successful for children with insomnia, anxiety, and asthma. In contrast, exercise could reduce tension by a reduction in energy and fatigue.

METHOD: Random assignment was made for twenty-four hyperactive and impulsive third-grade boys to one of three con-ditions—progressive relaxation training, strenuous exercise, or making objects with clay. The boys reclined on mats and pil-lows and were told how to relax. Standard adult relaxation training was somewhat modified for children's use. The exercise training, which was done outside or in a gym, consisted of agil-ity, power, and speed tasks. Over three weeks, each boy re-ceived five individual ten-minute training sessions. During the last three sessions, the children relaxed or exercised for ten min-utes and then solved problems requiring attention and concen-tration (card games and mazes). While playing these games, the relaxation group practiced muscle relaxation, and the exercise group did several thirty-second intervals of push-ups.

The boys were administered the Matching Familiar Figures Test (MFFT) and an abbreviated version of the Continuous Performance Task. Both exercise and relaxation training resulted in improved accuracy on the matching task but not on the performance test. Those boys who were less able to do the relaxation exercises did more poorly on the tests. The authors suggest that boys such as these might profit from more intensive relaxation training or biofeedback-assisted relaxation.

COMMENTARY: The details of the exercise and relaxation training are not described. However, there are many easily available relaxation training programs, and the exercises used appear to be those commonly found in physical education classes. Significant results were obtained in this study, and its techniques are economical and usable in any school setting. The qualitative findings concerning the effects of relaxation training are most promising. The hyperactive children who learned how to relax improved their performance the most. A properly planned program will allow overly active children to exercise and relax beneficially throughout the school day. School personnel can set up a program appropriate to the individual circumstances. Some children might respond very well to morning exercise and afternoon relaxation, others to just the opposite pattern.

SOURCE: Klein, S. A., and Deffenbacher, J. L. "Relaxation and Exercise for Hyperactive Impulsive Children." *Perceptual and Motor Skills,* 1977, *45,* 1159-1162.

Behavioral Treatment of Hyperkinesis

AUTHORS: K. Daniel O'Leary, William E. Pelham, Alan Rosenbaum, and Gloria H. Price

PRECIS: Daily report cards and individually selected rewards for reducing overactivity in the classroom

INTRODUCTION: Stimulant drugs have often successfully reduced hyperactivity and classroom disruption. However, they
have possible negative side effects such as suppression of
growth, increased heart rate, and elevation of blood pressure.
Also, drugs have not proved effective with 30 to 50 percent of
hyperactive children. Behavior therapy procedures have reduced
overactivity and disruption with hyperactive and retarded children.

METHOD: Nine children in grades 3 to 5 participated. They received extreme hyperkinetic scores (greater than 15) on the
Abbreviated Conners' Teacher Rating Scale. Eight other children with extreme scores served as a control group, and intervention took place over a ten-week period. Trained observers
rated the children during twenty-second intervals regarding
three hyperkinetic behaviors—moving around the room, fidget-
ing, and not attending to task. The children were not receiving
any behavior control drugs during the study. They were of average intelligence but at least one year below grade level academically.

   A therapist met with the parents, obtained information
about their child's behavior at home, and explained their role to
them. Suitable rewards for each child were determined by the
therapist and parents, while the therapist and teacher chose the
daily classroom behavioral goals for each child. Goals included
completing assigned math, helping other children, not fighting,
and bringing completed homework to school. Academic and
prosocial goals were used, and the children were not reinforced
directly for sitting still or paying attention. Each day, the
teacher gave the child a report to take home to his parents. If he
met the goals, the parents rewarded him. Care was taken to determine rewards that would be motivating. Some rewards used
were thirty extra minutes of television, a special dessert, game
playing with parents, and spending money. When four out of
five daily reports were positive, a weekly reward was given. This
might be a fishing trip, a dinner with a favorite relative, or a
family meal at a restaurant.

   In two instances, parents did not consistently reward their
children, and so a school reward system was arranged—one piece

of candy for one child at the end of the day and free library time for the other. The authors point out that the reward program should be modified if significant behavioral improvement does not occur. They note that, in the same way, no single drug or amount of drug is appropriate for all hyperkinetic children.

Statistics are presented regarding relative improvement on the two scales used. Significant progress was made, at least comparable to that reported with the use of stimulant drugs. Behavior therapy is seen as an alternative to drugs such as methylphenidate (Ritalin) and dextroamphetamine. In spite of the acknowledged need to combine medication with other remedial procedures, drugs are often prescribed as the only intervention. Although drugs may have short-term beneficial effects, long-term social and academic change are not likely to occur when only drugs are employed. The authors point out that children have reverted to original behaviors immediately after taking stimulants for a year and then discontinuing them. Drugs make social and academic learning possible, but they do not necessarily produce it.

COMMENTARY: The authors demonstrate a simple and effective means of reducing hyperactive behavior by reinforcing appropriate academic and social behaviors. The daily report cards and custom-tailored reward system appear to be the key ingredients and are readily adaptable to the wide variety of problems covered in our book. The authors point out that stimulant drugs are not used in the afternoon because they may reduce food intake and cause insomnia. They suggest that behavioral methods are particularly suited for parental use during the evenings. Their article, which was published in a pediatric medical journal, would be quite useful for school personnel and could serve as a useful communication between the school and a hyperactive child's pediatrician.

SOURCE: O'Leary, K. D., Pelham, W. E., Rosenbaum, A., and Price, G. H. "Behavioral Treatment of Hyperkinetic Children: An Experimental Evaluation of its Usefulness." *Clinical Pediatrics,* 1976, *15,* 510-515.

Behavioral Intervention with Hyperactive Children

AUTHOR: H. Thompson Prout

PRECIS: Operant conditioning, environmental manipulation, self-regulation, and biofeedback for reducing hyperactivity

INTRODUCTION: The author defines behavioral interventions as any nonmedical treatments for reducing hyperactivity. Reviews of the problems involved in drug therapy indicate that nondrug interventions should be emphasized. Data are cited concerning the problems that hyperactive children continue to have as adolescents and adults. A review of the literature suggests that intervention should begin before school age and that parents should be helped to structure the child's home environment.

INTERVENTIONS: The author provides a description of various approaches that have been taken to the problem of hyperactivity.

Psychotherapy. Although anxiety-caused hyperactivity should be treated by psychotherapy or a behavioral method, psychotherapy is not considered the treatment of choice by many authors. Literature is cited to show that, with neurotic children, psychotherapy has been successful 60 to 70 percent of the time but that it has had a success rate of only 15 to 40 percent with hyperactive children. The author concludes that psychotherapy should be employed only when hyperactivity does not interfere with the therapeutic process and when there are additional psychological problems.

Operant Procedures. Undesirable behaviors have been eliminated and new behaviors encouraged by operant conditioning. Attention can be conditioned as a means of inhibiting off-task behaviors. Tokens have been successfully used to reward intervals of attending behavior. Classmates may also receive tokens for the hyperactive child's improved attention. Adult social reinforcement has been successfully used to increase the amount of time spent on an activity. Another study successfully used a primary reinforcer (candy) and then switched to a secondary reinforcer (praise) to increase attention. The author cites a situation in which teachers were inadvertently reinforcing inappropriate behavior by attention. A token exchange system was instituted that reduced hyperactivity and destructive acts and increased attention and cooperation. The same type of management techniques have been successfully used by parents. Videotape feedback has been effective in teaching parents how to use behavior modification.

Environmental Manipulation. Various aspects of children's school or home have been changed. One study suggests that hyperactivity involves either the absence or the breakdown of self-control and that external control should be used and gradually lessened. Engineered classrooms have been used for hyperactive children. Intervals of fifteen to twenty minutes were used for various activities so that attention would be maintained. Sitting activities would not be scheduled for three consecutive time periods. Rather than grades, tokens were given for work completion. One study used a grade promotion to reduce hyperactivity. The hyperactive child controls himself better in the presence of larger children who do not tolerate impulsive outbursts. Background music and physical education programs have been employed with reported beneficial effects on hyperactivity.

Self-Regulation. One study used children to monitor one another's behavior. Another study successfully used self-directed verbal commands with cue cards that read "stop" and "think" and had cartoon illustrations. Motor exercises have been used to train hyperactive children to inhibit motor responses.

Biofeedback. Biofeedback is thought by some practitioners to be particularly well suited for hyperactive children in school in that it allows excessive muscle tension to be brought under voluntary control. Alpha-wave training has been employed with inconclusive results. Slow, even breathing has increased attention and performance in some hyperactive children. But again, results have not been definitive.

COMMENTARY: The author provides a valuable overview regarding interventions for hyperactivity. It should be noted again that psychotherapy is not seen as the treatment of choice. The various behavioral approaches cited are seen as effective or at least promising. Since hyperactive children usually continue to have adjustment problems, there is a need to provide services during the adolescent period. We believe that a combination of the approaches reviewed, tailored for the individual child, is more likely to be effective than one method alone. For example, the child could be taught self-regulation, the parents could use a positive reinforcement system, and the teacher could provide a structured, "engineered" classroom.

SOURCE: Prout, H. T. "Behavioral Intervention with Hyperactive Children: A Review." *Journal of Learning Disabilities,* 1977, *10,* 141-146.

Hyperactivity and Artificial Food Colors

AUTHOR: Terry L. Rose

PRECIS: Frequency and duration of hyperactive behaviors in two eight-year-old girls as caused and reduced by controlling intake of artificial food colors

INTRODUCTION: The author discusses Feingold's theory that eating "salicylate-like" compounds causes hyperactivity (B. F. Feingold, *Why Your Child is Hyperactive,* New York: Random House, 1975). The K-P diet eliminates many foods containing salicylates, such as apples, berries, pork, and tomatoes, as well as all artificial flavors and colors (including toothpastes, flavored medications, and mouthwashes). Many experimentally uncontrolled studies report dramatic improvement in hyperactivity as a result of the K-P diet. Rose highlights the methodological flaws, including the absence of experimental control groups, the lack of objective data, no controls for the placebo effect, inappropriate statistical methods, and the use of nonvalidated assessment instruments.

METHOD: Two eight-year-old hyperactive girls were on the K-P diet for approximately one year. They were given a cookie that contained a yellow artificial food color, tartrazine No. 5 (the children received .05 mg. of dye per kg. of body weight each day). The parents completed a log for significant behaviors, such as increased motor activity or changes in sleep patterns. Observers rated the children for on-task behavior, out-of-seat behavior, and physical aggression. Details are presented concerning the experimental design, double-blind procedure, placebo control, observer reliability, and how the data were collected.

Results indicated a relationship between consumption of artificial food colors and an increase in frequency and duration of out-of-seat behavior and a decrease in the duration of on-task behavior. The author discusses some problems that resulted from the opportunity to take fewer observations than desired and from the children's occasional nonadherence to the K-P diet.

COMMENTARY: This article addresses the current controversy over food additives. It is an objective, controlled study demonstrating that a particular food coloring did produce increased hyperactive behavior, as measured by out-of-seat behavior and less ability to remain on-task. This type of information could be useful for educational personnel in two ways. First, advice may be offered to parents with hyperactive children to reduce their consumption of additives. Second, some schools have already taken steps both to provide "natural" foods without additives and to eliminate "junk" foods from cafeterias and vending machines.

SOURCE: Rose, T. L. "The Functional Relationship Between Artificial Food Colors and Hyperactivity." *Journal of Applied Behavior Analysis,* 1978, *11,* 439-446.

Covert Positive Reinforcement in Treating Hyperactivity

AUTHORS: Edward A. Workman and Donald J. Dickinson

PRECIS: Teaching covert conditioning to a nine-year-old boy to reduce out-of-seat behavior, noise making, and rocking

INTRODUCTION: Positive reinforcement, extinction, time-outs, and response costs (all operant procedures) have been used to change negative school behaviors. However, school psychologists have to rely on teachers and parents to carry out these methods. In contrast, covert conditioning can be directly used by school psychologists in teaching children to control their own behavior. If a behavior is followed by a reinforcing event, then the probability of that behavior occurring again increases. In covert positive reinforcement (CPR), the reinforcing event (pleasant activities) and the behavior to be increased (for example, assertive or nonfearful behavior) are visually imagined. After vividly imagining appropriate behavior, the person imagines the pleasant activity. CPR has been successfully employed with adults to help them overcome phobias and with children to increase their positive self-statements.

METHOD: A very intelligent nine-year-old boy was considered hyperactive by the school and by his parents. An interview with his teacher revealed three specific classroom problem behaviors —out-of-seat behavior, rocking his chair, and making noises by hitting various objects. An objective observer was used to reliably measure the behaviors. After an eight-day baseline observation, CPR was begun. Twice per week (Tuesdays and Thursdays), thirty-minute sessions were held (for a total of six sessions).

Ten CPR trials were performed by the school psychologist during each session with the boy. The boy imagined himself quietly sitting in class with all four legs of the chair on the floor and looking straight at the teacher while listening to every word. He then imagined himself doing one of sixteen previously determined reinforcing activities. The boy was asked to list the things he would most like to do or to receive as gifts. Among the activities that he mentioned were flying the fastest plane in the world, scoring a touchdown, receiving a minibike, and being a war hero. The boy raised his finger to indicate a clear visualization. Target behaviors were imagined for fifteen seconds and reinforcing activities for thirty seconds. Satiation to a reinforcing activity was avoided by using ten different images during each session.

Statistics are presented that demonstrate significant reductions of the three target behaviors, and the teacher was pleased with the noticeable changes. The authors note that the boy spontaneously imagined scenes from the CPR training when he was tempted to perform one of the inappropriate behaviors. Rather than actively trying to imagine the scenes, they "just came to him." Additionally, he thought about the scenes almost every night before falling asleep.

COMMENTARY: This one case report clearly demonstrates the feasibility of using CPR in a school setting CPR is certainly worth considering as a method when teacher and/or parent cooperativeness is marginal or nonexistent. School psychologists may relatively easily accumulate their own data to determine which types of cases are most responsive to this approach. As seen throughout our book, a combination of methods may well be the most powerful and efficient procedure. While the psychologist is training a hyperactive child to use CPR, the teacher and parent could be positively reinforcing appropriate, focused, nonhyperactive behaviors. Also, the authors point out that the boy was motivated to change his behavior and willingly participated in the training. It may be worthwhile to consider using some powerful form of positive reinforcement to motivate children to learn CPR. Learning self-control and receiving natural positive feedback for improved behavior may then become a positive cycle that may be generalized to other behaviors.

SOURCE: Workman, E. A., and Dickinson, D. J. "The Use of Covert Positive Reinforcement in the Treatment of a Hyperactive Child: An Empirical Case Study." *Journal of School Psychology,* 1979, *17,* 67-73.

Environmental Stimulation

AUTHOR: Sydney S. Zentall

PRECIS: Reducing hyperactivity by optimizing classroom stimulation and lessening the need to produce stimulation through overactivity

INTRODUCTION: In spite of inconclusive findings, it has been widely accepted that hyperactivity is exaggerated by excessive environmental stimulation. The author proposes the alternative theory that environmental stimulation decreases (rather than increases) hyperactivity. The overstimulation theory proposes that hyperactive children have inadequate stimulus filters. A flood of undirected responses results from this unfiltered flood of stimulation. Therefore, environmental stimulation should be drastically reduced, and classrooms should have little visual, auditory, or tactual stimuli. However, the author points out that low-stimulation environments do not in fact reduce hyperactivity and that hyperactive children cannot be differentiated from normal children in high-stimulation environments (novel situations, games, movies, playground). Theoretically, a search for optimal stimulation may be occurring when children behave in a manner that permits more stimulation to reach them (increased verbalizations, activity, changing orientation by moving eyes or head).

The author reviews studies that demonstrate decreases in activity when sensory (visual or auditory) stimulation was increased. He also points out the similarity between the behavior of hyperactive children and people who are in situations of sensory deprivation; that is, both groups respond with increased activity and restlessness. Also, sensory-deprived individuals and hyperactives both show poor concentration, disorganized thoughts, and poor visual-motor skills. Stimulant drugs have been used to calm hyperactive children rather than making them more active (as happens with normal children). According to the author, the drugs serve to maintain an adequate arousal that reduces the underaroused hyperactive children's need to search for more stimulation through overactivity.

CLASSROOM ENVIRONMENTAL STRATEGIES: The practice of having gray, bare walls with individual study carels is not recommended. Instead, rooms should be divided into interest areas.

Color and Patterns. Each area should have bright posters and pictures. Bulletin boards with frequently changed material may be used. Research is cited to show that distant visual stimuli aids in the reduction of activity.

Movement. Some form of movement serves to provide varied stimulation; for example, desks can be turned to face windows. Pets (mice, guinea pigs, fish) or mobiles are also possible sources of stimulation.

Duration. Long exposure to repetitious tasks tends to increase activity, and this in turn decreases performance level. Therefore, tasks and activities should be relatively short to avoid satiation and increased physical activity on the part of hyperactive children.

Novelty. Long exposures to tasks lead to a loss of novelty and more hyperactivity. Novelty is enhanced by having children frequently change tasks. Research cited suggests that added stimulation should not be part of the task itself. Children may well have difficulty in separating the task from the added stimulation. Rather, other stimuli should be presented before or peripheral to the task.

Task Difficulty. Hyperactive and impulsive children do more poorly and are less persistent than normal children when presented with relatively difficult tasks. It is therefore essential to ensure success on tasks in order to maintain the attention of hyperactive children.

Large-Group Tasks. Hyperactive children have much difficulty in waiting and therefore do quite poorly in groups. They do much better in one-to-one situations. Some theorists have speculated that the high level of group stimulation leads to the poor performance of hyperactive children. Zentall suggests that the cause is the low stimulation caused by the long periods of waiting for teacher attention and the low teacher-to-child ratio in a group.

Self-Paced Tasks. Hyperactive children do better at tasks in which they can regulate the rate of progress. There are no waiting periods, and they can control the amount of stimulation.

Active Tasks. Hyperactive children also do better in tasks involving movement and active participation than in those that require waiting. However, activity should not interfere with performance; this may happen if children focus more on the activity than on the task. The author suggests not including activity during the early stages of learning and allowing activity only after task completion. Children could move to a different part of the classroom or deliver a message following task completion. They could do isometric exercises when they have trouble sitting still. Some children may benefit from having two seats if they can't stay in one.

Reinforcement. Positive reinforcement is frequently used to effectively increase appropriate behaviors such as sitting still. However, positive effects often are not maintained, and even partial withdrawal of reinforcement results in the elimination of the positive behaviors. Reinforcers may function as needed sources of stimulation, and hyperactive behavior may be the means that children use to obtain the needed stimulation. When reinforcement is reduced, other sources of stimulation should be substituted. However, hyperactive children can be taught to internalize reinforcement by using self-control strategies. They learn to talk to themselves in terms of planning ahead, stopping to think, being careful, correcting errors, and rewarding themselves.

COMMENTARY: The author argues very effectively that hyperactivity is related to understimulation, not overstimulation. He calls for careful use of high-stimulation environments to assess the effective aspects of increased stimulation. When isolation effectively results in less hyperactive behavior, he believes that the significant factor is the return to the more stimulating classroom. For those in education who have accepted the necessity of a reduction in stimulation, this article will serve as a provocative plea to reassess this widespread belief. In keeping with the philosophy of our book, *alternative* approaches should always be considered when planning for children. This is especially true when a child's hyperactive behavior is not responding to the methods being used. The success of brief intervals of exercise in reducing hyperactivity would lend support to the need of many hyperactive children for an active form of physical stimulation.

SOURCE: Zentall, S. S. "Environmental Stimulation Model." *Exceptional Children,* 1977, *44,* 502-510.

Additional Readings

Cunningham, S. J., and Knights, R. M. "The Performance of Hyperactive and Normal Boys Under Differing Reward and Punishment Schedules." *Journal of Pediatric Psychology,* 1978, *3,* 195-201.

Forty-eight hyperactive boys aged seven to twelve participated in a discrimination-learning study. Punishment (taking away marbles for incorrect responses) was more effective for both hyperactive and normal boys in promoting learning than reward (giving marbles for correct responses). Penalties increase attention and caution, whereas rewards distract children and increase impulsivity. Only the younger hyperactive boys did significantly better than normal children when punishment alone was used. Young hyperactive children should receive feedback after mistakes rather than after correct responses.

Gittelman, M. (Ed.). "Intervention Strategies with Hyperactive Children." *International Journal of Mental Health,* 1976, *8,* 3-138.

This entire issue is devoted to the effective treatment of hyperactive children. Specifically covered are stimulant drugs, cognitive behavior modification, behavior therapy, and training for parents. Hyperactivity is diagnosed too freely; and drugs are not only used too frequently but are often used before other methods have been tried. Hyperactive children who took Ritalin and those whose parents received behavior modification training improved equally, but parents who underwent training were more pleased with treatment. Suggested multidisciplinary approaches include environmental restructuring, specific training at home and school, concentration training, and movement therapy. There is a need to address the problems of immaturity, impulsivity, and restlessness that continue into adulthood. However, many hyperactive children do relatively well as adults. Cognitive behavior modification has successfully established inner speech control over impulsive and disruptive behavior. Hyperactive boys who attribute success to luck do better with an operant social reinforcement program, while those believing in effort benefit more from self-instructional training.

Henker, B., Whalen, C. K., and Collins, B. E. "Double-Blind and Triple-Blind Assessments of Medication and Placebo Responses in Hyperactive Children." *Journal of Abnormal Child Psychology*, 1979, *7*, 1-13.

Under very carefully controlled conditions, twenty-two hyperactive boys (seven to eleven years old) were rated as more difficult and disruptive when taking a placebo than when taking methylphenidate (Ritalin). Drugs are seen as being measurably beneficial, not as sufficient in themselves. The Conners' Abbreviated Symptom Questionnaire indicated fewer problems (such as restless, overactive, excitable, and impulsive behavior) when Ritalin was being administered.

Lambert, N. M., Sandoval, J., and Sassone, D. "Prevalence of Treatment Regimens for Children Considered to be Hyperactive." *American Journal of Orthopsychiatry*, 1979, *49*, 482-490.

This study identified 1.2 percent of elementary school children as hyperactive. In one year 58 percent of these children received stimulant medication, and an estimated 86 percent will take medication at some time. Treatment coincides with school stress, and multiple-treatment approaches are usually employed. In order of frequency, the most used treatments are medication, psychotherapy or counseling, special education, school consultation, diets, and motor therapy. The incidence of .76-percent use of stimulants is in contrast to reports of large numbers (10 to 15 percent) of children being forced to take amphetamines in order to remain in school.

Loney, J. "Hyperkinesis Comes of Age: What Do We Know and Where Should We Go?" *American Journal of Orthopsychiatry*, 1980, *50*, 28-42.

This is a recent overview of the improved state of diagnosing and treating hyperkinesis. There has been a shift in focus to viewing the problem as primarily one of inattention. Various behavioral treatment approaches have been successfuly tailored to the specific circumstances of inattentive hyperactive children. Stimulants do not have a paradoxical or diagnostic role with hyperactive children. Rather, the reduced hyperactivity is a by-product of the heightened efficiency and attentiveness that central nervous system stimulants cause in everyone.

Loney, J., Weissenburger, F. E., Woolson, R. F., and Lichty, E. C. "Comparing Psychological and Pharmacological Treatments for Hyperkinetic Boys and Their Classmates." *Journal of Abnormal Child Psychology*, 1979, *7*, 133-143.

Methylphenidate (20 to 40 mg. per day) was administered to hyperkinetic boys aged six to twelve. Intervention with a similar group took the form of consultation with the classroom teacher in order to increase teacher approval for appropriate behavior, decrease the intensity of disapproval, and ignore off-task behavior. As in other studies, teachers were found to be disapproving 80 percent of the time, and the change in being approving was a dramatic one. The effectiveness of both approaches was equal. Teacher consultation also led to improved behavior in the overactive classmates not focused upon.

McBrien, R. J. "Using Relaxation Methods with First-Grade Boys." *Elementary School Guidance and Counseling*, 1978, *12*, 145-152.

Deep muscle relaxation should be taught to hyperactive children rather than giving them drugs. Relaxation counterconditions anxiety and enables children to become calm and less distractible. Steps include the use of imagery, slow deep breathing, tensing and releasing muscles, and then only releasing muscles. Simon Says is used as a game format ("Simon says to let go and feel your eyes relax"). Imagery is used to help children imagine pleasant, comfortable scenes as they relax.

Minde, K. *A Parents' Guide to Hyperactivity in Children.* Montreal, Canada: Quebec Association for Children with Learning Disabilities, 1971.

This manual is useful for parents and teachers as a clear statement of the recognition of and interventions for hyperactivity. Hyperactive children need constant reinforcement, repetition, and help with their impulsive work habits. Specific suggestions include the making of realistic demands on the child, avoiding arguing, reinforcing any talent and providing successes, avoiding punishment but teaching cause and effect, and providing consistent praise.

Safer, D. J., and Allen, R. P. "Hyperactive Children: Diagnosis and Management." Baltimore: University Park Press, 1976.

Written in nontechnical language, this book focuses on the practical concerns of teachers and parents of hyperactive children. Various approaches are reviewed, with special attention to school management issues. Behavioral management techniques are presented in jargon-free language, and practical details of daily management are described.

Schulman, J. L., Suran, B. G., Stevens, T. M., and Kupst, M. J. "Instructions, Feedback, and Reinforcement in Reducing Activity Levels in the Classroom." *Journal of Applied Behavior Analysis,* 1979, *12,* 441-447.

A biomotometer is an electronic device that measures motor activity while providing auditory feedback (beeps). Instructions, feedback, and contingent reinforcement (toys or candy) successfully reduced motor activity in nine hyperactive children aged nine to thirteen. The beep indicated that the child was moving around too much, so a small number of beeps meant the likelihood of earning a reward. Too many beeps meant no reward.

Varni, J. W., and Henker, B. "A Self-Regulation Approach to the Treatment of Three Hyperactive Boys." *Child Behavior Therapy,* 1979, *1,* 171-192.

Hyperactivity should be seen from an interactional point of view, since hyperactive behavioral style was responsive to context changes. Self-instruction included adult modeling and self-verbalizations to guide performance. Self-monitoring involved a wrist counter to record time spent on academic tasks. Self-reinforcement was the earning of points based on improved behavior to purchase articles. Self-instructional training or self-monitoring did not improve performance in the absence of adult supervision. Combining self-monitoring with self-reinforcement in a clinic and then in school did lead to improved academic performance and decreased hyperactivity.

Weithorn, C. J., and Kagen, E. "Training First Graders of High-Activity Level to Improve Performance Through Verbal Self-Direction." *Journal of Learning Disabilities,* 1979, *12,* 82-88.

Impulsive, highly active first graders were successfully taught to use verbally mediated responses on multiple-choice tasks. Children told themselves what to do by describing aloud what they were looking for. If the picture was incorrect, they said "no" and repeated what they were looking for. If it was correct, they said "right" and marked it. Children were reminded to use these verbal self-instructions. Training was most successful for children with high activity levels and low language maturity.

Distractible and Inattentive Behavior

Distractibility is generally defined as having attention (or focus) drawn to an object different from the primary one or having attention drawn in different directions at the same time. Distraction or mental confusion also occurs as a result of conflicting thoughts or feelings. This confusion could be due to psychological or physiological (usually central nervous system) problems. When children are inattentive, they are not attending (looking or listening) appropriately. Attention span is the length of time an individual is able to concentrate, and attention is acknowledged as a basic skill underlying learning. Research has demonstrated that ability to pay attention clearly differentiates high and low achievers (J. V. Gilmore, "The Factor of Attention in Underachievement," Journal of Education, *1968, 50, 41-66). Estimates of serious attentional problems in children range from 5 to 10 percent.*

Attention deficits are central in the hyperactive syndrome; hyperactive children are unable to sustain concentration for more than a very short time. Many theorists believe that attention problems are frequently caused by a weakness in distinguishing figure from background or essential from nonessential information. This type of "stimulus equivalence" may underlie distractibility and inattentiveness (M. Gittelman, "Hyperactive Children: Types and Behavioral Interventions," International Journal of Mental Health, *1979, 8, 129-138). Methods for improving distractibility are extremely varied, including positive reinforcement of attention, conditioning, teaching communication skills (focusing and avoiding distractions or talking, listening, and observing), modeling, the use of peers as teachers, changing the environmental structure, self-instruction, self-monitoring, and stimulant drugs.*

Teacher Attention to Increase Student Attention

AUTHORS: Marcia Broden, Carl Bruce, Mary Ann Mitchell, Virginia Carter, and R. Vance Hall

PRECIS: Praising and increasing attentive behavior of two very disruptive second-grade boys

INTRODUCTION: Study behaviors of children have been improved by having the teacher give positive attention for appropriate behavior. In addition, students sitting nearby the children who were praised also showed improved study habits. Many teachers believe that one disruptive child increases the inappropriate behavior of nearby students. If that student improves, however, the others may also be positively influenced. The present study concerned the effect of social praise on the attentiveness of two second-grade boys who sat next to each other. They came from very economically deprived backgrounds, and their IQ scores were 60 and 72.

METHOD: Observers recorded appropriate attending to teacher-assigned tasks during ten-second intervals over a daily half-hour period. Attending behaviors were doing assigned writing or looking at the teacher if she was talking. Nonattending behaviors were being out of seat, talking, looking at peers, or any other behavior incompatible with attending to tasks. Speaking to the boys was defined as teacher attention. Baseline rate and recording procedures are described.

    After the boys' usual rate of attention was measured (baseline), the principles of positive reinforcement and their use in past studies were explained to the teacher. The teacher was asked to attend to and praise one of the boys whenever he paid attention appropriately and to ignore all his inappropriate behavior. After twenty-three days, the teacher stopped praising this boy and systematically began praising the other one for paying appropriate attention. The teacher then stopped attention to both boys for several days and followed that by praising both boys for paying attention. The statistical results are graphed and discussed.

Teacher attention dramatically increased the first boy's attending behaviors. At the same time, the neighboring boy's attention to tasks also increased significantly. The authors speculate that the second boy received some "spillover" of positive reinforcement from the teacher. This may have occurred because she moved close to both boys even when she was praising only one of them. Teacher proximity has been considered reinforcing by some researchers. Also, unintentionally the teacher had slightly increased her attention to the second boy when she was not supposed to. Finally, the second boy may simply have imitated the increasingly appropriate behavior of his neighbor.

COMMENTARY: The study clearly demonstrated that the appropriate behavior of a nearby student can be increased by improving the behavior of the target student: there was a drop in attention when positive praise was withdrawn and an increase in attention when praise was reinstituted. The implications for teachers are quite clear. Student attention (as well as many other appropriate behaviors) is increased by positive teacher reinforcement and the ignoring of inappropriate behaviors. The experimental support for the beneficial effect upon neighboring students is very strong. This should allay the concern of many teachers that other students may be adversely influenced by increasing attention to only one child. Many teachers have expressed the opinion that other children will become jealous and act up to get attention. This study demonstrates (as hundreds of others do) that systematic positive teacher attention is a very powerful influence on student behavior. The teacher who uses this method on one student may receive the additional benefit of improved behavior in others. This result could also influence the teacher to place two problem children near each other in order to influence both of them efficiently and positively.

SOURCE: Broden, M., Bruce, C., Mitchell, M. A., Carter, V., and Hall, R. V. "Effects of Teacher Attention on Attending Behavior of Two Boys at Adjacent Desks." *Journal of Applied Behavior Analysis*, 1970, *3*, 199-204.

Increasing Attention with a "Workclock"

AUTHORS: Vernon T. Devine and Jerry R. Tomlinson

PRECIS: Giving free time to an entire class for attentive behavior and stopping a clock and using time-outs for inattention

INTRODUCTION: Behavior management techniques have been successfully used to improve the behavior of entire classrooms. Methods have included tokens or free time for appropriate behavior and teacher praise. But token economies consume much teacher and consultant time, and maintenance of appropriate behavior has been a problem when the system is terminated. The following program has been used in more than forty classrooms with children who were management problems. Observations before and after the program were taken of seven third- and fourth-grade classrooms (129 children, 7 with behavior problems).

METHOD: The "workclock" used is a Meylan sixty-minute reset timer (Model 4861H) with a seven-inch face and a sound-activated switch. It can be turned on or off with a whistle that activates the switch. A psychologist told the class that the clock would be used to improve study habits and to give them a chance to earn free time. A specific amount of work time was required during a time interval (usually fifteen or twenty minutes less than the total time). The amount of free time earned was the time remaining on the clock. The clock ran as long as all students were in their seats, talking only when called upon, and attending (listening or working on assignments). If the rule was broken by anyone, the clock stopped until the behavior changed positively. Three strikes (stopping the clock) against a student during one period resulted in that student sitting in a time-out chair for one minute. That student made up the time spent in the chair during free time. Three time-outs, refusing to sit in the chair, or making noise while sitting resulted in being sent to the principal's office. At the office, a quiet area was provided where the child had to complete an academic assignment.

The clock was used during one academic period, which changed each day. During this time, teachers socially praised attentive behaviors. After five days, use of the clock was terminated, and all children were expected to complete their work before having free time. A strike was given when a child interfered with others (by being noisy or talking out). The teacher acted as a workclock by stopping the lesson and being silent until everyone was paying attention. Students quickly paid attention since time lost during instruction reduced the amount of free time. The psychologist's role is defined as that of a consultant who is to withdraw (after three to five work-completion periods) from the program once the teacher learns what to do. Quicker students have been successfully used to help other students to complete their assignments.

Observational procedures and statistical results are described. The workclock resulted in more positive classroom behavior for both referred and nonreferred students. The authors see this method as an alternative to token economies since it is easier to use, easier to eliminate, and requires less teacher time. Not only was attention improved, but there was a significant reduction in the differences among children in terms of attending behavior. The seven students with behavior problems no longer were very different from their peers in terms of paying attention. The authors stress that the workclock is a temporary device, that it should not be used permanently, and that teachers must learn the principles underlying the behavior change.

COMMENTARY: The workclock appears to be another effective method for both increasing attentiveness and improving assignment completion. It certainly provides an alternative for teachers who are philosophically opposed to allowing students to earn tokens for tangible rewards. The use of free time as a reward has been successfully employed by many teachers. Students may find their interests aroused both by the technical aspects of the equipment and the cooperative earning of free time by the group.

SOURCE: Devine, V. T., and Tomlinson, J. R. "The Workclock: An Alternative to Token Economies in the Management of Classroom Behaviors." *Psychology in the Schools,* 1976, *13,* 163-170.

Teaching Learning Skills
to Disturbed, Delinquent Children

AUTHORS: Salvador Minuchin, Pamela Chamberlain, and Paul Graubard

PRECIS: Teaching students how to focus attention and gather and order information

INTRODUCTION: The authors believe that delinquents very frequently show poor academic achievement in spite of possessing normal or superior intelligence. They wanted to develop a curriculum for helping children from disorganized families of low socioeconomic status. These parents often respond to children in a global and erratic manner and do not aid them in understanding and following rules. In solving conflicts, the children seek answers in the immediate reactions of others. They do not see their causal role and do not learn how to focus their attention on the problem. Additionally, the rules for communicating information through words are not well established. People do not expect to be heard, and communication occurs through yelling. Children attend to the person rather than to the content of the message. Since the school expects attention to abstract content, a conflict is inevitable.

METHOD: Sessions were held with six children in one classroom of a residential treatment center. In spite of an average age of ten years, the boys exhibited the communication skills of five-year-olds. They were told that they would learn to do well in school even if the teacher did not like them and that they might be able to eventually learn in a regular classroom. During the sessions, children observed each other behind a one-way mirror. They were taught to rate each other's responsiveness to being taught and to list behaviors that enhanced or interfered with learning. Money was given for each point earned for being receptive. The children who judged the others were also rated and earned points.

The ten meetings all centered on developing adequate communication skills—for example, listening, staying on a topic, taking turns, telling a story, asking relevant questions, categorizing and classifying information, and role playing. Games were used during each session. Listening was taught through "Simon Says"; the winners were those who could listen and pay attention. The children were also asked to repeat telephone messages exactly, and waiting, keeping directions in mind, and concentrating were discussed. Children were told to make noise (tapping, thumping, jangling keys, and so on) while one child spoke, and a discussion followed on how noise interferes with learning. Taking turns was demonstrated through giving each child a part to say in familiar nursery rhymes. The difficulties of listening for your part, talking in turn, and waiting for others to speak were covered. The logic in stories and conversations was specifically reviewed.

After five sessions the children were listening and were being heard by others. They were being judged positively, winning games, and earning money; in addition, the noise level had diminished. Two sessions took up categorizing. The children could ask Twenty Questions in order to learn what the object or correct answer was. Their ability to ask good questions increased, and they learned how to ask questions that would result in information relevant to solving a problem. Role playing was then used to allow them to practice their new skills. They had to discuss why they became so angry at someone that they turned to abuse rather than communicating effectively. Role-playing adults helped them learn what it is like to be an adult. The children, as observers, became skilled at identifying such mistakes as getting off the topic or asking irrelevant questions. During the last session increased self-awareness and the possession of new skills were apparent to all participants.

Ability to pay attention was markedly increased, and the

children learned to concentrate on achievement. Their serving as "judges" aided this process. They slowed their tempo and learned to listen, take turns, and ask good questions. They displayed more conceptual (rather than concrete) thinking after the sessions were completed.

COMMENTARY: The authors comment that they were surprised to see such a large amount of change in only ten sessions, but their observations fit the pattern that may be seen throughout our book. Specific, focused interventions can lead to efficient and rapid change. The children learned to avoid distractions and to focus their attention more accurately and for longer periods than before. The curriculum described is also usable for generally enhancing communication and social skills. Teachers should note that role playing, Twenty Questions, Simon Says, and the "judging" systems may be used in the classroom to improve listening, staying on a topic, and asking relevant questions.

SOURCE: Minuchin, S., Chamberlain, P., and Graubard, P. "A Project to Teach Learning Skills to Disturbed, Delinquent Children." *American Journal of Orthopsychiatry,* 1967, *37,* 558-567.

Group Counseling for Inattentiveness

AUTHORS: Robert D. Myrick and F. Donald Kelly

PRECIS: Structured group discussion of feelings and behavior with three first graders

INTRODUCTION: The authors review the rationale of group counseling for positive learning and the giving up of ineffective attitudes and behaviors. Common concerns can be effectively discussed in a group of two or more with a trained leader. Chil-

dren can express themselves concerning tasks and problems
typical of their developmental level. New understanding and behaviors that reduce conflicts are learned. But the authors are
concerned about the too general nature of the counseling literature and about the use of adult group procedures for children.
Traditional group experiences require verbal ability and a relatively long attention span. In the present study, a more structured approach was used to help children become aware of their
feelings and practice appropriate expressiveness. They were
taught to discuss themselves and others.

METHOD: The main problem was a seven-year-old boy who
was inattentive, restless, aggressive, and doing poor academic
work. Another boy was described as restless, hyperactive, bossy,
and an impulsive talker. A girl was careless, sought attention,
and frequently giggled. These three children participated in five
half-hour sessions held on five consecutive school days. Because
of their age, putting them in a larger group might have prevented their relating to one another and learning effectively.

Children were encouraged to take three roles—talker, listener, and observer. During the first meeting the counselor said,
"I would like to learn more about children your age and I think
you can help me. Perhaps, as a result of our meetings and your
talking to me and each other, you will also learn more about
yourselves." The counselor explained that the talker would have
one minute to say what he or she liked and disliked about
school. The listener could ask questions and try to repeat what
was said. The observer watched, later made suggestions to the
listener for better listening, and then joined the discussion. Immediately after, the counselor expanded, summarized, clarified,
and restated the feelings discussed. The second session began
with the counselor suggesting that they talk about teachers and
other adults. The children said that they liked teachers and
adults who paid attention to them, were nice, and let them do
what they wanted. They disliked being ignored, being told to sit
down and be quiet, and always having to do what they were
told. The third session focused on what is it like to feel good,
bad, happy, sad, and so forth. Pictures of children and adults
who were expressing feelings were discussed. Feelings related to

behavior were the topic of the fourth and fifth meetings. The children discussed what made them feel happy, sad, angry, or embarrassed. They were asked to tell about things that they did to cause these feelings in others. Throughout, the talker-listener-observer method was employed so that each child received feedback from the other two. They made comments to one another concerning their specific behaviors.

Classroom observations of the three children were made in order to assess the effects of counseling. Attending behavior was listening to the teacher, looking at children who were responding to lessons, doing desk assignments, and copying instructions. Nonattending behaviors were looking out the window, playing with objects, walking around, and talking out. The inattentive boy's attentive behavior continued to improve significantly during and after the sessions. Both the teacher and observer noted more interested and attentive behavior in class. The other boy also paid more attention and was less fidgety. No changes were observed in the girl's behavior. All three children said that they enjoyed the meetings.

COMMENTARY: The discussion method used in this study could be employed by educational personnel with experience in leading groups. One significant difference from other groups is the talker-listener-observer structure. Additionally, the leader is directive in the sense of setting the topic for discussion and guiding the conversation. The general procedure used for attentiveness is also readily adaptable to the other problem behaviors covered in our book. Too often, adults believe that a few meetings are not sufficient to influence children. This article is a useful reminder of the possible effectiveness of focused, time-limited discussions of feelings and behavior.

SOURCE: Myrick, R. D., and Kelly, F. D. "Group Counseling with Primary School-Age Children." *Journal of School Psychology*, 1971, *9*, 137-143.

Classroom Management Techniques
for Increasing Attention

AUTHORS: Joyce T. Simmons and Barbara H. Wasik

PRECIS: Seating arrangement, peer influence, and free time as methods to increase attending behaviors of first and third graders

INTRODUCTION: Classroom behavior has been changed most effectively by teacher approval for appropriate behavior. Another popular method is allowing students to earn free time or special activities by behaving appropriately. There is also some evidence that peers can be used to modify a child's behavior. Peer influence can be used indirectly by reinforcing an entire group only if all members act positively. This study investigated three methods or conditions for increasing the attention of students.

METHOD: Five students (four boys and one girl) were selected from a third-grade class because of their frequent inattention and noncompletion of assignments. Six boys were selected from a first-grade class for similar problems. Peer popularity was assessed by the teachers through a sociometric questionnaire. Observers recorded appropriate and inappropriate behavior, verbal interactions, and amount of work completed. The observations were categorized with the Children's Classroom Behavior scale only during independent work periods, when the teacher and aide were not present. Time intervals and specific definitions are described. There were two appropriate categories (paying attention or sitting quietly and preparing materials) and four inappropriate categories (activities inappropriate for time and place, unproductive activity, inappropriate attention getting, and aggressive or resistant behavior).

The following three conditions were used. (1) *Seating arrangement:* Small groups were formed on the basis of positive choices obtained from the sociometric ratings. A chairman was chosen in each group to be the most reinforcing peer for the inattentive child in that group. (2) *Peer influence:* The teacher asked everyone in each of the groups to help the target child do his or her work. Independent work such as creative writing, free-choice reading, and math was performed. Helping consisted of encouragement to start or continue working, help with spelling or reading a word, or help with understanding a math concept. (3) *Free time:* If the target child completed assigned work, his or her group received the positive reinforcement of thirty minutes of free time near the end of the day. The group could choose an outdoor play session or activities in the auditorium. Groups that did not earn free time remained in class with the aide and did academic assignments.

A detailed analysis is presented for results in the two grades. Teacher instruction to peers to positively influence one another did work for relatively long periods of time. But the target children in the third grade showed dramatically better attention as compared to the modest increase for first graders. Peer influence worked very well for both first and third graders without the need for any additional reinforcement. The authors speculate that children may be more responsive to requests to help their peers than to requests for being more attentive. Free time further increased attentive behavior, especially for the first graders. After the program, the target children appeared to be more popular than previously. They were more frequently chosen to be partners in class and on the playground and were invited to play after school.

The classroom teachers believed that the use of sociometric groups led to more cooperation among children and smoother functioning of the program. Also, the independent work periods required less teacher attention than they did prior to these groupings. The authors report that teachers are often needlessly concerned that small-group instruction leads to management problems. Instead, instruction offered to a large group often requires more time for behavioral management.

COMMENTARY: Educators should take careful note of this simple, economical, and effective method of increasing attention. Sociometric ratings are easy to obtain and may be strategically used for a variety of purposes. For example, social acceptance of unpopular students can be increased by pairing them with popular students on a project (M. S. Lilly, "Improving Social Acceptance of Low-Sociometric-Status, Low-Achieving Students," *Exceptional Children*, 1971, 341-347). Simmons and Wasik effectively used sociometric groups combined with instructions to the children to help one another and the reinforcement of free time periods to increase attentiveness. Their call to view peers as an important classroom resource is directly in keeping with findings in the impressive body of literature on group dynamics. Educational personnel might find very valuable practical guidelines for using groups effectively in R. A. Schmuck and P. A. Schmuck, *Group Processes in the Classroom*, Dubuque, Iowa: Brown, 1975.

SOURCE: Simmons, J. T., and Wasik, B. H. "Grouping Strategies, Peer Influence, and Free Time as Classroom Management Techniques with First- and Third-Grade Children." *Journal of School Psychology*, 1976, *14*, 322-332.

===

An Ecological Approach to Disruptive Classroom Behavior

AUTHOR: Susan M. Swap

PRECIS: Focusing on adaptive environmental responses rather than on the disturbance in a child

INTRODUCTION: The author reviews the idea that a child's disturbed behavior in the classroom is in large part a result of the interaction between the child and the classroom environment. She integrates Hewett's educationally based developmental model of behavior with Erikson's psychologically based model (F. Hewett, *The Emotionally Disturbed Child in the Classroom*, Boston: Allyn & Bacon, 1968; E. Erikson, *Insight and Responsibility*, New York: Norton, 1964). Children who have not reached a certain developmental level may show a variety of learning and behavior problems.

METHOD: Children who have not learned what Erikson calls "basic trust versus mistrust" show many disruptive behaviors. They may withdraw, seem impervious, and be unable to focus their attention. They do not trust others to offer them nurturance and consistency. Hewett calls this the "attention" level because of the child's inability to focus attention on relevant educational tasks. He states that the educational goal is to teach the children how to pay attention by encouraging their interests. Ways to do this include viewing slides, assembling very simple puzzles, and matching objects. Adults should give individual attention, provide immediate tangible rewards, and accept approximately correct responses. Hewett gives an example in which an adult draws a picture and gives the child warm acceptance for just being interested, and he also describes a process for turning passive attention into active collaboration. In it, the criteria for correctness are lowered in order to ensure success.

Swap discusses the need for the teacher to design an adaptive environment that is appropriate to the developmental level of children. For children with severe problems, a climate of safety, predictability, and consistency is necessary in conjunction with nurturance, acceptance, and individual attention. The basic trust stage requires a degree of adult permissiveness for building the ability to attend and respond to educational efforts.

Adaptive environmental responses are suggested for the other developmental stages described. The author sees problem children not as "emotionally disturbed" or "sick" but as having difficulty in handling stressful situations. Another way of viewing child-environment interaction involves temperamental characteristics. Disturbance is seen as the result of the reactions of key adults to the child's temperament. For example, dealing with the crises in Erikson's "industry versus inferiority" stage requires persistence, low distractibility, and adequate attention span. The author stresses the need to consider the compatibility between children's temperament and teacher personality. Teachers should have a say about which children are enrolled in their classes or be provided with a variety of adult resources (aides and consultants).

The classroom should be adapted for children at different developmental stages. A quiet area could be used for those children needing security, predictability, and individual attention (Hewett's attention and response level). Children at the exploratory level require an area designed for multisensory stimulation and exploration. Teachers are seen as having to evaluate their own values and expectations, be flexible, and set specific goals for children (as guided by their specific stage of development).

COMMENTARY: Even though this article is a theoretical overview of developmental stages, we included it here for two reasons. First, it is a very useful reminder of the importance of considering the child's developmental level in relation to the environment. The criteria for success can be changed by changing the ecological system, and children can experience success no matter how deficient their responses had been. Second, part of the article is relevant to the most basic aspect of appropriate classroom behavior—attentiveness. Without adequate attention to educational tasks, learning is difficult if not impossible. An atmosphere of safety, predictability, and acceptance, as well as individual relationships, is needed for children to attend and respond appropriately to educational efforts.

SOURCE: Swap, S. M. "Disturbing Classroom Behaviors: A Developmental and Ecological View." *Exceptional Children,* 1974, *41,* 163-172.

Positive Reinforcement for Conditioning Attention

AUTHORS: Hill M. Walker and Nancy K. Buckley

PRECIS: Rewarding ability to withstand distractions in an underachieving nine-year-old boy

INTRODUCTION: Conditioning methods have been effectively used to improve a large variety of children's behaviors. This study was designed to improve attention and to generalize that skill to the classroom. A bright nine-year-old boy was paying attention to classwork only 42 percent of the time. He did not complete tasks, was provocative to peers, made loud noises and comments, and was very easily distracted. Placed in a special class, his social behavior and academic task rate improved. However, his inattention and distractability did not respond to teacher approval or to a reward system.

METHOD: Individual conditioning was performed in a setting in which distractions could be controlled. The room contained only a table, two chairs, and a lamp, and there was very little external noise. A programmed mathematics text was the material to be learned during five daily forty-minute sessions (ten-minute periods with three-minute breaks). The boy was told that a click would sound during certain time intervals in which no distractions occurred. The adult would then enter a check mark on a sheet. If the boy paid attention to the click, this would be considered a distraction, and he would lose a point earned during that time interval. A model could be purchased with 160 points (check marks).

Attending was defined as looking at the page, doing problems, and writing answers. Nonattending was any behavior incompatible with task performance, such as looking away, holding something between his eyes and the work, or making any extraneous marks on the paper. A detailed analysis of his behavior is presented and discussed. Since he was able to consistently earn points, the length of the time interval was increased (30 seconds were added each time until he reached 600 seconds). Points were proportionally increased, so that he earned twenty points for paying attention for 600 seconds. Withdrawing the reinforcement led to a return to base rate (the number of nonattending behaviors before conditioning took place).

Generalization was then attempted by reinforcing his attention in the classroom. The teacher awarded one check mark for each interval of attentive behavior. Different time periods were used (variable-interval schedule); these averaged to thirty minutes. He reconditioned quickly and paid attention over 95 percent of the time. The teacher praised him for earning points. The authors believe that a conditioning procedure should first be used outside the classroom. Once the inappropriate behavior is brought under control, the procedure can be used effectively in the classroom.

COMMENTARY: This article illustrates a simple yet effective method for use by educational personnel. For example, the school psychologist, social worker, or guidance counselor can work with a child for a few sessions and, once success is reached, communicate the effective method to the teacher. The striking aspect is that attention and the ability to withstand distraction can be directly conditioned. It is up to the imagination of the adult to determine exactly how to condition a child to ignore distractions and pay attention to the teacher's voice or to tasks. Depending upon the age of the child, a game can be played in which the child practices not becoming involved in any kind of distraction. We have successfully used this technique by having children work on tasks while the adult whispers, walks back and forth, taps the desk, and so on. Most children are pleased and proud of their new ability to ignore distractions.

SOURCE: Walker, H. M., and Buckley, N. K. "The Use of Positive Reinforcement in Conditioning Attending Behavior." *Journal of Applied Behavior Analysis*, 1968, *1*, 245-250.

Contingency Management for Increasing Attention

AUTHORS: Anita E. Woolfolk and Robert L. Woolfolk

PRECIS: Training fifty-four inattentive elementary school children to earn rewards by paying attention to taped instructions

INTRODUCTION: Paying attention is a skill that underlies

learning, and it often differentiates high and low achievers. Contingency management has been effectively used to increase attention. Students receive tokens that can be used to purchase rewards for various study and listening behaviors. However, it has been difficult for teachers to define "attention" in a reliable manner. The authors review a study that used the ability to detect an instruction ("touch your nose") and make the appropriate response as an indicator of attention.

METHOD: In contrast to the study they reviewed, the Woolfolks used an instruction relevant to the lesson content. For example, "some goats have short hair, touch your hair." A motor response was required in response to the "vigilance signals" employed. The lessons were modifications of the Listening Skills Program (Science Research Associates). The research design included two control groups (one receiving no tokens and one receiving regular classroom instructions). In addition, some teachers received instructions concerning reinforcement principles while others did not. This training consisted of two and one-half hours of discussion and role playing in which teachers learned to pay selective attention to attending behaviors and to ignore inattention. The six most inattentive children were selected from three classes in grades 1, 2, and 3. Two measures of attention were employed. An "attention-rating instrument" was used by an observer to rate eye contact and body orientation indicating attention to tasks. A "vigilance score" represented the number of correct responses made to the teacher's signal instructions.

For four weeks, the students participated in thirty-minute sessions during the school day in small groups of six with specially trained teachers. Both teacher and audio taped presentations were used, including stories, songs, sound effects, and other listening activities. The children were told to listen carefully and follow the instructions of both the teacher and the tapes. During each session, ten directions (preselected at random times) were given; these included "touch your nose," "raise your hand," and "close your eyes" as part of the lesson. Each child received one point for responding appropriately within two seconds. The teacher scored points by moving a wooden bead (a total of ten) on a wire with each child's name on it). In this way, children received immediate feedback about the accuracy of their responses. During the second week, a group bonus point was given if all students responded correctly (each child received one additional point). Initially, points could be used to buy candy, but after the first week, points were used to play with special toys.

Statistical results are graphed and discussed. During the sessions, the method elicited and maintained student attention. High levels of attention were shown throughout the four-week training period. These students were enthusiastic and task oriented, while the students in the control groups were inattentive and frequently disruptive. However, the significantly improved attention did not transfer to the regular classroom, and the inattentive students did not pay more attention even to the regular classroom teachers who had been trained to give increased praise for attentive behavior.

COMMENTARY: This article highlights the ability of children to increase their attention, as well as the need to plan for the transfer of beneficial effects to the regular classroom. One way to do this would be to train children and then design a classroom program that used signals throughout regular instruction. Children would then have to be alert in order to earn both short- and long-term rewards. For example, each student could be given a work sheet and told to check a specific box when the teacher uses certain key words. Any method might be considered that could make paying attention to the content being presented more fun or more rewarding.

SOURCE: Woolfolk, A. E., and Woolfolk, R. L. "A Contingency Management Technique for Increasing Student Attention in a Small-Group Setting." *Journal of School Psychology,* 1974, *12,* 204-212.

Additional Readings

Barkley, R. A., and Cunningham, C. E. "Stimulant Drugs and Activity Level in Hyperactive Children." *American Journal of Orthopsychiatry,* 1979, *49,* 491-499.

A review of the literature indicates that stimulant drugs improve hyperactive children's attention span and sustained concentration. The present study demonstrated that the stimulant methylphenidate (Ritalin) increases attention span even in an informal, highly stimulating setting (a gymnasium). However, gross motor activity level in informal settings is not decreased, as is seen in more restrictive, formal settings.

Breitrose, H., and Nixon, S. "Production and Evaluation of a Film About Behavioral Techniques to Increase Task-Oriented Behavior." Stanford, Calif.: Stanford University, 1970 (ERIC Document Reproduction Service No. ED 041 342).

"Behavior Modification in the Classroom" is a twenty-one minute film about operant conditioning techniques in elementary classrooms. The role of the school psychologist and the training of teachers are demonstrated in this unrehearsed film that illustrates positive reinforcement and modeling. Misconceptions, such as the belief that operant conditioning is a mysterious form of manipulation and that reinforcement is bribery, are dispelled. Evaluation demonstrated that the film was effective in conveying information and favorably influencing people's attitudes toward these methods.

Clements, J. E., and Tracy, D. B. "Effects of Touch and Verbal Reinforcement on the Classroom Behavior of Emotionally Disturbed Boys." *Exceptional Children,* 1977, *43,* 453-454.

Tactile (touching, patting, hugging) stimulation and verbal praise effectively improved attention and accuracy of performance in solving arithmetic problems by nine-to-eleven-year-old boys. When a boy was attentive, the teacher firmly touched both his shoulders approximately every four minutes during each twenty-minute work session. Touch and verbal praise ("good job") were more effective than either touch or verbal praise alone.

Hallahan, D. P., Lloyd, J., Kosiewicz, M. M., Kauffman, J. M., and Graves, A. W. "Self-Monitoring of Attention as a Treatment for a Learning-Disabled Boy's Off-Task Behavior." *Learning Disability Quarterly*, 1979, *2*, 24-32.

An eight-year-old learning-disabled boy with attention problems learned to self-monitor his on- or off-task behavior. Every time he heard a tone on a tape recorder, he checked yes or no under the heading, "Was I Paying Attention?" On-task behavior and performance increased dramatically for handwriting and math. He next monitored himself without the tones and then used only self-praise for paying attention to the task. The improved attention continued and was still observable in a one-month follow-up.

Hewett, F. M. "Educational Engineering with Emotionally Disturbed Children." *Exceptional Children*, 1967, *33*, 459-467.

The teacher defines tasks, provides meaningful rewards for learning, maintains limits, and eliminates maladaptive behavior. A hierarchy of educational tasks is described, and specific methods are presented. The first step relates to inattention; attention is gained by using tangible rewards (food, money, tokens). Check marks are earned regardless of type of task, as long as the child functions as a student. Inattention, boredom, or daydreaming results in an immediate change of assignment.

Lewis, B. L., and Strain, P. S. "Effects of Feedback Timing and Motivational Content on Teachers' Delivery of Contingent Social Praise." *Psychology in the Schools*, 1978, *15*, 423-430.

Paying attention to classroom tasks can be effectively increased by social praise for on-task behavior. Comments such as "I like the way you're completing the worksheet" and "You're working nicely" increased the attentiveness of six-to-nine-year-old boys with behavior problems. Immediate feedback (a click of a counter) or delayed feedback (a graph of the teacher's praise statements) to the teacher did not increase the amount of praise given. However, delayed feedback plus goal setting increased both amount of teacher praise and degree of attentiveness. The key ingredient was the specific setting of a goal for the teacher to give a specified rate of contingent praise (one per minute).

Mischel, W., and Patterson, C. J. "Substantive and Structural Elements of Effective Plans for Self-Control." *Journal of Personality and Social Psychology,* 1976, *34,* 942-950.

Preschoolers earned rewards by working on lengthy tasks in the face of tempting distractions. Resistance to temptation was fostered by directing children not to pay attention to temptation (saying, "No, I'm not going to look") and by having children remind themselves about wanting to work for the rewards. However, these plans were effective only when the specific words to say to themselves were directly taught to the children. When only the nature of resisting temptation was explained, there was no improvement in their resistance to distraction.

Nixon, S. B. "Increasing Task-Oriented Behavior." In J. D. Krumboltz and C. E. Thoresen (Eds.), *Behavioral Counseling Cases and Techniques.* New York: Holt, Rinehart and Winston, 1969.

The distractible behavior of hyperactive second graders was reduced by having them watch a film of task-oriented and distractible behavior. Children were asked what the boy was doing when the film was stopped at a task-oriented moment. Rewards were given for recognizing attentiveness. The adult made comments about the boy in the film; for example, that his parents were pleased because he was paying attention and that he probably received prizes for working so hard. Correct identification of scenes not oriented to tasks were recognized by a matter-of-fact comment, with no praise or rewards.

Sykes, D. H., Douglas, V. I., and Morgenstern, G. "The Effect of Methylphenidate (Ritalin) on Sustained Attention in Hyperactive Children." *Psychopharmacologia,* 1972, *25,* 262-274.

Hyperactive children aged five to thirteen were impaired in their ability to sustain attention to visual or auditory stimuli. Ability to pay attention and performance on the Continuous Performance Tests significantly improved when methylphenidate was prescribed. Stimuli were more accurately defined, and there were fewer momentary lapses in attention. Gross inattentiveness (nonobserving responses) and impulsive responding were reduced. Methylphenidate results in less distractibility, better processing of information, and more appropriate responding in hyperactive children.

Wahler, R. G., and Erickson, M. "Child Behavior Therapy: A Community Program in Appalachia." *Behavior Research and Therapy,* 1969, *7,* 71-78.

Nonprofessional volunteers were trained to observe and modify reinforcement contingencies between the problem child and adults. They learned about positive reinforcement, extinction, and punishment. Attention to problem behavior was to be eliminated and social praise given for appropriate behavior. The program, which usually involved both the child's teachers and parents, was very effective. Two of the significantly improved behaviors included classroom and home study attentiveness.

Impulsiveness

Being impulsive is acting without prior thought or anticipation of possible consequences. Curbing impulsiveness sometimes means delaying immediate gratification and tolerating the frustration involved. In school, impulsiveness is especially prevalent in situations where the correct answer is not immediately obvious and must be selected from alternatives. Rapid inaccurate responding without sufficient deliberation has been called impulsive cognitive tempo. A slower and more accurate responding pattern in which alternative hypotheses are considered is called a reflective cognitive tempo.

Teachers are most familiar with children who impulsively blurt out, or write, the first answer that occurs to them. When tasks require it, motor-impulse control (restraining activity) is essential. Impulsiveness is a frequently noted characteristic of learning disabilities that are based upon central nervous system dysfunctions. An impulsive tempo is linked to poor school performance as well as to social difficulties. As high as 30 percent of young children have been considered to be significantly impulsive (E. Siegelman, "Reflective and Impulsive Observing Behavior," Child Development, 1969, 40, 1213-22). Other estimates start from 5 to 10 percent of school-age children. Recent methods for decreasing impulsiveness include self-verbalization (especially use of the words stop, look, and listen), self-reinforcement, modeling, requiring delay in responses, having children repeat or actually reenact behavior, increasing their concern about correctness, using reminder flash cards, and fantasy training.

Modifying Impulsive Tempo

AUTHORS: Douglas Cullinan, Michael H. Epstein, and Lois Silver

PRECIS: Modeling and self-verbalization to promote reflective problem solving in thirty-three impulsive, learning-disabled boys aged nine to twelve

INTRODUCTION: An impulsive cognitive tempo is one in which problems are solved by rapid but inaccurate selection of alternative responses. This impulsiveness is associated with poor performance in various areas, including inductive reasoning, perceptual skills, discrimination learning, reading, and arithmetic. Impulsiveness is frequently seen in children identified as hyperactive or underachieving. The authors report on various studies that tried to modify this impulsive cognitive tempo. Methods included teaching children to delay responding, reinforcing slow and careful responses, punishing errors, modeling slow and careful problem solving, and self-verbalization to be slow and careful. Results were increased time before responding and/or fewer errors. The present study used thirty-three learning-disabled boys, who were also impulsive as measured by the Matching Familiar Figures Test (MFFT). The MFFT requires finding a correct match to a standard figure.

METHOD: The boys were randomly assigned to a modeling, modeling plus self-verbalization, or control group. In the *modeling* group, the boys watched a six-minute videotape of a boy solving six MFFT items "reflectively." The boy first pointed to the standard figure, selected the important distinguishing features, and then selected the correct feature. The boy spoke aloud to himself to delay selection until he had checked each possibility: "It's probably best if I take my time. That way I won't make many mistakes. I'll look at two or three of these in the first row and see how they differ. Now I'll check the bottom three. I shouldn't just choose the first one that seems to be right. I better make sure and check the rest before deciding." In *modeling plus self-verbalization,* each boy immediately repeated the model's self-verbalization after viewing the tape. The boys in the *control* group saw a ninety-second tape of the items, but no model was shown to them. Different forms of the MFFT were given before they viewed the tape, immediately after they viewed it, and three weeks later.

Neither modeling nor modeling plus self-verbalization led to longer selection times. However, both groups did make significantly fewer errors when tested immediately after viewing the tape. There was no difference between the two experimental groups. Reduced errors were not seen three weeks later. The authors report that their findings are in contrast with other studies that showed reduction of errors only following slower response times. They speculate that learning-disabled children's response time may be more resistant to change than of normal children. Also, the learning-disabled children were not able to retain the more careful (although still rapid) problem-solving strategy.

COMMENTARY: This study highlights the possibly effective use of films without the necessity for having children imitate self-verbalization. This means that a film of reflective problem solving may be shown to large groups of children. The type of problem may be tailored to fit the age of the children and the subject matter in question. Schools can produce their own films in which appropriate peer models will be seen in action. Most important is the authors' point that reflective strategies should be repeatedly applied for several teaching sessions, using various problem situations. This is essential to promote both generalization and long-term (rather than only immediate) effects. Teachers could write brief scripts that would model reflective approaches to math problems, essay questions, test taking, and so forth.

SOURCE: Cullinan, D., Epstein, M. H., and Silver, L. "Modification of Impulsive Tempo in Learning-Disabled Pupils." *Journal of Abnormal Child Psychology*, 1977, *5*, 437-444.

Improving Efficiency in Impulsive Children

AUTHORS: Gail Digate, Michael H. Epstein, Douglas Cullinan, and Harvey N. Switzky

PRECIS: Teaching implications for modifying impulsiveness by required delay, direct instruction, self-verbalization, differentiation training, modeling, and reinforcement

INTRODUCTION: Problem solving requires the consideration of alternative hypotheses. Rapid but inaccurate responding to problems is called impulsive behavior, whereas accurate and slow responding is termed reflective. The Matching Familiar Figures Test (MFFT) measures cognitive tempo and distinguishes between children who use impulsive and reflective problem-solving strategies. A child must select the one out of six figures that is identical to the standard figure. A longer response time and fewer errors characterize a reflective tempo, while quick response times and more errors are typical of impulsive children. In reviewing the literature, the authors comment on differences between impulsive and reflective children. Impulsive children have more difficulty in inhibiting movement, processing information, performing perceptual and discrimination tasks, and using effective search strategies in problem solving. They also do more poorly on word recognition and arithmetic tasks.

INTERVENTION: Instructional methods should be modified for impulsive children.

Required Delay. The teacher makes sure that the child does not respond to a problem for a specified amount of time. This allows time for the child to observe, analyze, and evaluate. The teacher emphasizes that the child should think about the task during that time and that different problem-solving strategies could be tried.

Direct Instruction. Reflective children consider alternative solutions before responding. Impulsiveness is decreased when the teacher shows the children how to scan alternatives and use different problem-solving methods. This approach is essential for children with disorganized or nonexistent problem-solving strategies. If children have learned to delay responding with no improvement in performance, they should be taught to generate and consider alternative responses and to evaluate all possibilities before making a response.

Self-Verbalization. Children learn to tell themselves to proceed cautiously and to verbalize their behavior during tasks. This leads to more careful, deliberate, and productive work. The teacher must identify the appropriate type of verbal self-instructions that a child requires. Some examples follow: "Seven plus two equals what number?" "It's best if I take my time." "I shouldn't just choose the first one that looks correct, I better check the rest before deciding."

Differentiation Training. Impulsive children often search for an alternative that has features in common with a standard, while disregarding features that are different. Since alternatives usually have some features identical with the standard, a more useful approach is to look for differences. Looking for differences has led to better problem solving, less impulsiveness, and better academic achievement. Specific training would help students in detecting subtle differences or similarities before responding. Materials used in training should call for increasing skill in attending to dissimilar details.

Modeling. Observing reflective models, especially when they are positively reinforced, leads to a decrease in impulsivity. Modeling and self-verbalization have led to longer response times and increased accuracy. Children with low IQs responded better to a combination of watching a model who verbalized tactics and demonstrated visual scanning (tracing figures). Impulsive children could be seated next to reflective children to enhance imitation effects. The presence of an impulsive adult is detrimental to impulsive children, and very impulsive children should have experienced, reflective teachers.

Response Consequences. Positive reinforcement can increase reaction time and reduce errors. Methods used are corrective feedback, verbal and nonverbal reward, and task incentives. Feedback regarding inaccurate responses produced more correct responses than did positive feedback alone. One study showed that mild verbal or nonverbal punishment led to more reflective responses than did mild verbal or nonverbal reinforcement. Another study demonstrated that use of an imposed delay in answering, tutoring, and extrinsic reinforcement increased reflectiveness. Notably, there were improved accuracy and longer reaction times on a standardized achievement test.

COMMENTARY: This is one of the few research-oriented articles that directly discusses the teaching implications of research on impulsiveness. It is clear that the specific methods described are quite capable of reducing impulsiveness and promoting more reflective, accurate responding. The authors do caution that most studies have been done in laboratories rather than in classrooms and that the generalization and durability of reflective skills have not been adequately demonstrated. They call for creative and individually tailored approaches by teachers. This would require careful selection, planning, and evaluation of the effectiveness of the procedures employed. One role of a school psychologist, guidance counselor, or learning specialist would be to help a teacher to select the best method to use, as well as an appropriate means of assessing improvement (or lack of improvement). The effectiveness of the teacher's methods would be greatly enhanced by the parents' employing similar approaches to help children be less impulsive at home and in the community.

SOURCE: Digate, G., Epstein, M. H., Cullinan, D., and Switzky, H. N. "Modification of Impulsivity: Implications for Improved Efficiency in Learning for Exceptional Children." *Journal of Special Education*, 1978, *12*, 459-468.

Cognitive Training to Reduce Impulsiveness

AUTHORS: Virginia I. Douglas, Penny Parry, Peter Marton, and Chrystelle Garson

PRECIS: Modeling, self-verbalization, and self-reinforcement used to aid eighteen hyperactive boys to become more effective and less impulsive

INTRODUCTION: Cognitive and behavioral approaches have been used as an alternate to stimulant drugs for hyperactive children. Various disruptive behaviors have been reduced by consistent contingency management. However, the authors believe that it is not appropriate to rely on operant techniques to modify the behavior of hyperactive children. Positive reinforcement may increase impulsiveness in such children, and their attention may be turned away from the task and become focused on the reinforcement. Therefore, self-reinforcement and self-control should be used. Methods promoting better problem solving are also appropriate. In previous work, Douglas highlighted an attentional-impulsive problem, that is, an inability to "stop, look, and listen." Douglas saw hyperactivity and distractibility as much less important than the attentional-impulsive weakness. Therefore, training should be directed toward developing inhibitory control and better strategies for paying attention and sustaining it.

TREATMENT: The children who participated were all hyperactive, demonstrating excessive activity, impulsiveness, and attention problems. They had scored worse than average on two measures. Parents and teachers completed the Conners' Rating Scale for Hyperactivity, and the child completed the Matching Familiar Figures Test of Reflection-Impulsivity. There were eighteen boys; their average age was seven years, nine months (all were between six and eleven years old). The boys were trained over a three-month period for two one-hour sessions per week (a total of twenty-four sessions).

At least six sessions were conducted with each boy's teacher and twelve sessions with his parents. Parents and teachers learned the methods and helped the child use them. Often, they took part in the actual training sessions with the boys. They were taught contingency management for disruptive behaviors and how to give positive reinforcement when their child used the methods. Much emphasis was placed on helping the boys learn self-control, self-monitoring, and self-reinforcement. Teachers were to encourage the boys to carefully check their own work. Effective and independent coping was stressed for situations requiring care, attention, and organized planning. All the children needed to develop better inhibitory control.

While working on a task, the trainer talked out loud about the nature of the problem and the strategies used. At first, the child did the same. After a few sessions he spoke more softly and then only talked to himself. At times, the trainer and the child took turns telling each other how to proceed. Many games and tasks were used, including assigned academic work. The attempt was to promote generalization of strategies to academic and social situations. Children worked both alone and in pairs. The boys were told that they were intelligent but that they got into difficulty at home and at school because they were not using the "tricks" that they would be taught. These tricks or strategies would work in all kinds of situations. General strategies included various steps in stopping to define a problem, considering and evaluating various solutions before acting on any one, checking work and calmly correcting errors, sticking to a problem and doing everything possible to correctly solve it, and congratulating oneself for good work. Examples of the trainer's comments follow: "I must stop and think before I begin. What plans could I try? How would it work out if I did that? What shall I try next? Have I got it right so far? Gee, I made a mistake there—I'll just erase it. Now, let's see, have I tried everything I can think of? I've done a pretty good job!"

Modeling and some direct instruction were used to train children in search, focusing, and attentional strategies. They were taught to scan and explore visual, auditory, and tactual materials for essential similarities and differences. Sorting, arranging, and classifying were stressed. Examples of verbalizations during a visual task were: "I haven't looked at them all yet, I'd better keep going until I'm really sure. What I need here is one door, two windows, and a chimney on this side. Oh, oh! This one has all those things but it's still not quite right because it doesn't have a roof with marks like this." For a tactual task: "I feel a long, flat part. It feels like a handle. Then there are a lot of pointy things on the end. I bet I am holding a fork." Also stressed were planning ahead, thinking sequentially, and being organized: "I am going to make a list of everything I need for this school assignment. Then I'll mark each part off as I get it ready."

Training was also given in noting facts carefully and rehearsing facts to be remembered. During a card game the verbalization might be: "He's asking me for all of my threes, so I'll have to remember that he has threes in his hand." Remembering essential parts of a picture could lead to the following comments: "I'll have to look at the main things in this picture carefully so I can remember what I saw. The most important things I see are. . . ." Verbalizations were also taught concerning appropriate game playing and task cooperation. Comments are made regarding the importance of taking turns, figuring out the opponent's strategy, and being sensitive to others' motives and feelings. The authors describe various games and tasks that they used. For example, rearranging pictures in a logical order was used to teach sequencing. Also employed was carrying out a series of verbal instructions in an assigned order. A kitchen timer was always used to set an amount of time for working on an activity. As training progressed, longer time intervals were used.

The assessment measures are described. These included the Matching Familiar Figures Test, Story Completion Test, Porteus Mazes, Bender Visual-Motor Gestalt, memory tests from the Detroit Tests of Learning Aptitude, Durell Analysis of Reading Difficulty, Wide-Range Achievement Test (Arithmetic), and the Conners' Rating Scales for Parents and Teachers. The statistical analyses and results are described in detail. Cognitive training was clearly effective, and the children learned general principles rather than only task-specific response sets. Significant improvement on the measures occurred immediately after training and were still present three months later. The results on the different measures employed are discussed at length.

The training in considering consequences was thought to lead to less aggression and more effective tolerance of frustration. Although reading was not taught, there was significant improvement in listening and oral comprehension. This was thought to result from practice in reading written instructions and in listening more carefully to oral instructions.

COMMENTARY: The techniques described are readily adaptable to the classroom. Modeling by the teacher or a peer, self-verbalization, and self-reinforcement may be applied in a wide range of educational tasks. The goal is a familiar one—having children learn the general principles for becoming more effective and less impulsive. What the study does is offer specific practical methods and examples. The authors point out that it may be necessary to control impulsiveness before training children in focusing and search strategies. They have had children sit on their hands while organizing and verbalizing appropriate strategies.

SOURCE: Douglas, V. I., Parry, P., Marton, P., and Garson, Ç. "Assessment of a Cognitive Training Program for Hyperactive Children." *Journal of Abnormal Child Psychology*, 1976, *4*, 389-410.

Reinstatement for Increased Self-Control

AUTHOR: Dennis H. Karpowitz

PRECIS: Describing or rehearsing undesirable behavior as a means of making discipline more effective for first-grade boys

INTRODUCTION: The author cites research that reports immediate discipline to be effective for decreasing various undesirable behaviors. He also discusses the greater effectiveness of severe discipline compared to mildly negative discipline. The present study sought a means of making mild, delayed discipline effective. "Reinstatement" is defined as verbally stating or reenacting the original behavior. Studies have shown that reinstatement may make discipline more effective in preventing further undesirable behavior. The author defines discipline as communicating that a rule was broken and imposing punishment.

METHOD: Toys were made available so that ninety first-grade boys might be tempted to disregard instructions not to leave their seats and play with the toys. Conditions enhanced boredom: the children were supposed to look at a book containing only Russian words. Reinstatement consisted of telling the boys that the toys had been moved and the rule broken. Four conditions are described to test different aspects of discipline; two observers recorded and timed behavior.

In analyzing the various experimental conditions, the author concludĕs that discipline decreases the likelihood of repeated undesirable behavior even when discipline is delayed. Punishment in past studies often took the form of loud buzzers rather than more typical classroom punishments. The present study demonstrated that the typically employed methods of withdrawing material possessions (marbles) and verbal reprimands are effective. Verbal reinstatement involved a detailed review of the negative behavior: "You stopped reading the book, got up from your chair, came over to this table, and then played with some of the toys." This verbal reinstatement was as effective as the more elaborate reenactment of the behavior.

COMMENTARY: This article is included here even though the author does not discuss impulsiveness as such. However, the experimental conditions he used closely resemble the low frustration tolerance of children who impulsively give in to internal or external temptation. The method described is a specific alternative that teachers (and parents) can use to enhance the effectiveness of mild punishment. The impulsive undesirable behavior is succinctly described to the child and immediately followed by some disciplinary measure. This approach would be especially appropriate with children with poor memories and short attention spans. It serves as an excellent reminder to adults to make sure that children know what specific behavior is being punished.

SOURCE: Karpowitz, D. H. "Reinstatement as a Method to Increase the Effectiveness of Discipline in the School or Home." *Journal of School Psychology*, 1977, *15*, 230-238.

Modifying Impulsiveness in the Classroom

AUTHORS: Howard Margolis, Gary G. Brannigan, and Mary Anne Poston

PRECIS: Increasing reflectivity by peer modeling, self-instruction, rehearsal, concern about correctness, and improved visual discrimination

INTRODUCTION: Successful learning requires attention and careful consideration of concepts as well as time to reflect upon alternative solutions. The authors cite research to support the importance of assessing and remediating impulsive and impatient responses. They report that there has been success in making impulsive children more reflective and accurate. Impulsiveness is especially detrimental in situations where the correct answer must be chosen from alternatives. Word recognition, arithmetic achievement, and inductive reasoning are poorer in impulsive than in other children, who comprise about 30 percent of elementary school children. The authors reason that remedial activities usually do not affect the impulsiveness that prevents learning. Impulsiveness has frequently been measured by performance on the Matching Familiar Figures Test (MFFT), which requires matching one of six pictures to a standard picture. Fast response times and numerous errors indicate an impulsive approach. Impulsive children do not carefully or thoroughly examine material and pay little attention to details. Poor school performance is often the result of an impatient and disorganized approach, not of poor instruction or an intellectual or perceptual deficit.

METHODS: A variety of techniques that reduced impulsiveness in children are described.

Modeling. Children can learn a reflective cognitive style and improve performance on a variety of tasks. An adult model solves a visual-motor task or a complex problem while talking out loud regarding his actions and the demands of the task and thus reinforcing himself verbally. A child first observes the model and then does the problem with verbal self-instruction. Next, the child does the task while whispering and finally does the same task with silent self-instruction. In other instances, peer models who act reflectively have served to diminish the impulsive behavior of observing children. "High-status" peers demonstrated reflective verbal and behavioral cues while doing the MFFT. Another study showed that boys viewing a film of a reflective nine-year-old taking the MFFT successfully lowered their impulsiveness. The authors of the present study suggest the following strategies for teachers. First, have reflective, high-status models demonstrate reflective behavior (visually, verbally, or both) in a step-by-step manner. They should illustrate the necessary actions for a careful and successful performance on a particular task. Second, arrange for repeated exposure to the models on various tasks at the child's level. Third, plan for the shift from overt to covert rehearsal before and during the task. Fourth, help the child clearly understand the goal and the skills that are necessary to achieve the goal.

Inducing Anxiety. Studies are reviewed in which inducing concern and mild anxiety about being correct improved the performance of impulsive children. Telling children immediately after performance to "be more careful" has led to longer response times and fewer errors. Feedback is provided as to the accuracy of the response, and correct intermediate steps are positively reinforced. Margolis, Brannigan, and Poston caution that the effect of feedback and reinforcement must be carefully and individually assessed for each child. Also, delayed responses alone do not lead to better performance. Children may have to be taught specific strategies.

Attention. Impulsiveness was reduced by having third graders identify pictures that were different from a standard one. After this experience, they made significantly fewer errors on the MFFT. This type of "differentiation" training improves the ability to detect distinctive features. Teaching impulsive children to be aware of differences may increase their word recognition and general awareness of visual material. Another study showed that second graders became less impulsive after they had learned efficient scanning strategies. Rules were explained and demonstrated for analyzing visual material and comparing parts.

Visual Discrimination. Mildly retarded elementary school children became less impulsive after visual discrimination training. Short periods of daily training for seven weeks led them to make fewer errors and slower responses on the MFFT. Also, they were able to generalize their learning to a related but different task.

The point is made that impulsiveness interferes with learning in varying degrees, depending upon the nature of the task. Teachers should use trial lessons with one of the described techniques for at least two weeks. Most importantly, it must be remembered that the basic problem of impulsive children is their failure to attend to and consider alternatives.

COMMENTARY: The authors provide a valuable service to teachers by reviewing various research projects and pointing out their educational implications. Teachers and other school personnel can readily adapt the methods described above for individual students and individual situations. The potential in having students observe reflective models is enormous. It would be an exciting and productive educational experience for a school to produce a film showing peer models who are concerned about performance, are attentive, demonstrate the ability to discriminate details of a task, and talk to themselves about their appropriate behavior. Such a film could be used for clearly impulsive children and be followed by having them role play reflective behavior on a variety of relevant tasks. It could also serve as an educational reminder for all children as to the effectiveness of a careful and thoughtful approach to problems.

SOURCE: Margolis, H., Brannigan, G. G., and Poston, M. A. "Modification of Impulsivity: Implications for Teaching." *Elementary School Journal,* 1977, *77,* 231-237.

Self-Directed Verbal Commands
for Hyperactive Impulsive Behavior

AUTHORS: Helen Palkes, Mark Stewart, and Boaz Kahana

PRECIS: Reducing thoughtless, careless, and impulsive behavior of twenty boys by using stop, listen, and look flash cards

INTRODUCTION: The authors review theories that voluntary control of behavior is based upon internal verbal self-instruction. Improved performance would result if hyperactive children could learn appropriate self-directions. Participants in the study were twenty normally intelligent, middle-class boys aged eight and nine. The Porteus Maze Tests were used as measures of impulsiveness before and after the study.

METHOD: Four five-by-seven-inch visual reminder cards were used. Self-directed commands and ink-line drawings are shown. Card 1 had a stop sign, ears drawn around the word *listen,* and eyes drawn in the o's in the word *look.* The card read: "Instructions. This is a stop! listen, look, and think experiment. Before I start any of the tasks I am going to do, I am going to say: Stop! listen, look, and think! Before! I answer." Card 2 consisted of a stop sign, with the word *screech* written twice. Card 3 had a boy's head with huge ears and the word *listen* written five times. Card 4 was a boy's face with question and exclamation marks over his head and the instructions "Look! and Think! Before! I Answer." The training materials used were three tests: the Matching Familiar Figures Test (this required selecting a figure identical to a standard; the Embedded Figures Test (the children had to find a simple geometric design within a complex figure and trace it with their finger tip; and the Trail-Making Test (a dot-to-dot task using numbers and letters). Training was done in two thirty-minute individual sessions on consecutive days.

During the tasks, the four reminder cards were plainly visible on the desk. The children were told to read the first card, which would remind them of what to say. After reading it, they were told, "*Before* each task *you* must *Stop* whatever you are doing, then you must *Listen* to my directions, and then you must *Look* and *Think* before you make any answer or do what I tell you to do. OK, now, don't forget: the *important* thing is that *you* must give *yourself* these commands by saying each one aloud at the proper time." The instructions used for each task are described in detail. Whenever the children forgot a command, the task would stop until they verbalized the command. Throughout, the children were questioned to make sure that they were clear about the task requirements and the necessity of verbalizing what was printed on the cards.

The statistical results presented demonstrate that training improved performance on the Porteus Maze Tests. The previously slapdash approach to maze completion was significantly improved. The authors speculate that hyperactive children have not internalized external verbal commands and that they are seeking attention through disruptive behavior. They are usually receptive to being taught self-control and to learning to perform more adequately.

COMMENTARY: The authors point out the preliminary nature of their findings. However, more and more evidence indicates that this type of "cognitive behavior modification" does indeed reduce impulsiveness and promote reflectivity. In working with impulsive children, we have found reminder cards to be one of the most effective means of reducing impulsiveness both in the classroom and at home. The content and illustrations of the cards should be individualized according to the child's level of understanding and specific problem. For example, we have used: "Think How Others Will Feel About What You Say," "Don't Hit or Mom Will Have a Fit," and "Consider the Consequences." It is extremely helpful to have a reminder card both at home (on the child's desk) and in an inconspicuous place in his classroom desk.

SOURCE: Palkes, H., Stewart, M., and Kahana, B. "Porteus Maze Performance of Hyperactive Boys After Training in Self-Directed Verbal Commands." *Child Development,* 1968, *39,* 817-826.

Improving Impulse Control
Through Fantasy Training

AUTHORS: Eli Saltz, David Dixon, and James Johnson

PRECIS: Acting out fantasies as a means of increasing cognitive development and impulse control in preschoolers

INTRODUCTION: Imitating and pretending underlie cognitive development. But this type of sociodramatic play is not frequently engaged in by disadvantaged children. Several studies have found that sociodramatic play improved cognitive functioning in such areas as intelligence subtest scores, story interpretation, sequential memory, empathy, originality, problem solving, and verbal communication. In previous research, Saltz and Johnson trained preschoolers to enact different roles in such fairy tales as "The Three Billy Goats Gruff" and "Little Red Riding Hood" (E. Saltz and J. Johnson, "Training for Thematic-Fantasy Play in Culturally Disadvantaged Children: Preliminary Results," *Journal of Educational Psychology,* 1974, *66,* 623-630). Imaginative play permits children to free themselves from the immediate, concrete environment. The authors here make the distinction between thematic fantasy play (themes remote from personal experience) and sociodramatic play (themes from real, recent experiences such as visiting a fire station). Because time is compressed in thematic fantasy, children can learn the causes for the plot within ten to fifteen minutes. Viewpoints that predict that enacting fantasies will be a more effective learning experience than listening to them are reviewed.

METHOD: A sophisticated experimental design (analysis of variance) was used in order to assess the effectiveness of four methods: (1) thematic fantasy play—enactment of both fantasy and play; (2) fantasy discussion—children heard and discussed fairy tales but did not enact them; (3) sociodramatic play—children enacted realistic events only; and (4) control—children engaged in usual age-appropriate activities such as cutting, pasting, and categorizing objects. Participants were 146 children (ages three to four and one-half years) from lower-income families. The sessions lasted fifteen minutes per day, three days per week for approximately seven months.

Thematic Fantasy Play. At first, very simple fairy tales ("The Three Billy Goats Gruff" and "The Three Little Pigs") were used; later, more complex stories were acted out. The story was read to the children, they were shown the pictures in the book, and a discussion took place. An adult narrated most parts of the stories, and the children (who chose or were assigned roles) acted chiefly in pantomime. Each story required four to six sessions. Costumes were not used because they might have caused distractions, and minimal props were employed.

Sociodramatic Play. The sources of themes were common experiences (visits to a physician or grocery store) or outings conducted by the preschool (trips to a zoo, gas station, and so on). Upon return, children described and enacted the experience.

Fantasy Discussion. The fairy tales used for thematic fantasy were read and discussed. Questions were asked to see if the children understood what was happening in the tales. After hearing a story several times, the children told the story while viewing the pictures in the book.

Measures. The following cognitive tests are described: the Picture Test of Intelligence, the Story-Interpretation Test, the Fantasy Judgment Test, Sequential Memory of Stories, and an adaptation of Borke's Empathy Test. Different tasks were employed to measure delay of gratification (not touching a toy when told not to and sitting still for a specified time) as a means of assessing impulse control. The Matching Familiar Figures Test (MFFT) was used to assess impulse control by having the children find the one out of four figures that was the same as a standard figure.

Statistical results are presented and discussed. Thematic fantasy play led to increased intellectual performance, better ability to interpret sequential events, increased reality-fantasy discrimination, better delay of impulsive behavior, and increased empathy. On most cognitive and impulse-control tasks, better performance was reached through thematic fantasy and sociodramatic play than through fantasy discussion or the control activities. Thematic fantasy play was consistently more effective. The authors conclude that the significant element is play enactment, which encourages "pretend," provides "motoric feedback" from the actual performance, and permits children to learn through changing roles.

COMMENTARY: This article has direct implications for preschool programs. Impulse control and cognitive development are likely to be enhanced by having children act out fantasies (such as fairy tales) and play different roles. This technique may be used by both preschool and early elementary teachers. Most striking is the enhancement of children's ability to wait patiently and to delay having what they want. This research should encourage those teachers who use dramatic play to continue doing so and influence other teachers to begin using fantasy play as one of their teaching methods.

SOURCE: Saltz, E., Dixon, D., and Johnson, J. "Training Disadvantaged Preschoolers on Various Fantasy Activities: Effects on Cognitive Functioning and Impulse Control." *Child Development*, 1977, *48*, 367-380.

Additional Readings

Anderson, W. H., and Moreland, K. L. "Laboratory and Clinical
Studies of Self-Instruction in Children." Paper presented at
convention of the Association for the Advancement of Behavior Therapy, Chicago, November 1978.

Verbal self-control has been successfully employed with
educational and clinical problems, resistance to temptation, and
delay of gratification. Self-verbalizations should be brief and to
the point, and children should say what they are about to do
rather than what they have just done. Young children should
say instructions aloud, while older children can think the instructions. The verbalization should be task relevant, it should
tell the child how to behave and why he or she should behave
that way, and it should be consistent with the child's level of
moral comprehension. Preschoolers performed better when the
verbalizations served to prevent distraction from a task than
when the verbalizations were designed to facilitate performance.

Cole, P. M., and Hartley, D. G. "The Effects of Reinforcement
and Strategy Training on Impulsive Responding." *Child Development,* 1978, *49,* 381-384.

Thirty-six impulsive second graders were effectively
trained to wait longer before responding and to make fewer
errors on a visual matching task. Strategy training consisted of
part-whole analysis of common scenes and objects, systematic
scanning, and detecting dimensional differences. Strategy training combined with positive reinforcement (choice of food) was
more effective than strategy training alone for increasing response delay.

Kendall, P. C. "On the Efficacious Use of Verbal Self-Instructional Procedures with Children." *Cognitive Therapy and Research,* 1977, *1,* 331-341.

Self-instructions are step-by-step verbalizations of problem
definition, problem approach, focusing of attention, coping
statements, and self-reinforcement. Impulsive children lack
verbal mediation (they often think in pictures) and solve problems poorly (inefficient scanning of alternatives). Self-instruction has effectively lowered impulsiveness, and the author dis-

cusses the use of incentives to motivate children to learn this method. Planning is necessary if the new skill is to generalize to the classroom and to social situations.

Mock, K. R., Swanson, J. M., and Kinsbourne, M. "Stimulant Effect on Matching Familiar Figures: Changes in Impulsive and Distractible Cognitive Styles" (ERIC Document Reproduction Service No. ED 160 189).

Stimulants (Ritalin) differentially affected the cognitive style of fifty-five hyperactive children aged seven to fifteen. A learning task indicated that some children responded adversely (poorer performance). For the favorable responders, taking Ritalin resulted in lowered impulsiveness. Aggressive and impulsive children increased their decision time and made fewer errors than before. The withdrawn and distractible children bettered their performance by decreasing their overly long reaction times and making fewer errors.

Newman, A., and Kanfer, F. H. "Delay of Gratification in Children: The Effects of Training Under Fixed, Decreasing, and Increasing Delay of Reward." *Journal of Experimental Child Psychology,* 1976, *21,* 12-24.

Self-control requires a child to voluntarily tolerate delay in satisfaction. In a discrimination-learning task, first graders could earn a small reward (candy or a toy) or wait and receive a larger reward. Voluntary delay of gratification can be increased by practice on a learning task with increasing delay of rewards. Direct training of tolerance of delay is suggested.

Pressley, M. "Increasing Children's Self-Control Through Cognitive Interventions." *Review of Educational Research,* 1979, *49,* 319-370.

This is a very comprehensive, detailed, scholarly review of the latest research related to the enhancement of self-control. Many of the studies reviewed highlight young children's verbal control of their motor behavior. Self-verbalizations and attention training are very powerful methods for modifying impulsiveness. Children should be taught strategies that they lack in order for them to become less impulsive and more reflective. By appropriately deploying their attention, they learn to take more time in arriving at decisions and thus make fewer errors.

Ridberg, E. H., Parke, R. D., and Hetherington, E. M. "Modification of Impulsive and Reflective Cognitive Styles Through Observation of Film-Mediated Models." *Developmental Psychology,* 1971, *5,* 369-377.

Cognitive style can be effectively modified by viewing a model behavior impulsively or reflectively. Fourth graders with high IQs responded best to scanning methods or verbal cues used singly, while children with low IQs responded most effectively to the combined use of scanning and verbal cues. The film showed a nine-year-old boy impulsively (seven to ten seconds) or reflectively (twenty-five to thirty-one seconds) choosing the correct figure on the Matching Familiar Figures Test. Reflective verbalization consisted of describing the response slowly, not choosing the first figure that looked correct, and describing the strategy of checking the standard comparison figure. Scanning involved using a finger to point back and forth when comparing figures.

Yando, R. M., and Kagan, J. "The Effect of Teacher Tempo on the Child." *Child Development,* 1968, *39,* 27-34.

First graders were tested and selected as being impulsive (fast) or reflective (slow) responders in making decisions. Children in classes taught by experienced reflective teachers became more reflective during the school year. The increase in response time was most likely due to a combination of modeling and social reinforcement for delay and inhibition of responses. Extremely impulsive boys (especially those with reading problems) might be placed with temperamentally reflective teachers.

Messy and Sloppy Behavior

The term messy, *to some people, implies being dirty or untidy, while* sloppy *connotes carelessness. However, dictionaries use these words synonomously. Thus, to be messy or sloppy is to be careless, confused, disordered, or untidy. At school or at home a child may frequently get dirty and not wash, as well as be careless about belongings. Before age five, messiness is typical. By school age, some degree of neatness is both possible and expected in children. Their desks are supposed to be reasonably neat, their appearance relatively tidy, and their class and homework papers readable and not covered with marks or wrinkled.*

Messy children are often seen as having difficulty in adapting to social standards of tidiness and cleanliness. Some children, regardless of age, lack the organizational skills necessary for arranging and maintaining their property. Others may be rebellious, unconcerned, or not motivated to give up the earlier pleasures of irresponsibility and messiness. Adults sometimes serve as messy models to be imitated.

Outside school settings, therapy may consist of changing the psychological cause of messiness. For extremely disorganized children (often with central nervous system dysfunctions), specific skill training may be necessary. In schools, the usual methods for reducing messiness involve monitoring and positive reinforcement (a point system to earn rewards) for neatness.

Anti-Litter Procedures

AUTHORS: Robert L. Burgess, Roger N. Clark, and John C. Hendee

PRECIS: Assessing different methods, especially incentives, for removing litter in a theatre

INTRODUCTION: Three approaches to controlling littering in public places are legal sanctions (difficult to enforce), campaigns to change attitudes (ineffective), and discovering personality characteristics of litterers (this knowledge does not automatically lead to methods for controlling littering). This study assessed what approach would be most effective for decreasing littering.

METHOD: The following methods were tried after a baseline of amount of trash on the floor was recorded: (1) Extra trash cans were placed conspicuously (double the usual amount). (2) Before the regular film, an anti-litter Walt Disney children's cartoon film called "Litterbug" was shown. (3) Each entering person was given a litterbag and told that "this is for you to use while you are in the theatre." (4) Each person was given a litterbag, and during intermission an announcement was made that everyone should put his or her "trash into the litterbags and put the bag into one of the trash cans in the lobby before leaving the theatre." (5) Each person was given a litterbag and told that he or she would receive one dime for a bag of litter before leaving the theatre. If children returned empty bags, they were told to collect some litter and that they would then receive their dimes. (6) Each person received a litterbag, and an announcement at intermission stated that a free ticket to a special children's movie would be given for a bag of litter.

Baseline amount of properly disposed trash was 19 percent of the total litter. Litterbags resulted in 31 percent disposal, litterbags plus instructions 57 percent, and litterbags plus ten cents 94 percent. In a second theatre, baseline was 16 percent. Doubling trash cans had no effect, while the anti-littering film resulted in 21 percent disposal and free tickets in 95 percent.

The desirability of increasing trash cans in public places or of conducting anti-litter campaigns was thus not supported. Legal sanctions have been ineffective for decreasing littering. This study indicates that the best method is immediate positive consequences for anti-littering behavior.

COMMENTARY: Some method of positive incentives for not littering is possible in any public setting. Schools should employ this effective method for promoting a clean, healthful, and attractive environment and for teaching children good habits. Aside from money, there are a multitude of other rewards that can be used in schools. For example, rewards could be entrance to special events, playground use, special privileges, free time, and so on. This could be part of an overall point system in which points and privileges are earned for a variety of appropriate academic and social behaviors.

SOURCE: Burgess, R. L., Clark, R. N., and Hendee, J. C. "An Experimental Analysis of Anti-Litter Procedures." *Journal of Applied Behavior Analysis*, 1971, *4*, 71-75.

Modifying Preschoolers' Bathroom Behaviors

AUTHORS: Marjorie J. Taylor and Thomas R. Kratochwill

PRECIS: Teacher praise for improving such conditions as paper towel litter, unflushed toilets, dirty sinks, and running faucets

INTRODUCTION: A frequent concern in schools is inappropriate use of toilet facilities and the health hazards that might result. There is also much waste of water and paper goods. Litter is often carelessly discarded, and such actions as picking up litter, turning off water, and flushing toilets are often not positively reinforced. The authors review a number of studies in which behavior modification has been successfully used to decrease littering. In campgrounds and movie theatres, less litter resulted from paying children for bags of litter. Just telling students not to litter has been ineffective. In schools, natural reinforcers (praise) may be better than tangible reinforcers for promoting generalization of effects.

METHOD: Teachers complained to the consulting school psychologist that children were leaving many paper towels on the bathroom floor, not flushing toilets, stopping up sinks, and leaving faucets running. There were sixty-five preschool children; their average age was five years, two months. The study was conducted over a ten-week summer program, five days a week, from 10 A.M. to 2 P.M. Observations of the bathroom were made five times per day regarding the number of paper towels and toilet tissues on the floor, unflushed toilets, dirty sinks, and running faucets.

Children were instructed to flush toilets, clean sinks, turn faucets off, and put litter in the trash container. Eight teachers each entered the bathroom five times per day to instruct the children and reinforce appropriate behaviors. Only one teacher at a time was in the bathroom. Teachers did not do any cleaning and were told to react in the following manner.

Paper towels: Suggested teacher comments were: "Wow! Some children sure don't know where paper towels go! Do you? Can you show me?" "I wonder if you're fast enough to pick up all these towels before I count to five." Teachers praised children for cleaning up or when the bathroom was tidy.

Unflushed Toilets: Teachers instructed any children present to flush any unflushed toilets. If no children were there, the teacher would wait or ask a child to come in. Children were asked what was wrong, which toilet was not flushed, or if they remembered how to flush the toilet. They were then praised for being good helpers or for knowing how to keep the bathroom clean. Praise was also given to children who flushed toilets on their own. When all toilets were flushed, general praise was given.

Dirty Sinks: When water was left in a sink, the children present were asked to figure out a way of removing the water. Compliance or spontaneous cleaning was praised. Observation of clean sinks led to praise for any children present.

Running Faucets: Children present were instructed to turn off any running faucets. Teachers made comments such as, "Oh, no—Look at all the water being wasted." Praise followed compliance, spontaneous turning off of water, or the absence of running water.

All four problem behaviors were significantly reduced by the program. Prior to the study, monitoring and instructing the children had not reduced the problems. In effect, the teachers enlisted the aid of children to keep the bathroom clean. After the study, there were many incidents of spontaneous cleaning up by children.

COMMENTARY: This study suggests that adult praise, strategically used, is as effective as tangible reinforcers for promoting neatness and cleanliness. It is amply clear that messiness in children can be reduced by relatively simple techniques. The two key ingredients were monitoring (periodic observations) and praise for appropriate behavior. Not only can schools eliminate messy and sloppy behavior, but parents should be informed of the advisability of using the same approaches at home.

SOURCE: Taylor, M. J., and Kratochwill, T. R. "Modification of Preschool Children's Bathroom Behaviors by Contingent Teacher Attention." *Journal of School Psychology,* 1978, *16,* 64-71.

Additional Readings

Miller, R. L., Brickman, P., and Bolen, D. "Attribution Versus Persuasion as a Means for Modifying Behavior." *Journal of Personality and Social Psychology,* 1975, *31,* 430-441.

Fifth graders were taught to clean up after others and not to litter. Those belonging to an "attribution" group were repeatedly told that they were neat and tidy people. The teacher made many positive comments about neatness and being conscious of ecology. Those belonging to a "persuasion" group were repeatedly told that they should be neat and tidy. The teacher stressed how important neatness was, and "don't litter" signs were posted. Attribution was much more effective than persuasion in reducing littering; the authors consider persuasion to be a type of negative attribution (people should be what they are not).

Phillips, E. L. "Achievement Place: Token Reinforcement Procedures in a Home-Style Rehabilitation Setting for Predelinquent Boys." *Journal of Applied Behavior Analysis*, 1968, *1*, 213-223.

Points were given to boys aged twelve to fourteen for specific appropriate behavior and taken away for inappropriate behavior. Behaviors and points involved are listed, and graphs of the results are presented. Points were redeemable for privileges such as watching television, riding bikes, having snacks, and staying up late. Tidiness, punctuality, and amount of homework completed improved significantly. The yard, rooms, and bathrooms were much neater and cleaner than previously. Points leading to naturally available rewards are thus an effective and economical method for changing a variety of behaviors in predelinquent children.

Rickard, H. C., and Saunders, T. R. "Control of Clean-Up Behavior in a Summer Camp." *Behavior Therapy*, 1971, *2*, 340-344.

Eight emotionally disturbed boys whose behavior was impulsive, passive-aggressive, and undercontrolled participated in a study to improve cleaning of their cabin—its storage areas, cabinets, beds, and floors. Tokens worth one cent were earned for satisfactory completion of each task. A camp store that was open two nights each week offered merchandise valued from one cent to thirty-five dollars. Only twenty tokens could be spent for food items in one night. Significant improvement in cleaning occurred, similar to results with older children in institutions and schools.

Vogelheim, R. M. "Effects of Social Reinforcement on Poor Posture." *School Applications of Learning Theory*, 1970, *1*, 29-32.

Poor posture of a third-grade boy contributed to poor penmanship and messy papers. While studying, he was half out of his desk, feet in the aisle, and often rested his head on the desk. He was observed once a day for fifteen minutes by means of a fifteen-second-interval recording system. The teacher discussed with him the proper way to sit, and they agreed upon an acceptable posture. When he sat properly, the teacher told him how nice he looked. The teacher decided to praise him throughout the day and to ignore poor posture. Significant improvement occurred for posture and handwriting.

Daydreaming

The term daydreaming *is usually defined as pleasant, wishful imagining. Fantasies often serve to satisfy goals that cannot be attained in real life. There are many reports of shy children who often have vivid, grandiose daydreams. Children who engage in reveries can seem to be lost in thought. Serious difficulties occur when this happens at inappropriate times or when a great deal of time is spent daydreaming rather than engaging in everyday activities. Parents and teachers report that daydreaming children appear to be living in their own worlds. In class, they have a faraway look, are inattentive, and take too long to complete assignments.*

Typically, daydreaming serves as a means of feeling adequate for those children who are not successful in school. They picture themselves as famous heroes, while their daydreaming contributes to less success in school and less opportunity for receiving real recognition and praise than they would otherwise have. A vicious cycle is thus set up. Daydreaming is more satisfying than difficult classwork and serves as a substitute gratification and as a relief from tension. At times, daydreaming may cover deep feelings of sadness; in such cases, psychotherapy may be necessary. In school, point systems for rewarding attentiveness have been very effective in reducing time spent daydreaming.

Reinforcing Improved Classroom Behavior

AUTHORS: Ronnie N. Alexander and Cathy H. Apfel

PRECIS: Variable-interval schedules of reinforcement for decreasing daydreaming, talking out, and other nonattentive behaviors

INTRODUCTION: Positive reinforcement using tokens has been successful with a variety of behaviors and types of individuals. Tokens are exchanged for "backup reinforcers" (candy, toys, stars, grades, teacher approval). Five boys, ages seven to thirteen, were in a special class for children with behavioral disorders. After each fifteen-minute interval, tokens were given out for improved behavior. At the end of the day, the tokens could be exchanged for toys, candy, or free time. There was no behavioral improvement during a "communicative skills" period in which the children observed science experiments, played games, or completed art projects.

METHOD: The study was designed to improve behavior during the communication skills period through use of a variable-interval schedule of reinforcement. Attending behaviors were scored at the end of every three-minute period. Nonattentive behaviors included daydreaming (looking away), verbal (yelling, name-calling), and motor (out of seat, hitting, rocking); these were scored whenever they occurred during the forty-five-minute communication skills period. For two days, a bell was rung after every three minutes, and the teacher specified who had earned a token for those past three minutes. Afterwards, tokens were given on a variable-interval schedule of approximately every three minutes.

Providing immediate reinforcement did improve behavior during the communication skills period. Going back to the old system led to the same nonattentive behavior. The authors point out that relatively unstructured classroom activities are not well suited to fixed intervals of reinforcement. They note that intervals should be very short in order to influence behavior immediately. Longer intervals should be gradually employed, and children should be involved in efforts to control their own behavior.

COMMENTARY: This study illustrates the effectiveness of variable-interval schedules of reinforcement over fixed ones. Most researchers consider daydreaming to be a form of nonattentive behavior. The usual procedure is to reward attentive behavior and ignore daydreaming. However, resistant cases have been responsive when loss of tokens occurs for relatively long periods of daydreaming. This serves to make the children more aware of their loss of focus on their surroundings.

SOURCE: Alexander, R. N., and Apfel, C. H. "Altering Schedules of Reinforcement for, Improved Classroom Behavior." *Exceptional Children*, 1976, *43*, 97-99.

Using a Student to Modify Behavior

AUTHORS: Paul R. Surratt, Roger E. Ulrich, and Robert P. Hawkins

PRECIS: Using a fifth-grade student to reinforce four first-grade students for working and not daydreaming or engaging in other behaviors incompatible with learning

INTRODUCTION: Behavior modification has been successfully carried out by teachers acting as behavioral engineers. But this requires the selective observation of each child whose behavior is to be changed, and it is often impractical for a teacher to observe a large number of students. Other students, however, are abundantly available to be trained as behavior modifiers. In the present study, a fifth grader functioned as a student behavioral engineer with four first graders.

METHOD: Rather than completing work, the four first graders

daydreamed, walked around, and engaged in other inappropriate behaviors. A console was designed to record and
give feedback to the students about their behavior. When a student's behavior was appropriate, the operator pulled a switch
that turned a light on and activated a time meter. The student
engineer wore sunglasses that prevented the students from seeing his eyes. Sessions were held for ten minutes each morning,
while the teacher conducted a small reading group. The rest of
the class completed arithmetic problems at their desks. "Working" was defined as looking at the blackboard, counting, or
writing; during these activities the switch was on, and the time
spent working was recorded. The switch was off for any behavior other than working. "Percent time working" was the
working time divided by the total time of the session multipled
by 100. In another modification, a blue ticket was given for
studying harder than usual. The students could write on it what
they wanted to do the next morning, such as going to the gym
or the playground or engaging in other activities. In order to
avoid social isolation, they could choose a friend to take along
for the fifteen-minute reinforcement period. Each day, the
amount of work time needed to receive the ticket was increased
by two minutes. Those who did not meet the daily criterion
were told, "I'm sorry, you did not keep your light on long
enough today—please take your seat." The fifth grader was very
interested in the study, and his participation depended upon his
own academic performance. If his work was below average for
two consecutive days, he could not participate (this never happened). In sum, the response-contingent lights, combined with
special privileges for working hard, greatly increased the work
behavior of the four first graders. Six weeks after the study,
their performance was still significantly better than before the
intervention.

COMMENTARY: The study addressed many subtle questions
about the effects of vicarious observation and the student engineer's presence. However, the use of an older student to change
a younger student's behavior offers a quite promising approach.
Behaviors such as daydreaming may be greatly diminished by
having a student engineer observe the amount of time spent on

this kind of nonwork behavior. The study used an electronic console, but a simple hand timer (with or without a light) could be used. This type of student observation, along with positive reinforcement for improved behavior, would also be applicable to students who are easily distracted and have short attention spans.

SOURCE: Surratt, P. R., Ulrich, R. E., and Hawkins, R. P. "An Elementary Student as a Behavioral Engineer." *Journal of Applied Behavior Analysis*, 1969, *2*, 85-92.

Additional Readings

Chadbourne, J., and Foulk, B. "Daydreaming in School." *Teacher*, 1978, *96*, 56-58.
 Rather than being used only as an escape, daydreaming can be productive; that is, children can learn to daydream by choice rather than involuntarily. Guided fantasy can increase self-awareness and help students to concentrate. They learn to relax (for example, by pretending to be in a safe place) and to anticipate events by visualization. Fantasies are then verbalized by the children and unconditionally accepted by the teacher.

Hollon, T. H. "Poor School Performance as a Symptom of Masked Depression in Children and Adolescents." *American Journal of Psychotherapy*, 1970, *24*, 258-263.
 Poor school achievement is often attributed to laziness and daydreaming, when underlying depression is in fact the cause. Urging children to daydream less and study more may well increase their depression. Several case studies are presented. An apathetic fifteen-year-old boy who frequently daydreamed improved when his depression was recognized and treated with psychotherapy, medication, and counseling of his parents.

Procrastination
and Dawdling

Procrastination is commonly defined as intentionally and habitually putting off something that should be done. To dawdle is to spend time idly, fruitlessly, or lackadaisically (although not necessarily intentionally). In both cases, time is wasted. Procrastinating or dawdling leads to a lack of responsibility in children, so that they are frequently late for events and not prompt in handing in work. By age ten, most children understand the concept of time and have the ability to plan their time independently and to be punctual. Not being on time might be a rebellious means of winning a power struggle with adults. Wasting time may serve as an excuse for doing poorly, in the sense that you can't fail if you don't really try. Some children fear failure or success, while others are perfectionists and ineffectively try to do everything all at once.

Children under six years of age respond best when time and situations are clearly structured for them. For older children, specific step-by-step goals should be combined with rewarding consequences for accomplishment. In class, positive teacher attention (praise, physical contact) should be given for studying and assignment completion, while dawdling should be ignored. Privileges may be earned by decreasing time needed to complete work (as well as for improving accuracy).

Behavior Consultation for Increasing
Assignment Completion

AUTHORS: Harris Farber and G. Roy Mayer

PRECIS: Having a counselor consult with a teacher who uses positive reinforcement to ensure that completed assignments are handed in on time

INTRODUCTION: Behavioral approaches have been successfully used by counselors to help teachers in elementary schools become more effective in providing an environment conducive to learning. The present study involved helping a teacher cope with high school students in a large class in a Mexican-American neighborhood (barrio). A tenth-grade English teacher sought assistance because of the lackadaisical attitude of students toward completion of assignments.

METHOD: After observing the class, the counselor met with the teacher for seven sessions that lasted for five to fifty minutes. The goal was for students to complete individual study assignments as set by the teacher. Students could choose their own topic and difficulty level with teacher approval. The results were compared with the prior rate of assignment completion.

   The following behaviors leading to assignment completion were to be reinforced: being on time, starting to work, reading and writing, using the dictionary, following directions, and meeting due dates. During the first minute of the period, the teacher verbally praised the class and gave a small reward (school decal, used book, pen, or movie ticket) to a student whose behavior was appropriate. Two five-minute segments were used to praise desirable behavior as the teacher moved about the room. Undesirable behavior was ignored. At the end of the period, the teacher reviewed and praised desirable behaviors. Unlimited hall passes could be earned by meeting all due dates during the prior week. Record-playing privileges for the class were earned by completing 65 percent of assignments (a 90-percent completion rate was tried but it turned out to be unrealistically high).

Directions, prompts, and modeling were used to help the students learn appropriate behavior. Written and oral instructions specified how rewards could be obtained. On the blackboard was a thermometer showing the number of students who had completed assignments and the names of students who had earned hall passes. Completed assignments rose from 18 to 74 percent, and they were maintained at a 61-percent rate. When the teacher stopped the reinforcement for a short period (reversal phase), the completion rate dropped by more than half. Observed side effects were improved attendance and grades.

COMMENTARY: This study demonstrates the effectiveness of reinforcement techniques with inner-city high school students. The cause of the students' lackadaisical attitude is not addressed, however. It is possible that some had little academic motivation, that some were rebellious, or that some simply procrastinated in turning in assignments. However, in line with other studies, increasing student motivation was found to be a simple and effective solution to procrastination. The students wanted to complete assignments in order to earn the specific privileges of hall passes and playing records. Once again, the pairing of praise with rewards was demonstrated to be very effective.

SOURCE: Farber, H., and Mayer, G. R. "Behavior Consultation in a Barrio High School." *Personnel and Guidance Journal,* 1972, *51,* 273-279.

Modifying Lethargic Behavior

AUTHORS: Anthony J. La Pray and Jonell Chipman

PRECIS: Using candy to reward faster behavior of a nine-year-old girl

INTRODUCTION: A nine-year-old girl had a history of hypo-
thyroidism, general lethargy, slowness, absentmindedness, and
not completing tasks on time. These lethargic behaviors continued even after appropriate glandular treatment.

METHOD: The girl's classwork was inconsistent and below her
potential. Before the thyroid difficulty was discovered, she ate
large quantities of food without gaining weight and was generally lethargic. She rarely completed or handed in assignments.
After medical treatment, her absentmindedness improved and
she became more energetic. However, task completion remained
at the same low level.

Forty sessions took place during the lunch hour, immediately after she had finished eating lunch. Ten more sessions
were held after school. The teacher assigned her six tasks to
complete each time. Each task had been completed by a comparable peer within two minutes. The teacher left the room
after assigning the task and returned in three minutes. After
noting whether the task had been completed, she assigned the
next task. Baseline recording revealed erratic performance
(sometimes all tasks were finished and sometimes none).

Reinforcement consisted of a piece of candy for each task
completed on time. This resulted in a consistently high level of
performance, with at least five tasks being completed each time.
When reinforcement was stopped, her erratic low-completion
level returned. Classwork improved somewhat.

COMMENTARY: This brief study demonstrates the power of
tangible rewards to increase speed of responding. Many teachers
use classroom activities (free time, being a monitor, special
privileges) with the same effect. In this particular case lethargy
that began as a result of a physical condition appeared to continue because of habit or inadvertent environmental rewards for
lethargic behavior. Whatever the cause of their lethargy, children readily respond to a consistent course of rewards for more
desirable and effective behavior.

SOURCE: La Pray, A. J., and Chipman, J. "Application of Behavior Modification to Lethargic Behavior." *School Applications of Learning Theory*, 1970, *1*, 15-20.

Intrinsic Reinforcers for Assignment Completion

AUTHORS: Thomas F. McLaughlin and John Malaby

PRECIS: A combined fifth- and sixth-grade class earned privileges for handing work in on time

INTRODUCTION: Studies are reviewed that successfully used tokens and backup reinforcers (rewards) for improved classroom behavior. But these studies used rewards such as candy, toys, and comic books that are costly and not intrinsic to the classroom. Most of these studies took place in special settings, for example, an adjustment room or a special education or remedial class. Two recent studies used cost-free rewards such as free time or game playing. The present study to improve assignment completion used cost-free rewards (privileges were earned), took place with an entire class in a public school, and was conducted by one teacher.

METHOD: A combined fifth- and sixth-grade class of twenty-nine students was taught by McLaughlin. Assignments were considered complete if all exercises or tasks in spelling, language, handwriting, and math were performed on time. Students earned tokens (points) for desirable behaviors and lost points for undesirable behaviors. McLaughlin often praised students for earning points and calmly and matter-of-factly deducted points when necessary. The authors present a table that lists thirteen desirable classroom behaviors (such as neatness, taking notes, and being quiet) and how many points each earned. Undesirable behaviors that lost points were failing to complete assignments, chewing gum or eating candy, inappropriate verbal or motor behavior, fighting, and cheating. Points lost were the number of incomplete assignments squared (for example, five incomplete assignments would lead to -25 points). An incomplete assignment did not earn points, no matter how many items were correct.

The students determined the privileges to be earned, with the most desirable privileges costing the most points. The twelve privileges included sharpening pencils, seeing animals, taking part in sports, being on a committee, playing games, and being given special projects or jobs to carry out. Details of the exchange of points are described. Each Monday morning, points were exchanged for weekly privileges. Students kept their own records, and a student was made weekly banker to monitor the transactions.

The point system significantly increased assignment completion. Completion of tasks was initiated and maintained with this system; brief termination led to significantly decreased completion. The one student with the most difficulty in completing assignments was influenced the most by this method. Most students liked the program—twenty rated it favorably and only five unfavorably. Positive statements included: "I completed my work on time easier" and "I liked to earn the privileges."

COMMENTARY: Most striking is the ease of this method for significantly improving assignment completion. Instead of privileges being given randomly or to favored students, students earn privileges by demonstrating a variety of appropriate behaviors, including assignment completion. The usual procrastination that many students exhibit is readily handled by this method. With this approach, there is no need for punitive methods or negative statements to children or their parents. Students hand their work in on time because they are motivated to do so. The use of privileges (rather than tangible rewards) eliminates the philosophical opposition of those teachers who are resistant to using concrete rewards to "bribe" children. The amount of points earned or lost by specific behaviors must be custom-tailored by the teacher. Also, the system must work so that most students are able to earn privileges, and the amount of points should realistically reflect the actual importance of the work or behavior.

SOURCE: McLaughlin, T. F., and Malaby, J. "Intrinsic Reinforcers in a Classroom Token Economy." *Journal of Applied Behavior Analysis,* 1972, *5,* 263-270.

Additional Readings

Gardner, D. C., and Gardner, P. L. "Goal Setting and Learning in the High School Resource Room." *Adolescence,* 1978, *13,* 489-493.
    Goal setting increases the person's expectancy that goals will be achieved. Students with serious learning problems learned to complete tasks with the aid of the setting of specific goals. They were given spelling and vocabulary tasks, with one week to study for examinations. Feedback on past performance was provided, and they were asked to predict how many items they would get correct on the following day's test. Students reported studying hard in order to,meet their goals.

Hall, R. V., Lund, D., and Jackson, D. "Effects of Teacher Attention on Study Behavior." *Journal of Applied Behavior Analysis,* 1968, *1,* 1-12.
    Dawdling of elementary school children was effectively reduced by contingent teacher attention. An observer held up a piece of colored paper when a student was studying appropriately. The teacher then moved to the child and made a positive verbal comment and physical contact. Teachers systematically reinforced studying and ignored dawdling or disruptiveness. Teachers were informed of the results of each day's observations. One teacher gave almost no positive attention to any student, issuing only commands and reprimands. Changing that to positive attention resulted in improved behavior.

Hall, R. V., and others. "Modification of Behavior Problems in the Home with a Parent as Observer and Experimenter." *Journal of Applied Behavior Analysis,* 1972, *5,* 53-64.
    A five-year-old girl took excessively long in dressing herself, and it made no difference when her mother laid out her clothes and insisted on speed. But operant conditioning that used loss of television viewing time was dramatically effective. She was required to finish dressing within thirty minutes of awakening or she would not be allowed to watch television until 3:30 P.M. During a period of seventeen days, she lost television privileges only once.

Heider, J. P. "Time with the Psychologist as a Reinforcement for Work Completion." *School Psychology Digest,* 1979, *8,* 335-338.

Rather than artificial reinforcers, naturally available consequences should be used. This study used the opportunity to read to a reinforcing audience (the psychologist) as a reward for classroom task completion. A nine-year-old boy earned one minute with the psychologist for each check mark. In spite of a history of poor academic and social adjustment, there was an immediate and significant increase in his work completion.

McLaughlin, T. F., and Malaby, J. E. "Set of Procedures to Improve Accuracy of Performance and Decrease Time to Complete Mathematics Problems." *Psychological Reports,* 1974, *35,* 1092.

Points were awarded for decreasing amount of time taken by sixth graders to accurately complete math problems. Points were used to purchase classroom privileges. This method is easy to implement, requires little teacher time, and is enjoyed by most pupils.

Penny, H. A. "The Effects of Three Levels of Positive Reinforcement on Promptness Behavior." *School Applications of Learning Theory,* 1971, *2,* 13-18.

A second-grade boy was always late, never got his work done, and was always last in all classroom activities. A written "behavior program" was given to the teacher and parents. It laid down the rule to "be prompt" and outlined the specific behaviors expected. Check marks were given, and various rewards (free time, playing a game, and basketball) were earned according to the number of points accumulated. Daily notes of improved behavior were sent home and resulted in rewards at home. The child's promptness and work completion improved dramatically, and teacher and parental attitudes became more positive.

Slavin, R. E. "A Student Team Approach to Teaching Adolescents with Special Emotional and Behavioral Needs." *Psychology in the Schools,* 1977, *14,* 77-83.

A cooperative reward structure was used in instances in

which individual efforts contributed to the group goal and rewards earned were shared by group members. The time that students spent on tasks in the classroom was increased through
participation in the instructional technique called Teams-
Games-Tournament. Teams of seventh graders competed in
answering social studies questions. A weekly newsletter announced individual and team winners.

Voorhees, S. G. "The Use of a Structuring Technique to Increase Student Speed in Completing an Assigned Task."
School Applications of Learning Theory, 1970, *1,* 7-10.

Mildly retarded students (aged six to nine) were not completing assignments on time. A kitchen timer and the classroom
clock were used to show the students the fifteen minutes
allowed for arithmetic assignments. After nine days, only the
clock was used. Even though the students were not given any
rewards, dramatic improvement occurred. The chronological
structure enabled students to better gauge their time.

Poor Coordination

Physical coordination is the ability to use sets of muscles to accomplish a purposeful movement smoothly. Poor coordination leads to clumsy, awkward, ungainly, or accident-prone behavior. Clumsy children are unable to perform an age-appropriate activity smoothly and accurately. Poor coordination may be seen in large muscle groups (poor gross coordination of running, catching, and throwing) or in small muscles (poor fine coordination typically seen in awkward use of fingers). A lack of motivation or insufficient practice in a particular skill may cause poor coordination. Good coordination requires the intactness and maturation of the nervous system. A tendency toward clumsiness may be inherited, or it may be the result of a central nervous system dysfunction. For example, some children have a poor sense of visual-spatial relations, others cannot effectively integrate sensory information, and still others cannot coordinate a complex movement.

Remediation usually involves teaching the basic movement skills that underlie more complicated actions. Body awareness and relaxation, as well as visual-motor and sensory perception training, have been taught. Skills are then reinforced and corrective feedback is employed. A wide variety of games, obstacle courses, and trampoline activities are used for improving gross coordination.

Motor-Sensory Training with Music

AUTHORS: Sarah de Vincentis and Linda Johnson

PRECIS: Relaxation through music as a means of improving motor skills and self-control of children with behavior disorders

INTRODUCTION: Special education teachers need techniques to teach children cognitive skills and self-control. The following program was designed to improve motor responses, using music as a cue rather than depending upon verbal cues from an adult. Theoretically, developmental deficiencies would be remediated. Thirteen children aged six to eight had a variety of problems, including depression, withdrawal, and learning disorders. Most of them were below average in movement skills. Some of the children had relatively adequate coordination but also had excessive muscle tension and were very impulsive. All children had some deficiency in their sensory-motor response to the environment.

METHOD: *Body awareness* is necessary for developing voluntary motor movement. Body parts must be identified for the child, and their functions understood by him or her. The body's location and position in relation to the environment must also be perceived by the child. It is important for a child to have a positive body image, which is a reflection of his or her self-concept. Body awareness leads to a positive and strong self-image. *Body relaxation* techniques were included—particularly for those children who reacted impulsively to stress. According to the authors, control of muscular activity follows from becoming aware of tension. A calming effect was sought both for impulsive thoughts and for muscular tension. Every session ended with a relaxation exercise. Self-control was one goal of both gross and fine *motor training*. Once smooth gross motor movements have been acquired, fine motor control can be improved. Organizing and interpreting data are improved by *sensory perception training*. Students should learn to integrate information and generalize the knowledge to other situations.

Music (words and melody) was used to make the exercises

similar to dancing. The music, rather than an adult, served as external control in that the children's movements were guided by music. With familiarity, the children became more responsible for controlling their movements and the amount of space they used. All movements were in time to the music's rhythm and pace; folk music was selected because of its simplicity and clarity. The authors note that listening to music enhances attention, concentration, and memory and that for children with emotional or learning problems, music provides a sense of predictability and consistency.

Two fifteen-minute periods each day were devoted to this program. The following is an example of one such period. A tune-up was accomplished by stretching, touching toes, and deep breathing. Gross motor activities included creeping ("An Old Fish"), crawling ("Doggie Song"), and rocking ("Row, Row, Row Your Boat"). At the end, the children tensed and relaxed parts of their bodies. The morning and the afternoon began with motor activities because these should increase attentiveness in the time period directly following. The teacher reported improved impulse control, longer attention spans, and greater motivation following the exercises.

The program was carried out in the classroom, with the thought that its furniture would help to establish familiar boundaries. Masking tape was used to create a trail for the children to follow. Internal control was to be enhanced by the use of boundaries and the control of personal space. The authors have used this program in regular and special education classes for four years. Reported benefits are improved motor skills and better internal self-control.

COMMENTARY: Poor coordination was directly addressed in the classroom. Children learned to improve their movement skills in time to folk music, and the authors included relaxation methods that have become increasingly popular for reducing tension and impulsivity. They also used these activities to aid the children in attending to the academic work that followed. We could speculate that four brief exercise periods might be more effective for many children than two longer ones. Brief exercise could follow difficult academic periods, both as a reward and as a motor outlet of frustration and tension.

SOURCE: De Vincentis, S., and Johnson, L. "A Musical Approach to Motor-Sensory Training." Paper presented at the World Congress on Future Special Education, Stirling, Scotland, June 25, 1978 (ERIC Document Reproduction Service No. ED 158 478).

Treating Perceptual-Motor Disorders

AUTHORS: Benjamin B. Lahey, Mary Kay Busemeyer, Christiane O'Hara, and Vicki E. Beggs

PRECIS: Reinforcement and corrective feedback for improving the handwriting of four boys, ages seven to nine

INTRODUCTION: Psychologists are often involved in planning programs for learning-disabled children. Behavior modification is an alternative to training visual perception, perceptual-motor skills, and psycholinguistic processes. Inefficient learning is not viewed as a symptom of a disorder, but as a characteristic that must be changed. The present study focused on severe perceptual-motor disturbance in handwriting since this is often seen in children with learning disabilities and is resistant to traditional remediation. There had been success using reinforcement procedure with very mild handwriting problems. This study involved students with severe and pervasive perceptual-motor disorders.

METHOD: The first experiment involved a seven- and an eight-year-old boy. When copying words, they made many orientation and sequencing errors (called reversals or mirror writing). During each session, they copied their first name five times, five different words with four letters each, and five different geometric figures. A response was correct if it was clear, in proper sequence, and not more than a 20-degree deviation from horizontal. All drawings were done with a pencil on separate five-by-eight-inch cards. The drawings were scored, and rater reliability was quite high.

Two sessions of fifteen to thirty minutes each were held twice a day, four days per week. The children were told that the purpose was to help them with their printing. Their performance before treatment (baseline) consisted of fifteen copying responses each session, with no feedback or reinforcement for correct or incorrect productions. Treatment consisted of being told they were "right" and receiving a token for each correct production. Incorrect performance led to being told they were "wrong" and being shown the correct response. They were told why their production was wrong and were shown a correct illustration on a separate sheet of paper. Tokens were traded in at the end of each session (three tokens for one penny).

"Probe sessions" were held to assess the possible generalization of the training. They consisted of copying five new words, five new geometric figures, and the child's first name five times. No feedback or reinforcement followed these periodic trials. The results are presented graphically and discussed. Direct instruction did effectively remediate the severe perceptual-motor disorders. Errors of orientation and sequence were greatly reduced by the use of corrective feedback and reinforcement. The probe sessions demonstrated that the improvement generalized to other unreinforced handwriting performances.

A second experiment was conducted with two children with even more severe deficiencies. Two boys, aged eight and nine, had extremely poor handwriting. The procedure used was similar to that in the first experiment, with raisins being substituted for pennies with the nine year old. An additional problem of the other boy was added—shoe tying. Treatment consisted of teaching him to tie shoes by the standard "six-step backward chaining procedure." The loops were first pulled tightly, and praise was given after each correct response. For every three correct responses, one penny was given. After every third attempt, correct shoe tying was demonstrated (modeled). The boy soon began to tie his shoes properly, and he was praised and given one penny for each correct performance. Incorrect attempts led to corrective feedback.

Treatment resulted in improved handwriting for both boys and in better shoe-tying ability for the one who could not do that task. Generalization of handwriting skill was demonstrated for only one of the boys. The authors speculate that teachers usually do not provide useful feedback to students. Marks and smiling faces are placed on sheets with very little explanation of what they mean. Instead, systematic corrective feedback and reinforcement should be employed.

COMMENTARY: The authors see a need to convince teachers to use the specific type of instruction employed in their study. They see their experiments as confirming past success with reinforcement and corrective feedback for learning-disabled children. It does seem clear that poor handwriting and copying skills can be improved by this technique. However, generalization to other activities is also important. Teachers can periodically give corrective feedback under different conditions and in different subject areas to ensure the generalization of improved skills. We would suggest involving parents in the specific task of helping their children at home. They could be shown how to give positive reinforcement and corrective feedback. This is much better than simply commenting on sloppy work and insisting that children do their work over.

SOURCE: Lahey, B. B., Busemeyer, M. K., O'Hara, C., and Beggs, V. E. "Treatment of Severe Perceptual-Motor Disorders in Children Diagnosed as Learning Disabled." *Behavior Modification*, 1977, *1*, 123-140.

Kinetic Family Drawings

AUTHORS: Larry M. Raskin and Georgia Pitcher-Baker

PRECIS: Isolation-rejection, body concerns, and sibling rivalry indicated by drawings of fifty kindergarten and first-grade children with delayed perceptual-motor development

INTRODUCTION: There is considerable published information

on the usefulness of human figure drawings. They have been interpreted as unconscious projections of feelings, conflicts, and motivations and have been used as measures of mental maturity. Drawings also reflect a person's current concerns and attitudes, as well as the quality of his or her interpersonal relationships. Research by Burns and Kaufman demonstrated that action (kinetic) drawings yield more information about children than do static human figure drawings (R. C. Burns and S. H. Kaufman, *Kinetic Family Drawings (K-F-D): An Introduction to Understanding Children Through Kinetic Drawings,* New York: Brunner/Mazel, 1970). Kinetic Family Drawings require that the child draw everyone in his or her family in the act of doing something.

METHOD: The Martin Screening Test for Motor Disabilities and the Developmental Test of Visual-Motor Integration were used to screen 359 kindergarten and first-grade children for perceptual-motor problems. Arbitrary cutoff scores were used to categorize 123 children as developmentally delayed. Of this group, fifty were randomly selected for this study; fifty nondelayed children served as a comparison group. They were tested in a large room, separated sufficiently from one another to preclude copying. The authors suggest that drawings should ordinarily be administered individually and in conjunction with a comprehensive battery of psychological tests. The children were told the following: "Draw a picture of everyone in your family, including yourself, doing something. Draw whole people, not cartoons or stick people. Remember, make everyone doing something— some kind of action." When finished, each child was asked the names of the people and their activity.

Two independent raters scored the drawings for isolation-rejection, body concerns, and sibling rivalry. Isolation-rejection is indicated when children draw themselves separated from all other family members (separated by objects and lines or drawn on the back of the paper). Body concerns are indicated by poor integration of body parts, excessive shading, omission or exaggeration of parts, and excessive erasing. The raters used Koppitz's scoring system, which takes into account the age and sex of the child (E. M. Koppitz, *Psychological Evaluation of Chil-*

dren's Human Figure Drawings, New York: Grune & Stratton, 1968). Aggressive or competitive action (hitting, pushing, throwing or hitting a ball) indicated sibling rivalry. Reliability of raters was high; the only disagreements occurring for body concerns.

One or more emotional concerns were present for forty-three of the fifty children with perceptual-motor delays. The comparison group had twenty-two children with one or more emotional concerns. Sibling rivalry indicators were few, and the groups were not significantly different in this characteristic. According to the authors, these findings are useful for treatment. On the one hand, delayed perceptual-motor development suggests that a child may be suffering from feelings of isolation-rejection and interpersonal problems. Children and their families should be helped in these areas before the problems become worse. On the other hand, one should investigate the possibility of perceptual-motor delay if feelings of isolation and rejection are identified. The authors conclude that children with average intelligence who are relatively slow in their perceptual-motor development often experience feelings of isolation, rejection, and bodily concerns.

COMMENTARY: The authors suggest that kinetic family drawings would be useful as a group screening device in schools. Scores would indicate perceptual-motor problems and/or feelings of isolation and rejection, as well as bodily concerns. This approach serves the purpose of identifying perceptual-motor problems and possibly of indicating specific emotional problems. Children who feel isolated and rejected may well benefit from a few sessions with their families in which this concern is addressed. Even communicating this problem area to parents may help them focus more on their child's feelings. Children with difficulties in drawing may well benefit from corrective feedback from the teacher or a planned program to improve their skills.

SOURCE: Raskin, L. M., and Pitcher-Baker, G. "Kinetic Family Drawings by Children with Perceptual-Motor Delays." *Journal of Learning Disabilities,* 1977, *10,* 370-374.

Additional Readings

Applegate, E. "Large-Muscle Coordination." *Academic Therapy Quarterly,* 1968, *3,* 113-14.

Poor gross coordination leads to awkwardness, accident-proneness, and inability to stand quietly in line. A variety of exercises are described to improve coordination and social participation. Balls and beanbags can be thrown at various targets and in relay teams. The foot opposite the throwing arm must be put forward. Demonstrated and practiced jump-rope skills are very valuable. Another aid is the hitting back and forth of a rubber ball suspended from the ceiling by a sturdy, elastic rubber band.

Arnheim, D. D., and Sinclair, W. A. *The Clumsy Child: A Program of Motor Therapy.* Saint Louis: Mosby, 1975.

This book is meant for regular classroom teachers, special educators, and physical education instructors. Specific motor therapies are presented for children with inefficient motor skills. Developmental motor activities are used to teach the movement skills that underlie complicated coordination. Step-by-step procedures are detailed in order of their increasing complexity.

Bachara, G. H., and Zaba, J. N. "Learning Disabilities and Juvenile Delinquency." *Journal of Learning Disabilities,* 1978, *11,* 242-246.

There is a significant correlation between learning disabilities and juvenile delinquency. This study demonstrated that perceptual-motor training, tutoring, and special education significantly reduced delinquent acts of adolescents aged fourteen to sixteen. Visual-perceptual-motor training was tailored to the specific measured defect.

Reed, M., Black, T., and Eastman, J. "A New Look at Perceptual-Motor Therapy." *Academic Therapy,* 1978, *14,* 55-65.

A variety of activities were used to enhance integration of sensations, body image, visualization of space, motor skills, and cognitive adaptive methods as means of overcoming perceptual-motor problems. Many motor games and craft projects are described. The nine-to-12-year-old children also used videotape equipment for immediate feedback. Group interaction was used to foster more effective and adaptive social and work skills.

Taylor, D. C., and McKinlay, I. A. "What Kind of Thing Is Being Clumsy?" *Child: Care, Health, and Development,* 1979, *5,* 167-175.

Clumsiness may be due to central nervous system deficiencies, slow maturation, inappropriate arousal, or inadequate rehearsal of activities. Diagnosis is important since it can lead to a general direction for management and education. However, practical remediation is more useful than fully pinpointing the cause of clumsiness. Rehearsal by clumsy children is often insufficient. Schools and home should provide practice in cycling, swimming, ball control, and penmanship.

Trexler, L. K. "The Trampoline: A Training Device for Children with Perceptual-Motor Problems." *Academic Therapy Quarterly,* 1970, *5,* 145-147.

The trampoline is described as not being dangerous, contrary to what many people believe. Rythmically bouncing enhances body image and awareness of spatial relationships. Specific methods are described for gradually overcoming fear of the trampoline. After bouncing is learned, such activities as clapping, touching body parts, and closing of the eyes are added. Performing in sequence is suggested (three bounces, sit-drop, three bounces, knee-drop, and so on.

Trexler, L. K., and Lacey, H. M. "The Use of a Rope Maze in Developing a Perceptual-Motor Training Program." *Academic Therapy Quarterly,* 1968, *3,* 194-195.

Children with learning disabilities often cannot tie shoelaces, ride a bicycle, or catch a ball. They have not acquired the subskills underlying these activities. A rope maze was used to develop rhythm and body awareness, position, and control. Four pieces of half-inch rope about eight feet long were tied parallel to each other approximately eighteen inches apart and six inches from the floor. Without touching the ropes, children walk over, under, forward, and backward, through the created maze.

Crying

Crying is an inarticulate sound of distress, pain, or rage. It is most frequently a call for help. Forms of crying include sobbing (compulsive catching of the breath) and weeping (shedding tears). Crying in response to stress is an expected and frequent occurrence up to school age. From that point on, both intensity and frequency diminish with age. A very helpful distinction is made in the literature between respondent crying (reaction to painful or unexpected events) and operant or attention-seeking crying. It is operant crying that is the greater cause for concern. Unfortunately, the pattern is often set in infancy by well-meaning parents who inadvertently reward crying. They pick up, feed, or play with infants when they cry. Research during the infancy period makes it quite clear that adult attention to crying increases its frequency, while ignoring it has the opposite effect. There is a need for adults to be aware of the causes for crying without reinforcing operant crying.

Children need attention when they are not crying. In classrooms, teachers should praise children for coping with stress and should ignore operant crying. Also, when an overly sensitive child does not cry under stress, a favored activity can follow immediately (serving as a natural reinforcer). Time-outs (some form of interruption of ongoing activities) have been effectively used to quickly eliminate extreme crying.

Reducing Crying by Social Reinforcement

AUTHORS: Betty M. Hart, K. Eileen Allen, Jean S. Buell, Florence R. Harris, and Montrose M. Wolf

PRECIS: Having teachers ignore crying and praise coping responses in two preschool boys

INTRODUCTION: Respondent crying is a reaction to unexpected or painful events. Teachers must of course respond immediately to a child who cries as a result of a fall, being hit, or an accident. Operant crying is social: a child looks around, sees an adult, and then cries. If attention is not given, crying increases in loudness and intensity.

METHOD: Systematic positive social reinforcement was used with two four-year-olds who exhibited operant crying. During the morning, Bill cried more than any other child in the school. Any minor accident resulted in his crying until a teacher came over to him, while any frustration or threat resulted in his crying and screaming. In Alan's case, any accident or having anything taken from him led him to cry loudly. Both boys made eye contact with a teacher before crying and cried more and more loudly until a teacher came. The number of crying episodes was recorded on a pocket counter; graphs are presented showing baseline rates and rates after intervention.

All operant crying was ignored by the teachers, who were not to look at, speak to, or go to the child. If crying began near a teacher, she walked away or busied herself with another child. When the boys reacted appropriately to a fall or other minor mishap, teachers gave immediate approval and attention. When crying had clearly diminished, the teachers began to give attention to anything resembling crying (whimpering or sulking) and considerable attention to crying itself. This was done to reinstate crying and thus to prove that crying was a function of adult reinforcement. The reinstatement of attention for crying immediately resulted in the usual rate of crying (about five times per morning). Alan's crying pattern was analyzed, and the point was made that he was able to gain the teacher's attention by looking as if he were going to cry. When the teacher did not give immediate attention, operant crying clearly appeared.

COMMENTARY: This was one of the early studies that used reinforcement principles with children in a school setting. It provides a clear illustration of the power of adult attention to maintain or eliminate crying. While crying is ignored, more appropriate behavior is praised. A useful distinction is made between respondent and operant crying. Unfortunately, it is easy for teachers to pay attention to typical respondent crying, which then may foster the development of operant crying (to gain attention). Teachers should note that crying was easily reinstated by attention; this demonstrated that adults were inadvertently maintaining crying behavior. Adult attention may be used in the manner outlined to reduce any overtly inappropriate school behavior.

SOURCE: Hart, B. M., Allen, K. E., Buell, J. S., Harris, F. R., and Wolf, M. M. "Effects of Social Reinforcement on Operant Crying." *Journal of Experimental Child Psychology,* 1964, *1,* 145-153.

Overcorrection of Crying and Hitting

AUTHORS: Thomas H. Ollendick and Johnny L. Matson

PRECIS: Reducing disruptive behavior of two preschool boys by restitution and positive practice

INTRODUCTION: Overcorrection consists of mild punishment and reeducation. Individuals learn to be responsible for the effects of their misbehavior. First, the environment is returned to a condition better than that which existed before the disturbance (restitution). Second, the individuals repeatedly practice appropriate behaviors (positive practice). Overcorrection has been successfully employed with a wide range of people and problems. Although its effectiveness has been studied, the following components have not been investigated separately: (1) the verbal command not to perform a behavior; (2) restitution to overcorrect the disturbance caused by the behavior; and (3) positive practice of overly correct behavior.

METHOD: A two-year-old boy hit children or adults and cried uncontrollably when he could not get his own way. Scolding and spanking were unsuccessful in changing this behavior. Behavior ratings of hitting and crying were performed during fifteen-minute play periods with his mother (during which he could not get his way). The mother was instructed to say "No, Chris" when he hit or attempted to hit her (verbal warning). Then, the restitution phase was added during which he had to pat the hit area for thirty seconds and say that he was sorry ten times. For attempted hitting, he had to verbally apologize thirty times. Finally, he had to raise and lower his hitting arm forty times after each episode. Numbers of hits, attempts to hit, and cries are described for each phase. Restitution resulted in less hitting, but attempted hitting remained high until positive practice was put into effect. A three-month follow-up revealed no hitting or attempts at hitting and rare crying.

Shortly following the divorce of his parents, a two-and-one-half-year-old boy began to hit, bite, cry, scream and throw things. Scolding, spanking, and isolation were not effective in changing these behaviors. The number of hits and cries is listed for each overcorrection step. Saying "No, Bill" was followed by having him pat the hit area for thirty seconds and apologize ten times after each hit. However, introducing positive practice (having him raise and lower his arm forty times) led to an increase in hits. Doubling the restitution and positive practice led to a reduction in hitting. After three months, only one hit and occasional crying were observed.

The authors see overcorrection as effective in changing behavior that is resistant to traditional punishment. This approach works for relatively normal as well as for more disturbed children. In both cases discussed here, the mother had been instructed to first try positive reinforcement of appropriate behavior and ignore hitting and crying. This method had no effect. Bill appeared to react negatively to overcorrection and showed more aggressive behavior than did Chris. Bill improved when the punitive and educational aspects were doubled; this result suggests that the amount of overcorrection must be individually determined.

COMMENTARY: Crying decreased in both cases, even though it was not directly addressed. The authors point out that overcorrection of one behavior does directly affect interrelated behaviors. This finding suggests that one significant problem should be focused upon and changed. An accompanying behavior such as crying may often correspondingly decrease. Overcorrection is a very flexible method that may be judicially applied to any overt misbehavior. By implication, overcorrection might be applied directly to crying. Children can be warned not to cry, to speak softly and nicely for one minute, and then to smile and laugh for one minute. In school, it is up to the creativity of educational personnel to adapt this method to the individual circumstances. We believe that a positive moral point is made by using restitution and positive practice. Individuals are then held responsible for their actions and the effect they have on others.

SOURCE: Ollendick, T. H., and Matson, J. L. "An Initial Investigation into the Parameters of Overcorrection." *Psychological Reports*, 1976, *39*, 1139-1142.

Time-Outs for Crying

AUTHOR: Sidney K. Teel

PRECIS: Using a time-out room for a six-year-old boy who cried almost constantly

INTRODUCTION: The author points out that many teachers

use unconditional love in the hope that children will respond positively and give up their inappropriate behavior. Love and acceptance are often employed with children who cry frequently. If crying is a reaction to fear, offering a child love may serve to reassure him or her and desensitize the fear. However, persistent crying usually means that the child is seeking attention, and the best course may be to remove the child from the presence of reinforcers (a type of operant conditioning). In the time-out method discussed here, the child is isolated in an uninteresting room with nothing to do. The author sees this as a more humane procedure than scolding, humiliation, nagging, and so on.

METHOD: A six-year-old boy cried in school almost every day. Gradually, this increased to continuous crying, and he was transferred into a learning disabilities class. There, the teacher was generally loving but ignored his crying, verbally chastised him, and used corporal punishment. Since his crying became more intense, the procedure was instituted of matter-of-factly escorting him to the time-out room. The teacher avoided eye contact and did not speak to him. He came out as soon as he had stopped crying or after five minutes. If still crying, he was taken back to his seat and the lesson was continued. If crying did not stop in two minutes, he was returned to the time-out room.

Within two days the almost continuous crying diminished greatly. After that, crying was eliminated. The author points out that once time-outs are begun, they must be continued until the problem behavior is eliminated. If not, the behavior might become even more difficult to reduce. Although the teacher said that the procedure was very time consuming, the author believes that the two or three hours of teacher time required is relatively economical. When crying has been reduced, the usual methods of positively reinforcing appropriate behavior become feasible.

COMMENTARY: This simple time-out procedure has been effectively employed with a wide range of inappropriate classroom behaviors. It is particularly useful for crying, since frequent crying is usually annoying to both peers and adults. Not only are time-outs effective for eliminating crying, but they provide a valuable model lesson for others that a child will not be allowed to disturb others. Matter-of-fact removal makes this point without negative attitudes or punitive behavior on the part of adults.

SOURCE: Teel, S. K. "The Use of Time-Out Procedures in Diminishing Crying Behavior: A Case Study." *School Applications of Learning Theory,* 1971, *3,* 27-31.

Additional Reading

Yawkey, T. D., and Griffith, D. L. "The Effects of the Premack Principle on Affective Behaviors of Young Children." *Child Study Journal,* 1974, *4,* 59-70.

Operant crying occurs and is maintained because of the responses of others. Five-year-olds cried significantly less when the teacher employed the Premack principle, which states that a behavior is strengthened when followed by a behavior that is *often* voluntarily performed—a preferred or liked activity. The teacher said that she liked the way the child got up from a fall without crying. Immediately after, they engaged in a favored activity (high-frequency behavior), such as riding a bicycle, painting, or washing the blackboard.

3

Insecure Behaviors

The problems discussed in this chapter are all characterized by the presence of severe and debilitating anxiety. As Munroe states, "[anxiety] comes, in the course of development, to function as a signal of potential danger . . . the child's ego forms its own concept of the dangers confronting it . . . and its own methods of handling them. . . . The pain of anxiety and the threat can be warded off in various ways. . . . These methods of handling conflict tend to become more or less firmly institutionalized as 'mechanisms of defense' " (R. L. Munroe, *Schools of Psychoanalytic Thought*, New York: Holt, Rinehart and Winston, 1955, p. 91). The behaviors that characterize these disorders are symptomatic of intense anxiety and represent the child's attempt to "ward off" tension and keep it in check. For example, the school-phobic child may remain at home to avoid the anxiety associated with leaving his mother. The child is not afraid of school in itself but is afraid to leave the home and separate from his parent. The anxiety attached to school is thus displaced from its true source. The compulsive child is unable to tolerate deviations in his ritualistic pattern without experiencing extreme tension. Thus, the compulsive act is both a symptom and a defense. Electively mute children choose silence to protect themselves from the anxiety connected with verbal communication. They also find additional protection in other children, who speak for them or run their errands. The effeminate boy experiences tension through his inability to fulfill male sex-role expectations. His association with girls may help him avoid the anxiety of having to play the masculine role. Depression and low self-esteem are related in their focus on negative self-attributes and personal weakness. Depressed children and children with low self-esteem attempt to minimize anxiety and the risk of failure by withdrawing from life's activities.

Anxiety is a natural component of development and is experienced by every child. It has important survival value in that it motivates the child to learn about and avoid danger. It is typically displayed in its earliest form as "stranger anxiety" (at six to eight months of age) and as "separation anxiety" (at about one year). During the preschool years, the birth (or adoption) of a new baby, darkness, ghosts, or expectations of punishment are common sources of anxiety. These tend to disappear or change form, while other fears may require such further action as explanation, encouragement, modeling, and the use of simple behavioral techniques if they are to be eliminated.

While minimal anxiety is constructive and educational, intense fears can be crippling. When attached to certain stimulus conditions, they may lead to the defensive symptoms discussed in this chapter. Early sources of strong anxiety are often related to harsh, inconsistent parental standards, coupled with frequent negative evaluations of the child's behavior. Such treatment causes insecurity, damaged self-esteem, and the adoption of long-term defensive patterns. The true sources of anxiety become deeply buried, as neither the child nor the parent is able to communicate honestly and openly. As middle and late childhood progress, the actual concerns become less reachable and may be replaced by other unrealistic and intense fears. In this process, insecure behaviors develop.

The traditional strategy for children with these disorders has been to refer them to sources outside the school for in-depth psychotherapy. Under this treatment model, it was assumed that behavior would change as the child came to understand the hidden conflicts underlying the anxiety and to abandon his or her defenses. However, in each of the sections in this chapter, techniques are described that directly alter the behaviors and feeling states characteristic of these disorders. For example, combined cognitive and behavioral strategies have been employed to encourage depressed students to refocus their attention and practice pleasurable behavior. Similarly, effeminate boys have experienced success engaging in "masculine" activities with male role models and have modified feminine behaviors in response to behavioral contingencies. (While politics and treatment have collided on this issue, techniques are available for those who choose to use them.) For children with low self-esteem, procedures to prompt and reward positive self-statements, refocus feelings of helplessness, teach self-concept education (geared toward improving how children feel about themselves), and provide successful school experiences have shown promising results. Yoga has been used to reduce school-related anxiety in youngsters while strategies to gradually shape audible speech have been effective with elective mutes. Treatment for school-phobic behavior has emphasized a firm, supportive, and quick return to school.

These approaches demonstrate that disorders that have been typically referred for psychotherapy can be treated in the school. It is not necessary for feeling states to be altered before behavior change can occur. A number of articles in this chapter utilized attitudinal measures to show that behavioral changes resulting from treatment are accompanied by positive feeling changes.

Anxiety and Tension

Anxiety is a feeling of apprehensiveness, painful worry, or uneasiness. There is a doubt about one's capacity to cope with perceived threats. High anxiety may be indicated by such symptoms as agitation, crying, screaming, nightmares, poor eating habits, and breathing difficulties. Frequently, there are such accompanying physiological reactions as increased pulse rate and higher blood pressure, nausea, sweating, and tense muscles. The word tension *is used by some as synonomous with* anxiety, *but it more specifically refers to strained, tight, stiff, and stretched muscles.*

In the classroom, anxiety may be the cause of forgetfulness, lateness, apathy, angry bravado, or hyperactivity. Common forms of anxiety are test anxiety and public speaking anxiety. Some students become psychologically paralyzed by anxiety and are unable to seek alternative solutions to academic or social problems. Typically, anxiety is caused by insecurity (not feeling safe) or excessive frustration. Lowering parental and teacher rejection, for example, will lead to a decrease in anxiety. More than any other school behavior problem, anxiety is responsive to an amazingly wide array of techniques. Frequently employed are modeling, desensitization, relaxation, cognitive behavior modification, counterconditioning, meditation, and yoga. Among the techniques that have been successfully adapted for classroom use are psychodrama and behavioral rehearsal in which worries and possible solutions to them are acted out. Children trained to be more assertive frequently come to feel more competent and less anxious. Finally, there have been recent attempts in schools by rational-emotive practitioners to eliminate the kinds of faulty and irrational thinking ("shoulds," self-blame, exaggerating) that cause anxiety.

Self-Control Training

AUTHOR: Steven D. Brown

PRECIS: A ten-week course for controlling anxiety and increasing self-confidence and assertiveness

INTRODUCTION: The author reviews various approaches to mental health problems, such as training nonprofessionals to play roles previously restricted to professionals. Parents, teachers, and friends have been trained to change maladaptive behavior in individuals, but little effort has been made to teach troubled individuals to change their own and others' behavior. These self-help and preventive skills can be taught in well-designed psychosocial educational programs. In the program under discussion an educational rather than a group therapy approach was used to teach progressive relaxation, anxiety management training, idealized self-image, assertive training, and operant reinforcement principles.

METHOD: The course is designed to take thirty hours over a ten-week period. Each class lasts one and one-half hours (twice per week) and is conducted according to a lesson plan. The course objectives are explained, and the responsibilities of students and instructor are outlined. Successes are praised, while failures are sympathetically discussed. A major focus is on practicing the self-control procedure taught during that class and learning when to use it. Practical applications in real life are discussed, and homework assignments are given. Students are expected to practice the skills, keep a record, and describe situations where that skill can be used. Educational aids such as films, videotapes, and manuals are employed. This course was used with patients from various county mental health facilities in an effort to turn helpless individuals into students capable of learning new skills. An evaluation at the end indicated that course participation had reduced their anxiety and increased their self-esteem and assertiveness.

Relaxation. The course begins with progressive muscular relaxation training. Hands, arms, and face are made taut and then completely relaxed. Homework includes daily relaxation practice. The next class focuses on the neck, shoulders, chest, back, stomach, legs, and feet. Once they have learned relaxation, the students learn to breathe slowly while counting from ten to one. Then, they breathe while saying the word *relax* to themselves on each breath. At home, they make a list of relaxing situations and things that they do well (competency). Later, they learn to recognize tension and to use self-relaxation to counteract tension.

Anxiety Management. While relaxed, the students learn to imagine their relaxing and competency scenes. At home, they list anxiety- or fear-provoking situations. Examples of anxiety management by past students are reviewed. The students learn to imagine their least "nervous scene" in detail while remaining completely relaxed. Reactions are discussed, homework is to practice relaxing to the nervous scenes. There are overlaps of methods during each session. As students become more successful, more and more anxiety-provoking scenes are imagined.

Self-Image. Confidence is built through an idealized self-image procedure. The self-perpetuating cycle of negative thinking and inadequate behavior is described. Examples are given in which this cycle was reversed for past students. Appropriate, effective behavior in various situations is imagined. Homework is to apply the idealized images to real-life problems.

Assertiveness. The instructor explains that assertiveness is different from either passivity or aggressiveness. Demonstrations are given of these three types of responses to common situations. An assertive response shows in eye contact and facial expression, body posture and gestures, tone of voice, and message content. All students make a list at home of situations where they think more assertiveness is required. In class, they role play common situations, such as returning improperly cooked food in a restaurant. Feedback from others is offered, and more appropriate assertive responses are role played. Later, students act resistively by being hostile, overly apologetic, or passive while another student learns to react appropriately and assertively. During all classes, successes are praised, while failures are analyzed and role played until the problem is satisfactorily and assertively handled. When students become able to handle situations comfortably in class, they are then encouraged to try their new skills in real-life situations. The last meeting on assertiveness includes possible situations when being assertive is not appropriate. Also covered is learning to give and receive positive feelings and compliments.

Reinforcement Principles. Using rewards is discussed as a means of modifying one's own or others' behavior. Social behavior is learned. A film is shown to illustrate positive and negative reinforcement (punishment). Homework involves selecting someone's behavior (at home) and applying the principles learned to increase or decrease that behavior. Finally, reinforcement principles are used for self-change. The last class is a review of skills learned; questions are answered, and a reminder is given to apply the skills in real situations.

COMMENTARY: We present this article because it is one of the few models using an educational approach to improve and prevent psychological problems. The curriculum used appears particularly applicable to adolescents, although the ages of the students who participated were not given. With some modifications and parent involvement, it could be adapted for use with children. Clearly, a school could incorporate some of the methods in their ongoing health courses or in their counseling efforts. A brief course run by a school guidance counselor, social worker, or psychologist could be offered to students experiencing a high degree of anxiety. This format offers a specific way to control anxiety and thus prevent it from interfering with academic (and social) learning.

SOURCE: Brown, S. D. "Self-Control Skills Training." *Professional Psychology*, 1975, 6, 319-330.

A Rational-Emotive Program in the School

AUTHORS: Raymond Digiuseppe and Howard Kassinove

PRECIS: Lowering the anxiety and neuroticism of fourth and eighth graders by teaching them rational-emotive principles

INTRODUCTION: Rational-emotive therapy has been an effective treatment with disturbed populations. Literature is cited that demonstrates its usefulness with test anxiety, speech anxiety, and interpersonal discomfort. However, the value of rational-emotive therapy has not been demonstrated with normal schoolchildren. The 204 children participating in this program came from the fourth and eighth grades of a Catholic elementary school. The classes were randomly assigned to rational-emotive education, human relations education, or a control group. Sessions were taught for fifty minutes, one day per week for fifteen weeks.

METHOD: Faulty thinking produces negative emotions. It is the irrational negative beliefs about events that cause emotional upset. Three categories of commonly held irrational beliefs are "awfulizing" (exaggerating negative consequences), "shoulds, oughts, and musts" (unrealistic demands), and "statements of blame." Since rational-emotive therapy is based upon an educational model, classroom presentation is appropriate. Basic therapeutic principles are directly taught through lectures, discussions, and repetition. The stress is on developing attitudes of self-acceptance, risk taking, accepting uncertainty, and tolerating imperfection. A series of lessons were designed around the premise that thinking produces emotion and that emotional adjustment is enhanced by changing one's thinking.

An alternative program was taught to one fourth-grade class and one eighth-grade class. It was believed that adjustment would be enhanced by teaching psychodynamic principles of behavior. Concepts such as "our inner human drives" and "how personality traits develop" were taught. After a story was read and discussed, the adults reflected on the children's comments.

The two no-treatment classes (control group) participated in their regular health class, which was concerned with such things as nutrition and safety. The assessment methods are described, including the Idea Inventory (which tests eleven basic irrational beliefs) and the Children's Survey of Rational Beliefs (which tests knowledge of principles). Adjustment was measured by the Junior Eysenck Personality Inventory (neuroticism scale) and the State-Trait Anxiety Inventory for Children (trait anxiety scale).

The children were able to understand rational-emotive principles, and their emotional adjustment was improved as measured. Rational-emotive education led to fewer irrational beliefs and significantly less trait anxiety and neuroticism. Irrational thinking was reduced significantly more in the rational-emotive group than in either the human relations training group or the no-treatment group. Effects were stronger for the fourth graders, possibly because the eighth graders had already developed a more irrational philosophy of life.

COMMENTARY: The authors point out the need for more research to confirm their results. However, it is clear that teaching rational-emotive principles is feasible. We present this digest to alert readers to a specific teaching method designed to enhance emotional adjustment and to prevent emotional problems. The present study, as well as past research, indicates that decreasing irrational beliefs reduces anxiety. Test and speech anxiety have also been significantly decreased by rational-emotive approaches. The implication is that these methods may be applicable to the wide variety of problems covered in our book. Some of the principles and methods may be readily adaptable by teachers or counselors in existing courses or group meetings. Educators may obtain material from the Institute for Rational-Emotive Therapy in New York City.

SOURCE: Digiuseppe, R., and Kassinove, H. "Effects of a Rational-Emotive School Mental Health Program on Children's Emotional Adjustment." *Journal of Community Psychology*, 1976, *4*, 382-387.

The School Psychologist's Role
with Anxious Children

AUTHORS: Guy T. Doyal and Ronald J. Friedman

PRECIS: Psychodynamic and learning theory to diagnose and treat anxiety as illustrated by two case studies

INTRODUCTION: The authors see the school psychologist as responsible for both diagnosing problems in children and developing treatment strategies for these problems. They provide an overview of the cause and treatment of anxiety, which is seen as often impairing schoolwork. Psychoanalytic theory holds that anxiety is a danger signal that warns the individual to take protective action. Sexual and aggressive drives are seen as threatening to overwhelm the child's ego. In contrast, learning theory suggests that anxiety results when a neutral stimulus is followed and thus conditioned by a negative reaction. Test anxiety or being sent to the principal's office are examples in which anxiety is the result of past negative experiences. These kinds of anxiety are learned and evoked by specific situations, whereas general anxiety is nonspecific and caused by unconscious conflicts. Tension discharge over a long period (chronic anxiety) produces strain and fatigue. A panic reaction may result from extreme anxiety. Here, the acute discharge of tension may take the form of choking or nausea.

METHOD: Diagnosis of excessive anxiety is accomplished through classroom observation, psychological testing, or parent and child interviews. In the classroom, high anxiety may cause hyperactivity, short attention span, and distractibility. On psychological testing, the pattern resembles that seen with a hyperkinetic impulse disorder. If children are misdiagnosed as hyperkinetic, Ritalin or Dexedrine will not calm them down. A thorough psychological evaluation can distinguish between anxiety and hyperkinesis. Anxious children usually do not have markedly different verbal and performance IQ scores, whereas hyperkinetic children often show a fifteen-point (or more) IQ difference, as well as having poor visual or auditory perception and soft neurological signs (crossed eyes, mixed laterality, clumsiness, and poor hand-eye coordination). They usually do poorly on the Bender Motor Gestalt Test and the Wepman Auditory Discrimination Test. However, short attention span, distractibility, and hyperactivity are found in both hyperkinetic and anxious children.

The authors see actual or perceived parental rejection as frequently causing anxiety in children. Busy parents may communicate a lack of interest; the child interprets this as rejection that may possibly lead to abandonment. But children may be helped to understand and deal with the reasons for anxiety through a psychodynamic approach that uses the therapist-child relationship in a supportive and interpretive manner. Understanding leads to reduced anxiety within a trusting and confiding relationship. The learning theory approach centers around symptom reduction. After being taught to relax, the child is gradually exposed to more and more anxiety-provoking images. Anxiety diminishes since relaxation is incompatible with anxiety.

CASE STUDIES: A bright but anxious fourth-grade boy was doing poor academic work and had a negative attitude. During testing and interviews, he spoke of being rejected by his family. He saw his father as being too busy to spend any time with him. Poor grades were a means of getting even with his parents for lack of attention. The school psychologist helped the parents see that their son's hostility was due to his feeling of being rejected. Their guilt was handled by explaining to them the difference between actual and perceived rejection. The boy was pleased when his father soon after took him to a football game. In therapy, interpretations were made within the context of a good relationship between the boy and the therapist. The boy came to realize that doing poorly in school to get even with his parents was self-defeating. After six weeks, his grades rose from C's and D's to B's. After one year, his anxiety and hostility were gone, and his academic progress was good.

A bright fifth-grade girl was very anxious about giving oral reports. She couldn't sleep or eat and was nauseous when a report was in prospect. If she had to give a report after lunch, she vomited before giving the report. In five sessions, she was taught how to relax using systematic desensitization. A hierarchy of increasingly anxiety-provoking oral report scenes was imagined. The first scene was thinking about a brief oral report several weeks off. Eventually she had to think about giving a major report for a semester grade the next afternoon. Each time she relaxed until the scene caused no anxiety. Her anxiety greatly decreased, and after six months, she had no anxiety before oral presentations.

COMMENTARY: In a straightforward manner, the authors effectively applied two widely used psychotherapeutic methods in the school. To reduce anxiety, they call for lowering parental rejection (perceived or actual) of the child and using relaxation techniques directly with the child. This is a valuable reminder for school personnel that psychotherapeutic techniques are feasible, effective, and efficient when applied in school. Successful intervention does not require long-term therapy. There has been a trend to refer emotional problems to individual practitioners or mental health clinics. Unfortunately, this has often not been effective and has at times led students to feel alienated from the school. Assistance provided by the school enhances children's perception of the school as a positive, helpful place. Additionally, the authors offer some suggestions for the differentiation of anxiety from hyperkinesis. This distinction is particularly important since it should lead to different treatment approaches (see the section on hyperactivity in Chapter Two).

SOURCE: Doyal, G. T., and Friedman, R. J. "Anxiety in Children: Some Observations for the School Psychologist." *Psychology in the Schools*, 1974, *11*, 161-164.

Reducing Test Anxiety by Psychodrama and Systematic Desensitization

AUTHORS: David A. Kipper and Daniel Giladi

PRECIS: Using a structured type of psychodrama to reduce test anxiety in thirty-six college students

INTRODUCTION: The authors review the wide range of methods for reducing test anxiety. These include systematic desensitization combined with self-study instructions, autogenic relaxation, cue-controlled relaxation, self-counseling with relaxation, covert positive reinforcement, cognitive modification, rational-emotive treatment, implosive therapy, and modeling. Most of these learning theory approaches follow the principle that the client should face the source of anxiety without experiencing the anticipated catastrophic consequences. Although it comes from a different theoretical orientation, psychodrama permits operation of this same principle. In psychodrama, environmental and psychological experiences are simulated. Through acting, clients explore behaviors in a protective learning situation that permits the experiencing of new feelings. New responses that are both appropriate and spontaneous are developed.

METHOD: Participants were twenty-seven female and nine male college students who volunteered for a program to reduce test anxiety. They were assigned to thirteen sessions in one of three groups—systematic desensitization (ten students), structured psychodrama (fourteen), and a waiting-list control group (twelve). Pretesting and posttesting were performed with the Suinn Test Anxiety Behavior Scale and the Neuroticism Scale of the Eysenck Personality Inventory.

Systematic desensitization was accomplished through an adaptation of Wolpe's method for use in small groups (gradually desensitizing anxiety by presenting anxiety-producing images while the individual is relaxed). An introductory session focused on a description of the process and a sharing of test anxiety experiences. Muscular relaxation was directly taught by a counselor. During a two-week break, the students practiced relaxation by using an audiotape. A twenty-item test anxiety hierarchy was prepared, and sessions focused on having participants gradually progress from the least to the most anxiety-provoking item without experiencing anxiety. The counselor read the item, and the students imagined the scene. If all group members could imagine the scene three times for thirty seconds with no anxiety, the next item was begun. Each session began with a rehearsal of the last one or two items desensitized. At the end of each session, a discussion of experiences took place.

Structured psychodrama was a variation of Moreno's classic psychodrama procedure (acting out psychological conflicts through role playing). Instead of spontaneous situations, a structured format was used with each student. As in the desensitization procedure, small groups were used. After one introductory session, two sessions were used to practice techniques. The "empty chair" technique involved speaking to an imaginary person or behavioral quality (fear, anxiety, ambition). A helper then acted out the role of another person or an aspect of the student's personality. Following that, the students exchanged identities and acted out the opposite roles ("role reversal"). This "double" technique involved another student's acting out an aspect of one student's personality (a kind of inner voice). The double more fully expresses the actor's feelings in situations than the actor herself would do. Nonanxious situations (discussing what movie to attend) were used for practice. The same twenty-item hierarchy was used and enacted as in the desensitization group. At times one item (sitting at your desk the evening before the exam) was enacted. When appropriate, items were grouped together (sitting in a room and watching the instructor arrive with the examinations).

Test anxiety (but not neuroticism) was significantly reduced as indicated by the assessment methods and by the subjective evaluation of the students. Systematic desensitization has been the most frequently recommended intervention for test anxiety. In this study, structured psychodrama was equally effective. Psychodrama is thus a treatment alternative that may be more theoretically acceptable to some counselors. The authors point out that psychodrama uses catharsis and spontaneity, which behaviorists usually do not employ. Desensitization uses imagination, whereas psychodrama uses a simulation of anxiety-provoking situations (a type of simulated real-life desensitization).

COMMENTARY: We included this article even though it involved college students because the two methods discussed are applicable to (and have been employed with) children in elementary and high school. Moreover, there are many mental health professionals who have been trained to use psychodynamic methods and who reject learning theory approaches. We think that structured and time-limited psychodrama is an effective and inherently exciting approach to treating test anxiety.

SOURCE: Kipper, D. A., and Giladi, D. "Effectiveness of Structured Psychodrama and Systematic Desensitization in Reducing Test Anxiety." *Journal of Counseling Psychology*, 1978, *25*, 499-505.

Using the Classroom for Desensitization

AUTHORS: Richard J. Kravetz and Steven R. Forness

PRECIS: Reducing speaking anxiety in a six-year-old boy

INTRODUCTION: The authors review the successful use of desensitization for reducing anxiety in children. A hierarchy of increasingly anxiety-provoking situations is introduced in the presence of relaxing or rewarding stimuli until the child can be assertive and unafraid. A six-year-old boy was in a hospital school; psychotherapy and token reinforcement had not resulted in normal verbal communication (he was not speaking at all in his local school).

METHOD: The boy was placed in an "engineered" classroom where he worked on individual assignments and received check marks for completing work and following rules. Check marks could be used to purchase candy or small toys at the end of a week. With encouragement, he was able to read a story to a tape recorder and see how far he could make the volume needle move. However, he was later unable to read the same story in front of the class. Twelve sessions of desensitization were then carried out.

The boy was asked if he liked any heroes. The investigator (working as a classroom aide) reinforced the slight interest he expressed in Paul Bunyan, the legendary lumberjack. During the second session, he read the story of Paul Bunyan. In a discussion with the boy, the following increasingly fearful situations were discovered: reading to the investigator, to a roommate, to two classroom aides, to the teacher and aides, to the teacher, aides, and a few peers, and to the entire class. The most fearful situation involved asking questions or making comments at hospital ward meetings when all children, teachers, and staff were present. During each session, he was deconditioned by one stage. When he performed that behavior in the classroom, he received praise for doing so.

One session is described in detail. The goal of having the child read in front of the teacher and aides was described to them. A half hour before the class, the boy and the investigator went to the study room next to the classroom. The investigator described how big, strong, and assertive Paul Bunyan was. When he was then asked to imagine sitting with the teacher and the aides, the boy appeared distressed. The investigator told him to imagine that his big, strong friend Paul Bunyan was standing next to him and had just told everyone that the boy was his good friend and that they had better pay attention to what the boy was going to say. Next, he told the boy that Paul Bunyan was very interested in hearing him read the story. Further, if he read three pages of the story to the adults, he could play with electric trains during free time. The adults sat in a circle in front of a picture of Paul Bunyan. The boy read, held up the book so they could see the pictures, and answered questions.

The investigator thus used the image of Paul Bunyan to overcome the boy's unassertive behavior. Once he as able to relax during these descriptions, a reward (check marks or free time) was set for actually doing the behavior. After six weeks, he was able to participate, read, and speak freely in all situations. After discharge, he functioned well in a regular classroom.

COMMENTARY: The authors point out (directly in keeping with the philosophy of this book) that desensitization was effectively *combined* with positive reinforcement. Reinforcement alone had not been successful in promoting speech. Helpful to educators is the specific description of how a child's hero was used to desensitize anxiety. In class, the boy studied and drew pictures of Paul Bunyan. In contrast to the boy's unassertiveness, Bunyan's assertive characteristics were stressed. With appropriate consultation, this form of classroom desensitization may be effectively employed by teachers to help children overcome a wide variety of anxiety-provoking situations. Also, this article is a useful reminder to mental health professionals (working within or outside the school) that desensitization should be employed in *conjunction* with teachers. This is essential to ensure that behavior changes in real-life settings and not only in the office.

SOURCE: Kravetz, R. J., and Forness, S. R. "The Special Classroom as a Desensitization Setting." *Exceptional Children,* 1971, *38,* 389-391.

Meditation for Reducing Test Anxiety

AUTHOR: William Linden

PRECIS: Decreasing anxiety and increasing attention by teaching twenty-six third graders to meditate

INTRODUCTION: Meditation trains attention. Ordinary thought is stopped, and people become more aware of their environment and their own experience. Meditation increases electroencephalogram alpha waves, indicating a condition of relaxed alertness. Relaxation, being "in the present," and freeing oneself from distractions lead to the voluntary ability to lower anxiety. The improved attention leads to an increased ability to focus on a "figure" and resist distractions from the "background."

METHOD: Three groups (each with fifteen boys and fifteen girls) were randomly selected from a third-grade class in an economically disadvantaged neighborhood. The groups were meditation, guidance, and control. Three assessment measures were used. The Children's Embedded Figures Test was used to measure "field independence" (clear, systematic, and effective thinking and perceiving). In it children have to visually find a form hidden in a distracting background. Test anxiety was assessed by administration of the Test Anxiety Scale for Children, and reading achievement was measured by the Metropolitan Achievement Test.

A counselor conducted three guidance groups with ten children in each. They met for eighteen weeks for forty-five minutes once a week. The counselor focused on giving information and on how to develop and use good study skills. There were also two meditation groups of fifteen children each that met twice a week for twenty to twenty-five minutes for thirty-six sessions. In line with suggestions in the meditation literature, the room used was dimly lit, with little furniture and few distractions.

The children were told to assume a comfortable position that they could hold without moving. Their job was to pay attention only to themselves. While sitting quietly, they were to pay no attention to any distractions. They were to keep their minds on whatever they experienced. If their minds wandered, they were to gently bring their attention back to their breathing. If they were unable to do the exercise, they were to do nothing to interfere with the others. During a pause, the author asked questions related to the instructions, such as where their attention was and if they had observed their breathing. After initial reluctance, the group became more positive.

The children were able to learn to meditate. As measured by the tests, their test anxiety was reduced, and they showed more "field independence" (did better at picking out a figure from a confusing context). There was no improvement in reading scores. The guidance and control group did not show these gains (there was no difference between those groups). The author believes that the breathing exercise focuses and fixes attention and promotes the ability to ignore background distractions. Also, the children appeared to learn to voluntarily change their anxiety state, possibly by briefly meditating. Rather than anticipating failure or danger, they shifted their attention to their immediate bodily experience.

COMMENTARY: We have successfully used meditation (breathing and counting) to reduce high levels of anxiety in many children and adults. Linden's article lends empirical support to the feasibility of teaching young children to voluntarily focus their attention. This method is also clearly usable with distractible, impulsive children with short attention spans, and it may be used with groups or individuals. All the children in a classroom may well benefit from spending a few minutes per day just sitting and focusing their minds. Important messages are thereby communicated. Children are capable of focusing their own attention, and it is important that they be sensitive to their own bodily experiences.

SOURCE: Linden, W. "Practicing of Meditation by Schoolchildren and Their Levels of Field Dependence-Independence, Test Anxiety, and Reading Achievement." *Journal of Consulting and Clinical Psychology*, 1973, *41*, 139-143.

Desensitizing Anxiety to Improve Reading

AUTHORS: Sarah Denney Muller and Charles H. Madsen, Jr.

PRECIS: Group desensitization or reading placebo for reducing anxiety in twenty-eight seventh graders with reading problems

INTRODUCTION: Systematic desensitization has been successfully used with fearful children and adults, individually and in
groups. The authors believe that anxiety leads to inefficient
reading, and they review a successful real-life desensitization of
the reading problems of an eighth-grade girl. According to them,
real-life desensitization is probably more effective than use of
imagination. In many students, classroom reading is associated
with negative reactions (anxiety).

METHOD: The Children's Manifest Anxiety Scale and a Self-
Report Reading Scale were administered to seventh graders, and
twenty-eight students were selected. Students sat on gymnastic
mats placed next to a wall. Two weekly thirty-minute sessions
were held for a total of twenty sessions. Students were randomly assigned to a desensitization or a reading placebo group.

Students in the *desensitization group* were told that the
tests showed that they tended to become nervous or anxious,
especially when reading aloud, and that they probably didn't
enjoy reading as much as they could and had some reading difficulties. Two thirty-minute sessions would be held each week in
order to help them with these problems. Participation was voluntary and all selected did volunteer. Progressive muscular relaxation was taught for all parts of the body. Each muscle group
was tensed for five to seven seconds and then relaxed. Each session consisted of fifteen minutes of relaxation and presentation
of the following standard fear hierarchy: sitting in a classroom,
studying before reading, going to a reading group, teacher reading to the group, teacher asking a question about the reading,
teacher asking a child to pronounce words, listening to someone
else read aloud, reading aloud, and teacher scolding the child
for a reading mistake. These scenes were described and imagined
by the children. The final step involved actually reading aloud
(real-life desensitization). Students kept their eyes closed for
the whole session, except of course when reading aloud. The
last seven sessions included reading aloud for increasingly longer
times.

The *reading placebo training* group listened to the same
introductory remarks as the desensitization group had. Stories
were read to them for the same amount of time as the other

group. They also read short stories (from the Science Research Associates Reading Laboratory III kit) aloud during the last seven sessions.

Since both groups were equally effective in reducing reading anxiety (it was reduced much more in them than in a no-contact control group), muscular relaxation did not result in greater anxiety reduction. Although anxious, the students were able to perform the real-life rehearsal of reading aloud. Students commented that when the adult read to them, they came to realize that there was nothing to fear and that reading aloud could be fun. The authors report that the students objected to sitting on mats and that comfortable chairs should be used. Of the twenty-eight students, twenty-six reported that they had benefited from the study. There were indications that there was generalization of fear reduction to other activities, such as participating in sports and camp-outs and giving reports in class.

COMMENTARY: As the authors indicate, a very striking finding was that muscular relaxation did not increase the effectiveness of desensitization. This suggests that behavioral rehearsal (reading aloud to a small group) should be the first (and maybe the only) step necessary to reduce reading anxiety. Also, as in other reports, group desensitization was effective. The fact that individual sessions are not necessary, allows for a more effective and efficient use of staff time. This study is directly in line with the many reports of the success of a gradual step-by-step increased actual exposure to any anxiety-producing situation.

SOURCE: Muller, S. D., and Madsen, C. H., Jr. "Group Desensitization for Anxious Children with Reading Problems." *Psychology in the Schools,* 1970, 7, 184-189.

Relaxation Through Yoga

AUTHORS: Gary Seiler and Kathleen Renshaw

PRECIS: Tension reduction and stress prevention by practicing yoga in the classroom

INTRODUCTION: Research indicates that yoga can reduce tension, relieve stress, improve vitality, increase calmness, and produce a sense of well-being. When a classroom atmosphere appears tense, practicing hatha yoga can lead to a relaxed and refreshed feeling in class members. The authors discuss the high incidence of stress-related problems, including hypertension and cardiovascular and gastrointestinal illnesses. Stress reduction is sought through the use of cigarettes and alcohol, with negative side effects and no alleviation of stress.

METHOD: Yoga is an ancient practice with a great deal of research support for its effective therapeutic value. It is composed of a series of psychophysiological methods that combat and prevent tension and fatigue. In the Western world most people practice hatha yoga (the other four branches are karma, bhakti, jnana, and raja). Hatha yoga involves physical postures or exercises, breath control, mental concentration, and deep relaxation. The natural self-regulating tendency of the organism is enhanced. Rather than being a physically fatiguing exercise, yoga affects the nervous system and endocrine glands and increases energy. The authors believe that it is beneficial even to practice part of the yoga system for a few minutes a day. The system is readily adaptable for children. They point out that yoga is not a religion but a system of self-realization. A state of awareness is reached in which one controls one's mind and feelings rather than being controlled by them. A person does not have to be in very good physical condition to do yoga, and it is as beneficial to the fragile, shy child as it is to the aggressive bully.

A table is presented listing the benefits of yoga and how it works. Some selected excerpts follow. Body awareness is increased and tension decreased by stretching and breathing.

Stamina, energy, and health are promoted by increased lung capacity, better circulation, and stimulation of internal organs. Concentration and attention span are improved by focusing on breathing and increasing the oxygen supply. Children of any age can learn to achieve deep states of relaxation. While their muscles are being strengthened, children learn to distinguish between tense and relaxed muscles. Renshaw has reported observable positive changes in the attitude and behavior of adolescents in an inpatient psychiatric unit who practiced yoga for half-hour sessions twice a week (K. Renshaw, "Adolescent Yoga Program," Unpublished manuscript, Las Vegas Mental Health Center, 1977). Less hyperactivity, more appropriate behavior, and better communication were reported. Preadolescent awkwardness is diminished by the poise, balance, and coordination developed through yoga. Also, yoga makes it possible to resist childhood diseases more effectively.

In school, yoga may be useful to both teachers and counselors. Students learn to cope with stress and relax. Less hyperactivity, increased attention span, and tension reduction are possible benefits. Preventing tension and coping effectively with stress also lower susceptibility to disease. Practicing yoga, and using it when experiencing stress, will prevent an episode of stress from leading to more and more anxiety and tension.

The authors suggest that readers consult books on yoga, and they cite recent works. They also suggest the following procedure: Students should each have a yoga towel, and there should be regular yoga class breaks. The room should be quiet, each student should have ample floor space and the teacher should quietly demonstrate the postures. The teacher must also be aware of any student's physical limitations. Respect for limitations, acceptance of differences, and noncompetitiveness should be emphasized. The authors suggest the following beginning exercises for children—"balloon," "tree," "paper clip," "cobra," "locust combination," and "sponge." Children enjoy the exercises and often say that it makes them feel good. They find yoga to be interesting, and they enjoy imitating animals.

COMMENTARY: This article suggests that yoga is beneficial for many different problems (tension, hyperactivity, poor concentration, psychosomatic problems, and so on). Clearly, yoga may be employed as both a preventative of and a cure for anxiety. The authors call for the practice of yoga by children in schools. Educational personnel who are experienced might conduct yoga breaks in their own classrooms. It would be relatively easy for a teacher, a volunteer, or a hired yoga instructor to conduct yoga exercises in the school. There have been many reports of group exercises being relaxing and beneficial in Chinese schools and business places. The noncompetitive nature of yoga might make it a useful and widely acceptable method for individual psychophysiological improvement.

SOURCE: Seiler, G., and Renshaw, K. "Yoga for Kids." *Elementary School Guidance and Counseling*, 1978, *12*, 229-238.

Psychogenic Illness in the Schools

AUTHOR: Virginia M. Thompson

PRECIS: Relieving stress by promoting security, being supportive, and providing a school mental health program for effectively coping with anxiety

INTRODUCTION: The author distinguishes three classes of psychogenic illness. The malingerer consciously pretends to be ill in order to escape such activities as going to school or taking a test. The fact that "symptoms" seem to disappear as soon as the school day begins or the test is over reveals the child's real motives. The child with hypochondriasis does not necessarily complain of sickness but constantly worries that he or she may be seriously ill. Older children are more likely to behave this way than younger ones. While some may use this tactic to avoid school or other events, hypochondriasis may also be a reaction to stress or an expression of unsatisfied emotional needs. However, the most serious of the psychogenic disorders are psychosomatic illnesses. These are actual physical conditions often caused by stress or tension. Asthma, ulcers, and migraine headaches are some of the many physical disorders believed to be influenced by emotional stress. They usually require both medical and psychological treatment.

Research has demonstrated a strong relationship between stress and physical reactions. Sweating and increased breathing are examples of the body's response to everyday tension. However, when the child's needs for order, safety, and belonging are threatened, intense fear builds and psychogenic illness may result. For example, one child may be upset by the presence of a substitute teacher, while a visit to a divorced parent can threaten another child's feelings of belonging. In a third, a poor grade may validate feelings of worthlessness and result in escape through illness.

RECOMMENDATIONS: With proper guidelines, school personnel can minimize the stress that leads to psychogenic illness.

First, teachers can promote feelings of security and belonging in the classroom while still challenging students academically. The tone of the class should communicate acceptance, and the teacher should be consistent and reliable.

Second, both the physical arrangement of the room and the schedule of activities should be ordered, even if change is necessary at times.

Third, support for a child (and his parents) during periods of increased stress may prevent the fears that lead to psychogenic illness. This support may be expressed in verbal reassurances or through an offer of help if it is needed.

Fourth, a school mental health program is necessary to teach children about the physical and emotional changes that they inevitably experience as they grow. This knowledge can prepare them to cope more effectively with problems and stresses.

Fifth, once psychogenic symptoms occur, the school nurse must try to identify the contributing factors. Learning difficulties, family chaos, social failure, and/or emotional problems may all play a role. A medical evaluation may be necessary to determine the degree of physical causation. The nurse may have developed relationships with many students and might use this rapport to help the child understand the reasons for his or her complaint. Together they might examine the pattern and frequency of the child's visits to the health office. Perhaps the child leaves certain classes for obvious reasons. These issues can be explored with the child. Such guidance can help students begin to face their problems and help lay the groundwork for long-term counseling.

COMMENTARY: The author argues that psychogenic disorders should not be interpreted as a sure sign of emotional disturbance. To help the child, school health specialists should work as a team to identify and treat the sources of stress that create the problem. By discussing psychogenic illness from the school's perspective, this article makes a valuable contribution. There are few, if any, discussions in the literature about this problem, even though it is not an uncommon one.

SOURCE: Thompson, V. M. "The School Nurse Looks at Psychogenic Illnesses." *Journal of School Health*, 1977, *47*, 519-521.

Additional Readings

Bower, E. M. "The Modification, Mediation, and Utilization of Stress During the School Years." *American Journal of Orthopsychiatry*, 1964, *34*, 667-674.

Anxiety-producing situations in school should not be avoided but should be used to help students develop immunity to stress. Teachers should anticipate normal crises and aid students to cope more effectively with them. Specific steps are discussed to make the first school experience more productive. Junior high school study classes are recommended for students to learn more about appreciating and communicating with young children—mainly so they will learn more about human behavior and themselves. Game playing is suggested as a means of increasing children's awareness of rules and their general coping ability.

Hendel, D. D., and Davis, S. O. "Effectiveness of an Intervention Strategy for Reducing Mathematics Anxiety." *Journal of Counseling Psychology*, 1978, *25*, 429-434.

Mathematics anxiety leads to poor performance and avoidance of math, especially in females. A counseling support group was formed to reduce anxiety in women returning to college. Techniques used included bibliotherapy (assigning appropriate reading materials that can serve to reduce anxiety), cognitive restructuring (changing what people say to themselves), keeping a math diary, weekly goal setting for math, learning study skills, assertiveness training related to asking questions, desensitization relaxation exercises (learning to relax muscles and feel calm), and math games.

Jaffe, P. G., and Carlson, P. M. "Modeling Therapy for Test Anxiety: The Role of Model Affect and Consequences." *Behavior Research and Therapy*, 1972, *10*, 329-339.

Test anxiety was effectively reduced in twenty-four college students by having them observe models taking tests. Contrary to results in past studies, viewing anxious models led to better grades, and viewing negative consequences led to less self-reported test anxiety. The authors speculate that viewing anxiety or negative consequences is similar to implosive therapy, in which clients are asked to imagine very terrifying scenes to alleviate their anxiety.

Leffingwell, R. J. "Misbehavior in the Classroom—Anxiety, a Possible Cause." *Education*, 1977, *97*, 360-363.

Maladaptive behavior is often caused by anxious reactions to test taking, speaking in front of a group, or being evaluated. Signs of classroom anxiety include hand wringing, twisting hair, squirming, inappropriate laughing, rationalizations, and withdrawing. The author makes specific suggestions to reduce classroom anxiety, such as more adequate preparation by the student, clearer guidelines by the teacher, and helping students set more realistic goals. The teacher should serve as a sincere, interested, nonthreatening model. Failure should be minimized by using several criteria for grading, giving several tests, and dropping the lowest test grade.

Mann, J. "Vicarious Desensitization of Test Anxiety Through Observation of Videotaped Treatment." *Journal of Counseling Psychology*, 1972, *19*, 1-7.

Test anxiety was significantly lowered and timed reading was improved for eighty seventh and eighth graders. Students viewed a test-anxious peer being desensitized by the author for six forty-five minute semiweekly sessions. While relaxed, the student imagined increasingly anxiety-provoking scenes; these ranged from the announcement of a future examination to bringing home a poor test to his parents. Three different treatment conditions did not alter the effectiveness of the basic vicarious desensitization and modeling approach (observing the tape). This method is economical and efficient. The author suggests that observing a desensitization tape without also viewing the time-consuming relaxation period does not reduce the technique's effectiveness.

Meichenbaum, P. H. "Cognitive Modification of Test-Anxious College Students." *Journal of Consulting & Clinical Psychology*, 1972, *39*, 370-380.

Insight-oriented therapy (more awareness of anxiety-producing thoughts) was combined with a modified desensitization procedure (coping imagery to handle anxiety and self-instruction to be attentive and not ruminate). Students were taught to make task-relevant statements to themselves and practice relaxation. They imagined themselves studying appropriately and relaxing, while breathing evenly and deeply if they became anxious. Test anxiety was significantly reduced as indicated by test performance, self-reports, and improved grades.

Miller, N., and Kassinove, H. "Effects of Lecture, Rehearsal, Written Homework, and IQ on the Efficacy of a Rational-Emotive School Mental Health Program." *Journal of Community Psychology*, 1978, *6*, 366-373.

A rational-emotive approach was successfully taught to ninety-six fourth-grade children for twelve daily one-hour sessions. Twelve irrational beliefs of schoolchildren were dispelled. These beliefs fall into three categories: exaggeration of reality ("awfulizing"); "shoulds, oughts, and musts"; and blaming self and others. Rational-emotive lectures were combined with behavior rehearsal and completing homework assignments. Irrational thinking, neuroticism, and trait anxiety all decreased significantly.

Parish, T. S., Buntman, A. D., and Buntman, S. R. "Effect of Counterconditioning on Test Anxiety as Indicated by Digit Span Performance." *Journal of Educational Psychology,* 1976, *68,* 297-299.

Pairing pictures of classroom scenes with positive words reduced test anxiety in twenty-three fifth and sixth graders. A neutral word was shown on a slide, then a school-related scene, and finally a positive word—each for five seconds. Therefore, classical conditioning can be used to lower anxiety and enhance school performance.

Robinson, C. M. "Developmental Counseling Approach to Death and Dying Education." *Elementary School Guidance and Counseling,* 1978, *12,* 178-187.

A program is described for discussing death and dying in order to reduce anxiety and eliminate irrational ideas and fears. The course is required for all seventh graders for seven and one-half weeks, fifty-five minutes every day. Activities used include films about dying, value interviews, role playing, discussing personal experiences, guest interviews, and writing a personal obituary.

Stanton, H. E. "Music and Test Anxiety: Further Evidence for an Interaction." *British Journal of Educational Psychology,* 1975, *45,* 80-82.

A slow movement of a Mozart symphony was played for college students. Test anxiety was reduced when music was played while students entered the room, sat down, and were given instructions. Music during the examination did not further facilitate performance, nor did it interfere with performance. Music appears to have a relaxing effect for highly anxious students.

Tobias, S. "Anxiety Research in Educational Psychology." *Journal of Educational Psychology,* 1979, *71,* 573-582.

This is a thorough and practical review of minimizing anxiety by modifying educational materials or by using test anxiety reduction methods. Materials should be reduced in difficulty level and increased in clarity of organization. The need to rely on memory should also be reduced. Methods reviewed to diminish anxiety include systematic desensitization, relaxation, self-control training, cognitive coping skills, (positive self-statements replace negative self-references), modeling, and vicarious observation of desensitization.

Wine, J. D. "Test Anxiety and Evaluation Threat: Children's Behavior in the Classroom." *Journal of Abnormal Child Psychology,* 1979, 7, 45-59.

Expecting an examination led to various effects on the behavior of fourth graders. Some children worked harder, asked for evaluations of their work from peers and the teacher, and became less fidgety. However, test-anxious children became less task-oriented (sat idly, appeared preoccupied, and were less attentive). Test anxiety is associated with caution, constriction, and a passive orientation. Therefore, cognitive methods for reducing test anxiety are more appropriate than approaches designed for emotional disorders.

Phobias

Phobias are exaggerated, irrational fears of an object, a class of objects, or certain situations. Feared situations are carefully avoided. Some feared objects (such as snakes) can be avoided without interference with daily activities. Other fears are more debilitating and reduce the child's opportunity for positive contacts with the environment. Bodily injury phobias, animal phobias, or noise phobias can greatly curtail a child's activities. Phobias are more prevalent in girls than in boys. Combinations of methods have effectively eliminated phobias. Techniques used include insight therapy, implosive therapy, and especially various forms of "brave models." In school and out, a widely used method is the gradual approach to feared situations while in a nonanxious state. This includes systemative desensitization and counterconditioning.

The most prevalent problem is school phobia. Children refuse to attend school and react with physical and emotional distress when in school. Somatic symptoms of nausea, stomachaches, and dizziness are typical. Dread about something in school is often combined with separation anxiety about leaving home. Children are often overly dependent and resentful toward parents (usually the mother), and their anxiety and ambivalence become displaced onto the school. Going to school may be equivalent to losing mother, while staying home is inadvertently reinforced by mother. School phobias are frequently categorized as acute or chronic, with an acute phobia calling for an immediate return of the child to school and parent counseling, and a chronic phobia requiring an intense intervention such as family psychotherapy. Incidence for true school phobia is approximately 2 percent, and it peaks between the ages of six and ten years. Aside from the methods mentioned above, schools have begun to systematically attempt to make school attendance more rewarding and staying home less gratifying. Attendance contracts with specific rewards and punishments have been employed. Rapid return of the child to school is widely recommended.

Rehabilitating School-Phobic Adolescents

AUTHOR: Constantine J. G. Cretekos

PRECIS: Two case reports illustrating rapid return to school, parent involvement, and use of an attendance contract

INTRODUCTION: Mildly neurotic elementary school children have been forcibly returned to school with success. But the author sees a need for a different approach with adolescents who exhibit "characterological school refusal." They are extremely anxious in school and usually have a history of anxiety in other situations. While in school, they become more and more anxious and fear being psychologically annihilated. The author suggests that a clinician can negotiate an attendance contract with adolescents while they maintain grade-level work, strive toward return to full-time school, and receive individual or family therapy. The attendance contract may involve daily tutoring with the regular teacher, a shortened school day (anywhere from fifteen minutes to three hours), or spending time in the principal's or counselor's office. Given the student's anxiety level, the clinician assesses what would be a reasonable amount of time for him or her to spend in school. Once the contract is drawn, it can only be changed by the agreement of all participants. The attitude strived for is an optimistic expectation for adolescents to spend as much time as possible in school even if they feel extremely ill.

METHOD: A thirteen-year-old boy had a long history of difficulty in attending school. He complained of blurred vision, fitful and short sleep periods, vomiting, and abdominal pains. Recent attendance was characterized by his being in school for one day and then missing two weeks. The author asked him how long he could stay in school in spite of feeling sick. The boy's response of four hours was seen as too demanding, and a compromise of two hours was suggested. After discussion, they agreed on school attendance from 8:30 to 11:15 A.M. The school guidance counselor then tried to reduce the teachers' hostility toward the boy for missing school so often. The counselor successfully explained his problems, and the teachers became more cooperative and willing to praise his attempts at consistent attendance. Additionally, the counselor helped arrange for him to obtain any academic work that he missed. He soon wanted to increase time in school, but the author suggested caution. In four weeks, they lengthened his school day to 1:00 P.M. and to a full day after another two weeks. The changed attitude of the teachers was instrumental in the boy's quick progress.

The author discusses situations where children panic when forced to attend school. He suggests home visits by the teacher and a few peers, who can encourage the child to return to school with them or to attend the next day. This permits the child to interact with people in his own home. Visits are most effective if they occur very soon after a child's refusal to attend school.

A home visit was effectively used with a twelve-year-old who was terrified of school and often became hysterical when forced to go to school. He frequently refused to go to school and had a history of fear of school and periodic absences. He constantly worried about school and was especially bothered during the lunch period and playground activities. His mother always had to drive him to and from school. He refused to discuss an attendance contract or see the author, who told him that he had to choose to be seen either at home or at school. Reluctantly, he agreed to office visits on a twice-weekly basis. An arrangement was made with the teachers and principal for individual tutoring by his teachers in all subjects. He participated in the tutoring sessions for the rest of the year but refused to have any other contact with adults or peers.

Next year, he was placed in a class for socially and emotionally disturbed children. He attended but was very anxious, and tranquilizing drugs were prescribed. He often left school after a few hours because of his panic reactions. On a day when he refused to attend school, the teacher and all class members visited him. While holding his dog for emotional support, he listened to his peers, who urged him to return to school. After a half hour, he returned to school and was not absent again. Gradually, he returned to regular classes. Follow-up revealed that he could now easily separate from his mother, that he had made a few close friends, and that he was attending school regularly.

The author sees an attendance contract as respecting an adolescent's need for independence. The student participates in determining a reasonable program for school attendance at a tolerable level of anxiety while therapy proceeds. As the student becomes more comfortable with partial attendance, time in school is increased. This technique is only effective with highly anxious students who want to attend school. Home visits are a clear demonstration of the interest and empathy of others.

COMMENTARY: The author describes a practical approach for returning highly fearful young adolescents to school. School personnel should find the concepts of an attendance contract and home visits to be useful alternatives in responding quickly to a student's refusal to attend school. This article is in keeping with the growing trend to consider and alter as many aspects of the environment as possible. The attitudes of parents and teachers are crucial, and the time spent in enlisting their aid is well worth it. Interestingly, the author suggests that caution may have to be used with anxious adolescents. They may have to be slowed up in their eagerness to return to full-time attendance before they have become desensitized and have overcome the underlying cause of their fear of school.

SOURCE: Cretekos, C. J. G. "Some Techniques in Rehabilitating the School-Phobic Adolescent." *Adolescence*, 1977, *12*, 237-246.

Natural Consequences and a Makeup Period for Eliminating School Phobia

AUTHORS: Daniel M. Doleys and Sam C. Williams

PRECIS: Cooperation between parents and school personnel for returning a phobic seven-year-old boy to school

INTRODUCTION: School phobia is characterized by refusal to attend school and by reactions of physical distress and disruptive behavior when the child approaches or is in school. From a behavioral viewpoint, avoidance behavior and the accompanying emotional responses result from the school's having acquired negative attributes for the child. The school may be seen as a form of punishment (academic failure or verbal or physical abuse from others), or positive reinforcement at home may be interrupted when the child goes to school (a form of time-out). To change this situation, school personnel should make being in school more reinforcing than being out of school.

METHOD: A seven-year-old boy was suspended from school for being disruptive. He refused to go to school with his mother, and only went if his father took him. In school, he would cry and try to leave. Return to school was effected by "successive approximations." To reduce the negative qualities of school, he was allowed to play inside or outside after 3 P.M. Then, he was taken to school at 2 P.M. and told to remain for the rest of the school day. Time in school was increased by taking him at 12 noon, 10 A.M., and then 8 A.M. Each Monday, he was taken at the same time that he began on the preceding Friday. Time increases occurred only when he had completed three consecutive days without a disruptive incident.

    School personnel acted as monitors and positive reinforcers. Quietness and work behaviors were praised. If the boy cried or became disruptive, his parents were called after he had been warned once. School personnel were not to remove him from class or discipline him in any way. If he was disruptive when one of his parents arrived, he was removed from the classroom and given two firm spanks and sent to a small room. He could return to class if he became quiet within ten minutes. If not, he was taken home and restricted to his room with no toys for the rest of the day. He could leave his room only by attending a makeup period at school. The make-up period, which took place after school or during the next morning, consisted of his quietly cleaning the classroom. This period prevented him from reducing school time by being disruptive, and the cleaning was used as an undesirable activity. He could go home only if he was quiet for the last ten minutes of the makeup period. At home, the parents were instructed to change their behavior. A list (reinforcement menu) was made of the positive consequences for the boy. This included watching television, playing outside or with toys, and so on. Each day that he remained in school without his parents having to come, he could choose one item. His two favorite activities (riding a minibike and visiting his grandparents) were withheld until he attended school full time.

The authors present a table showing the incidents that occurred and at what times. Within sixteen days, the boy was back in school full time. He was spanked by his parents four times and attended three makeup periods. A four-month follow-up revealed regular school attendance, acceptable academic performance, and no disruptive behavior.

The authors believe that the child's phobic and disruptive behavior was inadvertently strengthened by release from school (negative reinforcement) and by being allowed to play at home (positive reinforcement). In another popular treatment approach, children are forced to stay in school regardless of their behavior. In the approach described here, however, school attendance is permitted only when behavior is appropriate, and this weakens the association between being in school and being disruptive. Rather than school personnel becoming more negative to the child, the parents administered the punishment. The makeup period is not recommended as a standard procedure and was only used because forced school attendance had not previously been effective.

COMMENTARY: As in other approaches to school problems, the authors used several methods here. In some instances, any one method might be successful. However, it is clear that the guiding principle was to make attending school more positive than not attending school. This is a useful reminder, since avoiding school and staying at home are very pleasurable to most children. Immediate parent involvement can be very effective. In this study, the parents served to remove the child from class, punish him, and reward appropriate behavior. This model could be very helpful for improving other problem behaviors. There are many studies that have demonstrated parental reinforcement of any appropriate school behavior to be a very powerful tool. This requires the time and energy for working with parents, especially with the more difficult families in which child management has not been successful at home. The school can become a positive resource both for improving school behavior and offering parents guidelines for helping their child.

SOURCE: Doleys, D. M., and Williams, S. C. "The Use of Natural Consequences and a Makeup Period to Eliminate School-Phobic Behavior: A Case Study." *Journal of School Psychology*, 1977, *15*, 44-50.

==========

Paraprofessional Treatment of School Phobia

AUTHORS: Arnold LeUnes and Sandra Siemsglusz

PRECIS: Using a college student to help a very fearful fourteen-year-old girl return to school

INTRODUCTION: In a school phobia, the school often serves as a focal point for the child's high level of anxiety. School brings out personal and social inadequacies. Often, the child is overprotected by a passive father and a dominant mother. Separation anxiety is fostered by the mother's subtle reinforcement of sickness, dependency, and not attending school. Anticipating going to school frequently makes these children nauseous (or causes them to actually vomit), while their health is fine on

weekends or holidays. They are usually socially inadequate, unassertive, and underachievers. But if action is taken quickly,
results are usually good.

METHOD: A fourteen-year-old girl had poor grades and had
missed fifty out of the first ninety school days. Parental threats,
bribes, spankings, and giving in to her demands had no effect.
She was often sick and screamed, kicked, fought, and vomited
before going to school. Her self-concept was poor (in spite of
the fact that she could be attractive and pleasant), and she had
few friends. The authors point out that previous assignment of a
homebound teacher reinforced the child's refusal to attend
school. Also, when she returned to school, a nurse unwisely sent
her home because of menstrual cramps. At this point, a college
student in a psychology course was assigned as a volunteer paraprofessional to work with the girl.

After a consultation, the volunteer was told to get the girl
to return to school and keep her there. The volunteer bought a
pin and a pennant, both stating "I am Somebody." For one
month, she picked the girl up and drove her to school, in spite
of begging, crying, and threats of vomiting. This removed the
parents from the conflict over school. For the first week, the
volunteer obtained permission to be somewhat late in getting to
school and drove the girl on scenic tours. This served to desensitize her fears. After school, they went to an ice-cream parlor
and discussed recent events. Role playing, supportive help, and
monitoring school progress were employed in therapy. The girl
also participated in brief group therapy.

After two months, her attendance was perfect, her grades
had improved, and the volunteer stopped driving her to and
from school. Teachers, counselor, and nurse all reported observable improvement in her behavior. However, she remained
relatively quiet and withdrawn. Further paraprofessional involvement was planned to improve her social assertiveness and
peer relationships.

COMMENTARY: This article serves to point out the value of
using paraprofessionals with children and adolescents. There are
many labels for such helpers—companionship therapists, volun-

teers, big brothers or sisters, aides, and so on. Paraprofessionals have been successfully employed with a wide range of behavior problems. The volunteer in this case devised her own strategies for bolstering the girl's self-confidence and for lessening her early morning anxiety about school. When using volunteers, most professionals plan strategies and carefully supervise the volunteers' interventions on a weekly basis. Simply put, teenagers and young adults can serve as competent models for fearful, inadequate, or withdrawn children to emulate.

SOURCE: LeUnes, A., and Siemsglusz, S. "Paraprofessional Treatment of School Phobia in a Young Adolescent Girl." *Adolescence*, 1977, *12*, 115-121.

An Overview of School Phobias

AUTHORS: James E. McDonald and George Sheperd

PRECIS: Theories, subtypes, and outcomes of treating school phobias

INTRODUCTION: School phobia is a more complex neurosis than school truancy. The anxiety of phobic children is intense, and their behavior is restricting and socially embarrassing. School attendance is characterized by irrational fears and acute anxiety; phobic children often dread something in school and fear separation from home. Dizziness, nausea, and stomachaches are typical somatic complaints. The seriousness of this problem may be seen by the consequences of not attending school— delayed learning, poor academic performance, and poor peer relations.

OVERVIEW: Psychodynamically, anxiety (especially concerning separation from home) becomes displaced on the school. School-phobic children often have high needs to excel but become apprehensive when facing school challenges and demands. Home serves as a source of comfort and gratification. In contrast, learning theorists see school situations as becoming fearful through conditioning. By remaining home, children avoid the anxiety associated with school. They receive secondary reinforcement through parental attention, toys, and television viewing. Anxiety may be expressed in many ways, such as crying, withdrawal, irritability, worry about harm to a family member, sleeplessness, and apprehension. Psychosomatic symptoms include abdominal pain, diarrhea, nausea, earaches, headaches, muscle spasms, enuresis, and dysmenorrhea. Family patterns are characterized by interdependence, isolation from the community, immature marital relationships, preoccupation with death and separation, and clinging mother-child relationships.

School phobia and truancy should be recognized as different entities. School-phobic children are extremely anxious and have somatic complaints. Also, upon fleeing school they go straight home, while the truant usually remains away from home. The authors present a table that shows the various ways that school phobias have been classified. "Mild acute school refusal" is quickly and effectively treated when there is good cooperation between school and home. Older children with "severe chronic school refusal" usually have a generally maladaptive personality. Individual therapy and family counseling are recommended for them.

"Separation anxiety" is a concept that has been proposed by a number of theorists. Mother and child have a mutually hostile and dependent relationship in which both may fear separation and abandonment. Psychoanalysts see symbiotic mother-child relationships as causing school phobias. Children become overly dependent upon overly protective mothers, and the anxiety and resentment of these children become displaced on the school. According to learning theorists, school phobia is a learned maladaptive pattern of behavior. A disturbed mother threatens to reject or abandon her child, who associates going to school with losing mother. Staying home from school is reinforced by fear reduction, pleasurable activities, and maternal attention.

METHODS: Treatment approach depends upon the type and severity of the problem and the theoretical orientation of the therapist. However, early return to school is agreed upon by all as being necessary. Psychoanalytically oriented approaches focus upon improving the insight and ego strength of patients and restoring family equilibrium. Individual therapy for the mother is indicated due to her hostility, inner conflicts, and dependency. Psychodynamic treatment has been concerned with the role of all family members. Children have unrealistic self-concepts, and poor school attendance is often related to family power struggles. Insight therapy tries to change parental attitudes and the child's self-image, while at the same time reducing the fear of school.

Learning theorists provide objective interventions to reduce fear and avoidance of school and to lessen separation anxiety. Adaptive responses are induced by contingent reinforcement. Positive reinforcement follows the adaptive response (operant conditioning). Also, the child is reinforced for each small step toward returning to school (shaping). There is a gradual exposure to feared situations. Another approach is systematic desensitization; in it, the child learns to relax while listening to threatening situations. From least to most threatening, the child (while relaxing) becomes less anxious to imagined or real situations. An alternative is to pair an enjoyable activity with the feared situation (counterconditioning). The pleasurable reactions gradually overcome the fearful responses. Finally, anxiety may be diminished by presenting vivid, scary scenes (implosive therapy). Children experience intense anxiety with no dire consequences, and the anxiety response is dramatically reduced.

Treatment outcomes and follow-up studies are reported. Desensitization (both imagined and in real life) was successfully used to eliminate a ten-year-old boy's fear of school, death, and separation from mother. While relaxed, he imagined scenes of going closer and closer to school. Then, gradual steps were taken to go to school and then remain in school for longer and longer periods. Other cases from the literature are presented to illustrate the successful use of parental reinforcement along with classical and operant conditioning. Favorable outcomes and successful follow-ups are reported.

COMMENTARY: The authors call for educators to be quick to recognize and obtain immediate help for school-phobic children. They favor interdisciplinary learning theory approaches, which lead to stable adaptive behavior. These behavioral methods are seen as being economical, reliable, and efficient. In spite of their preference, they also provide a very useful overview (including easy-to-read tables) of different approaches. In our view, there is a growing professional awareness that different types of problems do indeed require different forms of intervention. In some cases, intensive but brief psychodynamic family therapy may be dramatically successful. This occurs when there are conflicts, hostility, dependency, and power struggles among family members. Combinations of methods are now being employed much more frequently than in the past. The child can be desensitized and the parents simultaneously counseled, while the teacher uses positive reinforcement in the classroom.

SOURCE: McDonald, J. E., and Sheperd, G. "School Phobia: An Overview." *Journal of School Psychology,* 1976, *14,* 291-306.

Implosive Therapy for a Bodily Injury Phobia

AUTHORS: Thomas H. Ollendick and Gerald E. Gruen

PRECIS: Two sessions for reducing symptoms of sleeplessness, hives, and asthma in an eight-year-old boy

INTRODUCTION: Although anxiety-producing situations can be avoided, the fear associated with the situations remains. Implosive therapy focuses on extinguishing these conditioned stimuli (situations). The original traumatic events are recreated by having clients imagine scenes. Sights, sounds, and smells are imagined with intense anxiety, which diminishes as the clients realize that nothing is really happening to them. This reduced anxiety generalizes to real life, and there is no longer any need to avoid that situation. Implosive therapy has been successfully used with adults, and a successful application was reported with a thirteen-year-old school-phobic boy.

METHOD: In the present study, an eight-year-old had many fears and was afflicted with hives, asthmatic bronchitis, and sleepless nights. Of primary concern was his fear of bleeding to death from a bodily injury. His fear began at three and one-half years when a sister was born with a disease that prevented her blood from clotting. He was afraid of the dark, storms, bugs, monsters, and being alone. Psychological testing revealed average intelligence, a poor self-concept, and hostile feelings.

Two implosive therapy sessions were held one week apart. He was asked to vividly imagine the described scenes and then to say how he felt. Each scene was continued until there was a visible reduction in anxiety. An example is given in which he trips, hits his head, and blood trickles all over him. While he is crying and lost, hundreds of rats bite him and tear pieces of flesh off him. After each session, the therapist assured him that he was fine and taught him how to relax. At home, he marked a calendar with a green X when he slept well and a red X when he had trouble sleeping. His parents were told to compliment him for green X's and ignore red ones.

During both sessions, the boy was extremely anxious, wept, trembled, screamed, and tried to leave. At the end of each session, he was physically and emotionally exhausted. His parents were warned that at first he might have more sleep problems, which he did. However, his sleep gradually improved. He played more with his sister and was reportedly having more fun in school. After six months, no problems with hives or asthma occurred.

COMMENTARY: The authors believe that children are good candidates for implosive therapy since they are usually highly suggestible (especially between eight and fourteen years of age).

This study is presented for three reasons. First, it is a good example of an effective use of a specific technique. Alternative techniques are important, especially when progress is not being made with more traditional approaches. Second, since it was successfully used with a case of severe school phobia, this method may be useful for other fears typically occurring in school. Many children are quite fearful of being physically hurt, embarrassed, or teased. Third, it is an economical, quick method that may be employed by a trained mental health professional at school or in the community.

SOURCE: Ollendick, T. H., and Gruen, G. E. "Treatment of a Bodily Injury Phobia with Implosive Therapy." *Journal of Consulting and Clinical Psychology*, 1972, *38*, 389-393.

Desensitizing School Fears

AUTHORS: H. Thompson Prout and John R. Harvey

PRECIS: Illustrating that desensitization procedures are most effective when combined with other techniques in treating school phobias and other academic anxieties

INTRODUCTION: A variety of fears and anxieties interfere with school learning and performance. When the principles of reciprocal inhibition are applied, however, an anxiety-provoking situation is weakened by being paired with a response that is antagonistic to anxiety. Systematic desensitization typically employs deep muscle relaxation with increasingly anxiety-provoking imagined scenes.

SCHOOL PHOBIA: Each year, 17 out of every 1000 schoolchildren refuse to go to school. The authors present a variety of past studies in which this problem was addressed. Traditional systematic desensitization has been successfully used with separation anxiety. One study dealing with a variety of phobias effectively used desensitization, removal of secondary gains, and training in coping and assertive behaviors. A 13-year-old school-phobic girl was helped by combining desensitization (which did not lead to school return) with parental reinforcement of school-approach behaviors. Another study reported that social praise and consumable reinforcers were necessary to reward participation in treatment. When an inarticulate nine-year-old boy could not respond to desensitization, a real-life desensitization approach worked. Gradual approaches were used. After the boy first walked to school on Sunday with the therapist, tokens were then used to maintain regular attendance.

Other studies have successfully used variations of real-life desensitization. A 13-year-old-boy would not attend school and was very fearful of literature and math classes. Implosive therapy was effectively used: the boy vividly imagined being in a darkened classroom while being physically and verbally abused by peers. In another instance, an eight-year-old girl imagined her hero being afraid of and not going to school. Using "emotive imagery," she was told to imagine herself reassuring her hero and modeling assertive behavior. For many cases of acute, neurotic school phobia, rapid referral, parent involvement, reduction of secondary gains, and forced school attendance have been successful. The counterconditioning approaches noted above were often paired with removal of secondary gain, relaxation, positive reinforcement of attendance, and assertiveness training. Treatment was usually brief (a median of twenty-one days), and phobic behaviors did not recur.

The multiple-treatment approach led to over 80 percent effectiveness. Often, younger children must be presented with anxiety-inhibiting images in a modified form. Aside from the usual desensitization methods, counterconditioning may be accomplished by having the child imagine school scenes and pleasurable activities together. Often, rewards are helpful in reinforcing any actual steps toward returning to school. At home, all children should not be permitted to watch television or engage in pleasurable activities (prevent secondary gain). In school, children can effectively use relaxation to reduce anxiety. The authors recommend daily sessions for quick school return. Most cases should require a maximum of six weeks.

TEST ANXIETY: High school students have reduced test anxiety through the use of relaxation training and systematic desensitization in a group. Highly anxious fifth and sixth graders responded very well to group desensitization. Observing others being desensitized (vicarious desensitization) successfully reduced test anxiety and increased academic performance for seventh and eighth graders. Favorable results have been achieved in from two to ten weeks (four to twenty sessions). After desensitization, real-life exposure is necessary. Students could practice test taking, giving speeches, or reading. The authors recommend the development of structured group programs for test, reading, math, and speech anxieties.

COMMENTARY: This valuable overview shows that desensitization is an effective, economical, and flexible method. Fears of school attendance, test taking, or other school-related performance may be dramatically diminished in a relatively short time. This review supports our contention that combined approaches are the most effective form of intervention. While a child's fears are being counterconditioned, more appropriate coping behavior should be taught and reinforced. The many positive experiences with group and vicarious approaches are proof that economical methods can and should be developed and that individual sessions are not always necessary. Fearful students might beneficially watch films of students being desensitized. Finally, this review should alert professionals to the value of using some form of desensitization with fearful children.

SOURCE: Prout, H. T., and Harvey, J. R. "Applications of Desensitization Procedures for School-Related Problems: A Review." *Psychology in the Schools,* 1978, *13,* 533-540.

Automated Direct Deconditioning of a Phobia

AUTHORS: Peter A. Wish, Joseph E. Hasazi, and Albert R. Jurgela

PRECIS: Pairing music and feared noises to desensitize an eleven-year-old boy

INTRODUCTION: Children's fears have been eliminated by pairing feared objects with pleasant events (such as eating). Deconditioning phobias in children is difficult because many children find it hard to visualize events and because real-life desensitization may not be possible. Also, children may be unmotivated to practice at home. Therefore, an automated direct deconditioning method was designed for home use.

METHOD: An eleven-year-old boy had been afraid of explosives for nine years. At two years, he had been frightened by a fireworks display, and his mother picked him up and quickly left. Before referral, he became afraid of other loud noises such as thunder and jet engines. Any loud noise led to intense fear and somatic complaints (severe headaches and nausea). His activities were severely hampered, and he spent much time avoiding or running away from loud sounds. In class, his hiding and fear were disruptive to others.

A fear hierarchy was established by having the boy rate a list of fifteen sounds on a scale from 0 to 100. The sounds, from least to most disturbing, were the surf, balloon pop, cork pop, pistol shots, rifle fire, machine-gun fire, twenty-one-gun salute, cannon fire, battle sounds, rocket launching, explosions, sonic boom, thunderstorm, firecrackers, and fireworks. Two half-hour sessions were used to train him in progressive muscular relaxation. He practiced relaxing for fifteen minutes three times per day. Since he liked music, his favorite record was selected to serve as a source of relaxation. Also, since he was afraid of noises, it was thought that pleasant sounds would be a good counterconditioning agent. The forty-minute record was recorded on four tracks of an eight-track stereo tape. The other four tracks were used to superimpose the hierarchy of feared sounds. Each sound was recorded five times, with an average interval of about thirty seconds. The sounds came from professional sound-effects recordings.

There were three sessions per day for eight days. The session lasted five minutes on the first day, ten minutes on the second, and so on. Thus, the child was listening to the whole tape by the eighth day. The volume was increased each day, and he listened with earphones in a dark room after relaxing himself. His parents controlled the length of the session and the volume of the recording. If he became anxious, he was to shut the tape, relax, and then turn it back on. But this never became necessary. After each session, his parents praised him and gave him one baseball card.

He completed the program and was able to listen to the feared sounds at high volume without anxiety. Several real-life exposures were carried out, and he showed no fear at all. After nine months, there was no evidence of any fear of loud noises.

COMMENTARY: As the authors point out, several different procedures were used. The unique element is the automated procedure that can be economically carried out at home or in school. Sounds are easily tape recorded, and videotapes may be used for visual fears. Children might participate more actively and feel more involved and responsible if they were allowed to control the time and volume by themselves. This approach appears similar to that taken by those who assign special kinds of homework to fearful children. By reading about and drawing pictures of feared situations, the children became desensitized. The present approach is very promising for many fears, since the setting, as well as the music, can be made as relaxing as possible. Some children might respond very well when relaxing in a warm bath. A school psychologist might consider making a tape with feared events (noises, teasing, criticism, yelling), superimposing this on a favorite music tape, and having the child play it at home.

SOURCE: Wish, P. A., Hasazi, J. E., and Jurgela, A. R. "Automated Direct Deconditioning of a Childhood Phobia." *Journal of Behavior Therapy and Experimental Psychiatry*, 1973, *4*, 279-283.

Additional Readings

Chess, S. "Marked Anxiety in Children." *American Journal of Psychotherapy*, 1973, *27*, 390-395.

Treatment of phobic symptoms depends upon the diagnosis of the underlying disorder. Four diagnostic groups are described. Anxiety and speech disorder are common in "developmental delay." Techniques employed may include reassurance, tranquilizers, parental guidance, speech therapy, hearing aids, special education, and psychotherapy. An eight-year-old boy with "organic brain disorder" and school and loud noise phobias is described. A special protective school environment was prescribed. Panic states were treated in a seven-year-old boy with a "neuotic problem." Treatment was psychotherapy focused primarily on his need to obtain approval in an inappropriate manner. Finally, a bee phobia was present in a five-year-old girl with "childhood schizophrenia." Tranquilizers, parental guidance, and psychotherapy were employed.

Franks, C. M., and Susskind, D. J. "Behavior Modification with Children: Rationale and Technique." *Journal of School Psychology*, 1968, *6*, 75-88.

In this very useful review, a broad-spectrum approach to school phobia is discussed. Techniques covered include systematic desensitization, classical and operant conditioning, and teaching principles of reinforcement to parents. The crucial role of the parents is outlined. Behavioral methods lead to less parental guilt and more parental control and effective involvement.

Goldberg, C. "School Phobia in Adolescence." *Adolescence*, 1977, *12*, 499-509.

Five cases of adolescent school phobia are described in terms of the psychoanalytic classification scheme of Melitta Sperling, who regards school phobia as being related to the anal-sadistic phase of instinctual development. A distinction is made between common school phobia (which involves an external precipitating event) and induced school phobia (long-standing parent-child psychopathology). The anal-sadistic phase is predominant in school-phobic children, along with ambivalence, narcissism, and omnipotent magical thinking. Treatment is based upon analyzing each of the five cases in dynamic terms, returning the adolescent to school, and working with family members.

Graziano, A. M., DeGiovanni, I. S., and Garcia, K. A. "Behavioral Treatment of Children's Fears: A Review." *Psychological Bulletin,* 1979, *86,* 804-830.

This is an exhaustive, outstanding, and scholarly review of behavioral concepts, norms, and fear-reduction methods. The shortcomings of past research are pointed out, and specific proposals are made for more adequately studying childhood fears. Systematic desensitization and contingency management have not been demonstrated to be effective. Verbal mediation techniques are seen as promising, and the most frequently used and reliable method is modeling. Modeling has been successful with two types of fears—everyday, common ones (animals, the dark, water, examinations) and fears of dental and surgical procedures. Fearful children observe models coping with the fear, and they then attempt to face the fearful object or situation.

Johnson, S. B. "Children's Fears in the Classroom Setting." *School Psychology Digest,* 1979, *8,* 382-396.

This is a review of theory and treatment of school phobia, social withdrawal, and test anxiety. Young children with school phobia have a good prognosis, and many brief intervention strategies are effective. However, the literature contains many contradictory opinions and findings. For example, some writers see brief intervention as appropriate for acute-onset school phobias and psychotherapy as appropriate for chronic types, while others suggest the reverse. Psychotherapy, operant programs, and counterconditioning have reportedly been successful. Social withdrawal due to fearfulness has been improved by prompting, shaping, stimulus fading, reinforcement, and modeling. Test anxiety has mostly been diminished by counterconditioning and more recently by the teaching of cognitive strategies. The author suggests that the teaching of skills and preventive approaches be employed.

Lazarus, A. A., Davison, G. C., and Polefka, D. A. "Classical and Operant Factors in the Treatment of a School Phobia." *Journal of Abnormal Psychology,* 1965, *70,* 225-229.

A nine-year-old boy was effectively treated by a real-life desensitization procedure. The strategy employed involved his taking increasingly difficult fearful steps. A model was developed for two types of fears. Classical conditioning (reinforcer paired with the stimulus) is used when avoidance is based on extreme anxiety. When avoidance is based mainly on secondary reinforcers, operant conditioning (reinforcer contingent on a response) is suggested. In the case cited, both methods were used. Reciprocal inhibition was employed for the high anxiety, and rewards were given contingent upon school attendance.

Miller, L. C., Barrett, C. L., Hampe, E., and Noble, H. "Comparison of Reciprocal Inhibition, Psychotherapy, and Waiting-List Control for Phobic Children." *Journal of Abnormal Psychology*, 1972, *79*, 269-279.

Sixty-seven children with various fears were treated by one of two methods. Reciprocal inhibition (mainly systematic desensitization) was used to help children and parents to develop ways of gradually experiencing fears without anxiety. In psychotherapy, children were encouraged to express their feelings and conflicts. Awareness then led to the development of alternative coping mechanisms. Both methods were effective, but the measure of success depended upon which outcome criteria were employed. Treatment of fears depends upon a number of variables, and neither treatment method was demonstrated as being superior.

Weinberger, G., Leventhal, T., and Beckman, G. "The Management of a Chronic School Phobic Through the Use of Consultation with School Personnel." *Psychology In The Schools*, 1973, *10*, 83-88.

A consultant removed from the scene selects and assigns roles to strategically placed adults. A fifteen-year-old boy with a chronic school phobia was effectively treated by the school psychologist (the consultee), who involved the father as the main change agent. The role of the consultant is spelled out, including the need for him or her to give concrete and detailed advice and to be willing to revise plans. Adults must counteract the child's power maneuvers and fear avoidance.

Compulsive-Perfectionistic Behavior

Being compulsive means to feel compelled to do certain acts, usually in a repetitive, stereotypical way. A perfectionist regards anything short of perfect as unacceptable. Products must be completely accurate and flawless. At the extreme are children who are compulsively perfectionistic; that is, things must be done in a certain manner or they become very upset. If the compulsive behavior is not performed, they experience a great deal of anxiety. Compulsive children are often orderly, fussy, punctual, and overly conscientious. In addition, compulsive children are often obsessive, and there are many studies of such children. An obsession involves the occurrence of repetitive, persistent, often irrational thoughts. Compulsiveness is most common between eight and ten years of age. In school, compulsive children are excessively careful, do work over and over, and must have perfect desks and work papers or they become upset.

Overly high teacher or parent expectations can lead to compulsive behavior. Children often become compulsive as a means of feeling safe or of avoiding anxiety or real problems. There is some evidence that compulsiveness due to guilt and compulsiveness due to anxiety respond to different approaches (either resolving the guilt or desensitizing the anxiety). Compulsive perfectionism has been successfully desensitized by a variety of behavioral methods. In school, compulsive behavior can be made less gratifying, while noncompulsive, less perfectionistic behavior can be rewarded. Quickness and only brief checking can replace compulsive slowness and repetitive checking of work.

Behavioral Treatment of Childhood Neurosis

AUTHORS: Teodoro Ayllon, Stephen W. Garber, and Mary G. Allison

PRECIS: Strategies for eliminating a five-year-old's obsessive-compulsive need to play with electrical devices and sleep with his parents

INTRODUCTION: According to psychoanalytic theory, neurotic behavior is caused by repressed unconscious conflicts over aggressive and sexual impulses. Parental demands for conformity in such areas as weaning, toilet training, and sexual behaviors conflict with the child's demands 'for gratification. Unresolved conflicts cause anxieties that are expressed as neurotic symptoms. Other psychodynamic theories also see symptoms as signs of underlying conflict and therefore do not treat the symptoms directly. Behaviorists analyze behavior in its contemporary rather than its historical context. Treatment focuses on altering the current environmental contingencies that maintain behavior and the developing of desirable behaviors.

METHOD: A five-year-old boy resisted going to sleep and often crept into his parents' bed (possible conflict concerning sexual impulses). He compulsively switched lights on and off and unplugged appliances (possible reaction formation against antisocial and aggressive impulses). In general, he was uncooperative with parents and did not follow instructions. Traditional psychotherapy and counseling of his parents had been unsuccessful. The parents' typical reactions to his behavior were analyzed, and they were taught to make his maladaptive behaviors less rewarding. They were told to discontinue spanking him, trying to understand his behavior, or reasoning with him.

Ritualistic Sleeping. The child frequently got up during the night and slept with his parents. His father's efforts to keep him out of the bedroom were unsuccessful. The parents were told to meet all requests for play and refreshments before bedtime. If he stayed in his own bed, during the night, he received eight tokens, which could be exchanged for daily activities (watching television or a movie, visiting friends, and food treats). All communication after bedtime was to stop; if he came to his parents' room, he was to be matter-of-factly returned to his bed.

Obsessive-Compulsive Behavior. He stared at lights while rapidly switching them on and off. At home and elsewhere he unplugged appliances and unscrewed bulbs. Light switching resulted in his having to return half his tokens. Additionally, he had to spend thirty minutes alone in his room without the opportunity to earn tokens. When light switching or unplugging occurred outside the home, he was sent home, was paid half his tokens, and had to stay in his room for thirty minutes.

His uncooperative behavior was handled by a similar approach. Compliance led to praise and one token, whereas noncompliance resulted in his having to spend fifteen minutes in his room. Within three weeks, all behaviors had dramatically improved. He was invited to other children's homes, developed friendships, and appeared happier and less obstinate. The parents were pleased with the miraculous change; a two-year follow-up showed continued improvement and no compulsive or ritualistic behavior.

COMMENTARY: As the authors note, behavioral strategies had a unifying influence on the parents and helped them to follow specific procedures. The approach outlined is valid for parents and/or teachers to employ with compulsive children. At times, adults are put off by the apparent simplicity of making maladaptive behaviors less rewarding. However, it is abundantly clear from this study (and similar research) that compulsive behavior can be eliminated without creating any negative consequences. At the same time appropriate behavior should be taught, encouraged, and rewarded. The approach outlined here is appropriate for compulsive behavior in the classroom, such as wanting to turn in perfect homework or test papers, lining up or arranging pencils and materials, and repetitive behavior (tapping, noises, talking, adjusting clothing, and so on). Teachers can easily institute a token reward system, along with penalties and time-outs for inappropriate behavior. Finally, it is very effective when teachers and parents agree to follow the same approach to changing a child's problem behavior.

SOURCE: Ayllon, T., Garber, S. W., and Allison, M. G. "Behavioral Treatment of Childhood Neurosis." *Psychiatry*, 1977, *40*, 315-322.

Using a Relationship with the Teacher to Increase Socially Appropriate Behavior

AUTHORS: Gary G. Brannigan and Robert Reimondi

PRECIS: Improving self-acceptance and reducing compulsive rituals in an eleven-year-old boy

INTRODUCTION: An eleven-year-old boy attended a day school for emotionally disturbed children. He was very anxious, hyperactive, and distractible. Apparently to reduce anxiety, he engaged in many rituals. He counted buttons on others' clothing and items in a room, recited numbers or the alphabet, and frequently asked the same questions repetitively. When confronted with his behavior, he changed the topic or left the room.

INTERVENTION: Because of the boy's poor social skills and considerable anxiety, it was decided to focus upon developing a close interpersonal relationship between him and his teacher. They worked on assignments together, with the teacher helping him to focus on the tasks. In spite of his reluctance, they went places together, played catch, went ice skating, and so forth. When he hid, the teacher would find him and initiate some kind of physical contact such as tickling. His anxiety decreased considerably as a result of engaging in activities in which he did not have to speak. Redirecting his attention was effective in stopping him from continuing in inappropriate activities (such as picking at his skin). The teacher served as a model of appropriate behavior and frequently suggested alternative behaviors that he could engage in. He was told that, instead of hitting out when angry, he should walk away or say what was on his mind.

Increasing his awareness, understanding, and acceptance of feelings (his own and others) was very important. He was taught to label his feelings and to cope more adequately with them rather than allowing them to overwhelm him. The teacher often put these concepts into words, telling him, for example, "You seem angry." Also, the teacher did not become angry or retaliate when his behavior was inappropriate (hitting or spitting). The relationship between boy and teacher was intense and carried through to both academic and recreational activities. After three months, it was clear that the relationship had become a good one. The child was able to express his feelings in a relatively appropriate manner, and he became much less aggressive and anxious.

COMMENTARY: This article provides an example of intervention through development of a relationship rather than through use of a specific technique. Reducing anger, anxiety, and rituals was approached through bettering and intensifying the child's relationship with his current teacher. Many different types of approaches were employed within that relationship. For example, feelings were labeled verbally, the teacher was very accepting and nonpunitive, and specific suggestions were made to the boy as to better alternative behaviors. The lesson is that children will respond positively when they are able to relate to a caring person. Anger and anxiety often diminish when such a relationship is fostered.

SOURCE: Brannigan, G. G., and Reimondi, R. "Psychoeducational Strategy with the Emotionally Disturbed Child." *Academic Therapy*, 1979, *15*, 77-80.

Sensory Extinction of Compulsiveness

AUTHORS: Arnold Rincover, Crighton D. Newsom, and Edward G. Carr

PRECIS: Eliminating sensory stimulation to reduce ritualistic light switching of two eight-year-olds

INTRODUCTION: Compulsive rituals usually involve repetitive, persistent, and irrational motor behavior sequences. These behaviors often disrupt classroom or social functioning. Theoretically, compulsions are avoidance behaviors that are negatively reinforced by reducing the probability of some feared event. Treatment has usually focused on reducing anxiety by systematic desensitization or extinction (preventing the response). But reviews of the pertinent literature have concluded that behavior therapy has not been particularly effective for diminishing compulsive behavior. The authors point out that some rituals may be maintained by positive reinforcement (operant conditioning) rather than by the usual compulsive avoidance behavior. Since anxiety is not involved in these cases, anxiety-reducing methods would predictably not be effective. Ritualistic light switching has been called compulsive and is fairly common in developmentally delayed children. The present study investigated the possibility that light switching was motivated by illumination changes (sensory stimulation) rather than by anxiety avoidance.

METHOD: Two severely disturbed eight-year-olds engaged in excessive light switching, which disrupted hospital activities. The girl had been diagnosed as schizophrenic and the boy as retarded. Their play and social skills were virtually nonexistent. They were at different hospitals, and the slightly different procedures used for them are both described, as are the time intervals when the children were observed. In essence, there were two steps. First, the switch was altered so that it no longer worked the light. Second, all sound was eliminated so that there was no clicking (or other) sound when it was switched. Daily sessions were held for twenty to thirty minutes in a laboratory and in a classroom. Statistical results are presented, including results of a reversal period during which the usual sensory stimulation took place.

The light switching was eliminated or significantly decreased by removing the usual sensory consequences (this is called sensory extinction). One child responded immediately when the illumination changes (visual consequences) were removed. The other child's ritualistic switching stopped only when the clicking noises (auditory consequences) were removed. The method used was convenient and required little time or effort. The authors see sensory extinction as providing a valuable means for finding a powerful reinforcer for a child. The child who required elimination of the clicking sound would probably respond to the use of auditory stimulation as a reward. Also, it is essential to determine whether the behavior is motivated by avoidance or by positive (sensory) reinforcement. The appropriate intervention can then be determined (such as systematic desensitization for avoidance rituals).

COMMENTARY: This article is directly applicable to those disruptive and quasi-compulsive classroom behaviors that are maintained by sensory stimulation. Some annoying repetitive tapping sounds could be of this nature. Some children may have a need to seek visual stimulation (constantly looking out a window or at a neighbor's activities). Once the probable cause (motivation) of the behavior is determined, a specific method should be employed to eliminate it. Sensory extinction, desensitization, and relaxation are all relatively economical and efficient methods. Additionally, the valuable suggestion is made to use a child's sensory seeking in a more productive manner. For example, the sound-seeking child might be allowed to periodically play percussion instruments as a reward for appropriate academic or social behavior.

SOURCE: Rincover, A., Newsom, C. D., and Carr, E. G. "Using Sensory Extinction Procedures in the Treatment of Compulsive-Like Behavior of Developmentally Disabled Children." *Journal of Consulting and Clinical Psychology*, 1979, *47*, 695-701.

Additional Readings

Lindley, P., Marks, I., Philpott, R., and Snowden, J. "Treatment of Obsessive-Compulsive Neurosis with History of Childhood Autism." *British Journal of Psychiatry,* 1977, *130,* 592-597.

A young man had a history of rigidity, excessive tidiness, and many compulsive rituals. Operant conditioning (modeling, real-life practice, and response prevention) and social skills training were successfully employed. Compulsive slowness and checking were significantly reduced by using systematic rewards. Earned tokens were used to purchase privileges.

Pollack, J. M. "Obsessive-Compulsive Personality: A Review." *Psychological Bulletin,* 1979, *86,* 225-241.

This is an exhaustive review of studies of obsessive-compulsive personality. Psychoanalytic as well as other proposed theories have received little empirical support. Obsessive-compulsive individuals often have obsessive-compulsive parents who provide rigid, compulsive parenting. Ambivalence about expressing hostility may lead to the trait of obstinacy. Behaviors discussed include overconscientiousness, indecisiveness, excessive orderliness, and perfectionism.

Rosen, M. "A Dual Model of Obsessional Neurosis." *Journal of Consulting and Clinical Psychology,* 1975, *43,* 453-459.

Treatment of compulsive rituals or obsessive thoughts is based upon the discrimination between guilt or anxiety reduction as the cause. Two case studies illustrate the different approaches necessary. A twelve-year-old boy compulsively tied his shoelaces, hitched up his socks, and repeated sentences. Anxiety about accidents and a knee ailment were eliminated by relaxation, desensitization, and environmental manipulation (a leg cast). Desensitization was not effective for an obsessive young woman whose problems stemmed from feelings of guilt and worthlessness. But assertiveness training and role playing were effective.

Silverman, J. S. "Obsessional Disorders in Childhood and Adolescence." *American Journal of Psychotherapy,* 1972, *26,* 362-377.

Psychoanalytic diagnosis and treatment of obsessive-compulsive disorders in children are reviewed in detail. The author describes a five-year-old boy who indulged in compulsive behavior and verbalizations (rude words), as well as in obsessive-aggressive fantasies. The therapist became his ally in helping him develop his cognitive capacity so that he could understand his difficulties. Age-appropriate defenses against anxiety were strenghtened rather than abruptly removed.

Poor Self-Esteem

Self-esteem is defined as a person's feelings of self-worth. This is usually determined through self-report, observations of behavior, and, more formally, through so-called self-concept surveys. Self-esteem may be measured in a variety of categories, including academic, social, physical, and family self-esteem. Although a positive relationship exists between self-esteem and academic achievement, not all types of self-esteem are influenced by school-based interventions. Self-esteem is clearly affected by the attitudes of significant adults in the child's life. Whether improved self-esteem directly causes improved school performance has not yet been resolved.

Success Counseling to Build Self-Concept

AUTHOR: Kenneth R. Washington

PRECIS: A strength-oriented humanistic counseling technique to aid disadvantaged students develop success strategies

INTRODUCTION: Traditional counseling methods focus on the personal problems that must be resolved if self-esteem is to grow. Success counseling is an alternate approach that emphasizes personal strength and success potential to enhance self-concept. This "success" orientation allows participants to concentrate on positive goal-setting activities rather than on individual weaknesses or on conditions that create helplessness. The author regards this approach as extremely useful in helping economically disadvantaged minority youth develop self-esteem and a sense of control over their lives. The conditions under which these students live create feelings of worthlessness and make them feel that they lack power to change events. Techniques such as success counseling attempt to alter these feelings.

SUCCESS COUNSELING: Through a series of group exercises led by a facilitator, adolescents receiving success counseling are able to become more aware of their abilities and personal power. They also find in their peers a source of support and encouragement. In exercise one, the facilitator develops a sense of acceptance and trust among group members. Discussions are held in small groups about personal goals, experiences that lead to good feelings, and influential life events. The leader must also be willing to contribute personal experiences as a way of demonstrating and modeling trust. As similarities emerge in the histories of individual group members, they become more willing to reveal themselves.

Exercise two focuses on the sharing of personal success experiences. After describing some personal successes, the facilitator explains that the term *success* has an extremely broad meaning and can include awards, school honors, making house repairs, or assisting a grandparent. The facilitator then asks students to talk about their own successes. This experience increases their awareness of their positive attributes and success potential.

In exercise three the group identifies the personal attributes of each member that contributed to his or her successes and discusses how these strengths can be used to achieve future goals. This support helps self-esteem grow and creates a safe climate in which ideas and feelings can be expressed. This accepting atmosphere also encourages the sharing of personal problems.

COMMENTARY: The author has used this technique to begin building the self-confidence of inner-city students facing college. It has also been helpful with personnel in low-income day-care settings. As staff members came to view themselves more positively, they felt more able to affect the self-concepts of the children in the centers. Success counseling does not solve all problems, but is one way that mental health professionals can give disadvantaged youth the confidence to attempt changes in their lives. It is also applicable to students at all economic levels who suffer from low self-esteem. When individuals can focus on positive attributes instead of on their helplessness, they are often more able to use their strengths to achieve success.

SOURCE: Washington, K. R. "Success Counseling: A Model Workshop Approach to Self-Concept Building." *Adolescence,* 1977, *12*(47), 405-409.

Self-Concept Change Through Art Counseling

AUTHORS: Kinnard White and Richard Allen

PRECIS: Allowing preadolescents to discuss their work in the accepting atmosphere of an art room to increase their awareness of personal attributes and to "tune in" to their creative selves

INTRODUCTION: The unique characteristics of preadolescence, along with the limitations of the public school setting, make counseling this age group a challenging task. Preadolescents differ from adolescents in such attributes as their relationship with adults, their language, and their social status. Furthermore, counseling contacts in schools are often irregular, limited in time, and established with unwilling students. New approaches are needed that will be relevant to preadolescence and practical within the schools. The authors feel that art counseling is one such technique. With art as the medium, counselors can form positive relationships with preadolescents and use artwork to encourage expression of feelings. In this way, problems common to these youngsters can be explored in a nonthreatening atmosphere.

TREATMENT: This paper compared art counseling with traditional nondirective counseling on the development of positive self-esteem. Thirty students in a summer residential school program were administered a self-concept scale and then divided into two equal groups. One group received art counseling at least ninety minutes every weekday for the eight-week summer term, while the other group participated in daily nondirective counseling sessions.

In art counseling the teacher-counselor spent time with individual students, stressing their unique creative abilities and encouraging work on brief, successful projects. Students evaluated their own artwork, examined the reasons behind their creations, and compared their finished products with intended goals. Using art as a basis for personal discussion, the counselor urged students to express their feelings about their work and themselves. Throughout the program a sharing of feelings was accepted and encouraged.

After the eight-week semester, self-concepts were remeasured. Students in art counseling showed significantly greater improvements in self-concept than those in the nondirective group. In addition, measures taken fourteen months later showed a maintenance of gains in the art-counseling group compared with no change in the others.

COMMENTARY: School mental health specialists have begun to recognize that preadolescents are different from both children and teen-agers. Thus, therapeutic techniques and academic programs appropriate for elementary and high school settings are not necessarily practical for this age group. In order for school personnel to establish working relationships with preadolescents, they must understand these differences and plan strategies around them. The authors have demonstrated the use of the art room in this effort. Their study also seems to question whether traditional nondirective techniques can, by themselves, promote change in these youngsters. Perhaps more directive approaches need to be incorporated into mental health programs when they are designed for these students.

SOURCE: White, K., and Allen, R. "Art Counseling in an Educational Setting: Self-Concept Change Among Preadolescent Boys." *Journal of School Psychology,* 1971, *9*(2), 218-225.

Teaching Self-Concept to Preadolescents

AUTHORS: Jerome L. Schulman, Robin C. Ford, and Patricia Busk

PRECIS: Improving self-esteem and accurate self-appraisal through a "self-concept unit" taught in the classroom

INTRODUCTION: The authors describe a prepackaged mental health unit to improve self-concept in children. This unit, which can be taught by teachers with a minimum of planning, involves film clips, discussion, homework, and classroom assignments. The unit focuses on four major themes: (1) understanding the meaning of self-concept; (2) recognizing how behavior reveals self-concept; (3) examining the influence of friends, family, and others on self-concept; and (4) discussing how self-concept affects behavior. These themes are developed in a sequence of twelve lessons with accompanying class activities.

SELF-CONCEPT UNIT: In lessons one to three, students define "self-concept" and, with the aid of film clips, discuss how people's opinions of themselves influence their behavior. They learn to distinguish between positive and negative self-esteem by examining five people outside the class and deciding whether their self-concepts are high or low. Bragging as a reflection of self-concept is also considered. In all these activities students are encouraged to relate self-concept issues to their own feelings and behaviors and to identify with the situations and people described.

Lessons four and five center on how others influence our view of ourselves. Students view and discuss another film clip and write a composition based on the theme of the clip. Lessons six to eleven develop several topics. The notion of "self-acceptance" is introduced, and students are taught the importance of accepting personal strengths and weaknesses as part of a realistic self-concept. The teacher helps them assess their positive and negative attributes, appraise their self-concepts, and examine possible improvements. Film clips depicting a father-son relationship and reactions of students to a newcomer at school highlight parental, peer, and adult influences on self-esteem. In the final lesson students learn that a person can often choose among various ways to act or feel. The class activity involves comparing their self-appraisals with the appraisals of classmates.

This unit was tested with sixth, seventh, and eighth graders on its ability to improve both self-concept and self-appraisal accuracy. Students were administered self-esteem and self-rating questionnaires before and after the unit. Results clearly demonstrated improvement in self-concept and accuracy of self-judgments following participation in the program. Eighth graders seemed to benefit more than younger children, suggesting an increasing ability in older students to utilize course content for personal growth.

COMMENTARY: This research validates the importance and practicality of "emotional education" in the schools. Subjects once handled only by specialists in counseling problem children can now be introduced by the teacher in the regular classroom to further the psychological development of all children. This article highlights some of the important themes and topics that should be included in a comprehensive self-concept unit. However, teachers who present this material must be sensitive to the feelings that students express during the course. The authors suggest involvement of a school psychologist or counselor to advise teachers on the handling of sensitive material and to guide them in the most effective presentation of activities. It is also recommended that teachers who are uncomfortable presenting such nontraditional material not be pressured to do so. While the authors note that teachers derived personal benefit from their participation, it is likely that these teachers entered the program with initially high levels of sensitivity. The classroom should not be a training ground for teachers who find such topics hard to teach. The anxiety of these teachers could be unproductive, if not harmful, to students.

SOURCE: Schulman, J. L., Ford, R. C., and Busk, P. "A Classroom Program to Improve Self-Concept." *Psychology in the Schools,* 1973, *10,* 481-487.

Reinforcing Positive Self-Esteem in Elementary School Children

AUTHORS: Norma Hauserman, Jay S. Miller, and Frances T. Bond

PRECIS: Increasing the self-esteem of students by rewarding them for making positive self-statements

INTRODUCTION: According to the authors, individuals with low self-concepts rarely make positive statements about themselves. However, it may be possible to increase the frequency of these self-statements in children and thus alter their attitudes about themselves. In this study, thirty children from kinder-garten through grade 4 were rewarded for positive self-state-ments in an effort to improve their self-esteem. These children had scored low on a measure of academic self-concept and had been rated as low in self-confidence by their teachers.

TREATMENT: The children were observed for forty days dur-ing regular classroom activities. When a child in the treatment group behaved in an obviously successful way (perhaps helping another child or completing an assignment), the teacher, aide, or student assistant·prompted the child to say something good about himself. The request to "tell me something good about yourself" was made directly to the child. After making the posi-tive self-statement, the child was reinforced with a hug, pat, a statement such as "I'm proud of you," or a similar action. This was done eight times per day for each treated child. If the child had trouble making a positive self-statement, the teacher mod-eled one that the child then repeated. Reinforcement was then provided.

After the treatment ended, the self-concept measure was readministered. Four weeks later it was given a third time. Dur-ing this four-week period no prompting occurred, but children were periodically rewarded for positive self-statements. Com-pared to a no-treatment group, these children showed a signifi-cant increase in their self-concept score after the forty days of observation and maintained the increase after four weeks of no prompting. The authors note that every child in the treatment group maintained the four-week increase.

COMMENTARY: This study demonstrates that reinforcing chil-dren's positive self-statements increases their measured self-esteem. Other research has also shown that self-concept mea-sures improve when children are encouraged to make positive personal comments and are then rewarded for their statements. This technique is easy to use in the classroom and requires little effort other than prompting and rewarding. In addition, the in-creased frequency of positive self-statements that results from reinforcement should lessen the need for prompting. Although there is no clear proof that improved self-concept is a direct cause of better learning, many studies have shown that self-confident students achieve more, make friends more easily, and more often become leaders than do other student. Techniques that may help students achieve these goals are therefore valuable to teachers, school psychologists, and counselors.

SOURCE: Hauserman, N., Miller, J. S., and Bond, F. T. "A Behavioral Approach to Changing Self-Concept in Elementary School Children." *The Psychological Record,* 1976, *26,* 111-116.

Attribution and Self-Concept Improvement

AUTHORS: Richard L. Miller, Philip Brickman, and Diana Bolen

PRECIS: Attributing skill and effort to students to help them improve confidence and achievement

INTRODUCTION: Teachers usually expect their students to work hard and do well. In this paper the authors describe two kinds of statements that teachers may use to communicate these expectations. First, they may try to persuade students that they should work harder and do better. Comments such as "You should be getting better grades" or "Try harder" are often used. Second, teachers may encourage improvement by telling students that they *are* well motivated and successful. Phrases such as "You are a good student" and "You really work hard" are used here. In the authors' opinion the second type, or "attribution statement," is more effective in promoting desired student behaviors and attitudes. The attribution treatment helps the student feel capable and effective while the first type, known as the "persuasion statement," indicates to the student that the desired behaviors are lacking. In part one of this study the authors controlled littering by attributing neatness to students. Part two tested the effect of these statements on self-esteem and achievement in arithmetic.

PERSUASION VERSUS ATTRIBUTION: Ninety-six second graders in an inner-city public school were given a self-esteem questionnaire that included math-related self-esteem questions. They also took an arithmetic achievement test. Each student was then exposed to one of several treatments. In the *attribution treatment* students were regularly informed that they were skilled in math (attribution of ability) or were excellent workers (attribution of motivation). This feedback was given each day through verbal statements by teachers, letters from the teacher and principal, and medals. Comments and letters stated, "You are doing very well" or "Very good work" or "Keep trying harder." Sometimes letters were sent home. Medals read "good student" or "hard worker." In the *persuasion treatment* children were told that they *should* be good in math (ability) or *should* work harder (motivation). Comments, letters, and medals were delivered in the same manner as in the attribution treatment. A reinforcement treatment was also included that praised students for their progress in math. A control group received no treatment.

After students had undergone treatment for eight days, the self-esteem and math tests were readministered. The attribution treatments produced the highest and most significant increases in math self-esteem and achievement. The reinforcement groups also increased their scores but not as steeply as the attribution students. In addition, when the achievement test was given again two weeks later, students in the attribution treatments showed increased math scores while the persuasion groups declined. The reinforcement groups displayed a very slight increase. Finally, attribution treatments were found to be even more effective for low-ability math students than for high performers.

COMMENTARY: Teachers are more likely to improve self-esteem and achievement when they encourage students to feel capable and motivated. This approach motivates students to work harder in order to live up to these positive attributes. Telling students that they should do better emphasizes negative attributes, raises the youngster's defenses, and does not encourage desired changes. This is especially true for low-functioning students who, in other studies, also responded more eagerly to positive feedback than did successful students. Attribution is a powerful technique and is probably used informally by many teachers. However, the authors caution against applying these results uncritically. In their study, for example, attributing success to low performers was difficult for some teachers, and the principal declined to participate in one phase of the treatment after three days. If the school staff does not support a treatment approach, it will probably not be used; or if used, it will not be implemented as intended. It may be necessary to modify attributions in order to maintain consistency with actual student performance. In some instances the psychologist may first increase performance through a variety of behavioral interventions before suggesting the use of attributions. This might help the teacher feel more comfortable when attributing success to an improving student.

SOURCE: Miller, R. L., Brickman, P., and Bolen, D. "Attribution Versus Persuasion as a Means for Modifying Behavior." *Journal of Personality and Social Psychology,* 1975, *31*(3), 430-441.

Self-Esteem and an Alternative School

AUTHORS: Marlene Strathe and Virginia Hash

PRECIS: Improving adolescents' self-concept through a self-contained alternative school program

INTRODUCTION: The authors note that students who misbehave and/or fail may view themselves as unworthy and unable to succeed. Alternative schools are designed to help these students feel capable and successful in a school setting. This investigation assessed the impact of an alternative school project on the self-esteem of forty-nine junior high and high school students aged fifteen and sixteen. Participating students had dropped out or had been expelled from school because of educational difficulties. The program, which was run by the public school's board of education, involved three hours per day of self-contained classroom instruction in basic skills. Each class had one teacher for eight students, and advancement was based on demonstrated competency in a given skill area.

SELF-ESTEEM: Measures of self-concept were taken at the beginning of the school year and after the first semester of involvement in the program. Results showed that the younger adolescents made self-concept gains after only one semester while older students did not enhance their self-concept during that time. The authors conclude that early identification and placement in alternative schools are necessary to improve the self-concepts of failing students. For older students more time may be needed to demonstrate gains in self-esteem.

COMMENTARY: Traditional school programs are not always appropriate for all students. Alternative schools have developed in many forms to educate youngsters who do not succeed in traditional classrooms. Many of these students find school unsatisfying and have a low opinion of themselves even though they may be intelligent and capable. Some are disruptive in class. Usually, a major goal of such programs is to improve the student's self-esteem in order to increase his or her chances of future academic or vocational success. As shown here, one semester of alternative schooling may be "too little, too late" for older adolescents. However, programs with more innovative formats may be effective for these students. Occupational or work-study experiences, student involvement in program planning, more informal student-teacher relationships, and peer-group support are examples of other techniques. As more is learned about self-esteem and its influence on learning, more effective programs will be developed.

SOURCE: Strathe, M., and Hash, V. "The Effect of an Alternative School on Adolescent Self-Esteem." *Adolescence,* 1979, *14*(53), 185-189.

Additional Readings

Ammerman, M. S., and Fryrear, J. L. "Photographic Enhancement of Children's Self-Esteem." *Psychology in the Schools,* 1975, *12*(3), 319-325.

Suspecting a link between body image and self-esteem, the authors developed a phototherapy approach to enhance the confidence of fourth graders with low self-esteem. Children took pictures of partners in various prescribed poses for five photography sessions. Three days after each session children were helped to paste the pictures in photography scrapbooks while they expressed feelings about the pictures and wrote brief comments under them. During these meetings the experimenters maintained a friendly and helpful but nondirecting manner. After five weeks of the program, childrens' subjective ratings of self-esteem were no higher than pretreatment measures or control-group ratings. However, *teacher* ratings of self-concept behaviors on the Coopersmith Behavior Rating Form were significantly higher after treatment. While both treatment group and control group improved, the treatment group was rated significantly higher than the control group. These findings suggest that higher self-esteem may be reflected in behavior before a youngster can subjectively report the change.

Brown, J. A., and Macdougall, M. A. "Teacher Consultation for Improved Feelings of Self-Adequacy in Children." *Psychology in the Schools,* 1973, *10*(3), 320-326.

Teacher behaviors influence how children view themselves and classmates. Thus, an in-service program was developed that allowed elementary teachers to examine, discuss, and modify their interactions with children in the classroom. The purpose was to help students improve their self-perceptions. In six weekly two-hour sessions teachers explored such topics as the relationship between feelings and learning, how self-perceptions are learned, how adults interact with and affect childrens' behaviors, and the teaching of socialization skills. Teachers shared videotapes of their interactions in the class to analyze their behaviors, examine and model other approaches, and receive peer praise for positive interactions. As a result of teacher training, students rated themselves as more adequate in their peer and teacher relationships. It was also found that a significant correlation existed between teachers' perceptions of pupils and acceptance of these pupils by the class. It appears that teachers' views of a student may be transmitted to the class and thus be expressed in the attitudes of the class toward the child. Finally, the teacher's perceptions of a student were found to be related to the student's self-rating of performance on school-related tasks, but not in personal-social behavior. While teachers may influence a student's school-related self-concept, they do not necessarily influence his or her personal self-confidence.

Coopersmith, S., and Silverman, J. "How to Enhance Pupil Self-Esteem." *Today's Education,* 1969, 28-29.

Children may fail in school because they feel they are unable to succeed. Thus, they often turn to daydreaming or misconduct in an effort to bolster an inadequate self-image. Teachers can help change a child's self-concept by first examining their own attitudes about children, developing self-respect and feelings of personal worth, and maintaining a realistic sense of self. They must set consistent yet reasonable classroom standards and refrain from ridiculing or humiliating a student. The teacher who communicates genuine caring for the student will enhance the child's self-esteem. Giving children the right to express ideas or disagree with established rules makes them feel valued and respected. Grading should balance praise with supportive criticism, and students should feel that there are ways to overcome poor marks. Challenging students to use their abilities helps them test their limits and adds to their confidence. These suggestions are crucial to building self-confidence and promoting successful school experiences.

Curtis, J., and Altmann, H. "The Relationship Between Teachers' Self-Concept and the Self-Concept of Students." *Child Study Journal*, 1977, 7(1), 17-26.

For fourth, fifth, and sixth graders, this study found that (1) teachers with high measured self-concepts tend to have students who rate themselves high in self-esteem; (2) teachers rated high on self-concept tend to evaluate their students more positively than do teachers low in self-concept; (3) students tend to accurately assess their teacher's ratings of them; (4) students who perceive their teachers as rating them highly tend to rate themselves highly. These correlations support the importance of teacher self-concept in determining the attitudes students have toward themselves.

Krasnow, A. "An Adlerian Approach to the Problem of School Maladjustment." *Academic Therapy*, 1971-1972, 7(2), 171-183.

The author describes an intelligent boy with strong feelings of inferiority who was withdrawn, rebellious, sensitive to criticism, and underachieving. In Adlerian terms, Bob's position as a middle child between two sisters influenced his attempts to resist authority figures by refusing to learn and undoing efforts to teach him. His tutor used an Adlerian approach within a psychoeducational framework to build a relationship and encourage motivation. One technique allowed natural and logical consequences (rather than coercion) to provide the incentives. For example, when Bob arrived late to the tutoring room, he would find that the teacher had left to meet other obligations. When he acted out, his behavior was ignored rather than punished. When no reaction followed his misconduct, its ineffectiveness was reinforced for him. Coupled with respect for his decisions and actions, successful experiences, and the encouragement of personal insight, this approach induced motivational changes and helped Bob to understand how he had used his problem to achieve negative goals. Once this was verbalized, he became more cooperative. Positive behavior was reinforced, preferred activities were provided, and his ideas were given acceptance. Personal interests were incorporated into lessons and games, student-teacher role reversals were tried, and other activities were used to make learning more enjoyable. Successes were given great attention, and Bob was made to feel helpful to teachers on projects. Academic remediation was woven into these approaches. At times he acted as a tutor for a second grader, bolstering his own self-concept while learning math and language facts as he "taught" the child. By the end of the year, significant progress was noted. Children readily respond to educational strategies when respect and concern for them are combined with nonpunitive firmness.

Lane, J., and Muller, D. "The Effect of Altering Self-Descriptive Behavior on Self-Concept and Classroom Behavior." *Journal of Psychology*, 1977, *97*, 115-125.

When students are praised for writing positive self-descriptions, their self-concept improves. Fifth graders with low self-concepts wrote eight essays (two per week for four weeks) designed to elicit self-descriptive statements about school performance and other school-related personal characteristics. Some students (group P) received five written rewarding statements that were placed near their underlined positive self-statements. Rewarding statements such as "I like that" or "good thought" were used. Others received the same written praise for impersonal statements (group G), while a third group (group C) received no specific praise. Results showed a marked increase in the number of positive self-descriptions for group P over the four weeks. There was no change for groups G and C. On measures of self-concept, group P showed a significant increase in intellectual self-concept as compared to the G and C groups. No differences among groups were found on measures of social and personal self-concept. Finally, teachers did not rate the groups differently on achievement-related school behaviors after treatment. These results show that reinforcing positive self-statements increased self-concept only in the area specifically related to the content of the self-descriptions. This supports the "factor-specific" model of self-concept as opposed to a model that stresses a general, all-inclusive self-concept.

Ruedi, J., and West, C. D. "Pupil Self-Concept in an 'Open' School and in a 'Traditional' School." *Psychology in the Schools*, 1973, *10*(1), 48-53.

This article compared an open to a traditional classroom structure in terms of measured self-concept in fourth to sixth graders. In the traditional class students covered the same material together, sat in rows facing the teacher, worked in silence, were sometimes grouped for instruction by achievement level, and were tested at the same time. In the open class, students had more freedom to choose subjects or projects and worked at their own pace. Lectures were rare, and students often conferred with each other and gave each other tests. Parental participation was encouraged, and students were responsible for their own progress. Self-concepts were not found to differ in these two groups. While students in the open classroom viewed teachers and school more positively, children in the traditional class felt more academically adequate. The authors caution against using a single criterion such as self-concept to judge a school program.

Summerlin, M. L., and Ward, G. R. "The Effect of Parental Participation in a Parent Group on a Child's Self-Concept." *Journal of Psychology*, 1978, *100*, 227-232.

Parents of kindergarten and second-grade students participated in a six-session study group that presented the Systematic Training for Effective Parenting (STEP) program (D. Dinkmeyer and G. McKay, *Systematic Training for Effective Parenting: Parent's Handbook*, Circle Pines, Minn.: American Guidance Service, 1976.) After the program, parents showed a significant change in attitudes toward their children when compared with parents in a no-training group. Specifically, they became more accepting of their child's feelings and trusted their children more than they had previously. Furthermore, the children of these parents rated themselves as higher in self-concept than the children of the nontrained parents. They were particularly more confident about their acceptance by peers and their ability to help others in social situations. It appears that positive parental attitudes were communicated to the children and emerged as improved self-esteem. Such research documents the influence of the parent on the child's developing self-concept.

Gender Disturbance

Gender-disturbed children display attitudes and behaviors most commonly associated with children of the opposite sex. Since boys outnumber girls by fifteen to one in referrals for gender disturbance, virtually all reports of treatment deal with atypical sex-role development in boys. These children are typically unhappy and anxious. They are often ridiculed by peers of both sexes and usually carry their sexual preferences into adolescence and adulthood if untreated. While the issue of altering gender preference has political overtones, the need to relieve the depression and anxiety of all children, whether gender-disturbed or not, is rarely debated in public forums. The articles in this section focus on school-based treatments for gender disturbance.

Modifying Sex-Role Behaviors and Attitudes

AUTHOR: Robert D. Myrick

PRECIS: Developing a strategy to alter peer preferences and attitudes toward school in an effeminate fourth-grade boy

INTRODUCTION: In elementary school, boys who have not adopted traditional sex-role behaviors are often teased and ostracized by peers, rejected by adults, and considered deviant or potentially homosexual. As young as age three, males are expected to begin displaying such qualities as aggressiveness, physical activity, independence, and rebelliousness. For boys who prefer feminine behaviors, intensive psychotherapy is typically recommended for the family as well as the youngster, and most treatments are conducted outside the school. In this case study, the author reports how the counselor worked with teachers in the school to change the sex-role attitudes and behaviors of a fourth-grade boy.

CASE STUDY: Jerry was an intelligent boy and a good student. But his teacher was concerned because he preferred the company of girls, did not relate well to boys, and was unhappy. The other boys called him a sissy, and he seemed to be adopting speech patterns, mannerisms, and interests usually associated with girls. Rather than counsel the boy privately, the counselor worked with the classroom and gym teachers to encourage peer acceptance, increase masculine sex-role behaviors, and promote positive attitudes toward school. The physical education teacher tutored Jerry for five weeks in the basic skills and rules of football. In gym class, Jerry was encouraged to use these newly learned skills and was praised out loud in front of his classmates for his success. At times he was called upon to demonstrate certain skills to the class. Meanwhile, his classroom teacher seated him next to the most popular boy. They were required to work together on various classroom activities, and Jerry was thus provided with a positive masculine model. The teacher also led classroom discussions about making friends in which Jerry listened to peers and expressed his own fears and anxieties.

Jerry's behavior and attitudes showed modification in five areas:

1. On the playground Jerry's playmates changed dramatically from girls to boys after the first week of treatment.

2. In the lunchroom he chose to sit with the boys the day after he had first played football; after five months, he was still sitting with the boys.

3. In gym, Jerry's choice of activities switched to more aggressive games, and from then on he chose sports such as basketball and softball that were more popular with the boys than with the girls.

4. Jerry's popularity with classmates rose sharply. From an isolate, Jerry became the eighth most popular boy in class, and the fourth most popular among the boys.

5. Jerry's attitudes regarding boys and girls changed. Boys and school became more valued, while no change occurred in his attitude toward girls. Interestingly, his view of how others judged him was negatively changed; he felt that he was perceived by peers as less important and less valued than before. This feeling seemed related to his increased desire for interpersonal success and to the importance he now placed on his social image.

COMMENTARY: Three strategies were used by the counselor to modify undesired sex-role patterns. First, desired behaviors were encouraged, tutored, and publicly reinforced. Second, a classmate provided a model of desired sex-typed behavior. Third, classroom discussions were focused on friendship and the sharing of personal feelings. There is, of course, intense controversy about treatments to alter sex-role behaviors and attitudes. Many argue that the standards for sex roles reflect the biases and rigidities of the culture and should not be used to label children as deviant. Others contend that children who experience gender-role confusions suffer emotional distress and social rejection and need help to change. Myrick does not debate these issues in his article but outlines an approach for the school setting that avoids the need for outside intervention. He notes, however, that while behavior changes were dramatic, Jerry's self-esteem appeared to suffer. If the counselor changes behavior without considering the associated feeling changes, the client may be left in conflict, and new problems may be created. Opportunities must be provided to explore the emotions that accompany behavior changes, especially when such alterations are sudden.

SOURCE: Myrick, R. D. "The Counselor-Consultant and the Effeminate Boy." *Personnel and Guidance Journal,* 1970, *48*(5), 355-361.

Treating Gender-Identity Problems in a Young Boy

AUTHORS: George A. Rekers, O. Ivar Lovaas, and Benson Low

PRECIS: Home, clinic, and school treatment to reduce cross-gender confusion in all three settings

INTRODUCTION: The authors note that gender-role confusions in childhood often lead to later homosexuality, transsexualism, or other atypical sexual orientations. Thus, treatment should be started before childhood ends. Carl was eight years old when treatment began and had shown feminine behaviors since the age of four. His conversations were oriented to topics such as female clothing or cosmetics, and he was constantly ridiculed by male peers. He preferred to be with girls and liked to play with female-typed toys. He labeled himself a "fag" and a "sissy"; he was depressed, anxious, and socially isolated. Carl's mother had married four times since his birth and had given birth to two other children after Carl. Family therapy was unsuccessful.

CLINIC TREATMENT: Before and during clinic treatment, Carl's behaviors were recorded at home by his mother and an observer. These included feminine gestures, play acting the feminine role, feminine play with his sister, and masculine play with peers and his mother. Treatment in the clinic occurred in the waiting room for twenty minutes every one or two days. For the first six sessions, an assistant attended positively to all of Carl's conversation. In sessions seven to nine, the assistant looked away and picked up a magazine to read if Carl discussed feminine topics. Questions with feminine content were answered with such statements as "I'm not interested in that" and then simply ignored. If Carl talked on masculine or neutral topics, the assistant showed positive interest. In sessions ten to twelve, the assistant again attended to all of Carl's conversation. During treatment masculine-oriented speech increased while feminine speech decreased. However, changes did not carry over to the home so treatment was begun there.

HOME TREATMENT: After seven weeks of home observations, a token system was introduced. Carl's mother awarded him blue tokens for masculine play with his brother; these could be traded for rewards such as candies or television viewing time. After two weeks, a response-cost procedure was initiated. Red tokens were given for feminine gestures, and were subtracted from the blue tokens to determine Carl's reward. As feminine gestures were reduced, the response cost was extended to feminine speech and then to play with his sister. With this treatment, masculine play with his brother rose immediately, and after twelve weeks occurred outside the half-hour treatment period. For unknown reasons it dropped again sixteen weeks later. When response cost was added, all feminine gestures and speech decreased. Carl's play with his sister also dropped to virtually zero, as did play acting the feminine role, even though it was not a direct treatment target.

SCHOOL TREATMENT: Treatment was then initiated at school. After observing Carl's behavior for eighteen days, the teacher began each day by giving him ten points. Each time he was disturbing, rude, or bossy, he lost one point. At the end of the day he received two minutes of free time for each remaining point. After nine days these behaviors had been eliminated, and the system was applied to feminine mannerisms and speech.

After three weeks, both had decreased. When Carl was transferred to new classes in the summer and fall, all behaviors returned to their original levels. In the fall the teacher resumed the treatment for all behaviors, and they quickly ceased.

The total treatment lasted fifteen months, and reports from the home, school, and neighborhood indicated markedly reduced feminine behaviors. A fifteen-month follow-up treatment in an athletic program increased Carl's sports skills but only moderately increased his motivation to engage in sports. He also formed an attachment to a research assistant with whom he modeled appropriate masculine behavior and vented feelings of anger. Two individual psychological evaluations revealed no evidence of underlying cross-gender confusion, although feminine behaviors occasionally surfaced during periods of emotional stress. In addition, social acceptance increased, and in a new school Carl was considered well-adjusted.

COMMENTARY: One year after all treatments ended, feminine behavior was still absent, and Carl had made friends in school and at home. His relationships with girls were age appropriate, and he remained close to his sister. His parents considered him happy. This paper is one of the few to report a controlled procedure for the treatment of gender confusion in children. However, behavior changes occurred only in the setting in which the treatments were applied. Thus, if treatment occurs outside the school or home, it is unlikely that gains will transfer to these settings. The intervention should be carried out in the setting in which the desired behaviors are to be displayed.

SOURCE: Rekers, G. A., Lovaas, O. I., and Low, B. "The Behavioral Treatment of a 'Transsexual' Preadolescent Boy." *Journal of Abnormal Child Psychology*, 1974, 2(2), 99-116.

Additional Reading

Marlowe, M. "The Assessment and Treatment of Gender-Disturbed Boys by Guidance Counselors." *Personnel and Guidance Journal,* 1979, 128-131.

The author distinguishes two types of gender confusion. In *gender behavior disturbances* the boy prefers feminine clothing and cosmetics, shows interest in feminine play, and displays feminine gestures and speech. The boy with *cross-gender identification* manifests feminine behavior and expresses the wish to be female, with accompanying female-role fantasies. Observation of feminine play, parent and teacher reports of feminine behavior, projective testing, sociometric data, family interviews, questionnaires, and determination of mother-son versus father-son relationships all contribute to a diagnostic profile. The author considers early intervention essential because of the social rejection, anxiety, depression, suicidal risk, and high probability of later homosexuality, transvestism, and transsexuality evidenced in gender-disturbed boys.

Treatment is usually focused on a variety of techniques designed to increase masculine behavior and reduce feminine behavior and mannerisms. The ongoing efforts of Rekers and his associates to shape sex-typed behaviors through social reinforcement is noteworthy. Response-cost strategies, as well as self-reinforcement of masculine behaviors, have also been successfully applied by Rekers. Other techniques might include peer modeling, peer attention, and requiring cooperation between the target child and model boys. Magic Circle procedures can help promote awareness of, and feelings of belonging to, same-sex peer groups. Instruction in athletic and motor skills has also proven effective. The author stresses the need for cooperation between home and school to promote the carry-over of treatment gains from one setting to another. In homes where the father is absent or emotionally distant, the fostering of a relationship with a male model can offer companionship and empathy. When counseled, parents should be urged to encourage masculine behavior and discourage feminine interests. These varied approaches all strive for sex-role flexibility within the framework of one's own biological sex status.

◎◎◎◎◎◎◎◎◎◎◎◎◎◎◎◎◎◎◎◎◎◎◎◎◎◎◎◎◎

Depression

The major elements in depression are feelings of grief, loss, help-lessness, and guilt, along with a negative self-image. In children, depression may be masked by disruptiveness, acting-out behavior, lowered grades, and other symptoms, although lethargy and overt feelings of sadness may also be evident. In situations where masking behaviors occur, the reader is referred to other appropriate sections in this book for additional strategies. Bereavement over an actual loss is also included in this section, although it is usually less prolonged and less intense than the other kinds of depression considered here.

◎◎◎◎◎◎◎◎◎◎◎◎◎◎◎◎◎◎◎◎◎◎◎◎◎◎◎

Childhood Depression and the School Psychologist

AUTHORS: Ronald J. Friedman and Guy T. Doyal

PRECIS: Two case studies illustrating childhood depression with emphasis on the role of the school psychologist in detection and treatment

INTRODUCTION: In recent years depression has been increasingly acknowledged as a prevalent childhood disorder. While it is difficult to estimate how many children experience depression, it is clear that the problem deserves closer attention than it has received. Feelings of sadness that disappear after a short time are common in children and usually do not affect their physical, academic, and social well-being. However, more severe forms of childhood depression are often masked by hyperactivity, aggressiveness, physical complaints, poor achievement, and delinquent behavior. Because symptoms of childhood depression often affect school behavior and performance, the school psychologist should be aware of them and be able to decide when in-school treatment is appropriate and when other interventions are necessary.

Acute depression is usually short-lived and often has an identifiable cause, such as the loss of someone (or something) valued or the withdrawal of affection. It responds well to brief supportive counseling in which emotional support is provided while the child is encouraged to express the feelings of loss and/ or rejection. Teachers, parents, family members, and other interested adults should also be included in supporting the child in his grief. In most cases the families of these children can be helpful because the children are not grossly disturbed.

Chronic, long-term depression is more severe than acute depression. Symptoms include sadness, lethargy, threats of suicide, eating and sleeping difficulties, and expressions of helplessness. Chronically depressed children may live in families in which the mother is also chronically depressed and they may often experience rejection by parents. Intense feelings of helplessness and worthlessness may exist, with periodic episodes of acute depression. The severity of this condition typically requires long-term treatment and may involve the use of anti-depressants. Finally, the families of children who suffer from *masked* depression may also be highly disordered, and the necessary treatment may be similar to that for chronic depression. Teachers and parents should be aware that when depression is masked by other symptoms, using coercion or pressure to change these behaviors may only make the problem worse.

CASE STUDIES: The authors present cases that illustrate two types of depression:

1. Masked Depression—ten-year-old Chris was referred to the school psychologist by his parents even though his school performance was excellent. He had lost weight, was depressed, and was sleeping irregularly. Two years earlier he had been referred because of sleep disturbances and physical complaints. Counseling had reduced these behaviors. Two and one-half months before the current referral, Chris had witnessed the death of his younger sister. In weekly counseling sessions the school psychologist encouraged Chris to openly display his grief and share his fears about his own death. Within one month the depressive symptoms decreased, but Chris' mother reported that he had become defiant at home and had run away to visit his sister's grave. He was also increasingly disruptive in school. In this case, the authors note that the behaviors masking the depression developed as the overt symptoms disappeared. While his sister's death seemed to trigger this episode and might have led to a diagnosis of acute depression, indications of chronic depression that went back two years were evident.

2. Chronic Depression—at ten years of age, Alan, an only child, was referred for symptoms of depression, such as fatigue, physical complaints, and sleep disturbances. These symptoms had lasted for several years. His parents had been divorced one year before the referral, and he lived with his mother. When first interviewed he was hostile, but he became more verbal in later meetings. He cried when discussing his father but denied having intense feelings about him. Chris' hostility is viewed by the authors as an ineffective substitute for his chronic depression. He frequently acted aggressively to cover his sadness, but these episodes were quickly followed by guilt and withdrawal.

COMMENTARY: Depressed children and adolescents are difficult to treat because they will not acknowledge their depression and avoid confronting painful feelings. The therapist must first develop a close relationship within which the child is encouraged to express his feelings of rejection, loss, and worthlessness. Only when a solid rapport has been established can the psychologist begin to actively explore with the child the factors underlying his depression. Parents and teachers can play a supportive role in treatment after they are helped to understand that disruptive or hostile behavior may cover depressed feelings. In school it is crucial that the psychologist encourage teachers to refer depressed students and sensitize teachers to the symptoms and their destructive effects.

SOURCE: Friedman, R. J., and Doyal, G. T. "Depression in Children: Some Observations for the School Psychologist." *Psychology in the Schools,* 1974, *11*(1), 19-23.

Cognitive-Behavioral Therapy for Depression

AUTHORS: A. J. Rush, M. Khatami, and A. T. Beck

PRECIS: Using behavioral assignments to reduce depression in a college student

INTRODUCTION: Mildly to moderately depressed patients have found relief through both cognitive and behavior therapy. A combination of these treatments has been shown to be more effective than either one alone. These successes indicate the need for further investigation of cognitive and behavioral therapies with the chronically depressed, particularly those who have failed to maintain previous treatment gains or for whom other strategies have not been effective. The authors report three cases treated with a cognitive-behavioral approach. In one case, a twenty-four-year-old college student who had been suffering from depression for three years was seen for five sessions.

TREATMENT: The student had received drug treatments and psychoanalysis with no success. He was on a leave of absence from college because of his depression. During the first session he reported his past enjoyment of walking and observing nature. However, in his depressed state he focused only on negative feelings. The therapist suggested that after the session he walk to the college cafeteria and concentrate on his surroundings instead of on his feelings. The student phoned the next day to say that he had followed this advice and had had a delightful experience studying the architecture and gardens as he walked. When he reached the cafeteria, he felt better than he had in months and ate a hearty meal. For the next four visits the student was encouraged to participate in enjoyable activities and to write down satisfactions arising from them. He was also urged to begin doing academic work and, to increase its difficulty in a graded, step-by-step fashion. During sessions the therapist and client discussed his tendency toward negative self-judgments.

After two weeks of therapy, his depression (as measured by the Beck Depression Inventory) was within normal limits, and his academic performance had returned to full capacity. Follow-up twelve months later showed maintenance of these gains.

COMMENTARY: The authors demonstrate how a student's negative misconceptions can be altered through behavior assignments, graded tasks, and guided evaluation of personal attributes. As a result of the behavior changes produced by the assignments, depressive feelings were altered and self-esteem was enhanced. These techniques may prove acceptable to students who are unwilling or unable to explore their feelings. The non-threatening quality of an appropriate behavior assignment and graded task might work with students whose depression creates hostility toward traditional affective approaches.

SOURCE: Rush, A. J., Khatami, M., and Beck, A. T. "Cognitive and Behavior Therapy in Chronic Depression." *Behavior Therapy*, 1975, *6*, 398-404.

Additional Readings

Lewinsohn, P. M. "Activity Schedules in Treatment of Depression." In J. D. Krumboltz and C. E. Thoresen (Eds.), *Counseling Methods*. New York: Holt, Rinehart and Winston, 1976.

Depressed individuals are treated by directing them to engage in activities that are reinforcing and enjoyable. After making out lists of enjoyable and meaningful activities from prepared master lists or previous clients' choices, the present clients then monitor their own behavior by indicating at the end of each day which activities they engaged in and by rating their moods. Reinforcement is provided for increased activity level. In this study depressed clients were rewarded for activity increases with increased therapy time. The therapist was nondirective, listened with interest, and focused empathetically on the feelings and comments of the clients. The goal was to develop in clients a positive attitude toward the therapy. Results showed an increase in selected activities and a decrease in measured depression. For the future, the authors suggest broadening the range of activities available to the clients and using different kinds of reinforcers. Directive as well as nondirective therapies have also proved useful. Increasing the reinforcing characteristics of the environment is but one of many treatment approaches to depression. Attention to interpersonal relations and to internal feeling states is also important.

Meyers, J., and Pitt, N. W. "A Consultation Approach to Help a School Cope with the Bereavement Process." *Professional Psychology*, 1976, 559-564.

When two youngsters from the same parochial school died within one month, discipline problems increased, crying and apathy were observed, bomb scares were reported, rumors circulated of an impending third death, and younger children experienced death-related fantasies. A consultant psychologist held a series of workshops to help teachers cope with these behavioral and psychological consequences. Four themes were covered: (1) the importance of allowing children to talk out their sad feelings rather than protecting them from the topic of death; (2) understanding the three stages of mourning (protest/denial, despair/disorganization, and reorganization) and how they relate to the students' behaviors; (3) the importance of tuning into and expressing one's own feelings of grief as a staff member; and (4) specific recommendations for helping students express their grief, such as setting aside time for classroom discussion or dealing with feelings as they spontaneously surface in class. Teachers were urged not to pressure students to talk and to do only as much as they felt comfortable doing. This program promoted communication about death and allowed the school to help children deal with these feelings. Teachers expressed their personal feelings in the workshops, and many initiated classroom discussions. After the workshops, discipline complaints declined.

Elective Mutism

Electively mute children speak only in restricted settings and only to a select group of people. Children with this disorder will speak normally in certain situations, then become totally silent if the setting is changed or new people enter the room. Elective mutism has been highly resistant to traditional psychodynamic treatment. However, behavioral strategies in the school have demonstrated a good record of success. Several examples are presented in this section. A related disorder is reluctant speech, in which a very low frequency of speech is displayed in certain settings. This problem is considered less difficult to treat than elective mutism because some speech is already present.

Guidelines for Managing Elective Mutism

AUTHORS: Ronald Friedman and Nicholas Karagan

PRECIS: Suggestions for home and classroom management of elective mutism

INTRODUCTION: The authors view elective mutism as learned behavior. Silence is learned because it reduces the anxiety associated with speaking. This reduction of tension is rewarding, so the pattern of remaining silent is maintained and becomes resistant to change. Attempts to force speech from the child fail because the pressure of having to speak increases the fear and fortifies the mutism. Yet the elective mute usually displays no speech, language, or other communication disorder, has no physical defect that would inhibit talking, and has the intelligence to produce well-developed speech. The child has simply learned to fear speaking. This is particularly serious in school, where emphasis is placed on verbal activity. In addition, because the child will speak to family and/or friends (particularly his or her mother), the problem may not be detected until the school years.

GUIDELINES: The authors urge patience in working with electively mute children and suggest seven guidelines for classroom and home management:

First, do not use punishment or bribery to force speaking. This will increase insecurity and maintain silence.

Second, involve the child in all regular group activities.

Third, in settings where the child seems at ease, speaking should be encouraged through such tasks as reading or storytelling.

Fourth, parents should have familiar visitors at home to help the child speak with others in a nonthreatening setting.

Fifth, nonverbal activities with adults should be encouraged at home and in class. Opportunities to speak should be provided but not forced. The teacher or parent should speak normally to the child.

Sixth, if a good relationship exists between teacher and

child, the teacher may carefully try to encourage the child to speak in private. Answers of one word may be sufficient at first, but the teacher should stop urging the child to speak and continue with nonverbal activities if the child becomes anxious. A tape recorder or other objects such as cards or books can be used to create interest and increase the child's sense of security. As small successes occur, attempts to elicit other responses should be made. If speech progresses in private, this procedure can be moved to the classroom. There, the teacher may occasionally ask the child a question that requires only a simple answer and may have the child continue with nonverbal activities. Gradually, the teacher may introduce the child to activities in small groups. Most importantly, verbal participation should be encouraged with support and a lack of pressure.

Seventh, speaking with strangers should be attempted with familiar people present at home and in school. The child should never be pressured to speak but should be slowly encouraged to do so.

COMMENTARY: The main point of this article is that caution should be used when introducing a mute child to verbal activity. Before the child will speak, he or she must feel more competent and less anxious than usual. This can occur only through careful management of the speech settings. The authors note that with these guidelines, mute children seen at the psychological diagnostic clinic at the University of Iowa have improved in school. The teacher and parent were able to promote speech with patient handling and proper consultation.

SOURCE: Friedman, R., and Karagan, N. "Characteristics and Management of Elective Mutism in Children." *Psychology in the Schools,* 1973, *10*(2), 249-252.

Classroom Treatment of Elective Mutism

AUTHORS: Ross W. Colligan, Robert C. Colligan, and Maxine K. Dilliard

PRECIS: Using behavior modification techniques in the classroom to treat an electively mute student

INTRODUCTION: Electively mute children will not speak in everyday social situations and usually talk only to a limited number of close family members and friends. Among clinicians, opinions about the cause and appropriate treatment of elective mutism vary widely. Some view elective mutism as a symptom of underlying neurosis or personality disturbance and recommend individual psychotherapy, play therapy, parent counseling, or, in some cases, hospitalization. Others describe it as learned behavior that can be remedied through behavior modification techniques at home, in school, or in other noninstitutional settings. In this paper the authors chose a behavioral approach to treat an eleven-year-old boy with long-standing mutism.

Peter was a shy preschooler who talked to younger children but rarely to peers or adults. He did not speak in school but was an alert, popular, and successful student who communicated through notes and gestures. Efforts by school specialists to develop speech were unsuccessful. In grade 5 Peter's teacher and one of the authors of this article developed a plan to encourage Peter to speak in the classroom.

INTERVENTION: Treatment was organized in three stages:

Stage One—for six weeks Peter and his teacher held daily conversations designed to build a close, trusting relationship in which the teacher would become a powerful source of approval for Peter. The teacher stressed the importance of speaking to others and offered to work with Peter to reach this goal. Peter was required to participate in these talks but could respond in any way he wanted. After a few weeks he had to write some of his answers and at times imitate oral and motor behaviors performed by the teacher. Included were activities used by speech therapists to shape sound production. During this stage Peter developed a positive relationship with the teacher but would not imitate sounds.

Stage Two—to encourage him to speak in the classroom, Peter was shown the teacher's tape recorder and was asked to make a recording at home to share with the teacher. He made the recording and was praised lavishly. He was then asked to make a recording in the private conversation room in school and was again praised for his compliance. From then on, he recorded privately all language-oriented classwork. After five sessions of such recordings (and with Peter's knowledge), the teacher stood outside the private room with the door slightly open and listened to Peter while he was taping. At the end of three weeks Peter was able to record with the teacher in the room.

Next, to encourage transfer of speech to the classroom, a new plan was introduced in which students were required to ask for their class books. For Peter, asking out loud was shaped in the following eight steps: (1) whispering "book" to the teacher outside the classroom; (2) whispering "I need a spelling book, please"; (3) whispering the whole sentence but saying only "book" aloud; (4) saying the sentence aloud; (5) whispering "book" in class; (6) whispering the sentence in class; (7) whispering the sentence and repeating "book" aloud in class; (8) saying the sentence aloud in class. When Peter did not respond for ten days, the teacher designed an aversive situation to create stress for him. Students were told that they would have to request desks for the afternoon if Peter did not perform step one by noon. To resolve the stress and obtain social approval, Peter took the first step and was rewarded energetically by the teacher and students. The remaining steps were completed in eight weeks. Two weeks later he was talking normally in class and receiving much praise from his peers.

Stage Three—to encourage Peter to speak outside the classroom, school personnel were asked to talk to Peter and request answers. He was also sent on errands to practice speaking. By the end of grade 5, Peter's speech was no different from that of other students. Follow-up during the summer and one year later showed no reduction of speech.

COMMENTARY: This case illustrates how elective mutism can be treated in the classroom without the need for expensive hospitalization or psychotherapy outside the school. The teacher's influence as a social reinforcer, along with the gradual shaping of the target behavior, helped Peter achieve the goal. Further encouragement was provided by arranging for peers to reinforce talking rather than silence. The authors point out that this program was implemented by a teacher who was not an expert in behavior modification. Behavioral techniques can be employed without long-term training, can be learned through consultation with school specialists, and can be applied in the classroom during the school day without interfering with classroom routine. While this particular procedure seemed to require a sizable commitment on the teacher's part, less intrusive approaches are available.

SOURCE: Colligan, R. W., Colligan, R. C., and Dilliard, M. K. "Contingency Management in the Classroom Treatment of Long-Term Elective Mutism: A Case Report." *Journal of School Psychology,* 1977, *15*(1), 9-17.

Additional Readings

Bauermeister, J. J., and Jemail, J. A. "Modification of 'Elective Mutism' in the Classroom Setting: A Case Study." *Behavior Therapy,* 1975, *6,* 246-250.

The authors describe treatment of an eight-year-old Puerto Rican boy who was mute in the classroom but verbal outside. In class, hand raising, answering questions from the teacher, reading aloud, and completing assignments were targeted for reward, and minimal criteria were set for their display. The homeroom teacher (and later the English teacher) socially reinforced each occurrence and gave the boy a star at the end of class if he met the preset behavior criteria. At home his mother awarded a big star for every fifteen stars earned in school, with the promise of a bicycle for three big stars. Obvious and sometimes dramatic changes in target behaviors were effected, in addition to increased peer interaction and active requests for help with work. Progress was being maintained at a one-year follow-up. The authors stress that this simple in-class procedure does not interrupt classroom routine and that it resulted in quick change with generalization of gains.

Scott, E. "A Desensitization Program for the Treatment of Mutism in a Seven-Year-Old Girl: A Case Report." *Journal of Child Psychology and Psychiatry,* 1977, *18,* 263-270.

The author describes a four-week treatment of mutism. Although six and one-half years old, Linda had not spoken outside her immediate family and would not communicate in class. In treatment Linda read into a tape recorder and answered taped questions while the therapist gradually moved into the therapy room until face-to-face positioning was achieved. Since Linda enjoyed contact with the therapist, she was allowed to sit on the therapist's lap and have some candy as the taped sessions were played back. The therapist then began to read the questions directly while Linda answered into the recorder. After five sessions her answers had to be directed to the therapist. Finally, both entered the therapy room together, answered questions, and played a game in which Linda had to ask questions. New adults were introduced to promote carry-over of speech. New settings such as the classroom were also tried but proved too anxiety provoking. Thus, the procedures were repeated by the therapist in a more structured fashion in a corner of the classroom. Students were gradually introduced into the corner as Linda answered questions and then transferred back to the entire class along with Linda. Finally, the teacher took over from the therapist. In addition, two classmates were instructed in prompting Linda to speak. Three months later success was being maintained. During the summer break Linda responded to her mother's questions at home and, once back in school, ran errands, made requests, and sang in music class.

Williamson, D. A., Sanders, S. H., Sewell, W. R., Haney, J. N., and White, D. "The Behavioral Treatment of Elective Mutism: Two Case Studies." *Journal of Behavior Therapy and Experimental Psychiatry,* 1977, *8,* 143-149.

Two case studies utilized shaping, positive and negative reinforcers, time-out, reinforcer sampling, and fading strategies. In case one, a third grader was silent in school but verbal at home. Initially a shaping and modeling procedure was used in which the boy imitated the mouth movements of blowing and the sounds of "ah" and "cat." Money was the reinforcer; time-outs were used for noncompliance. Next, words were prompted and rewarded with ten-minute rest breaks and money. If the boy did not respond, he was left alone for twenty minutes to sit in his chair and look at the wall. Treatment was then transferred to the classroom. When this failed, clinic sessions were reinstated, and increased verbal responding was reshaped. After several sessions, the number of adults present was increased to three. Then the child was again required to answer in front of his class. At two-week and one-year follow-ups the third grader was displaying normal speech with peers and teachers. In case two, a seven-year-old girl was initially treated with shaping and modeling. This resulted in unvoiced but not vocal approximations to speaking. The mother was then used to apply shaping procedures, but the girl would only respond if the therapist was outside the room and only partially visible. Next, reinforcer sampling was used. Roller skates were introduced, and the girl was told that she could use them at home for three days if she responded vocally to the therapist. She was then told that she could keep them for her own if she read for ten minutes to her class. Both steps were successful, although she would not respond when a different therapist worked with her for one session. Finally, fading was accomplished through a classroom procedure in which the girl could earn money and a class party by reading to the class. One month later no reinforcement was required.

Williamson, D. A., Sewell, W. R., Sanders, S. H., Haney, J. N., and White, D. "The Treatment of Reluctant Speech Using Contingency Management Procedures." *Journal of Behavior Therapy and Experimental Psychiatry*, 1977, *8*, 151-156.

Reluctant speech is defined as a very low frequency of speech in particular settings. In one case, eight-year-old Mike spoke readily at home but only in a limited way in school. In treatment he received a token for each instance of speech to classmates. A small group of five friends was used at first to minimize his fear of attention from the entire class. This group was gradually increased to twenty students. Tokens could be traded for stars, which were displayed on a chart; after forty-five speech episodes, the class would earn a party. After five days Mike earned the party, and rewards were changed to privileges. One-year follow-up showed a maintenance of gains. The second treatment involved Kenneth, a seven-year-old with reluctant speech. For eight fifteen-minute sessions over three days, he received tokens for prompted or spontaneous speech. Both types of speech increased and generalized in the presence of a second therapist who delivered no rewards. Two months later, increased speech was being maintained. At home tokens were given for comments to nonfamily members; the tokens were redeemable for toys and privileges. This increased Kenneth's verbalizations. Follow-ups at two months and one year showed continued progress. Treatment of reluctant speech is less complex and time consuming than treatment of elective mutism because some verbal responding is already present.

4 ◎◎◎◎◎◎◎◎◎◎◎◎◎◎◎

Habit Disorders

◎◎◎◎◎◎◎◎◎◎◎◎◎◎◎

A habit may be defined as a behavior pattern that is (1) repeated frequently and often excessively; (2) well established and often resistant to change; and (3) displayed with an almost involuntary regularity. This chapter deals with habit disorders that may seriously affect school attendance, academic progress, and social success with peers and adults. For example, children who soil or wet regularly may soon develop a characteristic odor that can lead to teasing, social ostracism, or teacher reluctance to interact with them. Likewise, children who publicly masturbate may cause great discomfort in school personnel. Although such masturbation is not typically performed with a sexual intent, teachers may regard it as a form of sexual deviation and as symptomatic of emotional disturbance. The next step is often referral to an alternative school placement. For the adolescent, unprotected sexual intercourse increases the risk of pregnancy. Pregnant teenagers often withdraw from school, losing the chance to complete their high school education. Similarly, students who abuse alcohol and/or drugs may regard themselves as helpless in the face of home and school problems and may either drop out or continue their pattern of school failure. Finally, poor study habits, lack of motivation, and disorganization can affect students of all ages and create conflicts with parents and school authorities.

In the schools most interventions for habit disorders have focused directly on changing behavior and/or attitudes rather than on probing the presumed underlying historical causes for the problem. The reasons for this here-and-now approach are compelling. First, each day that the behavior persists, learning may continue to be disrupted, and relationships with students and teachers may worsen. These immediate problems require that the symptoms themselves be modified, with later attention given to deeper personality issues, if necessary. Second, the varied responsibilities of the school psychologist (or other school mental health practitioner) rarely allow time for in-depth psychodynamic treatment with one student or small groups. Behavior-oriented strategies may be developed by the psychologist and then implemented and/or maintained by the teacher or parent with ongoing consultation. This frees the practitioner to reach a greater number of students, parents, and staff members. Third, behavioral strategies have proved most effective in the treatment of habit disorders.

The approaches described in the section on Poor Academic Performance best represent the variety of techniques in use in the schools. In addition to teacher-controlled reinforcement contingencies, students have been taught to self-monitor and reinforce their own progress. Parents and principals have been added as reinforcing agents to broaden the utility and appeal of behavioral techniques. In response to criticism about the use of punishments (such as time-out and response cost), new emphasis has been given to rewarding those behaviors that are incompatible with a maladaptive pattern. For example, it has been found that students will more readily increase their performance to *obtain* positive rewards than to *avoid* negative ones. This approach shifts the tone of treatment from an emphasis on punishment to a stress on reward for adaptive responses. Reward for academic improvement has also been found to decrease disruptive behavior, and this finding has influenced strategies designed for classroom disturbance.

One other increasingly common technique is the group contingency. When consequences for a total class are dependent on the behavior of each student (or one student), the resulting social influence positively affects behavior. The selection of a group contingency will depend on such classroom variables as (1) the degree of expected peer pressure on nonperforming students; (2) the potentially negative side effects of withholding rewards from performing students; and (3) the number of students in the class requiring intervention. Since group and individual contingencies are often found to be equally effective, some writers have suggested using an individual approach for one or a few students; for larger groups, however, a group contingency may be more efficient and more easily implemented.

The interventions for substance abuse and sexual behavior have been somewhat different from those for other habit disorders. It has become clear that teaching factual information alone does not change attitudes, alter abusing behavior, or, in the case of sexual behavior, reduce the risk of early pregnancy or venereal disease. An added problem is convincing students to believe the information they are given and to apply it in making responsible decisions about drugs, alcohol, and sex. The most effective programs have incorporated peer-group support, peer counselors and teachers, student involvement in program design, communication skills training, and such attitude-change approaches as values clarification.

Poor Academic Performance

Poor performers typically function below the levels predicted by intellectual and educational assessments. They are often described as possessing the "behavioral repertoire" necessary for academic success but as being unmotivated, disorganized, unresponsive, bored, or lacking the necessary study skills and habits. The term underachievers *is sometimes used to describe these students. The articles in this section cover a range of techniques for increasing performance rate and accuracy. Many of the problems considered in other sections of this book also result in lowered classroom performance, and the reader is referred to those sections for discussion of other techniques.*

A Home-School Reinforcement Program
to Improve Academic Performance

AUTHOR: R. J. Karraker

PRECIS: Instructing parents how to provide home reinforcements when their children bring home satisfactory school reports

INTRODUCTION: The author notes that parents can deliver powerful rewards and punishments to their children that are unavailable in the classroom. This resource can be used by the school in developing a combined home-school reinforcement program. Parents can be taught to systematically respond to their child for improved or successful academic performance. The author investigates three such methods of instruction and their effects on student achievement.

HOME-SCHOOL PROGRAM: Students in three second-grade classrooms were selected on the basis of teacher judgments of underachievement. Throughout the study their performance was measured by the percent of correct responses on daily math assignments. The children each day brought home report cards that indicated satisfactory or unsatisfactory math performance. A smiling or frowning face with a check-box next to it represented each of the two categories. To receive a satisfactory check, the child had to maintain or increase her performance from the previous day.

Parents were instructed in the home delivery of rewards in one of three ways:

First, five sets of parents received a letter describing the purpose of the program. The daily report card was explained as well as the procedure for checking the smiling or frowning face. Parents were asked to choose a reward that could be presented to the child for a satisfactory check. This could be a treat, a special favor, or other appropriate item. They were also instructed to praise the child for her good work but not to punish the child for an unsatisfactory grade; the parent was told to simply examine the card and then walk away. If no card was brought home, no comment was to be made. The parent was to ask the child about it but was not to punish the child or respond negatively.

Second, five different sets of parents were invited to school for two one-hour conferences held one week apart. The first conference described how behaviors are learned, the basic principles of reinforcement, some child management strategies, and the importance of consistency in implementing these techniques. In the second conference the report card was introduced and explained. Parents rehearsed home responses to the card and discussed child management issues.

Third, six sets of parents were invited to a fifteen-minute conference, and the report card procedure was explained to them. No additional information or training was provided.

For ten days prior to the program, student performance on the math assignments was measured. Then for ten consecutive days the children were given their marked report cards, so that they could examine their grades. After a few minutes the teacher collected them; the children did not take them home. In the third ten-day period they brought their cards home, and parents delivered the instructed responses.

In the pretreatment phase, the median for correct math answers was 47 percent for the "two-hour conference" students, 77 percent for the "fifteen-minute conference" students, and 58 percent for the students whose parents received only letters. When report cards were handed out but not brought home, performance increased about 4 percent, with a range of 2 to 6 percent. When cards went home, the median for correct answers for the "fifteen-minute" students rose to 91 percent while the other two groups increased to 100 percent.

COMMENTARY: Home-school management programs are effective methods of improving academic performance. This extremely powerful and flexible technique has also been used to control poor school attendance and a variety of disruptive behaviors. Its potential utility with other school-related problems justifies expanded research. In addition, the author found that a letter or a fifteen-minute conference was as successful as two one-hour conferences, indicating that the procedure can be implemented with a minimal expenditure of time. Teachers will find this technique useful because it increases achievement and gives them specific information that they can share with parents. For parents, structured involvement in their child's school progress may enhance their relationship with him or her and provide additional motivation for the child to improve. This first real participation by parents in their child's education may itself produce positive change.

SOURCE: Karraker, R. J. "Increasing Academic Performance Through Home-Managed Contingency Programs." *Journal of School Psychology,* 1972, *10*(2), 173-179.

Goal Setting to Enhance Learning

AUTHORS: David C. Gardner and Paula L. Gardner

PRECIS: Setting goals to improve test performance in students with learning problems

INTRODUCTION: Research has shown that the performance of goal-setting students is consistently superior to students who do not set goals. The authors applied this finding to high school students in a resource room setting. Students attended the resource program one hour a day, five days a week, for help in a variety of subjects. They were variously diagnosed as educable retarded, as learning disabled, or as having learning problems. For this study two lists of high-interest spelling and vocabulary words were developed from the state driver's manual. Students had one week to study the first list and were then given a spelling and vocabulary test. During the second week, list two was assigned, and students were instructed to prepare for similar tests at the end of the week. One day before this second set of exams, students met with their teacher individually to set test goals. They stated to the teacher how many words they expected to spell and define correctly. Test results from the first week were shared with the students before they set their goals. Students were also asked not to discuss their goals with one another.

The results of the second week's tests were significantly higher than the scores from the first week for both spelling and vocabulary. No student earned a lower mark on the second set of tests than on the first. Furthermore, students reported applying themselves harder to try to meet their goals.

COMMENTARY: This study lacks many experimental controls, and the authors themselves stress that it was not intended to be a rigorous investigation. Rather, it represents an attempt to apply the findings of other well-designed studies to the practical classroom issue of increasing the quality of student work. Goal setting is easy to implement, works with students of varying intellectual abilities, and can be applied with no special training in virtually all subject areas. It can supplement other more complex intervention strategies and develops within the student an expectation of success that he or she may then work to fulfill. For these reasons it is a powerful motivational tool.

SOURCE: Gardner, D. C., and Gardner, P. L. "Goal Setting and Learning in the High School Resource Room." *Adolescence,* 1978, *13*(51), 489-493.

Self-Management of Academic Performance

AUTHORS: Laura L. Humphrey, Paul Karoly, and Daniel S. Kirschenbaum

PRECIS: Comparing the effects of self-reward and self-punishment on work rate in a second-grade reading class

INTRODUCTION: Children can self-regulate and administer

their own rewards in the classroom without external management by teachers or other adults. In this article the authors explore whether students can also self-punish as a way of altering behavior. Response cost is a form of punishment that has been effective in modifying academic and disruptive behavior without producing negative side effects. Thus, a self-imposed response-cost procedure was implemented in a second-grade reading class. Academic performance was measured by the number and accuracy of reading papers completed, as well as by the accuracy of reading workbook answers. Disruptive classroom behavior was also recorded.

METHOD: The response-cost procedure was carried out as part of a classroom token economy system. During a two-hour morning period, the teacher met with reading groups while other students worked on individual reading assignments. They rewarded or fined themselves with tokens depending on the rate and quality of their work. Performance on the various reading measures was first recorded for ten days before the treatment started. Then, at the beginning of each treatment day, each child received two cups, one with the child's name on it and the other labeled "bank." Eight children began treatment by self-rewarding for ten days and switching to the response-cost procedure after a ten-day no-treatment period. Ten other students performed in the reverse order.

Self-Reward. "Banks" were filled with plastic chips, and children transferred tokens into their cups according to predetermined performance criteria. They corrected their own work by using answer keys, checked their scores against the self-reward schedule printed on the key, and rewarded themselves with the proper number of tokens.

Response-Cost. Cups were filled with tokens, and "banks" were left empty. Children fined themselves for inaccurate or incomplete work by transferring chips from their cups to the "bank" according to criteria printed on their answer keys. Throughout the treatment, rewards and fines were equal. Thus, if each incorrect answer was fined two tokens, each correct answer earned two tokens.

While both self-reward and response-cost procedures improved work rate in the reading class, self-reward was always more effective. Six of the eight students who self-rewarded improved reading rates 100 percent or more initially, while only four of ten response-cost students improved that much. In addition, during the no-treatment phase between the switch in conditions, the reward group maintained a 75 percent increase in work rate, while the response-cost group returned to a rate only 5 percent above pretreatment levels. No change in accuracy of performance occurred for any group throughout all treatments. Although workbook accuracy was not self-rewarded or punished, the performance of the first self-reward group exceeded that of the first response-cost group. Disruptive behavior declined in the course of the study but was highly variable.

COMMENTARY: Techniques to motivate academic performance that can be managed by students are highly economical for the teacher and do not require her to constantly evaluate and reward (or punish). This study demonstrates that students as young as second graders can self-assess and self-reinforce their behavior with periodic supervision. While both self-reward and self-imposed response cost were effective without reducing quality of work, the authors note several possible reasons for the superiority of the self-reward technique. First, response cost required subtraction and fining for inaccurate or incomplete work. While older students may have no trouble with these procedures, they may be difficult for second graders. Second, response cost requires students to work to avoid failure and focuses their attention on poor performance. These factors can foster negative self-evaluations, thereby slowing work rate. When students are given the option, working for reward would seem to be a more effective motivator than working to avoid punishment.

SOURCE: Humphrey, L. L., Karoly, P., and Kirschenbaum, D. S. "Self-Management in the Classroom: Self-Imposed Response Cost Versus Self-Reward." *Behavior Therapy,* 1978, *9,* 592-601.

Encouraging Achievement
Through Positive Grading Practices

AUTHORS: Richard A. Brown and Jordan Epstein

PRECIS: Helping low achievers improve their performance through positive grades and comments

INTRODUCTION: When teachers grade papers, they often mark the incorrect responses while ignoring correct answers. The authors argue that highlighting errors consistently punishes the poor student and provides little motivation for him or her to improve performance, while the good student is able to escape such punishment by doing well. Contrary to the belief of teachers that comments do not influence poorer students, it has been found that lower achievers respond better to positive statements on test papers than do higher achievers.

METHOD: The authors explored these issues by testing the effects of positive and negative grading procedures on the performance of high and low achievers. For five days students in seventh- and eighth-grade math classes worked on daily five-minute addition drills consisting of 112 problems. For the classes receiving immediate feedback, papers were scored and returned at the end of the class period. Some classes received immediate *positive* feedback in the following way: (1) a *C* was written next to each correct answer; (2) the total number of correct answers was written at the top of each paper; and (3) positive comments were written on the paper if the student equaled or surpassed the previous day's score. Examples were: "This is a great paper" or "Keep up the good work."

Classes receiving *negative* immediate feedback were treated in the opposite way: (1) a check was placed by each wrong answer; (2) the number of incorrect answers was written at the top of each paper; and (3) negative comments were written on papers that had either the same number of wrong answers as the previous day's papers or a greater number. Comments included: "Too many wrong," "Careless work," or "Not fast enough."

No-feedback classes received their scores at the end of the five days.

On the basis of the score on the first drill, students were grouped into high and low achievers. After five days, the major finding was the large improvement made by the low achievers in the positive feedback classes. This contradicts teacher expectations that low achievers are least responsive to grades. While it is true that low achievers are most likely to be unaffected by *critical* grades and comments, positive feedback seems to increase their desire to improve.

COMMENTARY: Many teachers use reinforcing rather than punishing grading procedures without realizing the potent motivational effect that this feedback can have on low-performing students. Grades and comments as a form of positive feedback are a natural part of the learning process and require no alterations in teaching style or class routine. Clearly, errors that need correction or skills that need improvement should not be ignored and should be pointed out in the teaching process. But recognition through positive grades is a strong incentive to low-achieving students and may represent one of the few instances in which they are praised for academic effort and acknowledged for positive attributes.

SOURCE: Brown, R. A., and Epstein, J. "Interaction of Achievement Level and Reinforcing Properties of Daily Grading Systems." *Education*, 1977, *98*(2), 131-134.

Reality Therapy and Underachievement

AUTHORS: Howard Margolis, Cindy Muhlfelder, and Gary Brannigan

PRECIS: Stressing responsible behavior to motivate a high school underachiever

INTRODUCTION: This paper describes a fifteen-year-old boy with a history of underachievement and aggressiveness. Mark lived with his mother and two siblings but often slept at his grandmother's house because of conflicts with his mother. He saw his father occasionally but against his mother's wishes, since she felt that his father was a bad influence. Mark also spent time with an uncle who was suspected of supplying him with drugs and liquor. In first grade Mark was described as bright but overactive and unable to listen.

INTERVENTION: Mark spent one period each day in a special math class for disruptive underachievers. Louise, a special education major in college, worked with him to develop what "reality therapy" defines as responsible behavior. In school this consisted of obeying conduct rules, behaving appropriately in front of peers, interacting with others responsibly, and fulfilling graduation requirements. Louise worked with Mark to achieve these goals through several strategies:

1. Discussing Topics of Interest—Louise established a trusting relationship with Mark by initiating neutral conversations or "small talk" and gradually working up to more meaningful topics. As Mark became more relaxed with her, he was willing to discuss such personal interests as the air force, auto mechanics, and his desire to be a lawyer. Louise allowed Mark to show off his expertise and impress her. On several occasions she accompanied him to the weight-lifting room and let him instruct her on lifting techniques. As a result of Louise's acceptance, he grew more comfortable with her.

2. Social-Personal Standards—Louise always communicated her concern and respect for Mark and her belief in his ability to develop and attain reasonable goals. When work was assigned in class, she always remained task oriented with Mark, instructing him in math concepts, praising his efforts and mature behavior, holding him to responsible work habits, and stressing his ability to succeed.

3. Structuring Math Work—Mark's math work was sequenced and broken down to maximize success and provide frequent immediate feedback for completion of tasks. New mate-

rial was not presented until Mark had mastered all previous operations.

Before long Mark began to behave more responsibly and to improve in math, and he also started to meet graduation requirements. Three months after leaving, Louise returned to talk to Mark. He felt that he was pressured by most teachers but said that he had enjoyed how Louise worked with him. He seemed more interested in graduating and reported better grades than he had before the intervention began.

COMMENTARY: Louise dealt with the here-and-now reality of Mark's behavior rather than dwelling on his past difficulties or the reasons for them. She set standards for responsible behavior and held him to them but she also showed respect for his needs and talents and made him feel valued. This directive approach requires active teacher participation, as well as willingness to spend time developing trust with a student who typically gives and receives negative feedback. The teacher avoids asking the student why the behavior occurred; instead, she helps the student recognize its positive and negative consequences and how the behavior helps or hinders him in attaining realistic goals. The intent is to help the student develop the skills and confidence that will motivate him to work for responsible goals.

SOURCE: Margolis, H., Muhlfelder, C., and Brannigan, G. "Reality Therapy and Underachievement: A Case Study." *Education,* 1977, *98*(2), 153-155.

The Principal's Influence
on Academic Performance

AUTHORS: Rodney E. Copeland, Ronald E. Brown, and R. Vance Hall

PRECIS: Using principal praise and attention to increase math and reading performance in elementary school students

INTRODUCTION: The school principal can have a powerful effect on members of the school community. For example, principals have been able to influence such varied behaviors as attendance, punctuality, and disruptiveness through planned contacts with students and parents. In this paper the authors first demonstrated how a principal altered the attendance patterns of three students, and they then assessed the effects of the principal's actions on the academic performance of individual students and entire classes.

STUDENT TREATMENT: Three fifth graders who were described as unproductive received individual daily tutoring in reading and arithmetic and were rewarded by the principal for their progress. In reading, a different word-recognition list (composed of ten words) was practiced each day and tested the next day. Responses were scored in front of the student, and the number of correct responses was written on the list. Math tutoring consisted of addition drill in which the student worked on a math sheet for five minutes. The sheet was then scored, and the number of correct problems was placed at the top.

To begin treatment, the principal saw each boy and told him that he would like to see him improve in word recognition, math, or both, depending on the condition. In reading, the student was immediately taken or sent to the principal if he pronounced eight or more words correctly on his test. The principal praised him and asked him to return the next day if he again answered eight or more words correctly. In math, each boy had to correctly solve a specified number of problems to receive attention from the principal. With the introduction of principal contact, each boy increased his performance in both reading and math.

CLASS TREATMENT: The highest- and lowest-achieving third-grade classes in an elementary school worked on math sheets for five minutes daily. Student scorers graded the sheets, and scores for each child were displayed on a chart. After a few weeks, additional lists were made of students who improved their scores from the previous day, as well as of students with the five highest scores. The principal entered the classroom and asked those on the "improved" list to stand. He praised their progress, expressing the hope that everyone could be praised the next time. He then repeated the procedure with the five highest scorers. This treatment occurred twice a week for three weeks and resulted in a considerable increase in daily math scores in both classes. Only nine of the seventy-four students did not show any improvement.

COMMENTARY: The authors point out that students who do not perform well in school usually receive negative attention from the principal. This tactic is rarely successful in improving their performance. The procedures described here were successful because they focused on productivity rather than nonproductivity. As noted in other articles in this section, academic improvement is more likely to occur when students work to obtain positive rewards rather than to avoid negative consequences. If both the teacher and principal combine to reinforce progress, this "positive" strategy may be even more effective. For the principal this intervention allows for brief yet positive interactions with students. It also capitalizes on the principal's power to influence classroom performance.

SOURCE: Copeland, R. E., Brown, R. E., and Hall, R. V. "The Effects of Principal-Implemented Techniques on the Behavior of Pupils." *Journal of Applied Behavior Analysis*, 1974, *7*, 77-86.

Behavior Modification in an Open Classroom

AUTHORS: Donald Ascare and Saul Axelrod

PRECIS: Using points with an individual and group contingency to improve work rate in fifth and sixth graders

INTRODUCTION: In an open classroom the responsibility for learning is primarily with the student. The teacher rarely conducts the class but instead moves about the room guiding students in their own self-selected activities. Instead of rows of desks, the room is divided into areas where students work on learning tasks at various levels of difficulty. This arrangement requires self-motivation, yet not all elementary students are able to direct their own learning. The authors developed a behavior modification plan for children who had difficulty functioning in an open classroom. It was a token system providing both individual and group rewards contingent upon the performance of twenty target students.

METHOD: Fifth and sixth graders in four open classrooms were required to complete five assignments a week in each of their subject areas. They were permitted to schedule their work as they pleased. Twenty of the children were not working effectively even though such corrective steps as structuring their day and providing specific work directions had been taken. These students were placed on the token reinforcement system. They were scheduled by their teacher to spend one hour in each of four learning areas and were observed every ten minutes. If they were working on their assignments, the teacher recorded a plus sign that was worth five points. If not, a minus sign was recorded. When the token program began, the teachers shared their observations with the class using two different methods. Two teachers recorded each observation at their desks and wrote the results for each child on the blackboard after each one-hour period. Two other teachers recorded each observation directly on the blackboard. If the student earned a predetermined number of points (forty for each student), he or she received fifteen minutes of extra free time at the end of the day.

In the group contingency target students could also earn extra free time for their classmates if their combined total exceeded a prespecified criterion. This was the number of points each student had to earn multiplied by the number of students in class who were in the program.

As improvements were noted, individual and group criteria were increased; these changes were posted daily. After fourteen days, a no-treatment period was instituted. Nine days later the system was reintroduced. As a result of the program, every target student in each of the four classes improved his percentage of time working. Some increased their rate by as much as 75 percent. When the program was stopped and then reinstituted, the rate fell and rose accordingly, clearly indicating that work output was being influenced by the program.

COMMENTARY: In this treatment the authors combined an individual token reinforcement system with a group contingency to motivate students in an open classroom. Token economies are also easily applied in traditionally structured classrooms and have been studied most often in these settings. Furthermore, using free time as a natural reinforcer made it unnecessary to expend funds for candy or toys. Schools are relying less on material goods as rewards and are turning to activities and naturally occurring events such as free time, visits to the library, helping the teacher, and/or choosing the learning task. Disregarding philosophical arguments, the authors have demonstrated the compatibility of an externally managed behavioral plan within a self-directed open classroom.

SOURCE: Ascare, D., and Axelrod, S. "Use of a Behavior Modification Procedure in Four 'Open' Classrooms." *Psychology in the Schools*, 1973, *10*, 243-248.

The Helper Therapy Principle

AUTHOR: Joseph A. Durlak

PRECIS: Unmotivated students improve their academic performance and social skills by working as student helpers

INTRODUCTION: Students who tutor others often derive as much benefit from the process as those they help. They may experience reduced behavior problems, better self-concept, increased social skills, and improved academic performance. The Elementary Student Aide Program described by the author operates under this "helper therapy principle," utilizing ninth graders who are considered to be unmotivated underachievers. The goal of the program is to develop in these students the habits and skills necessary for academic and social success. Prospective aides volunteer or are recommended by the school staff. If they commit themselves to work for one semester, they are interviewed by the counselor to determine their motivation and their understanding of helper responsibilities. Once selected, they are assigned to a supervising elementary teacher and participate in tutoring students, correcting papers, setting up classrooms, supervising playground activities, and organizing class projects. Tasks and schedules are determined jointly by the aide and supervisor. Through this program, student aides fulfill their elective course requirements. Aides work a full morning or afternoon every school day and receive academic credit based on the supervising teacher's evaluation and grade.

PROGRAM EVALUATION: Evaluation of the program focused on its "helper therapy" effects. Questionnaire responses from supervisors and aides indicated positive self-concept changes, improved interpersonal relations, and better work habits in participating students. Parents reported improvement in the children's behavior at home and less trouble in school and with peers. They felt strongly that the program was a valuable technique for teaching responsibility. Academic performance was also considered an important measure of the program's success. Aides achieved an average grade of B+ for the program, and the grade for forty-six out of the fifty students exceeded their required course grades. In a comparison group of students only sixteen out of fifty received higher grades in their electives. Furthermore, unlike the comparison group, aides significantly improved their required course grades over the preceding semester. Moreover, negative report card comments for the aides were markedly reduced or eliminated, while the comparison group had no such reduction. In general, the "helper therapy principle" was supported by the results of this program.

COMMENTARY: The aide program consumed 50 percent of the day and was a major part of the student's educational experience. Like other alternative school projects, its goals were different from those of traditional academic programs and were realized through innovative practices. Its success demonstrates that students can be motivated to learn if the definition of learning is not confined to academic mastery alone. Schools must broaden their concept of "achievement" if they are to educate unmotivated students and must recognize that the classroom format is not the only method available. The counselor or school psychologist can coordinate such programs and thereby reach a larger "turned-off" population than is possible in a one-to-one or group setting. While the teacher must spend a certain amount of time in planning and supervising the program, the added freedom gained more than compensates for the time spent.

SOURCE: Durlak, J. A. "Ninth Graders as Student Aides: Making Use of the Helper Therapy Principle." *Psychology in the Schools,* 1973, *10*(3), 334-339.

Self-Recording Study Rate

AUTHORS: Marcia Broden, R. Vance Hall, and Brenda Mitts

PRECIS: Having a student self-record her own study behavior in class

INTRODUCTION: Most behavior modification programs require the cooperation of the classroom teacher. However, when the teacher is unwilling or unable to participate, the student or someone outside the classroom may have to implement the procedure. In this paper the authors examined the effect of student self-recordings on a variety of behaviors. The experiment discussed here investigated the effect of self-recording on study rates.

CASE STUDY: Liza, an eighth-grade student, wanted to improve her D— grade in history, but counseling sessions failed to change her performance. The teacher conducted the class as a routine lecture but asked periodic questions. When approached by the counselor, the teacher showed himself sympathetic to Liza's problem but said that the demands of the course made it impossible for him to attend to Liza's study behavior in class. Thus, a self-recording procedure was tried.

An observer recorded Liza's study behavior in class throughout the program. Teacher attention directed to Liza was also recorded. "Studying" included facing the teacher, taking lecture notes, facing a student who was answering a question, or responding when called on by the teacher. "Not studying" was defined as talking or being out of her seat, facing the window, handling nonschool items such as a comb or makeup, and working on unrelated assignments.

To begin the program, Liza met with her counselor and was given a sheet of paper with three rows of ten squares printed across the page. He instructed her to record her studying behavior at various times during the history class by placing a plus sign in a square if she was studying and a minus sign if she was not. She was to score herself according to her behavior at the moment she thought of it; there was no set schedule for her recordings. The sheet repeated these directions and had a space for the date. After reviewing the definition of studying with Liza, the counselor asked her to make sure that she picked up and turned in her sheets daily. Weekly meetings were held to review the self-recordings and to praise Liza for good study behavior. On days fourteen to eighteen treatment was stopped; it began again on day nineteen. Ten days later Liza's teacher was asked to participate by praising Liza's study behavior whenever he could. After about eight more sessions, self-recordings were discontinued, and teacher attention was withdrawn four sessions later.

When Liza began to self-record, her study behavior increased from 30 to 78 percent of the period. It dropped to 27 percent during the no-treatment phase and increased to 80 percent when the recording sheets were reissued. The request for the teacher to praise her increased Liza's study rate to 88 percent and also increased the number of times that the teacher attended to her. When self-recording was stopped, Liza's rate stabilized at 77 percent and remained there when teacher attention was withdrawn. Follow-up sessions approximately one week apart for three weeks showed Liza maintaining her study rate. Her grade at the end of the term was a C.

COMMENTARY: As the program progressed, Liza self-recorded fewer times per class and made no recordings on an increasing number of days. Furthermore, her self-recordings often varied widely from those of the observer who was simultaneously rating her throughout the program. (The variations, on a day-to-day basis, ranged up to 29 percent; on one day, Liza recorded her study behavior at 63 percent, the observer at 92 percent.) However, this did not affect her high study rate and indicates that the very act of self-recording was enough to modify her study behavior. As her teacher noticed increased studying, he was willing to pay more attention to her. The authors note that self-recording can strengthen a desired behavior to the point where a teacher will be more willing to reward it. Teachers who are reluctant to praise infrequent behaviors may thus be encouraged to participate in behavior management programs or perhaps initiate such simple techniques on their own.

SOURCE: Broden, M., Hall, R. V., and Mitts, B. "The Effect of Self-Recording on the Classroom Behavior of Two Eighth-Grade Students." *Journal of Applied Behavior Analysis,* 1971, *4,* 191-199.

Additional Readings

Block, J. "Effects of a Rational-Emotive Mental Health Program on Poorly Achieving, Disruptive High School Students." *Journal of Counseling Psychology,* 1978, *25*(1), 61-65.

This study compared the effect of rational-emotive and human relations training on low-income black and Hispanic students. All had low grades and records of frequent truancy, cuts, lateness, and serious misconduct. Treatment groups met for forty-five minutes each day for twelve weeks. The rational-emotive group was structured around set themes with a highly active and directive leader who encouraged role playing, self-questioning, the honest expressions of feelings, and direct confrontation. Activity exercises and homework assignments were also used. The goal was self-examination and cognitive restructuring (see W. Knaus, *Rational-Emotive Education: A Manual for Teachers,* New York: Institute for Rational Living, 1974). The human relations leader was less directive and tried to reflect and clarify feelings for members of the group. The goal was to aid adjustment through an understanding of psychodynamic behavior principles. In each session the leader made a short presentation with follow-up discussion (see E. Bullis and E. O'Malley, *Human Relations in the Classroom,* Wilmington: The Delaware State Society for Mental Hygiene, 1947). After treatment and at follow-ups, grades were significantly higher, disruptiveness was lower, and instances of cutting class were lower for the rational-emotive than for the human relations group and a waiting-list control group. A structured, action-oriented approach seems more effective with this population than a passive, reflective format.

Carter, J. L. "Application of Biofeedback/Relaxation Training
to Exceptional Children." *Journal of Clinical Child Psychology,* 1978, *7,* 23-25.

Biofeedback/relaxation techniques were used to help children aged five to eight with academic difficulties to control
stress and benefit from the learning process. Children listened
for ten minutes to taped relaxation exercises that used visual
imagery, and they then practiced handwriting. Afterwards they
received biofeedback/relaxation training individually for ten
minutes. Leads were attached on the flexor muscle of the pre-
ferred-writing forearm, and a visual display presented readings
of myographic muscle action. Children were instructed to watch
the display and keep the readings of muscle action as low as
possible. This procedure occurred twice a week for five weeks.
The children were also given muscle relaxation tapes to use at
home three nights a week. Results showed improved performance on intellectual, achievement, and perceptual-motor tests.
Handwriting was also improved. Parents and teachers reported
more well-adjusted behavior, and in one study measured self-
concept was more positive.

Daudargas, R. W., Madsen, C. H., Jr., and Scott, J. W. "Differential Effects of Fixed- and Variable-Time Feedback on Production Rates of Elementary School Children." *Journal of Applied Behavior Analysis,* 1977, *10,* 673-678.

Third-grade students were given reports to take home each
Friday describing the amount and quality of their work during
the week. Minimum daily work requirements were listed along
with the number of weekly assignments completed for each academic area. Parents were not asked to sign or return reports.
Assignment completion was defined as 85 percent accuracy. For
this study the fixed reporting schedule was varied. After one
week of Friday reports, students were told on the following
Monday that some reports would go home each day but that
they would not know whose until the end of the day. Seven to
nine students received reports each day, with each child getting
at least one per week. The schedule was varied so that fixed and
variable reporting was alternated over a five-week period. Variable reporting resulted in a marked increase in correctly completed assignments. When this condition was implemented for

the second time, completed assignments jumped 154 percent, indicating a high rate of completed extra assignments. Both students and teachers indicated a preference for variable reporting.

DeVries, D. L., and Slavin, R. E. "Teams-Games-Tournaments (TGT): Review of Ten Classroom Experiments." *Journal of Research and Development in Education,* 1978, *12*(1), 28-38.

Teams-Games-Tournaments (TGT) does not require a new curriculum but allows learning to be enhanced through a classroom reward structure different from the usual ones. It has three primary components. First, the class is divided into four or five student teams of equal overall achievement level. Team members work with one another to drill newly learned material and practice for tournaments. Second, once or twice each week students of equal achievement levels from each team compete for points in tournaments. Points are accumulated weekly, and team standings are published in a class newsletter. Third, games are played during tournaments to test skills and subject matter (for a detailed description see R. E. Slavin, *Using Student Team Learning,* Baltimore: Johns Hopkins University, Center for Social Organization of Schools, 1978). Research conducted with nearly 3,000 students in grades 3 to 12, showed TGT to increase academic achievement, to promote mutual student liking and cross-racial friendship, and to enhance those attitudes that support academic performance. Increased positive attitudes toward school were less consistently expressed. All three components were found to be important in producing the beneficial effects. The TGT structure uses skill diversity among students as an asset, creates increased interest in basic skill work, and harmonizes peer interactions with the learning process. A variety of TGT formats have been developed at the Center for Creative Leadership in Greensboro, North Carolina, and at Johns Hopkins University.

Greenwood, C. R., Hops, H., and Walker, H. M. "The Program for Academic Survival Skills (PASS): Effects on Student Behavior and Achievement." *Journal of School Psychology,* 1977, *15*(1), 25-35.

The Program for Academic Survival Skills (PASS) is a behavioral treatment package designed to improve achievement-related behaviors such as paying attention in class, working, and volunteering. Teachers of grades 1 to 3 were trained to identify academic survival skills, record them in class, and apply individual and group reinforcements to develop them in their students. Teachers set class rules based on the display of survival skills (for example, looking at the teacher while directions are being given). When rules were followed for specified time periods, students were rewarded with free time, recess, or other activities. As students came to meet the criteria for appropriate behavior, standards were raised until the children had to demonstrate survival skills for three consecutive days at 80 percent before rewards were given. PASS increased survival behaviors in reading and math and maintained them one week after termination of the program. Significant gains in reading achievement, along with similar but nonsignificant gains in math, were made by first graders. No significant gains were shown in grades 2 and 3. The authors speculate that younger students may be more sensitive to PASS procedures than older ones. Two-year followup analyses are planned.

Jackson, R. M., Cleveland, J. C., and Merenda, P. F. "The Longitudinal Effects of Early Identification and Counseling of Underachievers." *Journal of School Psychology,* 1975, *13*(2), 119-128.

Underachieving students were identified and then provided with psychological services during the fourth, fifth, and sixth grades. The services were described as adult centered, that is, mobilizing the adults in the child's life rather than counseling the child directly. Diagnostic techniques determined factors underlying poor achievement, while efforts were made to alter teacher and parent attitudes toward the child's problems. Meetings were held with parents, teachers, resource personnel, and others to plan prescriptive teaching goals and discuss other methods for working with the child. The child's strengths were stressed, so that adults might reevaluate and respond to him or her more positively. Personnel were urged to use such existing resources as tutoring and summer school to aid the child's learning. Six years later when they were high school seniors, the median class ranking of the target students was significantly higher than that of a control group. Scores on standardized achievement tests were also higher. Six months after graduation from high school more target than control students had followed through on their plans, and after one year the target students were as successful as control students in pursuing post-high school education. Psychological services (as defined in this article) seem to promote long-term positive outcomes.

Markle, A., Rinn, R. C., and Goodwin, B. "Effects of Achievement Motivation Training on the Academic Performance of Underachievers." In press.

Achievement Motivation Training teaches students to improve achievement-oriented thinking as a way of raising academic performance. Based on the pioneering work of McClelland and his associates (for example, D. C. McClelland, J. W. Atkinson, R. A. Clark, and E. L. Lowell, *The Achievement Motive*, New York: Appleton-Century-Crofts, 1953), this approach has been adapted for use in the schools. In this study, older children and adolescents identified as underachievers were trained over five sessions. In session one, students learned about achievement motivation, wrote stories and scored them on the amount of achievement imagery they contained, heard a lecture on motivation, and were assigned homework on goal setting. Session two dealt with motivation techniques and included group storytelling as a way to practice applying achievement imagery to lifelike situations. Homework was discussed and reassigned. Session three involved a presentation on classroom behavior, study habits, and test-taking skills. In session four, career and academic values were discussed. Students told achievement-oriented stories about two pictures, and study goals were reassessed. Session five focused on personal academic strengths and included tips and exercises on using time productively. Posttreatment evaluation demonstrated the effectiveness of the program in improving grade point averages.

McLaughlin, T. F., and Malaby, J. E. "The Comparative Effects of Token-Reinforcement with and Without a Response-Cost Contingency with Special Education Children." *Educational Research Quarterly*, 1977, 2(1), 34-41.

Nine- and ten-year-old special education students worked under a token system. They received points for appropriate

behavior and academic performance and lost points for disruptiveness and poor achievement. Exchange of tokens for privileges was made periodically. During this study students performed a daily tracing task and received ten points for
maintaining or increasing work rate. After a specified number of
sessions, response cost was added, and points could then also be
lost if the work rate was not maintained or increased. Under the
combined treatment, work rate was higher than under tokens
alone or under a no-treatment condition. However, token reinforcement was more effective than no treatment. No negative
effects of token loss were observed, even though students expressed preference for the token reinforcement condition over
the combined condition. The decision to use reinforcement
alone or with response cost requires consideration of classroom,
student, and program characteristics.

Perkins, J. A., and Wicas, E. A. "Group Counseling Bright
    Underachievers and Their Mothers." *Journal of Counseling
    Psychology,* 1971, *18*(3), 273-278.
    Bright male underachievers and their mothers participated
in separate group counseling sessions. First, counselors were
trained to develop specified levels of accurate empathy, positive
regard, and genuineness (see C. B. Truax, and R. R. Carkhuff,
Toward Effective Counseling and Psychotherapy, Chicago:
Aldine, 1967). Training involved rating taped therapy sessions,
practicing and rating responses to taped client statements, and
role playing. Counselors then established three counseling
groups in their schools. In group one, ninth-grade underachievers were counseled. In group two, underachievers were counseled during the day and their mothers in the evening. In the
third group, mothers were seen, but there was no student contact. Sessions were unstructured and focused on whatever
concerns participants chose to discuss. The emphasis was on
attitude change through a nondirective, introspective approach.
After twelve weekly one-hour sessions, the students in all three
conditions improved their grade point averages when compared
to a no-treatment group. Greater improvement was seen in the
self-acceptance of students when mothers were involved in
counseling. In fact, when mothers *only* were counseled, student
self-esteem was improved as much as when counseling involved

mothers and sons. After five months, improvement in grades was being maintained only in the two "mothers only" groups. It was concluded that achievement and self-acceptance can be positively influenced by counseling mothers of ninth graders. Boys of this age are still responsive to maternal influence. Thus, parent counseling skills should be developed and used by school counselors.

Richards, C. S. "Improving Study Behaviors Through Self-Control Techniques." In J. D. Krumboltz and C. E. Thoresen (Eds.), *Counseling Methods*. New York: Holt, Rinehart and Winston, 1976.

This approach uses bibliotherapy to help college students self-monitor their studying behavior. Typed handouts provide a standardized set of self-monitoring instructions that are distributed during a series of group sessions to college volunteers. These handouts describe self-monitoring as a simple observing and recording procedure that helps the student keep track of study habits. Daily records and cumulative graphs are kept of pages read and hours studied. These are totaled weekly. Goals for the following week are set that can be compared with actual achievement and self-reinforced if they are reached. Variations on this approach have deleted graphs and simplified the recording of study behavior to make the process as easy to implement as possible. Other studies have shown that gradually reducing therapist contact results in more positive grade changes than when steady contact is maintained. In addition, the less aware students are about their study habits, the more they benefit from self-monitoring because of the enhanced feedback effect. Self-monitoring is a technique for behavioral self-control that reduces the need for continued outside assistance.

Rie, H. E., Rie, E. D., Stewart, S., and Ambuel, J. P. "Effects of Ritalin on Underachieving Children: A Replication." *American Journal of Orthopsychiatry*, 1976, *46*(2), 313-322.

Underachieving children in kindergarten through grade 5 were given up to 20 mg. of Ritalin twice each day for fifteen weeks. All had displayed inattentiveness, distractibility, or disruptiveness but were not emotionally disturbed, physically disabled, brain damaged, or retarded. After treatment of the students, teachers rated them as less active, less distractible, more attentive, better achieving and less disruptive. However, objective measures showed no positive effect of the drug on reading, math, and spelling and no change in intelligence, achievement, and perceptual tests. The children were also clinically judged as less energetic, less emotionally expressive, and more lethargic than previously. No evidence was found that Ritalin improves learning. In fact, teachers may misinterpret behavior changes as improved achievement, and true learning problems will thus remain masked. It is recommended that Ritalin be used sparingly, in combination with other treatment approaches, and with frequent review of the need for continued use.

Wilson, S. H., and Williams, R. L. "The Effects of Group Contingencies on First Graders' Academic and Social Behaviors." *Journal of School Psychology*, 1973, *11*(2), 110-117.

A first-grade class received five minutes of free time if each student completed his or her writing assignment with six or less errors in a twenty-minute period. A choice of activities was available during free time. Five extra minutes were added for no misconduct. Each instance of misbehavior reduced free time for the class by one minute. After three weeks of treatment, the children's appropriate behavior and work rate increased significantly, although there was no carry-over of improved behavior outside the immediate setting. The utility of applying group contingencies for managing large classes was stressed.

Enuresis-Encopresis

Enuresis is the "involuntary urination by a child four years old or older," while encopresis is the "repeated involuntary defecation into clothing . . . occurring in children four years or older." (C. E. *Schaefer,* Childhood Encopresis and Enuresis: Causes and Therapy, *New York: Van Nostrand Reinhold, 1979, pp. 151, 4). For this section enuresis is further classified as nocturnal wetting and diurnal wetting. The reader will note that articles on enuresis appear only in the Additional Readings at the end of this section. Only about 5 percent of wetting is strictly diurnal, and virtually no research exists that deals specifically with enuresis in the classroom. Furthermore, in the 20 to 40 percent of cases in which both daytime and nighttime wetting occur, treatment is directed to the nocturnal problem. The articles cited here suggest ways in which the school practitioner can advise parents in planning treatments for wetting. For a comprehensive description of enuresis the reader is referred to the source cited above, as well as to C. E. Schaefer and H. L. Millman,* Therapies for Children: A Handbook of Effective Treatments for Problem Behaviors, *San Francisco: Jossey-Bass, 1977; and C. E. Schaefer, H. L. Millman, and G. F. Levine,* Therapies for Psychosomatic Disorders in Children, *San Francisco: Jossey-Bass, 1979.*

Treatment of Soiling
in a Resource Room Setting

AUTHORS: Thomas W. George, Juanita Coleman, and Pamela Williams

PRECIS: Using behavioral techniques in the resource room to modify the soiling behavior of an eleven-year-old boy

INTRODUCTION: The authors report the treatment of an educable mentally retarded black child attending regular class with resource room support. Frequent soiling had been evident since kindergarten, creating severe peer problems and making it difficult for teachers to stand close enough to the child to provide help.

TREATMENT: Treatment began with a conference involving the student, two friends, and the resource teacher. When questioned, his friends indicated that they liked to play with him when he did not smell. When they left, the student admitted the problem and began to cry. The plan to reduce his soiling was then described to him. He would report to the resource teacher each morning after coming to school, as well as between each class. If he had no odor, he would earn a star to place on a progress chart that would later be displayed in the resource room and explained to classmates. If soiling occurred, he would be sent to clean and change himself and would receive no star. He would also be asked to use the toilet before returning to class even if he had not soiled upon checking in. Successful days would be rewarded with toys or candy.

During the eleven days of treatment the boy had ten clean days. When treatment was stopped for six days, soiling occurred on four. The resource teacher then met with the boy to express concern about the new soiling behavior and discuss a new plan. In this phase he would not be allowed to attend gym or take part in school Christmas activities on days when he soiled. In addition, if he soiled on more than three of the remaining sixteen days before Christmas vacation, he would not be allowed to attend the school Christmas party. He was no longer required to check in with the resource teacher and received no stars or toys. He was still told to clean up if he soiled and was still praised for remaining clean. His regular teacher was also asked to remind him to use the bathroom and to inform the resource teacher when soiling was detected. The resource teacher kept in daily contact with the boy and allowed him a rewarding activity (such as running an errand) if he had not soiled. Under these conditions the boy soiled the first three days, then remained clean until the Christmas party.

After Christmas, the resource teacher met with the boy to praise his cleanliness and to tell him she was sending a letter of success to his parents. She also asked the classroom teacher to continue praising the boy for not soiling, to tell her if he soiled, and to ask him periodically if he needed to use the bathroom. Over the next five months only two soiling incidents occurred. These were followed by conferences with the resource teacher in which she offered the boy support. Six months into the next year, no soiling had occurred.

COMMENTARY: As noted in other studies, the elimination of encopresis not only rids the student of an annoying, unpleasant behavior but often leads to increased social success. In this case the boy also developed an increased concern for his personal hygiene and appearance, while also improving his academic performance. It is not uncommon to find that once disturbing behaviors are reduced, students are much more able to devote their energies to school tasks. Also worthy of note is the direct approach taken in discussing the situation with the student and in establishing mutual awareness of the problem. This sharing can be an effective part of treatment by providing the therapist with insight into the student's awareness of a problem and his possible resistance to, or acceptance of, a treatment plan. Furthermore, the resource room teacher is often the adult most trusted by students involved in a resource program. In the resource room, students may feel free to vent frustrations and discuss problems. Enlisting these specialists in programs to modify behavior should be seriously considered by school personnel.

SOURCE: George, T. W., Coleman, J., and Williams, P. "The Systematic Use of Positive and Negative Consequences in

Managing Classroom Encopresis." *Journal of School Psychology*, 1977, *15*(3), 250-254.

Behavioral Treatment of Encopresis

AUTHOR: Elizabeth A. Scott

PRECIS: Using social reinforcement and withdrawal of attention to eliminate soiling in an eight-year-old boy

INTRODUCTION: Encopresis, or faulty bowel control, may have many causes, ranging from poor toilet training or psychological conflicts to poverty, low intelligence, need for attention, or anger. Whatever its cause(s), encopresis in school may be controlled through behavioral strategies. In this case, a disadvantaged, disruptive eight-year-old boy of limited intelligence and with a long history of encopresis was treated during the school day. No medical cause for the problem was uncovered. Although David was learning effectively in a special school placement and was less disruptive than he had formerly been, inappropriate soiling continued. Most of his brothers and sisters had been taken from his mother at birth because of her limited ability to care for them. She was aided by social service agencies, yet David's home was a severely depressed setting. Deprivation and needs for attention were considered to be major factors in his encopretic behavior.

TREATMENT: David was observed to soil in the morning before school and after meals. His teacher would clean him and change his clothes when he soiled in school. When treatment was initiated, however, the teacher brought David to the bathroom each hour to praise cleanliness or appropriate use of the toilet or to display anger and disapproval for soiling. This proved unsuccessful because praise and anger provided David with equal attention, and because the teacher's frustration inhibited her ability to provide positive as well as negative feed-back. Therefore, beginning with week seven of the study, a nurse was enlisted to carry out the intervention by applying differential reinforcement and time-out. David was taken to the toilet by the nurse each hour and was praised for cleanliness or proper voiding; he was then allowed to play in a special room with the nurse's full attention for about thirty minutes. David also posted stars for cleanliness on a prepared poster. However, if he had soiled, he was left to clean himself and was not taken to the room to play. This procedure virtually eliminated enco-presis during the first week. After five weeks toilet visits were reduced to after meals only. One week later session lengths were decreased first to twenty minutes, then to ten minutes. For the next two weeks David was rewarded in class and in the final two weeks was placed under the teacher's control with the nurse totally absent. Soiling behavior remained infrequent.

COMMENTARY: The author points out that David knew how to use the toilet properly before treatment was initiated. Thus, it was possible to deliver verbal instructions and assume that David knew what to do. The extent of toileting skill should be assessed before such strategies are implemented. If competence in this area is not evidenced, the behavior may need to be shaped before techniques are used to increase its frequency. Furthermore, the procedure described required the availability of an additional staff person for several months. It is doubtful that most schools would consent to this kind of expenditure to treat one student. But this technique may be utilized in a class where an aide is readily available to provide the reward, leaving the teacher free to continue the lesson. This is more likely to occur in a special education classroom than in a regular setting.

SOURCE: Scott, E. A. "Treatment of Encopresis in a Class-room Setting: A Case Study." *British Journal of Educational Psychology*, 1977, *47*, 199-202.

Additional Readings

Allgeier, A. R. "Minimizing Therapist Supervision in the Treatment of Enuresis." *Journal of Behavior Therapy and Experimental Psychiatry*, 1976, *7*, 371-372.

A response-cost procedure was used to control enuresis in eight- and eleven-year-old sisters. Each morning they recorded on a chart on the refrigerator whether they had urinated during the night. No contingency was attached to urination, but the girls were penalized one tenth of their allowance for not signing in and fifty cents for lying. After five weeks they were denied fluids after six o'clock in the evening (including dinner) until they were dry for three consecutive weeks. Daily self-monitoring continued. Over twenty weeks both showed a decline in nighttime accidents. No accidents were recorded for weeks fifteen to twenty. This procedure minimized professional involvement and was easy for parents to monitor. It may not be as effective when family problems are severe, when the child cannot self-monitor, or when physical factors contribute to wetting.

Berg, I. "Day Wetting in Children." *Journal of Child Psychology and Psychiatry*, 1979, *20*, 167-173.

The author notes that there is surprisingly little information available on daytime wetting in children (diurnal enuresis). In one study approximately 28 percent of children with nighttime wetting (nocturnal enuresis) also had daytime episodes. Estimates of enuretic children who wet only during the day range between 1 and 10 percent, with girls predominating over boys. Most cases of daytime wetting involve children with primary enuresis who have never experienced extended periods of dryness. Complaints of urgency and increased frequency of micturition have been associated with daytime enuresis. Urgency refers to the strong need to rush to the toilet to void and to an inability to delay beyond a few minutes. Both urgency and frequency have been linked to "bladder instability," a condition in which premature voiding reactions occur in the bladder before regular distention of the bladder walls takes place. Another study has suggested that daytime/nighttime wetters do not void completely when they go to the toilet, but further study is needed here. It has also been found that with boys daytime wetting is related to encopretic incidents. Other relationships between diurnal wetting and physical processes also bear investigation.

Studies examining psychogenic issues have been inconclusive. Results in one case indicated that 40 percent of mothers of daytime wetters rated them as "nervous" compared with 20 percent of the mothers of daytime/nighttime wetters. Other research suggests that wetters with a daytime component have more problems than nonwetters. Teachers also tend to rate daytime/nighttime wetters as more disturbed than students in the general population, with boys showing antisocial behaviors and girls neurotic disorders. Diurnal wetters have been found to be less willing to use the toilet than nocturnal wetters. Perhaps one reason for reports of more problems in daytime wetting relates to the greater embarrassment and teasing experienced by daytime than by nocturnal wetters. Mothers also report feeling that daytime wetting is more related to disobedience than is nocturnal wetting. This attitude may affect their responses to the child. As for treatment, diurnal wetting has received virtually no attention. Reports suggest that treatment of nocturnal wetting can improve daytime accidents. However, a study using retention control training and a bell and pad technique for nocturnal wetting showed no positive carry-over to daytime wetting. Few treatments have been applied to daytime wetting itself.

Donahue, G. T., and Reing, V. A. "Teacher-Moms Help Emotionally Disturbed Pupils." *Nation's Schools*, 1966, *78*, 50-52.

This project was part of an individualized therapeutic educational program for emotionally disturbed children. Volunteer women from the community were invited to work with children in conjunction with a teacher supervisor and members of mental health consultation services. Moms were advised by the supervisor while they provided instruction to the children and evaluated their progress. Periodic meetings were held with the psychologist, psychiatrist, and school administrators. The goal was to phase the children back into regular classes, and careful attention was given to the timing of the child's return to normal schooling. In one case, an eight-year-old schizophrenic child with severe soiling problems progressed rapidly in the teacher-mom program. Soiling ceased, home relationships improved, and by third grade he was in regular class on a half-time basis. In grade 6 he was attending as a full-time regular student.

Pedrini, B. C., and Pedrini, D. T. "Reinforcement Procedures in the Control of Encopresis: A Case Study." *Psychological Reports,* 1971, *28,* 937-938.

Since he enjoyed reading, a fifth grader was rewarded with a book coupon for each class period in which he did not soil. A daily total of eight coupons was possible. After he had earned forty coupons, his mother bought him a book of his choosing. Additional criteria were set for more books, and the boy charted his progress toward gaining coupons. Soiling was dramatically reduced in school over eleven weeks, although only slightly improved at home. Peer relations improved, and during seven months of the following school year only one accident was recorded.

Sadler, O. W., and Merkert, F. "Evaluating the Foxx and Azrin Toilet-Training Procedure for Retarded Children in a Day-Training Center." *Behavior Therapy,* 1977, *8,* 499-500.

This study compared the Foxx and Azrin method with no training and with a scheduling method in which children were toileted four times per day (see R. M. Foxx and N. H. Azrin, *Toilet Training the Retarded: A Rapid Program for Day and Nighttime Independent Toileting,* Champaign, Ill.: Research Press, 1973). The Foxx and Azrin technique worked better than the other two methods, successfully eliminating daytime wetting in the school setting, and generalizing to the home. However, the fact that considerable staff effort was required created mixed feelings of satisfaction. Refinement of this successful technique was suggested.

Schaefer, C. E. *Childhood Encopresis and Enuresis.* New York: Van Nostrand Reinhold, 1979.

This book covers the causes, physiology, toilet-training practices, and treatment approaches associated with encopresis and nocturnal enuresis. The research and related literature are thoroughly described, with emphasis on behavioral, psychodynamic, counseling, and other treatment strategies. For enuretic children, the bell and pad conditioning technique has been the most consistently effective intervention, and a detailed discussion of this procedure is given. The research on retention control training is also discussed. Encopretic children seem to respond most readily to behavioral strategies involving rewards and penalties for appropriate or inappropriate defecation. The book ends with specific suggestions for conducting the treatment process and further research.

Masturbation

Masturbation and sex play are natural and common in young children of both sexes and occur in conjunction with developing sexual curiosity. It is crucial that parents and teachers distinguish between a natural developmental interest in the genitals and excessive or inappropriate public masturbation. In examining the causes of excessive masturbation, some writers view it as an attempt to relieve undue tension and associated depression or even as a way to avoid interpersonal relationships. One article in this section suggests that rubbing the genital area in response to irritation from daytime enuresis may inadvertently reinforce masturbatory pleasure and that this may trigger excessive display of the habit. Treatment should carefully avoid associating masturbation with anxiety to prevent future maladjustment. Child specialists consistently caution parents against adopting a rigidly punitive attitude toward sexual curiosity in young children. An open, realistic approach that appropriately responds to children's questions will promote healthy attitudes in them.

Reducing Excessive Masturbation
at Home and School

AUTHORS: Larry N. Ferguson and George A. Rekers

PRECIS: Using a combination of behavioral techniques to control public masturbation in a young girl

INTRODUCTION: Play therapy, drugs, reinforcements, and punishment have all been used to reduce compulsive masturbation. Although children are expected to masturbate, attempts are usually made to eliminate excessive masturbation. The authors describe the use of a nonpunitive behavioral treatment with a four-year-old girl expelled from a private preschool for public masturbation. The procedure was used in the clinic, home, and school and involved the girl's mother and teacher.

HISTORY: When Jane began to masturbate at home, her parents reprimanded the behavior but were not overconcerned. At school, her teacher noticed her rubbing her hands under her dress and distracting other students. This occurred daily without letup. The school suspended her out of fear that other children would copy her behavior. At the clinic she displayed excessive dependency, immaturity, distractibility, and impatience. She was easily upset, enuretic, and isolated from peers. During the initial interview at the clinic with her mother, she masturbated repeatedly.

TREATMENT: Jane's mother and teacher agreed to define masturbation as standing, sitting, or lying down with the hand in the genital area. Jane and her mother called masturbation "itchy-ootching," so this phrase was used during treatment. For the first two weeks Jane visited the clinic three times per week to talk with the therapist or play with toys. The frequency of masturbation was recorded by the therapist for ten minutes, then by the mother and therapist together for another ten minutes. The mother was also instructed to record masturbation at home. For four sessions Jane played with toys for the first ten minutes and received two M&M's from the therapist for not masturbating. Then the procedure was repeated for the next ten minutes with the mother present. For the remaining forty minutes, the therapist and mother talked while Jane regularly received M&M's for not masturbating. The delivery of the reward was gradually switched to the mother. As Jane earned M&M's, she was praised for playing quietly. During this time no masturbation occurred.

At home Jane's mother gave her two M&M's and praise for each successful fifteen minutes. If masturbation occurred, she was told to do something else and was rewarded with an M&M if she complied. If not, her mother would instruct her to stop "itchy-ootching." When she complied, her mother rewarded her with candy and offered another activity. After twelve weeks masturbation occurred only once in seven days of observation. Jane was allowed to return to school four weeks after her suspension; her behavior there was observed by the therapist. Masturbation usually occurred during quiet periods when Jane was restless and distracted. The teacher was instructed to intervene in the same way as the mother had done at home but was asked to praise Jane rather than give her candy.

After Jane had been back in school for two weeks, clinic sessions were ended. By the seventh week masturbation stopped at home, and Jane returned to school as a regular student. No incidents occurred during the first three days. When masturbation reoccurred at home during week nine, the mother instructed Jane to stop, and she turned off the television set for five minutes if Jane threw a temper tantrum. Masturbation was completely eliminated after two weeks. After six months it occurred only infrequently. After nine months Jane was transferred to a longer kindergarten program in which she masturbated once a day and, as a result was expelled from the school. At twelve months her mother reported infrequent masturbation at home and rarely needed to intervene. Psychological testing revealed that Jane felt insecure and had ambivalent feelings toward her mother but that she had increased her self-control. Incidents of wetting also decreased. Two years later Jane had stopped public masturbation. Masturbation at home was treated as normal and was observed only twice.

COMMENTARY: In this treatment verbal intructions were combined with the reinforcement of competing responses to reduce public masturbation. The occasional time-out procedure by the mother (no television for five minutes) was effective in reducing tantrums and might also have been used in school if needed. Instead of being punished for masturbation, the child was directed toward alternative enjoyable activities and reinforced for taking part in them. This approach is not unique to masturbation or difficult to apply in schools. The school psychologist can implement these techniques with the cooperation of the parent and teacher. However, because adults are highly sensitive to the genital play of children, they often overreact to masturbation as a unique problem or as indicative of emotional disturbance. Educators are also prone to these misconceptions. With the help of the teacher, the school treatment of public masturbation can proceed in the same manner as treatment for other inappropriate behaviors.

SOURCE: Ferguson, L. N., and Rekers, G. A. "Nonaversive Intervention in Public Childhood Masturbation: A Case Study." *Journal of Sex Research*, 1979, *15*(3), 213-223.

Punishing Public Masturbation

AUTHORS: J. William Cook, Karl Altman, Jeanne Shaw, and Marsha Blaylock

PRECIS: Eliminating public masturbation by squirting lemon juice into the mouth

INTRODUCTION: Severely retarded students frequently masturbate in class and probably will not respond to traditional positive reinforcement techniques. In this case the excessive public masturbation of a seven-year-old physically disabled and retarded youngster threatened his placement at home and in a community special education class. The use of electric shock to eliminate the behavior was rejected on legal and ethical grounds. Since lemon juice had been used as a mild but effective punishment for other behavior, its effectiveness was tested here.

TREATMENT: Public masturbation had been a problem for this boy for four years at home, in school, and in the institution in which he had lived from age 3 to 6. His parents were considering reinstitutionalization if the behavior remained uncontrolled. Before the lemon juice procedure was implemented, an attempt was made to reduce masturbation by following it with a loud "No!" and hand spanking. This tactic increased the adult attention he received, and masturbation became even more frequent. Ignoring the behavior was also found to be ineffective.

Lemon juice treatment was initiated in school and later at home. When the boy put his hand in his pants toward his penis, the teacher or aide squirted 5 to 10 cc. of unsweetened lemon juice from a bottle into his mouth. Within nine days, in-school masturbation was reduced to zero and stabilized there after day sixteen. On the forty-third day, the treatment was begun by his mother at home and in public. Masturbation in public was reduced to zero by the thirteenth day, with no relapse over a six-month follow-up period.

COMMENTARY: This simple procedure proved highly successful with a severely retarded boy in a special education classroom and enabled him to stay in a less restrictive school and home setting. It is unlikely that this technique would be needed with nonretarded students. They tend to respond when competing behaviors are encouraged and positively reinforced. Punishment always raises ethical questions, and it is advisable to weigh the benefits of a behavior change against the aversive technique to be used. The lemon juice technique was only mildly aversive, especially when weighed against a possible return of the child to an institutional setting. Whatever the consequence, however, the least negative contingency should always be tried before moving to more aversive strategies.

SOURCE: Cook, J. W., Altman, K., Shaw, J., and Blaylock, M. "Use of Contingent Lemon Juice to Eliminate Public Masturbation by a Severely Retarded Boy." *Behavior Research and Therapy*, 1978, *16*, 131-134.

Overcorrection to Eliminate Masturbation

AUTHORS: James K. Luiselli, Carl S. Helfen, Bruce W. Pemberton, and John Reisman

PRECIS: Applying positive practice overcorrection to modify public masturbation

INTRODUCTION: In positive practice overcorrection, the child is required to perform exaggerated responses that are incompatible with the target behavior. This technique has been used successfully in place of the more controversial and aversive electric shock procedures. The authors here applied positive practice overcorrection to the treatment of compulsive public masturbation in a disturbed and retarded eight-year-old boy. Masturbation occurred in his public school treatment program and involved rubbing his zipper to stimulate his penis. This behavior interfered seriously with academic instruction. In a previous treatment setting he was allowed to masturbate in a certain spot at specified times. This proved unsuccessful in controlling his behavior.

POSITIVE PRACTICE OVERCORRECTION: Treatment was applied during small-group desk work in which structured training tasks were presented and reinforced in four-minute intervals. For the first four days the boy earned one token for each completed task and received praise two or three times per minute for behavior that was incompatible with masturbation. Tokens could be exchanged for treats. Masturbation was ignored.

Beginning on day five, the boy received "overcorrective functional movement training" if he masturbated. He was told to stand by his desk and was instructed by his teacher to raise his arms over his head, extend them in front of his body, extend them by his sides, and wrap them across his chest. Each position was held for three seconds. This cycle was performed four times with simultaneous teacher demonstration. If he refused to comply, he was physically guided to perform the motions. After twenty-nine days treatment ended, and the boy's behavior was observed one, three, and six months later. When tokens alone were given, masturbation occurred during 58 percent of the four-minute intervals. When overcorrection was introduced, masturbation dropped to zero within four days, occurred only 4 percent of the time during the treatment period, and was absent throughout the one-year follow-up.

COMMENTARY: Overcorrection quickly eliminated masturbation in this youngster. The authors also note that the success of the procedure allowed appropriate behaviors to emerge and be reinforced. However, this technique may require the presence of more than one adult in class, especially in the early stages when frequent training episodes are likely. In addition, since physical correction may be necessary, parental understanding and approval of the technique are strongly recommended. While parents should always be told when a treatment is implemented in class, strategies that involve physical contact should probably receive written parental consent. This case also demonstrates the flexibility of overcorrection. When first developed by Foxx and Azrin, overcorrection training lasted five minutes, and positions were held for fifteen seconds (R. M. Foxx and N. H. Azrin, "The Elimination of Autistic Self-Stimulatory Behavior Through Overcorrection," *Journal of Applied Behavior Analysis,* 1973, *6,* 1-14). In this case, a modification with less aversive requirements was successful.

SOURCE: Luiselli, J. K., Helfen, C. S., Pemberton, B. W., and Reisman, J. "The Elimination of a Child's In-Class Masturbation by Overcorrection and Reinforcement." *Journal of Be-*

havior Therapy and Experimental Psychiatry, 1979, *8,* 201-204.

Additional Reading

Wagner, M. K. "A Case of Public Masturbation Treated by Operant Conditioning." *Journal of Child Psychology and Psychiatry,* 1968, *9,* 61-65.
An eleven-year-old girl who masturbated in class was rewarded with periodic reinforcers on a fixed schedule for increasing intervals between masturbation episodes. Negative verbal comments were given for masturbation. The behavior was eliminated and did not reappear throughout the school year.

Thumb-Sucking/Nail-Biting

Thumb-sucking and nail-biting are common habits among children and adolescents. Each behavior affects close to one half of the child population between the ages of zero and sixteen. Thumb-sucking becomes more socially inappropriate with age and can result in teasing, rejection by peers, labels of immaturity, and perhaps dental malocclusion. Nail-biting continues to affect as many as 25 to 36 percent of college students. Aside from the annoyance and pain of torn cuticles or ripped nails, bitten nails are unattractive and, for some, cosmetically embarrassing. Nail-biting has been treated through the use of bitter substances on the nails, habit reversal training, negative practice, hypnosis, self-monitoring, electric shock, and other techniques. Thumb-sucking treatments have included some of the same approaches, as well as pacifiers, mittens and a variety of rewards and punishments. One article in this section attempts to treat the underlying anxiety often associated with these habits through relaxation training.

Controlling Thumb-Sucking
Through Social Reinforcement

AUTHORS: Edward A. Skiba, L. Eudora Pettigrew, and Steven E. Alden

PRECIS: Using praise and attention to reinforce behaviors incompatible with thumb-sucking

INTRODUCTION: Social reinforcement has been used to control a variety of behaviors in the classroom. In this paper thumb-sucking was reduced in three third-grade girls through the systematic use of praise and attention. Audrey sucked her thumb at home and in class, especially when she could not complete difficult classwork. Betty was a moody, demanding child who had peer problems and a negative attitude toward teachers. She sucked her thumb at any time and became uncooperative when denied attention. Carol was a well behaved, successful student who sucked her thumb when tired or not busy.

TREATMENT: The children were considered to be thumb-sucking when the thumb touched the lips or entered the mouth. One week before treatment began, observers attended each student's class twice while the experimenter taught fifty-minute lessons. These were orientation and practice sessions for the observers. Beginning in the second week and continuing twice a week for eight weeks (sixteen sessions), the experimenter taught for fifty minutes in each class while the observers noted the thumb-sucking rate for each child. In sessions one to four, rates were recorded while no treatment was being applied. During sessions five through eight, the experimenter delivered praise and attention to each target student as he taught the class. He rewarded her for folding her hands or arms on her desk or for writing in her notebook. These behaviors were selected because they were felt to be incompatible with thumb-sucking. Because of the behavior management demands of the classroom and the need to provide a meaningful lesson, no predetermined reinforcement schedules were developed. Social reinforcement was delivered at various times during the fifty minutes in a way that would not interrupt the lesson. For sessions nine to twelve treatment was terminated and was then reinstated for sessions thirteen to six-teen.

Audrey's level of thumb-sucking showed a decrease of about 50 percent during the first reinforcement phase. When treatment was stopped during session nine, her thumb-sucking jumped to a rate three times higher than her pretreatment level but quickly lowered in sessions ten to twelve. When reinforce-ment was introduced the second time, her thumb-sucking dropped to levels similar to those in the first reward phase. Betty's pretreatment rate was lower than Audrey's or Carol's. When social reward was started, Betty's thumb-sucking was markedly reduced but then returned to pretreatment levels dur-ing sessions nine to twelve. It decreased to very low levels during the final praise condition. Carol's was the lowest rate of all three students during both reinforcement phases, and it did not increase when social attention was withdrawn during lessons nine to twelve.

COMMENTARY: This procedure closely approximates the teacher's natural reinforcing behavior under actual teaching con-ditions. The authors point out several difficulties that affected the results of this study. First, teaching a classroom crowded with eight-year-olds is not conducive to delivering consistent reinforcement, and the absence of a predetermined reward schedule makes it difficult to assess the treatment's effective-ness. Second, providing reinforcement twice a week for fifty minutes may not be sufficient to produce desired changes. Daily rewards by the teacher may be more productive. Third, the be-havior of teachers, parents, and peers toward the thumb-suckers was not controlled or examined. These influences may seriously affect the treatment results. One approach to this problem might be to have parents also reward children at home. Com-bined home-school reinforcement strategies have been shown to be powerful techniques with such problems as truancy and poor academic performance, and they might prove useful here.

SOURCE: Skiba, E. A., Pettigrew, L. E., and Alden, S. E. "A Behavioral Approach to the Control of Thumb-Sucking in the

Classroom." *Journal of Applied Behavior Analysis*, 1971, *4*, 121-125.

A Group Contingency to Eliminate Thumb-Sucking

AUTHORS: Joel A. Ross and Bruce A. Levine

PRECIS: Making rewards for a fourth-grade class contingent on reduced thumb-sucking in one student

INTRODUCTION: The authors note the lack of research on methods to control thumb-sucking, despite the social and health-related benefits of reducing this behavior. Their approach was to reinforce the classmates of a nine-year-old when he refrained from thumb-sucking for a specified time period. This method stems from the successful application of similar group contingencies to other maladaptive patterns in the classroom. Previous efforts at control by the boy's parents had been ineffective, and severe malocclusion of the upper and lower teeth was evident.

TREATMENT: For five days prior to treatment, the frequency of thumb-sucking was noted. When the intervention began, the teacher informed the class that she would place a check mark on the blackboard each time that she observed the boy's thumb in his mouth. If less than fifteen checks were recorded for each of two consecutive days, every child in the class, including the thumb-sucker, would receive a piece of candy. A criterion of fifteen was selected as reasonable on the basis of previous observations in which the child sucked his thumb an average of twenty-five times per day.

After five days, the group contingency was terminated, then reinstated five days later. The intervention immediately and dramatically reduced thumb-sucking to almost zero. When the contingency was stopped for five days, thumb-sucking increased sharply but disappeared when the program was reinstated.

COMMENTARY: This technique allows the teacher to control thumb-sucking without interrupting the routine of the class. As a result of its success, the boy's popularity increased, even though he continued to suck his thumb at home. At this point, the school psychologist might involve the parents in delivering positive and/or negative consequences at home to reduce the behavior in that setting. The authors are unclear as to which program components produced the boy's change. They identify the candy, teacher approval and reminders, and peer pressure as possible influential factors. Further research would be needed to isolate the contribution of each element. However, they state that this simple procedure may also prove effective with other maladaptive classroom behaviors such as crying, tics, social isolation, head banging, and masturbation.

SOURCE: Ross, J. A., and Levine, B. A. "Control of Thumb-Sucking in the Classroom: Case Study." *Perceptual and Motor Skills,* 1972, *34,* 584-586.

Habit Reversal Training to Eliminate Nail-Biting

AUTHORS: R. G. Nunn and N. H. Azrin

PRECIS: Using a multistep treatment program to control nail-biting in children, college students, and adults

INTRODUCTION: Despite the common occurrence of nail-biting, no treatment has yet effectively eliminated this habit. Nunn and Azrin's habit reversal procedure has greatly reduced nail-biting, but relapses have occurred, preventing the growth of attractive nails. In this article, Nunn and Azrin report on a refinement of their method to reduce relapses, to treat a wider variety of nail-biters, and to provide a more valid assessment of treatment success. Thirteen clients aged eleven to thirty-eight reported nail-biting problems and were treated by two graduate students. Photographs of the clients' hands were taken before treatment and one month after the program. Fingernail-biting was defined as hand movements causing damage to nails, cuticles, and surrounding skin. The total procedure was conducted in one two-hour session.

HABIT REVERSAL PROCEDURE: The frequency of nail-biting was recorded both one week and one day before treatment. Clients began the habit reversal session with an "awareness training" procedure. They learned to focus attention on such habit-related behaviors as picking their cuticles, their skin, or their nails, looking at their nails, resting their hands on their faces, and interlocking their fingers. They learned to distinguish these actions from other "nonbiting" movements and to increase their awareness of situations in which nail-biting might occur. Next, they engaged in "competing activity" exercises in which behaviors opposite to nail-biting were learned. They practiced manicuring their nails and were taught other responses for social situations, such as holding something with both hands or clenching their fists. Clients were instructed to use these competing responses for about three minutes when trying to prevent or stop the habit. The third step was "fingernail-biting control motivation." To increase the desire to stop nailbiting, the client and counselor engaged in an "inconvenience review" to discuss the social and personal problems created by the habit. The client was requested to ask his friends to praise his efforts and success and to remind him to use the competing responses when nail-biting occurred. The counselor also called the client on the telephone each day to encourage these activities, reducing the calls to twice weekly after several weeks.

The technique of "symbolic rehearsal" required the client to imagine potential nail-biting situations and to demonstrate with explanations the appropriate competing behaviors that he or she would use to avoid or stop the behavior. The client was also urged to seek out situations in which nail-biting was likely to occur and practice competing behaviors while in the situation. Finally, instructions were given to inspect and repair nails, cuticles, and skin each night.

One day after the session, average nail-biting for all clients was reduced by 90 percent, and nail-biting was eliminated completely after the first week. One month later no clients were biting their nails. The effectiveness of the treatment was validated by the fact that nail-biters not given training showed no reduction in their nail-biting rates. After sixteen weeks clients were still maintaining their gains. Two clients relapsed during stressful situations, but they were retrained successfully.

COMMENTARY: The habit reversal procedure seems to be effective with children, making it appropriate for use by school psychologists. In other articles the authors have demonstrated its effectiveness with thumb-sucking, as well as with head-jerking and other neck and shoulder tics. The procedure described above can be presented in one session, and the student would be easily available for follow-up. Children as young as five years old can participate with appropriate parental guidance and reinforcement. School specialists considering this procedure should also refer to the article by Azrin and Nunn on habit reversal for a thorough explanation of procedures ("Habit Reversal: A Method of Eliminating Nervous Habits and Tics," *Behavior Research and Therapy,* 1973, *11,* 619-628). A frequent criticism of these techniques is that once the target behaviors are eliminated, other symptoms of the underlying disturbance will appear. No such symptom substitution was reported in the study digested here.

SOURCE: Nunn, R. G., and Azrin, N. H. "Eliminating Nail-Biting by the Habit Reversal Procedure." *Behavior Research and Therapy,* 1976, *14,* 65-67.

Cue-Controlled Relaxation for Nail-Biting

AUTHOR: Billy A. Barrios

PRECIS: Teaching college students to self-initiate states of relaxation as a way to control nail-biting and other tension-related
behaviors

INTRODUCTION: Nail-biting affects as much as one third of
the college population. A variety of techniques have been applied to this problem—hypnosis, putting bitter substances on
the nails, habit reversal training, and numerous behavior modification strategies. However, nail-biting is sometimes viewed as a
reaction to tension, and these procedures have not provided the
client with the skills to deal directly with anxiety; they have
focused primarily on reducing the habit itself. Cue-controlled
relaxation attempts to teach the client how to cope with varied
anxiety-provoking situations, including those that promote the
nail-biting habit. Two college students with long-standing nail-
biting behavior were treated with this approach. They considered their problem serious and were eager to break the habit.
Nail lengths were measured before and after treatment, and the
students were asked to indicate their frequency of nail-biting
each day. The procedure was fully explained to each student before treatment began.

CUE-CONTROLLED RELAXATION: In this technique clients
are taught to use a cue word (for example, *calm* or *control*) to
induce a state of relaxation. The students in this study were
seen individually for five daily sessions. They were first trained
in deep muscle relaxation as described by D. A. Bernstein and
T. D. Borkovec in *Progressive Relaxation Training: A Manual for
the Helping Professions,* Champaign, Ill.: Research Press, 1973.
Then a cue word was repeatedly paired with the relaxed state in
the following steps:

1. The therapist repeated the cue word aloud and syn-
chronized it with the student's exhalations. As the student
exhaled, he or she subvocalized the cue word along with the
therapist. This was repeated five times.

2. The student subvocalized without the therapist's aid for fifteen additional trials.

3. The student focused on his or her relaxed state in silence for one minute.

4. The cue word was subvocalized upon exhalation for twenty trials.

5. The student was urged to practice the relaxation exercises and the cue-word association procedure each day.

In each session a state of relaxation was achieved, and the cue word was subvocalized in two sets of twenty repetitions. After the third session the students were instructed to use the technique in everyday instances where nail-biting might occur. Upon identifying increases in tension, they were to begin exhaling and subvocalizing the cue word. They were encouraged to do the same whenever any tension-filled situation was encountered.

After two weeks, and again three months later, nail length and nail-biting frequencies were measured. On both occasions nail lengths had increased significantly for each student. One student reported that daily nail-biting had decreased from a pre-treatment rate of twenty-seven incidents to two and one-half incidents a day after two weeks. At three months, the rate was down to one bite per day. The other student noted similar improvement. In addition, both indicated that they were using cue-controlled relaxation for public speaking, test-taking, and similar activities.

COMMENTARY: The authors point out the need for well-designed studies of cue-controlled relaxation. However, they emphasize its potential application to a variety of tension-related life experiences. Both relaxation techniques and self-control strategies have been used effectively with younger children as well as with college students and adults. It seems likely that cue-controlled relaxation, which combines both elements, can be taught to elementary school students with positive results. As a preventive technique it may help children and adolescents cope with the tensions that lead to such varied behaviors as substance abuse and thumb-sucking. Its potential should be further explored.

SOURCE: Barrios, B. A. "Cue-Controlled Relaxation in Reduction of Chronic Nervous Habits." *Psychological Reports,* 1977, *41,* 703-706.

Additional Readings

Vargas, J. M., and Adesso, V. J. "A Comparison of Aversion Therapies for Nail-Biting Behavior." *Behavior Therapy,* 1976, *7,* 322-329.

Three aversive techniques for reducing nail-biting were compared. Each method was applied in three weekly ten-minute meetings. Some nail-biters received electric shock to the finger when they made nail contact with the mouth. Others engaged in negative practice in which they were instructed to gnaw on their nails for ten minutes during their sessions with the experimenter and to do the same for three minutes each night. The third group had a bitter substance ("Thum") applied to their nails. After tasting the material on their nails, they were given a bottle to use daily. In addition, half the subjects in each group monitored their nail-biting by filling out daily charts and marking each biting instance on index cards. Results showed equal effectiveness of all three methods, with self-monitoring subjects superior to those who did not monitor. Awareness of nail-biting seems to be crucial in its reduction.

Waber, C. "The Use of Operant Conditioning Techniques to Eliminate Thumb-Sucking Behavior in a Third-Grade Child." *School Applications of Learning Theory,* 1971, *2,* 7-12.

Kim was treated by her teacher with a token system. She selected reinforcers from a predetermined list and earned tokens toward her choices for not thumb-sucking. She was not told about the target behavior, only that she might learn what it was in the course of being rewarded for its nonoccurrence. Kim received a token for every thirty seconds that she did not suck her thumb during the first half-hour session. This was increased by thirty seconds on each of the next two days. For the last three days she earned fifteen tokens for not sucking her thumb through the entire thirty minutes. So that she would transfer nonsucking to other times, Kim was given a fifteen-point ticket to take to gym class if she did not suck her thumb during the whole period. She was also able to earn tokens intermittently during the day in class for increasingly longer periods of not sucking her thumb. With this intervention thumb-sucking decreased to almost zero. When her mother discovered its success, she expressed a willingness to try it at home.

◎◎◎◎◎◎◎◎◎◎◎◎◎◎◎◎◎◎◎◎◎◎◎◎◎◎◎◎

Speech Disorders

In this section speech disorders are classified into stuttering, articulation problems, and low-intensity speech. Stuttering has been defined as a disturbance of the smooth rhythm of speech—a disturbance that arises from a complex blending of physiological, neurological, psychological, and social factors. It may be displayed as (1) interjections of sounds, syllables, words, and phrases; (2) repetitions of words and phrases; and (3) prolongations of sounds and syllables. Articulation errors usually occur as omissions, substitutions, and distortions of speech sounds. Low-intensity speech is speech at such a low volume that the speaker may be inaudible beyond the distance of a few feet. The importance attached to verbal facility can result in severe social, academic, and personal consequences for the child with atypical speech. As others wait for an acceptable communication, the anxiety and damage to self-esteem experienced by these children take their toll. While there are numerous theories about their cause, speech disorders are generally viewed as multifaceted problems requiring psychological assistance as well as speech therapy. This section illustrates techniques that have been successful with these problems.

◎◎◎◎◎◎◎◎◎◎◎◎◎◎◎◎◎◎◎◎◎◎◎◎◎◎◎◎

Reinforcing Verbal Fluency in Stutterers

AUTHORS: Walter H. Manning, Phyllis A. Trutna, and Candyce
K. Shaw

PRECIS: Using tangible and verbal rewards to increase fluency
in young stutterers

INTRODUCTION: Positive reinforcement of fluency is an
effective therapeutic technique for child and adult stutterers.
However, it is not clear whether verbal or tangible rewards are
more likely to promote fluent speech. To test this, the authors
compared the effect of verbal praise versus prizes, toys, and
candy on the disfluent speech of three children aged six to nine.
All three were receiving speech therapy in school.

METHOD: Each student met with Trutna for fifteen minutes to
talk on a variety of self-selected topics. A stopwatch was used
to record the time intervals during which speech was totally
fluent. From these, an average fluency-time interval was obtained. During training, the student was reinforced for remaining fluent for the average fluency interval. In addition, before
the first training session, students told the therapist what comments they wanted to hear and what prizes they wished to
receive for being fluent.

    Training session I was divided into three ten-minute peri-
ods. Before training, the student demonstrated fluent and disfluent speech at the instructor's request and was told to use
only fluent speech. The instructor showed the student a matrix
divided into thirty-six squares and indicated that he would
check each box if the student continued to speak without stuttering. The student then spoke freely for ten minutes, and the
instructor checked a box if the student remained fluent for the
predetermined average time interval. During the second ten-
minute period the instructor delivered the selected verbal praise
as she checked each box. For the final ten minutes prizes were
given as each box was checked.

    In training session II stuttering, rather than fluency, was
reinforced. Session III returned to a reinforcement of fluency

except that prizes were given first, then verbal praise, and then check marks alone. About two months later another fifteen-minute session was held to determine whether changes in speech had been maintained.

CASE STUDIES: SK was a six-year-old boy whose primary stuttering problem was the repetition of syllables, words, and phrases. His average fluency interval during the initial session was two and one-half seconds. As a verbal reinforcement SK selected, "That's very good talking," and chose army toys for his tangible reward. During training SK's speech was clearly controlled by the reinforcing contingencies. His number of fluent intervals increased when he was reinforced for fluency and decreased when stuttering was rewarded. Reversing the order of reinforcers had no effect. Prizes and verbal praise were equally effective and slightly more powerful than marks alone. At the follow-up two months later, his stuttering had decreased further.

CR, an eight-year-old girl, interjected "umm" into her speech and also displayed prolongations and occasional repetitions. "Good speech" was her verbal praise, while dolls, candy, coloring materials, and a ball were the tangible rewards she selected. Her fluency interval was one and one-half seconds. CR responded dramatically to the reinforcers, regardless of their order of presentation. Marks alone were slightly more effective than verbal praise or toys but were less effective when stuttering was reinforced. Stuttering decreased over the course of training and remained low at the two-month follow-up.

Nine-year-old KW stuttered primarily with interjections and single-word repetitions. Her fluency interval was two and one-half seconds. "You sounded real nice" was her selected verbal reward, while dolls, stuffed animals, candy, and coloring books were her tangible rewards. KW also increased her fluent intervals when reinforced for fluency. Verbal and tangible rewards were more effective than marks alone. Stuttering decreased and remained low at the two-month follow-up.

COMMENTARY: This study provides additional evidence of the effectiveness of behavior modification techniques with child stutterers. Three factors add to the power of this procedure: (1) allowing students to select their reinforcers; (2) choosing obvious behavior as a target; and (3) clearly specifying the reward conditions to the students. The authors also speculate that the phase that reinforced stuttering may have had therapeutic value by increasing the student's awareness of her ability either to stutter or to speak fluently. Since verbal and tangible rewards seem equally successful, this intervention does not require an expensive outlay for prizes, toys, or candy. This enhances its utility in a school setting. One might also try pairing marks with such other natural rewards as free time, visits to the library, or helping the teacher. Points can be given for each mark, which can then be traded for activities. Marks and points may be another way to increase the effectiveness of the approach without adding additional cost.

SOURCE: Manning, W. H., Trutna, P. A., and Shaw, C. K. "Verbal Versus Tangible Reward for Children Who Stutter." *Journal of Speech and Hearing Disorders*, 1976, *41*, 52-62.

Shaping Audible Speech in a Special Education Student

AUTHORS: Tom Evans, Laura Pierce, Robert York, and Lou Brown

PRECIS: Using smiles and verbal praise to increase the speech intensity of a retarded, disturbed young adolescent

INTRODUCTION: Although found less frequently, low-intensity speech may create communication difficulties as significant as those produced by stuttering or poor articulation. In the classroom it may force the teacher to remain close to the student, may prompt repeated requests to "speak up," and may severely limit student-teacher interaction. As instruction becomes more difficult, the teacher may also be forced to eliminate parts of the curriculum. Thus, the problem can result in reduced academic and social stimulation. Citing evidence of its effectiveness in increasing speech intensity, the authors made use of a reinforcement strategy to treat a fourteen-year-old boy attending a special education class.

CASE STUDY: At various times, S had been diagnosed as emotionally disturbed, retarded, and organically impaired. His measured intelligence was 35, and he had displayed low-intensity speech as early as age seven. A medical examination revealed no organic basis for the problem. In class S was inaudible but had been heard on rare occasions to speak with normal intensity.

Treatment was divided into four phases. The first three took place in the school's instructional materials center, while phase four was conducted in the classroom. In phase I S was required to imitate five individual words at normal intensity. They were spoken by the teacher, who was first seated face-to-face with S, then eight feet away from him, and finally fifteen feet away. The words were "no," "hello," "goodbye," "yes," and "Tom." The teacher modeled each word at normal intensity before S repeated it. If the word was correct and spoken at an appropriate intensity, he received smiles and verbal praise. If not, the word was remodeled, and he was told to speak louder. In order to progress to the next step, S had to repeat two presentations of the words correctly (previous assessment indicated S's ability to respond correctly to all words, phrases, and questions used in treatment).

In phase II treatment was repeated at each of the three distances; the following phrases were used: "Badger School," "Good morning, Mr. Evans," "Hello, Ms. Pierce," "Goodnight, mother," and "The weather is _____ ." Phase III was expanded to a series of questions, including "What is your name?" "What are we having for lunch?" "Where do you live?" Phase IV was conducted in class, and the classroom teacher asked the questions at each distance.

In each case, S had to respond correctly on two consecutive presentations. In addition, speech intensity at each distance for each phase was measured before the program began and was pretested again just before each treatment step was administered. This enabled treatment progress to be compared with original behavior and also allowed the teacher to measure progress from step to step.

Before the program started, S spoke at low intensities at all distances in all phases. In phase I the number of presentations needed for him to reach treatment goals decreased from six when face-to-face to four at distances of eight and fifteen feet. S mastered all three distances in phase I in twenty-five trials. Phase II was completed in eight instructional trials. In addition, at a distance of fifteen feet, S needed no instruction to correctly repeat the phrases; he was successful on the two pretreatment trials. In phase III he repeated the phrases correctly at both the eight- and fifteen-feet distances on the two pretreatment trials. Phase IV required no instruction at any distance. It was clear that training in earlier phases had transferred to the longer word lengths and distances.

COMMENTARY: This treatment is similar to strategies often used with electively mute children in schools. The desired response is shaped in an individual setting and then transferred to the classroom. In this case, S had already demonstrated his ability to produce the desired responses. Social reinforcement was used to shape its occurrence in the classroom. While the authors point out some flaws in their treatment design, they were able to demonstrate the effectiveness of a behavioral strategy with a retarded, disturbed child in a school setting. Such treatments allow for the education of handicapped children closer to the mainstream of regular school life.

SOURCE: Evans, T., Pierce, L., York, R., and Brown, L. "Increasing the Speech Intensity of a Retarded Emotionally Disturbed Student in a Public School Classroom." *Child Study Journal*, 1977, 7(3), 131-144.

A Time-Out Procedure for Young Stutterers

AUTHORS: Richard R. Martin, Patricia Kuhl, and Samuel Haroldson

PRECIS: Using a talking puppet in an experimental treatment to reduce stuttering in young children

INTRODUCTION: The authors note a lack of information about the effects of reward or punishment on speech disfluencies in very young children. They cite as one major reason the reluctance of speech pathologists to call the child's attention to his stuttering through such a procedure. Their article reports an experimental treatment of two children aged three and one half and four and one half in which a time-out procedure was used to reduce stuttering.

METHOD: To implement the time-out, the authors mounted a commercially produced puppet ("Suzybelle") on a chair inside a stage-box decorated as a house. The entire apparatus was positioned with its front flush against a one-way mirror. When lighted, the puppet and the house could be seen by a child sitting on the other side of the mirror but when the lights were turned out, the puppet disappeared. As the child talked with the puppet, the experimenter listened for disfluencies. When the child stuttered, the lights were turned out for ten seconds, cutting off the conversation and "timing-out" the puppet.

CASE STUDIES: JC was three and one-half years old and stuttered severely. His parents felt that he was getting worse, although no speech therapy had been initiated. He was introduced to Suzybelle and talked with her for three twenty-minute sessions each week. Time-outs were begun in session four after the first ten minutes. When JC stuttered for two seconds or longer, the lights were turned off, and Suzybelle went silent and disappeared for ten seconds. From sessions seventeen to thirty-one, time-outs occurred no matter how short the duration of the stutter. After session thirty-one time-outs were discontinued. Results showed an increase in speech rate and a decrease in stuttering to almost zero. Infrequent stuttering was maintained eleven months after the time-outs ended and carried over to home speaking. It also carried over to monthly, no-treatment "probe" sessions that were held throughout the treatment period. These "probes" were twenty-minute meetings in which JC and a different experimenter talked without the puppet.

SS was four and one half. She stuttered less severely than JC but with significant associated muscle tension. Time-outs were begun ten minutes into session five. Treatment ended after ten minutes of session fifteen. In this case speech output did not increase, but stuttering decreased to almost zero. As with JC, her fluency remained intact after treatment ended, carried over to the probe sessions, continued outside the treatment setting, and was being maintained thirteen months later.

COMMENTARY: Noting that their procedure is experimental, the authors make no claim regarding its therapeutic effectiveness or application to other stuttering populations. However, it is presented here because it represents a potentially viable approach to reducing stuttering in young children. It might be useful to test this technique on kindergarten or young elementary school children in an attempt to broaden its potential. Children in middle and late childhood remain responsive to play-oriented treatments and might benefit from this adaptation of time-out. These results also suggest that focusing a child's attention on his stuttering is not necessarily detrimental. In fact, increased awareness may have enhanced the effectiveness of the technique.

SOURCE: Martin, R. R., Kuhl, P., and Haroldson, S. "An Experimental Treatment with Two Preschool Stuttering Children." *Journal of Speech and Hearing Research*, 1972, *15*, 743-752.

Additional Readings

Bailey, J. S., Timbers, G. D., Phillips, E. L., and Wolf, M. M. "Modification of Articulation Errors of Predelinquents by Their Peers." *Journal of Applied Behavior Analysis*, 1971, *4*, 265-281.

Residents of Achievement Place, which conducts a token economy rehabilitation program for predelinquent boys, were treated by their peers in the facility. In the first study four peers treated a thirteen-year-old resident. They were present when the experimenter gave words to the boy on cards, which pinpointed his articulation errors. The peers were instructed to identify and correct his mispronunciation of specified words. They earned points for their judgments but received no guidance on how to correct errors; the boy could only lose points. After several sessions the peers worked with the boy on their own. Several sessions later each peer met with and instructed the boy individually. If the boy mispronounced a word, the peer trainer modeled the correct method until the boy was successful, while points were earned and lost as before. Finally, the treatment strategy was refocused, and the peer had to identify *correctly* pronounced words in order to earn points. After treatment, the boy improved his articulation on almost 90 percent of the trained words, and the results generalized at 40-percent effectiveness to a control list of matched words. Two months later improvement was being maintained.

In the second study a twelve-year-old was treated by five peers individually. Articulation tests were administered before and after treatment, and the boy was required to use treatment words in sentences. Treatment cards presented pictures rather than words so as to avoid any pronunciation cues that printed words might provide. Results duplicated those in the first treatment, with improvement generalizing to sentences at a 65-percent accuracy rate. Tests of articulation also showed positive change. The success of the peers further supports the value of the Achievement Place Model (see E. L. Phillips, E. A. Phillips, D. L. Fixsen, and M. M. Wolf, *Journal of Applied Behavior Analysis*, 1971, *4*, 45-59).

Gendelman, E. G. "Confrontation in the Treatment of Stuttering." *Journal of Speech and Hearing Disorders,* 1977, *42,*
85-89.

In this procedure the stutterer confronts a threatening person or situation perceived as a trigger for the stuttering response. In preconfrontation training the person becomes aware
of prestuttering and stuttering muscular activity to increase his
or her sensitivity to stuttering in the feared situation. Then the
specific circumstances under which stuttering occurred are identified. Finally, the precise words of the stuttered interchange
are recalled as are the underlying thoughts that preceded and
accompanied the stuttering. As these elements are discussed, the
threatening components of stuttering experiences begin to
emerge. These often relate to fears of rejection or fears of expressing intense hostility. Confrontations help the individual
defuse the anxiety associated with the feared person or situation. The stutterer arranges to meet with the feared individual
to discuss stuttering and related concerns. The therapist helps
the stutterer practice stating fears about the individual in non-
accusatory ways. This almost always results in favorable responses from the feared person, along with relaxation and a discharge of tension in the stutterer. Sometimes less feared
individuals are confronted first, with the most threatening people postponed until the stutterer's anxiety has been reduced. A
number of confrontations may be necessary to reduce or eliminate stuttering. The author reports treatment of two hundred
adolescent stutterers. Of forty cases followed up in this report,
thirty-six were cured or improved; of twenty-seven followed up
two-months to three years later, twenty-two maintained gains.

James, J. E. "The Influence of Duration on the Effects of Time-
Out from Speaking." *Journal of Speech and Hearing Research,* 1976, *19,* 206-215.

Adolescent and adult stutterers were taped as they spoke
on self-selected or suggested topics. In the time-out treatment
they were instructed to immediately stop speaking when a tone
sounded at each instance of stuttering. Four groups were exposed to time-out durations of one, five, ten, and thirty seconds. Results indicated that time-out significantly reduced stut-

tering for all four groups. Variations in time-out durations produced only slight differential treatment effects in favor of the long durations. Interruption of speaking rather than the length of silence seemed to provide the punishing effect.

Kaplan, N. R., and Kaplan, M. L. "The Gestalt Approach to Stuttering." *Journal of Communications Disorders,* 1978, *11,* 1-9.

The Gestalt approach views stuttering not as an isolated symptom but as an organized self-system arising within the total person. It is maintained by the individual's experience of himself or herself as an inadequate, deviant stutterer and by his or her inability to contact those aspects of the self that feel competent, speak fluently, and interact in comfort. Thus, stuttering is a system locked in by the stutterer's negative experiences. In Gestalt therapy the therapist encourages the stutterer to become aware of the here-and-now experiences that maintain stuttering. Tension, breathing, eye contact, and all other moment-to-moment behaviors are focused upon, so that those parts of the self that maintain the stuttering system may be explored. The therapy may also be used as a risk-taking experience in which the client tests the new behaviors that emerge from increased self-awareness. For example, one client discovered that his stuttering was in part related to his fear of criticism from his calculus teacher. This new awareness allowed him to understand his role in creating his own fear. With this new knowledge he practiced math-related fluent speech in his therapy group and experienced an increased sense of personal power. By attending to the stuttering behaviors and those aspects of the self that maintain them, the person expands his awareness to discover his or her fluent self.

Rustin, L. "An Intensive Group Program for Adolescent Stammerers." *British Journal of Disorders of Communication,* 1978, *13*(2), 85-92.

This describes a broad-based program for adolescent stammerers that combines a variety of treatment techniques. After the staff was trained in principles of learning, child assessment, and methods to establish fluency, the children were selected.

Motivation to be rid of the stammer was an important criterion for selection. The program itself employed the following techniques:

1. Progressive Muscle Relaxation Training—this method taught the difference between tension and relaxation, and it eventually included the muscles that affect speech. The importance of relaxation in fluent speech was stressed, and home training was encouraged.

2. Slowed Speech—the child was taught to slow his speech to the point where he no longer stammered. If necessary, aids such as a stopwatch or instructions to say only one word on each outgoing breath were used. (Slowed Speech was developed by N. H. Azrin and R. G. Nunn; see "A Rapid Method of Eliminating Stuttering by a Regulated Breathing Approach," *Behavior Research and Therapy*, 1974, *12*, 279-286.) An experienced child was used as a model when necessary.

3. Role Drama—this provided practice speaking in difficult situations, helped the child cope with stammering-related social situations, and allowed the child to act out stressful events and gain insight into the reasons for his social stammering.

4. Time-Out—this method was used only with children whose level of anxiety was low. The child was taught to stop speaking when he began to stutter and to turn around for one minute. When ready he turned back and resumed speaking. This method was helpful with children who used slowed speech and relaxation techniques effectively but needed additional fluency techniques for other situations.

5. Video Recording—this provided valuable feedback for self-awareness. Differences in one's own behavior when stammering or using fluency techniques may be observed.

Parents were invited to attend the training sessions, so that the treatment could be explained to them and they could be counseled on helping their children maintain fluency. Teachers were also contacted for similar purposes. The course stressed the stammerers' responsibility for progress and the importance of generalizing gains beyond the treatment setting. Tentative conclusions suggest that the program was effective.

Wahler, R. G., Sperling, K. A., Thomas, M. R., and Teeter, N. C. "The Modification of Childhood Stuttering: Some Response-

Response Relationships." *Journal of Experimental Child Psychology*, 1970, *9*, 411-428.

The parents of two youngsters aged four and nine with stuttering and articulation problems described secondary problem behaviors in addition to stuttering. Observations of these behaviors were made in the home and in the clinic playroom. The parents of the first child were then instructed on the use of a five-minute time-out procedure for the secondary oppositional behavior and on the differential reinforcement of cooperative behavior. The second child's parents were taught to shape sustained interactions with people and objects through praise of the child and to ignore shifts from one activity to another (overactivity). These behavior treatments resulted in a drop in the frequency of the target behaviors as well as a marked decrease in stuttering. While stuttering and other problem behaviors were shown to be functionally related, the nature of this relationship was unclear.

Substance Abuse

Despite the proliferation of substance abuse education programs in the late sixties and seventies, children and teen-agers continue to smoke, use alcohol, and take drugs. Studies have found that as many as two thirds to three fourths of high school students have tried smoking at one time or another. By seventeen, about 25 percent of the boys and 16 percent of the girls are regular smokers. It is rare to find a high schooler who has not had a drink, and alcohol abuse has in fact been discovered in children as young as eight to ten years of age. Estimates of alcohol use among teen-agers range from 30 to 80 percent. Other statistics suggest that about 2 to 6 percent of adolescents have one or more drinks per day. Drug abuse in the form of glue sniffing has been known to occur among children as young as six or seven. Statistics on drug use depend on the drug surveyed, with marijuana, amphetamines, and barbiturates more popular than hallucinogens and narcotics. Curiosity, peer pressure, feelings of alienation, personal problems, a desire to imitate adult behavior, and other factors contribute to substance abuse. Preventive educational strategies that extend beyond factual presentations are seen as the most effective approaches to this problem. Examples are presented in this section.

Drug Prevention in Elementary Schools

AUTHORS: Orin W. Sadler and Nancy R. Dillard

PRECIS: Using TRENDS—a peer counselor program—to prevent drug abuse in preteens

INTRODUCTION: The authors describe a drug abuse prevention program for sixth graders that used values clarification techniques, along with adolescents trained as peer teachers. Pre-adolescents may regard older teen-agers as more attractive models than adults and may be more willing to believe and imitate them. Thus, a peer-counseling approach to drug prevention may succeed where traditional educational approaches have failed. In this paper the authors speculate that sixth graders would prefer values clarification programs and teen-age leaders to lectures by adults.

TRENDS PROGRAM: The program was introduced in grade 6 to reach students about to enter junior high school, where drug use was more prevalent. High school students volunteered for the TRENDS peer counselor training program, and they were selected if they had at least a B average, had been recommended by their school, and had no drug abuse problems. A faculty adviser from each high school worked with the students and attended all meetings. During the eight training sessions, representatives from substance abuse clinics, from police and government agencies, and from the mental health and medical professions lectured and answered questions on all aspects of substance abuse. Topics included drugs, alcohol, smoking, law enforcement, childhood emotional development, and values education. Training also involved active participation in values clarification group activities. One session was also devoted to methods of preparing lessons, use of resource material, and other practical issues. A handbook that discussed substance abuse and outlined values clarification techniques was given to each student.

After training was completed, teams of teen-age counselors conducted drug education classes with sixth graders thirty minutes a day, one day a week for eight weeks. After the first get-acquainted meeting, students led their own sessions as they chose, lecturing, doing values clarification exercises, discussing issues, and summarizing the sessions. As a means of evaluating the program's effectiveness, other classes were conducted by adult teachers trained in values clarification or by teachers or students who gave lectures. Some classes did not participate in any program.

Questionnaires administered to sixth graders after the program indicated that they clearly preferred teen-age to adult teachers and that they had a slight preference for values education over lectures. The teen-age counselors were rated highly by school personnel, who also found the values approach useful. A test given to the sixth graders before and after the program showed no difference in learning between the values clarification and lecture classes, but more learning in these classes than in the classes that received no program. In addition, the authors report that the TRENDS program has continued in the school system studied and that the number of peer counselors being trained has grown. The fact that the sixth graders preferred the teen-agers and were effectively taught by them has resulted in continued community support for the program.

COMMENTARY: The preference for peer counselors over adult teachers was the strongest finding of this study and supports the trend toward the use of peers in prevention programs in the schools. The power of older adolescents to influence the attitudes and behaviors of younger students should be strongly considered in the development of such projects. However, the best mode of presentation seems less clearly evident. If the program goal is to increase student knowledge of drugs and their effects, teen-age or adult teachers giving lectures or using values education techniques would appear to be equally effective. Yet most programs have as their ultimate goal a reduction in drug usage and the development of attitudes that would minimize substance abuse. Teaching a knowledge of drugs does not accomplish this aim. However, if students prefer peer counselors and values education, it is possible that these approaches might make them more willing to adopt behaviors and attitudes

opposing drug involvement. As the authors point out, such findings await more long-term program evaluations.

SOURCE: Sadler, O. W., and Dillard, N. R. "A Description and
    Evaluation of TRENDS: A Substance Abuse Education Pro-
    gram for Sixth Graders." *Journal of Educational Research,*
    1978, *71*(3), 171-175.

Drug Education for High School Students

AUTHORS: John D. Swisher, Richard W. Warner, Jr., and
Edwin L. Herr

PRECIS: Comparing four approaches to drug education with
ninth and eleventh graders

INTRODUCTION: The authors question the wisdom of drug
prevention programs that focus exclusively on factual information. Some research has shown that increasing individuals'
knowledge about drugs may, in some cases, create attitudes
favorable to drugs or actually increase their use. Preventive
efforts must directly attack attitudes and behavior, as well as
provide information.

   In this paper the authors compare four drug prevention approaches used with high school students in grades 9 and 11. The
first was a typical drug abuse unit taught in health class. The
second approach involved "relationship counseling." Here, students met in groups to discuss drug abuse in an open-ended,
nondirective atmosphere. The counselor did not direct the
group and avoided expressing his views. His role was to help
group members express themselves and to come to understand
and accept varying points of view. He interacted in a warm, re-
spectful, and nonjudgmental way. The third approach was
"reinforcement counseling." This group met with the counselor
and two college students who were not drug abusers. Their role

was to serve as anti-drug models, actively steering the group to discuss why drugs should not be used. They reinforced attitudes opposing drug usage and praised students when they stated that they would avoid taking drugs in the future. The counselors also focused the discussion on alternatives to drug use. The fourth group was similar to the third, except that the anti-drug models were college students who were former drug abusers.

After training in relationship and reinforcement counseling techniques, counselors met with their groups once a week for six weeks. To assess the groups on knowledge, attitudes, and behavior changes resulting from the interventions, an achievement test, an attitude scale, and a scale measuring current drug usage were given to each participant. Results showed that exposure to each approach resulted in the same increase in knowledge, while attitudes toward drugs and patterns of drug usage remained unaffected by any treatment.

COMMENTARY: It appears that knowledge about drugs can be readily taught to students through a variety of techniques, including lectures, directive counseling, and nondirective group sessions. Changing attitudes and behavior is more difficult and does not necessarily follow from increased factual information. Since this article was written, more evidence has confirmed the need for programs that promote changes in attitude and behavior. However, for political as well as educational reasons, schools are sometimes reluctant to combine innovative with traditional approaches to drug education. In these instances the school psychologist or counselor can play a facilitative role, encouraging school officials to try new approaches, finding more successful strategies (for example, peer programs), and coordinating their development and implementation. Through these efforts the school mental health specialist can provide service to large numbers of students who may not need direct psychological intervention.

SOURCE: Swisher, J. D., Warner, R. W., Jr., and Herr, E. L. "Experimental Comparison of Four Approaches to Drug Abuse Prevention Among Ninth and Eleventh Graders." *Journal of Counseling Psychology,* 1972, *19*(4), 328-332.

Relaxation Training and Drug Abuse

AUTHORS: Bruce W. Bergland and Arthur H. Chal

PRECIS: Using relaxation techniques to reduce tension in a thirteen-year-old drug abuser

INTRODUCTION: The authors discuss relaxation training as one component of "systematic desensitization," a behavioral technique pioneered by J. Wolpe (*The Practice of Behavior Therapy,* New York: Pergamon Press, 1969). In systematic desensitization there are three essential steps: (1) listing a hierarchy of anxiety-provoking events; (2) using relaxation training; and (3) applying relaxation strategies while imagining the anxious events in the hierarchy. In this case the authors focus on relaxation strategies as tools to be used by the school counselor.

CASE STUDY: B was a thirteen-year-old boy from a broken home who had a pattern of serious drug problems, including use of marijuana, LSD, mescaline, and heroin. After being institutionalized for three months by his mother, he moved in with his father and entered the eighth grade, where he experienced severe academic and behavior problems. He was seen in counseling twice a week for five weeks. During counseling B reported frequent tension, particularly around authority figures such as the principal or teachers. He seemed interested in learning to relax in these situations, so counseling goals were developed around learning and applying deep muscle relaxation to relieve anxiety.

B trained in the use and application of differential relaxation through a forty-minute instructional tape that was played for three sessions. (This procedure is based on the work of Wolpe cited above and on descriptions provided by J. R. Emery in "Systematic Desensitization: Reducing Text Anxiety." For Emery's article see J. D. Krumboltz and C. E. Thoresen (Eds.), *Behavioral Counseling: Cases and Techniques,* New York: Holt, Rinehart and Winston, 1969.) The tape began by telling B to sit back in a chair, breathe deeply, and relax. He was then instructed to extend his arms and clench his fists more and more tightly during a slow count to five. At five he was told to relax his arms completely and let them fall, focusing on the difference between the previous state of tension and the current feeling of relaxation. With each muscle group, B practiced tensing and relaxing and thus learned to appreciate the difference between these two feelings. After the forty-minute sessions B and the counselor discussed the use of this procedure in tension-filled situations. As sessions progressed, B reported his increasing ability to use relaxation procedures when anxious and felt them to be more effective than the hospital medication he had received. In support of his reports, teachers indicated increased attention in class, better performance, and fewer behavior problems. B was also able to use relaxation to control his reactions when given a long and, in his opinion, useless assignment. He further stated with surprise and enthusiasm that deep feelings of relaxation were similar to being "stoned." Although it was not determined whether he actually ceased using drugs or maintained the treatment gains, the observed and reported changes at the time of treatment were significant.

COMMENTARY: The authors point out that one case study does not prove the utility of a counseling strategy. However, if some students abuse drugs because they cannot cope with tension, relaxation training may offer them a healthy alternative. Taped relaxation programs are well-regarded clinical tools and are readily available commercially. Tapes should be examined carefully to determine whether the technique and material suit the counselor's purpose. Furthermore, the counselor should help the student apply the technique outside the counseling situation and inform the student's parents of its intended use.

SOURCE: Bergland, B. W., and Chal, A. H. "Relaxation Training and a Junior High Behavior Problem." *The School Counselor,* 1972, *19*(4), 288-293.

Smoking Prevention Programs
for High School Students

AUTHORS: Jerrold S. Greenberg and Zenon Deputat

PRECIS: Comparing the effects of three smoking prevention approaches on immediate and long-term smoking patterns

INTRODUCTION: Although students are becoming more aware of the dangers of cigarette smoking, they are not smoking less. Education programs have failed to alter smoking habits and are rarely able to recommend specific steps to students on how to stop smoking. The need to modify smoking-related attitudes has been identified as a crucial component of smoking prevention programs. Other important elements include the use of peer groups, student participation in the planning of programs, inviting smokers to a school smoking clinic, and a critical assessment of life-styles that increase smoking risk. In this study, the authors compared the effects of the "scare" approach, the "fact" approach, and the "attitude" approach on the smoking habits of ninth, tenth, and eleventh graders who smoked at least five cigarettes a day. Each of the three programs ran for seven weeks and was preceded and followed by a questionnaire that measured smoking habits and attitudes. Five months later, the questionnaire was readministered to assess the long-term effects of the program.

METHODS: The authors described the different methods used in each of the three programs.

Scare Approach. The goals of this tactic were to create fear about smoking, promote negative smoking attitudes, and get students to stop smoking. Some of the activities included guest lectures on heart disease and emphysema, a demonstration that used cancerous laboratory animals, and films that depicted the deadly consequences of smoking. Homework assignments included writing a short story on how it would feel to choke to death or researching family members who had smoked and who had eventually died of heart attacks.

Information Approach. Smoking facts were presented in a

neutral, unbiased manner, but this approach had the same goals of increasing negative feelings about smoking and encouraging students to stop the habit. The physical effects of smoking were depicted in films and demonstrations, and guest speakers discussed the scientific relationship between smoking on the one hand and cancer, emphysema, and heart disease on the other. Pamphlets from the American Heart Association, the Lung Association, and the Department of Health, Education, and Welfare were assigned as readings, and class discussions stressed the advantages of giving up smoking.

Attitude Approach. Values clarification techniques and training in communication skills were used for this group. Again, the goals were to develop negative smoking attitudes and to encourage students to quit. Through a variety of activities students were led to discuss their values about smoking. For example, groups met to list the effects of smoking on various organs of the body. These lists were then mailed to friends and relatives. Students also dramatized a person's death from emphysema; and, after viewing a cancerous animal, they worked on a written assignment that began with the words "If I were that animal. . . ." They then shared their papers with partners. In one exercise students drew a heart with four chambers. In three of the chambers they drew a picture describing one advantage of smoking, a picture describing one disadvantage, and a picture of someone who loves them. In the fourth they listed three words this person would say to them to convince them to continue or to stop smoking. Students then exchanged the pictures with partners and discussed them.

Control Group. This group did not take part in a smoking prevention program.

At the end of the seven weeks each of the three treatment groups achieved a reduction in the number of students who smoked, with the "scare" approach showing the biggest initial drop. However, five months later, the "attitude" approach was maintaining the greatest long-term effect, with 29 percent of the students in that group still not smoking.

COMMENTARY: This article makes an important contribution by demonstrating that scare tactics and factual presentations have no lasting influence on the smoking patterns of teen-agers. School programs that incorporate values clarification techniques, peer-group activities, and discussions to share feelings and attitudes are more likely to modify smoking habits over time. Unfortunately, when substance abuse is discussed, smoking tends to cause less alarm than drugs and alcohol. This may be because health effects from smoking are usually slow to develop and because smoking does not alter behavior in the dramatic and immediate way that drugs and alcohol do. Although excessive smoking is considered a health risk, it is clearly more socially accepted than alcohol or drug abuse. Until nicotine abuse is viewed with the same concern as alcohol or drug abuse, schools will probably continue to place a low priority on smoking prevention programs.

SOURCE: Greenberg, J. S., and Deputat, Z. "Smoking Intervention: Comparing Three Methods in a High School Setting." *Journal of School Health*, 1978, 498-502.

Additional Readings

Harnett, A. L. "How We Do It: Suggested Guidelines for a High School Smoking Intervention Clinic." *Journal of School Health*, 1973, *43*(4), 221-224.

The guidelines presented here are based on the actual efforts of intervention clinics to help students stop smoking. First, the clinic should be part of the health curriculum. Second, it should be planned and implemented with students. Third, the clinic should utilize films and/or discussions to encourage smokers to examine their habit. For this purpose, a questionnaire such as the "Smoker's Self-Testing Kit" is suggested (National Clearinghouse for Smoking and Health, U.S. Department of Health, Education, and Welfare). Finally, the clinic should involve small study groups, each exploring and reporting on various topics—for example, the health consequences, the psychological and social dynamics, and the treatment of smoking. Evaluation of the program should consider the number who stop smoking, why others continue, problems in presentation, and suggested improvements. At the end of the article, films, pamphlets, and other resource materials are listed.

McIntire, J. T. "Complexities of Smoking Education." *Journal of School Health,* 1976, *46*(4), 234-235.

Instead of suspending students for early violations of school no-smoking rules, the author advocates treating smoking as a health problem. He describes a three-hour junior high school course that demonstrates to students caught smoking the consequences of the habit. The first hour uses film, discussion, and demonstration to depict smoking-related health hazards. In the second hour the school counselor examines the causes and social consequences of smoking, while in the final meeting students who wish to quit are helped to develop a plan. Follow-up guidance and reward are provided. This program reported an approximately 40-percent success rate in the school in which it was implemented.

Mitchell, J. E., Hong, K. M., and Corman, C. "Childhood Onset of Alcohol Abuse." *American Journal of Orthopsychiatry,* 1979, *49*(3), 511-513.

The authors studied eight alcohol-abusing children who had become alcoholic by age twelve or younger. Alcoholism was common among the parents and other relatives of these youth. Their families were generally unstable, with erratic discipline and no supervision of the children. Divorce was prevalent, and the children were depressed, alienated, and lacking in self-esteem. Delinquency was also evident in some. Almost all these children associated with peers who drank; because of their parents denial of drinking and disinterest, they were not questioned. In fact, parents seemed passively accepting of their children's behavior, and alcohol was available to the children in the home. In addition, school truancy and failure were the rule. The authors conclude that drinking is a "family disease." Children of alcoholics are at high risk and should be exposed to education programs in elementary school. Parents should be alerted to the hazards of alcohol abuse for themselves and their children. Treatment should be family oriented and not focused only on the abusing child.

Rose, S. E., and Duer, W. F. "Drug/Alcohol Education: A New Approach for Schools." *Education,* 1978, *99*(2), 198-202.

The Pattern of Healthful Living curriculum (Harris County Department of Education, Houston, Tex., 1975) is an affectively oriented drug and alcohol education program based upon the teaching of values and decision-making skills. Its goal is to help children make mature decisions about their drug-using behavior through the development of self-esteem, personal values, rational thinking, and interpersonal skills. It was tested in grades 6, 7, and 8 and was found to increase knowledge and positively affect attitudes toward drug abuse. The importance of well-trained, committed teachers was also stressed, as well as the need for adequate and readily available curriculum materials.

Sexual Behavior

The need for programs that encourage responsible sexual behavior is highlighted by the following facts: (1) in 1975, 19 percent of all births in the United States were to women nineteen years old or younger; (2) in the same year 13,000 births were to women under fifteen years of age; (3) the highest rate of increase in gonorrhea is occurring in the under-fourteen age group; (4) from 1957 through the 1960s, adolescent venereal disease rose over 400 percent. These figures indicate that the sex education programs instituted in the schools over the past twenty years have been largely ineffective. Recent approaches have gone beyond the giving of sex information and have emphasized such broader issues as human sexuality, responsible sexual activity, and sexual values formation. They have utilized peer groups and have avoided moralizing or preaching "proper" sexual behavior. The question of whether the school should offer sex education is less frequently asked than how it can do this most effectively.

Pregnancy Prevention for Adolescents

AUTHORS: Steven P. Schinke and Lewayne D. Gilchrist

PRECIS: Providing training in communication skills to help teen-agers reduce the risk of pregnancy

INTRODUCTION: The consequences of teen-age pregnancy are well documented. The authors note the medical risks to mother and infant, the mother's frequent need to leave school, her reduced earning power, the welfare dependence of teen-age mothers, and the increased potential for marital stress and divorce. Neither education programs nor health and contraceptive services have controlled teen-age pregnancies. Research indicates that the large number of early pregnancies may be related to the adolescent's inability to cope with his or her developing sexuality. Specifically, teen-agers may not know how to communicate with sexual partners in order to control sexual activity. For example, in one study, females reported difficulty in saying no to their boyfriends, while males reported embarrassment about discussing contraception. In other research, women with unplanned pregnancies scored low on measures of effective communication skills. In this paper the authors tested a pregnancy prevention approach that emphasized the training of interpersonal communication skills to help teen-agers manage sexual relationships and reduce their risk of pregnancy.

COMMUNICATION SKILLS TRAINING: Nine women and one male aged thirteen to nineteen attended an inner-city school program for parents and parents-to-be. They met for four two-hour group meetings. Session leaders first described ways to present oneself in social situations. They demonstrated the use of eye contact, posture, gestures, voice, emotion, and positive self-comments during social contacts. Students role played situations with group support and were urged to express feelings and act assertively. The following abridged example illustrates the role-playing technique used during the meetings.

Jeannie was concerned that her boyfriend Carlyle was visiting her late in the evening, making it difficult for her to get up early for school and her part-time job in the school office. Her mother was also complaining, but Jeannie could not tell Carlyle that she wanted him to visit her earlier. The dialogue begins as the group leader suggests role playing to help Jeannie respond to her boyfriend:

Leader: Pretend that I'm your boyfriend, and you're telling me how you want me to come over earlier.

Jeannie: Uh . . . Carlyle . . . uhmmm . . . you're not going to like this. My mother's been hassling me about you coming over all the time.

Leader (playing Carlyle): Well, tell her where to go.

Jeannie: Uh . . . well . . . uh . . . (breaking role) What am I supposed to say now?

Sandy: You let your mother do your talking for you? Just tell him what you want!

Annie: Tell him you've got to get up earlier than he does.

Leader: Let's role play the scene again. (Leader kneels down beside Jeannie's chair and gives frequent feedback and instructions while Jeannie practices.)

Jeannie: Carlyle. . . .

Leader: Look him in the eye.

Jeannie: Carlyle, I wish you could come over earlier.

Leader: Good! Don't play with your hair.

John (as Carlyle): What do you mean?

Jeannie: Well, I've got to get to bed earlier.

Leader: Keep looking him in the eye. Talk a little louder.

John (as Carlyle): Has your mother been bugging you about me again? You can tell her where to go.

Jeannie: Uhmm. . . .

Leader: Don't stall. Tell him what you want.

Jeannie: I'd like to get to bed earlier because I've got to get up early every morning to work in the office at school. If you could get to my house earlier, I could get to bed early enough, so I won't be wiped out every morning.

Leader: Great, very specific, very clear.

John (as Carlyle): If I come over earlier, your whole family will still be hanging around. Who needs what?

Jeannie: Let's try it out. (frowning) I'm tired of getting to
   bed so late.
John (as Carlyle, irritated): Oh, all right.

Jeannie practiced role playing until she and the group
members were satisfied with her responses. Overall, students became actively involved in the meetings, rated the role-playing
and feedback activities highly, and gave support to less involved
students. Many indicated that they had successfully used skills
learned here in real-life situations. Most planned to continue
attending.

COMMENTARY: There is no indication that this training by
itself reduces the risk of pregnancy in teen-agers. It would be
more reasonable to view this technique as one part of a total
program that would also include a sexual information component. A course on sexuality or a similar unit within a health
curriculum would be an appropriate educational addition if it
were taught by a knowledgeable, sensitive individual. The authors also note how the students supported one another while
practicing newly acquired skills. Peer support is a crucial element in such programs, especially when the sharing of feelings
and role playing are used as teaching techniques. Adolescents
often mistrust adults who tell them how they should behave.
When skills develop from the mutual efforts of peers, learning is
usually more effective and behavior change more likely.

SOURCE: Schinke, S. P., and Gilchrist, L. D. "Adolescent Pregnancy: An Interpersonal Skill Training Approach to Prevention." *Social Work in Health Care,* 1977, *3*(2), 159-167.

A Cognitive-Behavioral Approach
to Pregnancy Prevention

AUTHORS: Steven P. Schinke, Lewayne D. Gilchrist, and Richard W. Small

PRECIS: A four-step program based upon cognitive and behavioral strategies to reduce unwanted pregnancy

INTRODUCTION: The authors describe a comprehensive pregnancy prevention program for adolescents that rejects simple explanations for early pregnancy, such as a lack of sexual information or emotional disturbance. The problem is complex and arises from the sexual adjustments demanded of the teen-ager. In adolescence sexual intimacy becomes more likely to occur, but the social skills necessary to regulate such intimacy may not have developed. While it is possible to train these skills to some extent, a training approach alone is not sufficient. The four-step program outlined in this paper includes the training of communication skills but recognizes other components as being equally important

PREGNANCY PREVENTION:
Step 1: Information Access—the teen-ager must first be taught the basic facts about human sexuality, reproduction, and birth control. This includes relevant information about biology, contraception, the role of sexuality in adolescence, and so on. The presentation should be personally meaningful to the adolescent, easily understood, and complete. Later decisions and actions will then be based on accurate information.
Step 2: Information Acquisition—to ensure that students accurately receive and retain information, they may be divided into small groups where they summarize material and are quizzed periodically. Tangible or social rewards for high grades may be given as part of a reinforcement system to increase their knowledge. They may also be asked to develop solutions to realistic problems posed by the teacher as a way of demonstrating their understanding of sexual information. Through these exercises, misunderstandings or inaccurate knowledge can be detected.

Step 3: Decision Making—students use newly learned information to make decisions and plan actions. First, they learn how to change facts into personally meaningful "self-statements" that they can use in developing sex-related decisions. For example, a fact such as "unprotected intercourse risks pregnancy" becomes: "If I engage in unprotected intercourse, I risk pregnancy." After statements are personalized, they are practiced out loud with group support and reinforcement. Gradually the student progresses to making the statements privately, providing self-rewards for a specified number of repetitions. Throughout this step the group leader stresses to each student the real possibility of pregnancy and helps her use self-statements to consider the consequences of sex-related decisions and behaviors. The following is a possible sequence: "If I have unprotected intercourse, I risk pregnancy. I don't want to be pregnant so I must use birth control. I don't like the pill so I must consider other methods." Working through these options with group support helps train the students in decision-making skills.

Step 4: Decision Implementation—once decisions have been made, training is given in how to implement them. Students begin with a decision and then use communication skills training to practice the behavior. If a decision is made to use birth control methods, the student is then trained and practices the steps needed to request services from an appropriate agency. Effective behaviors are identified and rehearsed with group support. Students are then encouraged to test their skills outside and report back to the group.

COMMENTARY: This paper makes a valuable contribution to pregnancy prevention education by detailing the individual components of a pregnancy program and suggesting techniques to implement each step. It is a practical strategy built upon existing research. However, it may also stimulate additional research that will produce refinements in techniques.

SOURCE: Schinke, S. P., Gilchrist, L. D., and Small, R. W. "Preventing Unwanted Adolescent Pregnancy: A Cognitive-Behavioral Approach." *American Journal of Orthopsychiatry,* 1979, *49*(1), 81-88.

Values Clarification
in Venereal Disease Prevention Programs

AUTHORS: Don Breckon and Don Sweeney

PRECIS: Using values clarification techniques to encourage productive decision-making about prevention, diagnosis, and treatment of venereal disease

INTRODUCTION: The need for more and better quality venereal disease (VD) education programs in schools is clearly justified by the current sharp rise in VD, particularly among children and adolescents. The authors recommend beginning such
education as early as the upper elementary and junior high
school years. VD education should be introduced as part of a
required unit on communicable diseases and taught by someone
who can offer a fair, balanced presentation of facts. A teacher
who guides the students' learning and involves them in examining ideas will be more successful than one who preaches, lectures, or uses scare tactics.

TEACHING ABOUT VD: A successful VD education program
should cover prevention, early diagnosis, and treatment. But
facts alone are not enough. Through a values clarification approach students can examine their own feelings and values,
share other viewpoints, discuss the consequences of their behavior, and arrive at decisions that will help them use VD information to their advantage. Some of the activities used in VD values
clarification are:
    1. Who's Who in VD—students rank famous people on the
likelihood of their having had VD and discuss the reasons for
their rankings. In this game accurate and false conceptions are
shared about the kind of person who contracts VD.
    2. VD Top Ten—famous people who have had VD are dis-
cussed; the goals here are similar to those in the first activity.
    3. Role Play—students role play potential or actual situa-
tions, taking on the roles of parents, siblings, friends, or others
to increase their awareness of differing attitudes about VD, and
to practice using VD information in real-life situations.

4. Values Voting Line—students take a position on an issue related to VD and justify it. They are encouraged to analyze their personal attitudes and listen to alternative points of view.

5. What Would You Do If—realistic situations are presented for student response. For example, your fourteen-year-old brother tells you he might have VD or you see your favorite teacher coming out of a VD clinic. What would you do?

6. Popular Myths—common VD myths, their sources, their accuracy, and how they affect VD control efforts are listed and discussed.

7. Field Investigation—students seek VD information from libraries, local pharmacists, clinics, and other sources. They conduct surveys in the school and community to assess the attitudes of others toward VD.

COMMENTARY: Substance abuse and/or sex education programs that limit themselves to factual presentations do not result in desired behavior changes because they do not teach students how to use facts to make decisions. Values clarification attempts to promote such changes by focusing student awareness on the feelings and attitudes that affect their decisions. While little information exists on the effectiveness of values clarification in VD education, the authors note that teachers and students find the experience meaningful and that this approach has been successful in reducing drug abuse.

SOURCE: Breckon, D., and Sweeney, D. "Use of Values Clarification Methods in Venereal Disease Education." *Journal of School Health,* 1978, *48,* 181-183.

Sex Information Through Peer-Group Contacts

AUTHOR: Michael A. Carrera

PRECIS: Outlines the major components of a peer-group sex education training program at the high school or college level

INTRODUCTION: As a way of meeting the needs of high school and college students, sex information and education programs are making use of trained peer workers. Misconceptions about human sexuality have been exploited by the media and advertising and are sustained by the confusing ways that adults educate young people about sex. Peer programs allow students to obtain clear and accurate sexual information and to make knowledgeable decisions about their sexual behavior in an atmosphere of mutual respect and trust. The students are also provided access to counseling and contraceptive services if these are needed.

GUIDELINES: The author outlines the common attributes of existing programs as a guide to the planning of new services:

    1. Place—program settings are sometimes called rap-rooms or drop-in centers. Whatever its name, the room should be spacious, yet allow for private and small-group discussions. It should provide reading materials relevant to student sexual concerns and a referral book listing approved services (the author notes that high school referrals are usually made by the program's faculty adviser). Forms to evaluate the program's success and the skill of the peer workers may be made available and filled out anonymously. Students list their gender, major concerns, how they used the room, and how they learned about the program.

    2. Worker Selection—the author recommends allowing all interested students to enter the peer-training program and encouraging all grade levels to participate. Although there are risks to this approach, it preserves the spirit of the program and lessens the likelihood that peer workers will form cliques. The intensity of the training program tends to screen out uninterested students.

3. Teacher Selection—selection of the faculty adviser to train peer workers often determines whether or not the program will succeed, as well as the amount of school-community support it will receive. A sensitive, committed individual should be chosen—someone who is knowledgeable about human sexuality and has credibility with students. The author advises selecting a trained sex educator rather than importing different specialists for each training session.

During training the adviser must establish a strong relationship with student trainees and help them accept the continuing nature of their education. He must not allow them to adopt a "know-it-all" attitude after a few sessions.

4. The Training Program—three components make up the training experience. First, students must be given a solid understanding of human sexuality. Second, they must become sensitive to their own sexuality and how it affects their personal relationships. They must examine their sexual attitudes and understand how their values influence their judgments of others. Third, they must learn how to use their knowledge to help students who are seeking assistance. Through role playing and dramatizations students learn how to apply their training to probable rap-room situations. They practice communicating their knowledge, refine their strategies, and, in many instances, experience personal growth.

5. Community Outreach—early and ongoing discussions of program goals with community groups are crucial. Such discussions establish a climate of openness that can minimize conflict and reduce fears about the services to be provided.

COMMENTARY: The author stresses that properly trained peer-group leaders are an important source of *accurate* sex information for students. Students can discuss sexual issues with knowledgeable peers who share the same concerns and speak the same language. While each program must adapt itself to available resources, these guidelines provide a framework for the development of an effective peer project.

SOURCE: Carrera, M. A. "Peer-Group Sex Information and Education." *Journal of Research and Development in Education,* 1976, *10*(1), 50-55.

Additional Readings

Herold, E. S. "The Production and Use of an Attitudinal Film in Birth Control Education." *Journal of School Health,* 1978, 307-310.

"It Couldn't Happen to Me" (Perennial Education, Highland Park, Ill., 1975) is a film that focuses on the reasons why sexually active teen-agers do not practice birth control. Adolescents avoid contraception for many reasons: (1) belief that they cannot become pregnant; (2) the desire to avoid the hassles of contraception; (3) fear that parents will discover their sexual behavior; and (4) a lack of knowledge. In the film these issues are portrayed candidly. Pregnant teen-agers, as well as high school and college students and other credible peers, realistically discuss their experiences and attitudes about sex and contraception. Both sides of the birth control argument are presented by teen-agers who have been pregnant in an effort to promote attitudes favorable to birth control practice. The film's honesty and realism were favorably reviewed by adolescents and professionals in health fields, who suggested its use for students before the tenth grade. The authors see the need for further research to determine the film's influence on sexual attitudes and beliefs.

Mudd, E. H., Dickens, H. O., Garcia, C., Rickels, K., Freeman, E., Huggins, G. R., and Logan, J. J. "Adolescent Health Services and Contraceptive Use." *American Journal of Orthopsychiatry,* 1978, *48*(3), 495-503.

This article describes a program for high school students who have never been pregnant. The program was developed by the Family Planning Service at the University of Pennsylvania School of Medicine. It included a school and hospital component. In school, topics related to adolescent sexuality were discussed in six sessions of a health education or psychology class. Topics included pregnancy, menstruation, venereal disease, family planning, and sexual attitudes. Students could also request contraceptive and gynecological services at the Family Planning Service. They received examinations, counseling, and contraceptives anonymously and without charge. Of the girls who enrolled, only 10 percent had unplanned pregnancies over a period of two and one-half years. Most of these pregnancies occurred in the age group between sixteen and eighteen. These girls were less likely to keep their appointments and more likely to complain about and have difficulty using contraceptives. These girls also tended toward somatic conflicts that seemed related to their increased risk of pregnancy. The authors concluded that the current social milieu is not conducive to teenage contraceptive use. Teen-agers become pregnant not by choice but as a result of complex psychological and social factors. Contraceptive education and health programs can give teen-agers the information and support needed to avoid unwanted pregnancies.

Saxon, B. "Our First Five Years: Sex Education at Lee High School." *Journal of Research and Development in Education,* 1976, *10*(1), 30-35.

After five years of teaching sex education in a public high school, the author offers suggestions that may help others develop similar programs. First, begin with a program emphasizing sex information. Values and feelings can be introduced after the program has been established and teachers have become more comfortable with the material. Second, involve students and parents in program planning. Don't forget to ask students what they want to learn. Third, do not force students to take the course, but do not give in to a minority who may oppose sex education. Fourth, obtain administrative support even if it is quite passive. Fifth, have a consultant available to deal with difficult questions or to help present topics. Sixth, develop a personal awareness of sexual values in order to better help students clarify theirs. Seventh, decide how many of your own values you are willing to reveal to your students. Appropriate sharing of beliefs may encourage more openness. Eighth, investigate commercially produced materials (films, audiovisual material) for classroom use. The author also urges a team approach in which teachers plan together and provide mutual support in this new, and perhaps anxiety-provoking, venture.

Scales, P. "The Context of Sex Education and the Reduction of Teen-age Pregnancy." *Child Welfare,* 1979, *48*(4), 263-272.

The author describes examples of innovative sex education programs that involve the cooperative efforts of teen-agers, parents, and community resources. (1) A project in Minneapolis trained adolescents to provide health and sex information to peers in school, group home, and community settings. (2) Radio spots have been developed in which rock stars and athletes discuss sexuality. They have been aired across the country and used in classrooms. (3) Students have been urged to write articles for their school papers on pregnancy, parenthood, and related topics. This represents a readership of fifteen million students. (4) Theatre groups composed of teen-age actors have presented skits (with follow-up discussion) dealing with many aspects of sexuality. (5) Medical students in Washington, D.C., have met with students in weekly sessions to provide sexual information. (6) Syracuse University has sponsored sex education programs for parents to encourage parent-child communication. Studies show reduced pregnancy risk in the children of interested parents. (7) Private and government agencies are consolidating information on sex education programs and encouraging the development and dissemination of sex curriculums. It is clear that comprehensive sex education requires the input of all segments of society.

5 ◎◎◎◎◎◎◎◎◎◎◎◎◎◎◎

Disturbed Peer
Relationships

◎◎◎◎◎◎◎◎◎◎◎◎◎◎◎

Social interaction among schoolchildren has become a topic of considerable interest to teachers, therapists, and developmental psychologists. The obvious relationship between social skills and personality development has sparked this interest. Children who have difficulty relating to peers are likely to experience rejection, harassment, and generally hostile treatment from them. These negative reactions have an adverse effect on the child's self-esteem and serve to reinforce avoidance responses in the child that interfere with learning effective ways of relating to others.

Social science research conducted over the past thirty years has pointed to the following conclusions: (1) deviant

421

interpersonal interactions of preschool children (for example, social isolation and fighting) tend to persist through childhood and into adult life; (2) poor social skills in childhood are associated with adjustment problems in later life, such as juvenile delinquency, alcoholism, mental illness, and criminal acts; and (3) children's evaluations of one another are more predictive of future adjustment than the ratings of adults or mental health professionals. These findings indicate that the learning of cooperative social interaction is a crucial aspect of normal child development.

The importance of social development in schoolchildren has been acknowledged by educators. For example, John Dewey's concern for the development of the "whole child" required that school experiences provide the child with more than academic learning. Teachers, who are with their students thirty hours a week for forty weeks every year, are in a position to strongly influence the social and emotional development of children. In recent years there have been a variety of attempts to implement social development programs in the schools. Teacher- and peer-implemented intervention programs have been quite popular of late since they treat problems within the natural environment in which the problems occur. The most prominent social problems that appear among students in the classroom are aggressiveness, social withdrawal, and ethnic prejudice.

Childhood aggression is a serious problem and a frequent cause for referral of children to mental health centers. Follow-up studies indicate that aggressive children often exhibit a relatively high rate of antisocial behavior and other problems in later life. In the classroom, aggressive behavior can be particularly disturbing. Apart from disrupting ongoing instruction, aggressive acts by one child can lead to increased aggression by other children. To maintain a positive classroom environment for learning and social development, teachers must keep aggressive behavior at a low level.

Studies of aggressive children have associated them with the following personality traits: assaultiveness, quarrelsomeness, proneness to temper tantrums, fighting to settle conflicts, and ignoring the rights and wishes of others. Aggressive children tend to tease and embarrass others and to demand immediate compliance with their wishes. These children are generally unpopular, and their aggressiveness elicits similar responses from peers.

How one views the cause of aggression determines to a large extent how one acts to reduce it. Some professionals view frustration as a prime determinant of aggression and have thus treated aggression by attempting to remove abnormal causes of frustration, such as learning deficits or lack of adult attention. Others view aggression as a learned response and thus endeavor to help the children "unlearn" the behavior by strategies based on social learning theory.

Although the aggressive child is not easy to overlook in the classroom, the shy, withdrawn child is. This kind of child often seems to be in another world; he or she daydreams and engages in solitary, unconstructive activities that irritate those in the immediate environment. This pattern of withdrawal, once started, tends to reinforce itself and becomes more and more pronounced as time passes; hence, it needs to be diagnosed and changed as early as possible, preferably in nursery school. Fortunately, withdrawal has been found, in many cases, to be amenable to change without prolonged and intense psychotherapy.

Aggression

Aggression refers to unprovoked acts that inflict pain on another person. Physical aggression includes hitting, pushing, kicking, and bumping others; verbal aggression encompasses name-calling, derogatory remarks, threats, bossing, and teasing. Typically, children do not deliberately seek to hurt others; rather they act in an impulsive way to achieve their own ends. Aggressive children seek to fulfill their own desires or interests in an egocentric way, taking no heed of the rights of others. Observations of highly aggressive children in school reveal that they have "turned off" academically and pass the day by getting into trouble. Boys have been found to be more aggressive than girls. This difference appears early in life and has been observed in various settings and situations.

⦿⦿⦿⦿⦿⦿⦿⦿⦿⦿⦿⦿⦿⦿⦿⦿⦿⦿⦿⦿⦿⦿⦿⦿⦿⦿⦿

Psychosituational Classroom Intervention (PCI)

AUTHORS: Jack I. Bardon, Virginia C. Bennett, Paul K. Bruchez, and Richard A. Sanderson

PRECIS: Using direct intervention in the classroom to modify disruptive behavior, encourage academic performance, and promote cooperative interactions

INTRODUCTION: In Psychosituational Classroom Intervention (PCI) a psychologist (or other mental health professional) helps children with problems *in the classroom* while the teacher and students continue their regular classroom activities. Children are not removed from class for private meetings as in more traditional approaches but are helped to change their behavior in the place where the problems occur. To accomplish this, the psychologist uses many methods adapted for classroom use. PCI does not limit the choice of intervention strategies; it refers only to the place where the intervention occurs, namely, the classroom. The authors feel that PCI has several advantages for the psychologist working in schools: (1) it fosters a more realistic view of the psychologist's work by locating the intervention in full view of others; (2) it allows the psychologist to interact with teachers and students who are not usually involved with psychological services; (3) the psychologist can work on problems soon after they occur in the classroom; and (4) PCI allows the psychologist to work not just on the problem behavior but also on the classroom events that may create and maintain it.

PCI INTERVENTION: Jim, a second grader, was identified by his teacher as disruptive and troublesome, that is, as a child who got into fights and caused classroom disorganization and tension. A combined behavior management and counseling program had been tried, but the management plan had not been maintained by the teacher. Counseling alone outside the classroom setting was not considered an adequate remedy, so a PCI approach was attempted.

On one occasion, the psychologist entered the room and ignored the reports by other children (and the teacher) of Jim's misbehavior. He sat next to Jim, asked how things were going, and began to help him with schoolwork. As Jim relaxed, the psychologist calmly began to ask him about a recent fight, taking care not to be judgmental. Four other students were brought into the discussion and were asked about the fight, as well as about available alternatives to fighting back. After they contributed suggestions, the psychologist switched the topic to the consequences of fighting back and the particular problems that Jim faced when he fought.

On a second occasion, the psychologist was sitting next to Jim when Jim and a classmate named Judy began fighting over ownership of some plastic cups. Using the entire class, the psychologist determined how many cups were necessary for the classroom activity and guided Judy to ask, rather than push, Jim as a better way to get cups. She then asked for a cup, and Jim happily gave her one. He then gave cups to others, receiving and enjoying praise for his behavior.

A third example: Jim copied spelling words from others, while telling the psychologist he could not do the work on his own. The psychologist made suggestions about applying spelling rules covered in class and urged Jim to try spelling some words by himself. When he did this, the psychologist praised him for his success, emphasized his ability to work independently, and encouraged him to verbalize his success. The psychologist then convinced Jim to volunteer a correct answer to the class. When he did so, the psychologist talked about taking turns with classmates in the enjoyment of answering correctly. Jim was then able to read an answer in front of the class for which the psychologist praised him.

In each instance the psychologist entered the classroom, sat near Jim, and used naturally occurring or recent classroom events to initiate discussions with him. When it was appropriate, other class members were included, helped with problems, and praised for good behavior. In this way it was not obvious that Jim was the major focus of the intervention. The goal was to confront Jim with the causes and effects of his behavior in a nonjudgmental and supportive manner. By drawing in classmates and attending to their appropriate behaviors and responses, the psychologist used peer-modeling strategies to help

Jim observe and recognize possible alternative behaviors. While no long-term outcomes were reported, there was a decrease in the amount of disruption and tension during the psychologist's visits. Jim's teacher clearly felt a change in classroom atmosphere, and it was hoped that through her observations she might begin to recognize better ways of dealing with classroom problems.

COMMENTARY: When interventions requiring teacher involvement do not work out, it is often up to the psychologist or other mental health professional to develop a different strategy. PCI provides one such method. It has potential application to many classroom problems and can be used as one part of a total program involving behavior management, counseling, and consultation. Most interventions focus only on changing the student's behavior to make it more acceptable in class. Circumstances in the classroom that may cause problem behaviors are not usually treated as targets for change. PCI places the psychologist in the classroom, where both the problem students and the events that lead to problems can be observed as they unfold. The psychologist can then intervene immediately to alter potentially disruptive situations, encourage effort in schoolwork, or help students settle whatever difficulties come up.

SOURCE: Bardon, J. I., Bennett, V. C., Bruchez, P. K., and Sanderson, R. A. "Psychosituational Classroom Intervention: Rationale and Description." *Journal of Psychology,* 1976, *14*(2), 97-104.

Developing Self-Control in Aggressive Children

AUTHORS: Bonnie W. Camp, Gaston E. Blom, Frederick Hebert, and William J. van Doorninck

PRECIS: Teaching children to "think aloud" in a cognitive behavior modification program

INTRODUCTION: The "think aloud" program developed by the authors is designed to help aggressive young children improve self-control through the use of verbal mediation strategies. The program helps children verbalize a problem, develop plans for solving it, and evaluate the results. Games, dramatic scenes, and props are used to sustain the children's interest in the program.

Twelve aggressive second-grade boys participated in daily thirty-minute training sessions for six weeks. This experimental group was divided into two smaller groups of six children; a teacher was assigned to administer the program to each group. Normal and aggressive control subjects received no training.

INTERVENTION: A key element of the training program is to teach children to "think out loud," that is, to use overt self-instruction. The authors feel that problem solving is aided when children concentrate on answering four basic questions: What is my problem? What is my plan? Am I using my plan? How did I do? At first the teacher models the use of this cognitive strategy by talking out the answers to a specific problem or task. The children then play the "copycat" game; that is, they say aloud and in unison the standard answers given by the teacher.

To illustrate part of the "think aloud" approach to a relatively simple task, the teacher might verbalize the following plan for coloring shapes: "I'll go slowly. I'll be careful and stay within the lines. I'll outline the design first. Then I can go faster in the middle. OK, here I go." The children would then be asked to be "copycats" and say this plan aloud before starting to color.

After extensive use of the "copycat" game, the teacher gives the children cue cards to prompt them to verbalize aloud the four problem-solving questions, as well as the answers to them. The cognitive tasks (puzzles, mazes, and games) become increasingly difficult as the program progresses. Eventually the children are encouraged to repeat the four questions quietly to themselves.

After the children have become skilled in solving impersonal cognitive tasks such as puzzles, they are taught effective ways to solve interpersonal problems. Strategies include helping them to become more aware of feelings ("Does the child in the picture seem mad or sad?"), to think up several different solutions to a social problem ("What are some things you could do or say if someone pushes you in line?"), to respond empathically to others ("How do you think she felt when you took her toy?"), to anticipate possible consequences of one's actions ("What do you think might happen to you if you were caught stealing from others?"), to determine antecedents to emotions ("What are some of the things that get you mad?"), and to evaluate the fairness of outcomes ("Is it fair to others to take things that belong to them?"). In the particular study under consideration, the teachers dramatically enacted an individual child's reaction pattern, especially his aggressive reaction to frustration. Also, at various times during the six-week program the teacher suggested that thinking out loud in the classroom could help in figuring out how to complete schoolwork or get along with others.

Teacher ratings showed that both the trained and untrained aggressive boys improved in terms of aggressive behavior but that the trained group exhibited improvement on a significantly larger number of prosocial behaviors.

COMMENTARY: The authors developed this program because they noted that aggressive children tend to have normal verbal and reasoning abilities but fail to use these abilities to think through problems unless specifically asked to do so. Their natural inclination is to respond quickly and impulsively. However, when requested to "think aloud" before attempting a task, they can learn to inhibit their impulsiveness and reason to an effective solution. The authors suggest that in addition to encouraging children to think up a number of solutions to a social problem, teachers should reinforce solutions that are nonhostile in nature.

SOURCE: Camp, B. W., Blom, G. E., Hebert, F., and van Doorninck, W. J. "Think Aloud: A Program for Developing Self-Control in Young Aggressive Boys." *Journal of Abnormal Child Psychology,* 1977, *5,* 157-169.

===

Decreasing Aggression in Kindergarten Children

AUTHORS: Tanya Grieger, James M. Kauffman, and Russell M. Grieger

PRECIS: Effects of peer reporting on cooperative play and aggression

INTRODUCTION: The authors reasoned that having children report the friendly and cooperative acts of others to the whole class would be a natural and inexpensive way of reinforcing these acts and of decreasing aggressive interactions. The participants in this study were ninety children from the four kindergarten classes of two public schools.

INTERVENTION: For about six weeks the two classroom teachers set aside approximately ten minutes a day for "sharing time." At this time, each child was encouraged to name a classmate who had been friendly to him or her during play and to describe the friendly behavior. Any child so named was allowed to select a "happy face" badge from a hook on the wall. The children were discouraged from describing their own friendly deeds and received no badges for doing so. The teachers did not praise the children who received badges, nor did they hand out the badges. Whenever a child could not think of a peer who had been friendly, the teacher would say, "Perhaps tomorrow you will be able to name someone." Later, badges were no longer given out during sharing time, and peer praise was the only reinforcement provided.

Trained observers noted that the combined peer-praise and "happy face" procedure, the "reporting only" procedure as well as the peer-praise alone, increased cooperative behavior and decreased aggressive acts. A reversal phase, in which the children were asked to report unfriendly acts during sharing time, produced a decrease in cooperation and an increase in aggression.

COMMENTARY: The findings clearly indicate that children themselves can effectively direct their peers' attention to positive social interactions. Anecdotal reports from the teachers indicated that the reporting had a generally positive effect on the children's altruistic behavior toward one another. The teachers were particularly pleased that a number of children were now actively seeking the company of two isolated classmates. Even after the study had ended, the teachers continued to schedule sharing time for their classes.

SOURCE: Grieger, T., Kauffman, J. M., and Grieger, R. M. "Effects of Peer Reporting on Cooperative Play and Aggression of Kindergarten Children." *Journal of School Psychology,* 1976, *14,* 307-313.

Effective Use of Punishment in the Classroom

AUTHORS: R. Vance Hall, Saul Axelrod, Marlyn Foundopoulos, Jessica Shellman, Richard A. Campbell, and Sharon S. Cranston

PRECIS: Use of teacher reprimands to reduce aggressiveness in a seven-year-old girl

INTRODUCTION: The authors define *punishment* as "any consequence of behavior that reduces the future probability of that behavior." Clearly, punishment is widely used in our schools, since teachers do give detentions for classroom misbehaviors, send students to the principal's office, and require extra work from children who misbehave. The present study investigated the effects of punishment on specific problem behaviors in the classroom.

TREATMENT: The first case in this article involved Andrea, a seven-year-old deaf girl enrolled in a public school for the trainable mentally retarded. At every opportunity she would pinch and bite herself, her peers, the teacher, and visitors to the classroom. Andrea was so disruptive that it was impossible to teach her. Under the new strategy, whenever Andrea bit or pinched anyone, the teacher would reprimand her by pointing at her with an outstretched arm and shouting, "No!" Over the next eighteen days the average number of daily biting and pinching episodes dropped dramatically from seventy-two a day prior to treatment to five a day at the end of this period. When the teacher stopped reprimanding Andrea, the frequency of bites and pinches immediately rose to a mean of thirty a day. A return to the punishment procedure quickly reduced the bites to three a day. Andrea's decreased aggressiveness led her peers to interact with her more often.

COMMENTARY: Despite the misgivings of many educators, punishment does have a place in the classroom. Some children will simply not respond to any other method of control. Teacher reprimands are simple, easy to administer, and effective in quickly suppressing misbehaviors. If combined with teacher warmth and support, reprimands should not result in undesirable side effects, such as social withdrawal or resentment on the part of the child. But care must be taken to ensure that reprimands are not demeaning to the child. Ridicule, sarcasm, and name-calling should never be used to correct a child.

SOURCE: Hall, R. V., Axelrod, S., Foundopoulos, M., Shellman, J., Campbell, R. A., and Cranston, S. S. "The Effective Use of Punishment to Modify Behavior in the Classroom." *Educational Technology*, 1971, *11*, 24-26.

What to Do About Aggression

AUTHOR: Joanne Hendrick

PRECIS: Practical ways to prevent aggression in a nursery school

INTRODUCTION: Nursery school children require a great deal of vigorous and free play of their large muscles. However, teachers cannot allow direct expression of aggression during play—throwing things at others, biting them, hitting them with objects in hand, or outright insolence and defiance of the rules. At times it is necessary to physically stop a child from engaging in these acts. Apart from setting firm limits, however, teachers can find other ways to deal with the aggressive tendencies of children.

INTERVENTION: In the long run, the best way to handle aggression is to search for the underlying cause of this behavior and to try to remove it. It may be that the child's parents need guidance on how to help him feel less tense inside. Is the child coming to school hungry or sleepy? Perhaps there needs to be some change in the school environment. For example, does the child require an earlier snack, or does the program lack sufficient interest for him?

In the short run, the teacher should attempt to *sublimate* the child's aggressive feelings. Sublimation involves channeling the child's energies into acceptable outlets. Sublimation means providing plenty of materials (whether they are beanbags or dough), plenty of time, and as few restrictions as possible. Some activities that harmlessly drain off energy entail the use of large muscles, as in jumping off jungle gyms or boxes onto old mattresses, swinging, bike riding, climbing, sliding, throwing beanbags at a large face on a wall, hitting punching bags or bobos, hammering and sawing objects, pounding and squeezing dough, smearing finger paints, and tearing and crumpling paper.

Aggression can also be released by noise-making activities, such as pounding a drum or piano, dancing, yelling and playing loudly, and sitting on top of a slide and kicking one's heels hard. Dramatic play can help a child work off aggressive feelings. The classroom should be equipped with dolls, dollhouse furniture, rubber animals, costumes, and puppets. Water play is very effective for relaxing an out-of-control child. The child can wash cars or dolls in the housekeeping area. A running hose outdoors and lots of squishy sand and mud can result in a calm, happy day at school.

Apart from the sublimating activities described above, the teacher can use other indirect methods to handle aggression, such as kindly, one-to-one attention. A very effective technique is to consistently pay attention to a child a few minutes each day when she is doing positive things (and before she gets into trouble). It is also helpful to spot early warning signs of explosive situations. Thus, when an "angry monster" game is getting too high pitched, the teacher can distract the ringleader and get him involved in some other interesting activity. In addition, the teacher can be alert to certain children who tend to reinforce each other's negative behaviors. They should not be allowed to snack together or rest near each other, and the teacher should encourage them to form other friendships.

Other useful strategies include carefully planning interesting activities and scheduling active outdoor play right after periods of quiet activities, such as snack or story time. Opportunities for mastery are helpful, since aggressive tendencies are diminished when a child has done something constructive—for example, painting or learning to pump on a swing. Offering choices, whenever possible, encourages decision making and lessens defiance. A most helpful approach is to recognize, accept, and listen to a child's angry feelings without moralizing. Finally the teacher can encourage children to substitute talk for action. Before a child hits a troublemaker, the teacher can ask the child why he didn't like what the other child did. The teacher can then advise the child to *tell* the instigator how he feels rather than to act out his feelings.

COMMENTARY: The importance of providing acceptable outlets for tension and aggressive energy cannot be overemphasized. The more these energies come out in a constructive way, the less likelihood there is of an aggressive explosion. As this article points out, there is a wide range of acceptable substitutes and sublimations for releasing aggressive feelings harmlessly. To make sublimation work, the teacher needs to carefully plan activities in advance, provide plenty of materials, and be tolerant of noise and physical activity.

SOURCE: Hendrick, J. "Aggression: What to Do About It!" *Young Children,* 1968, *23,* 298-305.

Classical Conditioning and Childhood Aggression

AUTHORS: Thomas S. Parish, John Maly, and Ann Marie Shirazi

PRECIS: Use of classical conditioning to control aggression in elementary school children

INTRODUCTION: The goal of the present study was to reduce aggressive behavior in children through the application of classical conditioning procedures. This is one of the few studies reporting the use of classical conditioning with children. The subjects were sixty-five boys and girls from the fourth and fifth grades of a public elementary school in Oklahoma.

TREATMENT: The children were randomly assigned either to the experimental group or to one of two control groups. Children in the experimental group and in the first control group received four treatment sessions over an eight-day period. Treatment for the experimental children consisted of viewing a slide of a scene in which children were behaving aggressively in a playground setting. This was followed by a slide of a negatively evaluated word and then by a slide of a neutral word. This procedure was repeated thirty-six times during each treatment session. Examples of negatively evaluated words were "bad," "cowardly," "cruel," "evil," "selfish," and "unkind." The classi-

cal conditioning procedure involved pairing the pictures of aggressive acts with the presentation of negatively evaluated
words. It was hypothesized that in this way the children would
learn to negatively evaluate aggressive acts and thus reduce their
own aggressive behavior.

The children in the first control group received the same
treatment as the experimental group except that they were not
shown slides of negative words. Rather, they saw a slide of a
neutral word followed by a slide of an aggressive scene. To increase the attention of children in the experimental group and
the first control group, the experimenters asked them to say
each word out loud and to observe how each word was spelled.
Children in both groups were told that "this [was] a learning
experiment and that if they [paid] attention and [said] the
words shown on the screen ... they [would] probably become
better spellers." Children in the second control group did not
receive any of the previously mentioned treatment procedures.
Two days after the last treatment session ended, children in all
three groups were observed in the classroom by judges who recorded how many times the children engaged in aggressive acts
such as verbal assault, grabbing, hitting, kicking, pushing, pinching, and biting. An analysis of the data revealed that the experimental group committed significantly fewer aggressive acts than
did either control group. The two control groups did not differ
in the incidence of aggressive behavior.

COMMENTARY: Thus, children who viewed pictures of aggressive scenes paired with the presentation of negatively evaluated
words subsequently exhibited fewer aggressive acts in a classroom setting than children who had not experienced such a conditioning procedure. According to the authors, the implication
of this finding is that teachers do not have to resort to punitive
tactics such as reprimands or time-outs to reduce children's
aggressive behavior.

Other noteworthy findings of this investigation were that
aggressive acts by children occurred more frequently in classrooms where teachers showed a permissive orientation (unstructured, informal, and so on) than in classrooms where the
teacher was more restrictive (for example, insistent upon each

student's undivided attention). In the permissive classrooms, the children who were the same sex as their teacher tended to display more aggressive responses than did those children who were the opposite sex from their teacher.

SOURCE: Parish, T. S., Maly, J., and Shirazi, A. M. "Use of Classical Conditioning Procedures to Control Aggressive Behaviors in Children: A Preliminary Report." *Perceptual and Motor Skills*, 1975, *41*, 651-658.

Direct Intervention for Classroom Aggression

AUTHORS: Gerald R. Patterson, Joseph A. Cobb, and Roberta S. Ray

PRECIS: Using behavior modification procedures for aggressive-disruptive children

INTRODUCTION: Eleven aggressive-disruptive boys from different classrooms were treated by a "direct intervention" procedure. In this approach a professional consultant enters the classroom for a short period to demonstrate the use of behavior modification techniques, especially the use of rewards for appropriate behavior. The teacher and classmates of the problem child observe the procedures being modeled and subsequently administer them without outside assistance.

INTERVENTION: The problem child is first trained to pay attention in class and improve his work skills. This is usually accomplished by means of a "work box." This apparatus consists of a small box that is placed on the child's desk. The box contains a signal light and an electric counter that are readily visible to the child. Whenever the child attends in class or works at his desk, the consultant causes the light to flash and the counter to click. At first the child need attend or work only a little for the whole class ro receive extra recess time that day. Later, the child has to work or attend for longer intervals—for example, from sixty to one hundred seconds—to earn the group reward. The rewards, which are changed every few days, are chosen by the class. The work box usually produces immediate improvement in the child's work habits. And since the whole class benefits from his work, the problem child gains in "status" and peer acceptance. After a week or two, the teacher switches to a point system to reward the class for the child's behavior. The point system, in turn, is faded out after a few weeks, and then only teacher praise and approval are used to maintain the attending and work behaviors.

For some children the work box is not successful in reducing their aggressive and destructive behaviors. In these cases, time-out or contingency-contracting procedures are required. Time-out involves sending the child to a screened-off corner of the classroom for a period of one to ten minutes. Time-out needs to be applied consistently, that is, *each* time an aggressive behavior such as hitting or pushing occurs. Typically, time-out produces an immediate reduction in disruptive behavior. For extreme cases, the time-out will consist of sending the child home.

Contingency contracts are sometimes used to ensure that parents and school personnel work closely together. These contacts are written agreements entered into by parents, teachers, and the child. Typically, school personnel specify the behavior required for the child's continuation in school, such as a reduction in fighting or in throwing things in class or an increase in attendance. The teachers assign points for the fulfillment of these requirements, and the parents supply the reinforcement at home. For example, a certain number of classroom points each day might earn the child the right to watch television at home, to use his bicycle, to play outside, or to stay up later at night. The parents sometimes administer a penalty for certain misbehaviors at school. In some instances, whenever a child starts a fight, his mother takes him home, puts him to work for several hours, and then returns him to school. The contract ensures that the parents are in daily communication with the school and that all parties work together to solve specific behaviors such as fighting on the school bus or in the lunchroom. In addition to the procedures noted above, the disruptive child often needs tutoring in academic subjects. Parents can supervise a child's study at home when they are provided with programmed learning materials and training in effective teaching methods.

The authors report that this direct intervention approach was effective in substantially reducing the aggressive and destructive behavior of ten of the eleven children in the study. This improvement was being maintained at follow-ups three to six months later.

COMMENTARY: This comprehensive behavior modification program was carefully developed through seven years of research. Although it requires twenty to thirty hours of a consultant's time, it has the potential to bring under control the acting-out child who is in danger of being permanently expelled from school. Quite impressive is the fact that this technology has proved successful with extremely disturbed children in the classroom. The essence of the program is that parents and teachers decide on the specific behaviors they want changed and then spell out concrete rewards and penalties.

SOURCE: Patterson, G. R., Cobb, J. A., and Ray, R. S. "Direct Intervention in the Classroom: A Set of Procedures for the Aggressive Child." Paper presented at meeting of the Third Banff Conference on Behavior Modification, Banff, Alberta, April 1971.

A Time-Out Procedure in a Public School

AUTHOR: Raymond E. Webster

PRECIS: Use of time-out to control a highly aggressive boy

INTRODUCTION: The time-out technique involves placing a child in a quiet, boring environment as a punishment for inappropriate behavior. Varying durations of time-outs have been employed, ranging from two minutes to thirty minutes and, in a few instances, up to two hours. John, the subject in this study, was a thirteen-year-old boy who was enrolled in the sixth grade of a public school. He was referred to the school psychologist because he was exhibiting extremely wild and uncontrollable episodes of aggressive behavior. Recently he had injured two boys on the playground so severely that they had required hospitalization for head injuries. The boy had a long history of emotional problems, and traditional psychotherapy had proved unsuccessful in reducing his aggressive, disruptive behavior in the classroom and on the playground. John was currently being taught by a team of three teachers (two females and one male).

TREATMENT: After consulting with the school psychologist, John's teachers decided to record and try to modify his physically assaultive behaviors, which included throwing objects at children in the school, hitting other children with either his hands or an object, and kicking, biting, and pushing others. The teachers met with John to explain to him how these aggressive behaviors disrupted the class lessons and how unfair this infringement was. They stated that there would soon be a time-out imposed for any of the aforementioned aggressive acts. For time-out he would be sent to an eight-by-twelve-foot room that contained only a desk and a chair and had no windows. He could take his schoolwork and books with him, but he would have to stay in isolation for the duration of the class period in which he acted out. He would then go to his next class.

After this talk, John was given a five-day training period in which he was reminded of the consequences for a misdeed, but the time-out was not imposed. The next week one of the teachers escorted him to the time-out room for a misbehavior, while pointing out to him what he had done wrong, as well as his responsibility for his behavior. He was informed that when he stopped physically attacking others without provocation, the time-outs would end. The teachers recorded the number of times John was sent to the isolation room and the amount of time he remained there.

After ten weeks of this time-out procedure, John was no longer engaging in unprovoked aggressive acts. Prior to this intervention, he had been averaging over four such acts a day. During the first two weeks of the time-out procedure, he spent about sixty-five minutes a day in isolation. During the third week, however, there was a drastic reduction in time-outs: he averaged only eighteen minutes a day at this point. From this week on, his daily stay in time-out continued to decrease. After the seventh week of intervention he showed no self-initiated assaultive behaviors.

COMMENTARY: The results of this case study indicate that a simple punishment procedure, if carried out consistently and long enough, can eliminate aggressive behavior that had been both intense and frequent in nature. As soon as the boy's aggressive acts decreased, his teachers noted an increase in his spontaneous interest in schoolwork. Biweekly conferences between the psychologist and the teachers seemed to play an important role in supporting and encouraging the teachers.

SOURCE: Webster, R. E. "A Time-Out Procedure in a Public School Setting." *Psychology in the Schools,* 1976, *13,* 72-76.

Additional Readings

Ayllon, T., Garber, S., and Pisor, K. "The Elimination of Discipline Problems Through a Combined School-Home Motivational System." *Behavior Therapy,* 1975, *6,* 616-626.

To reduce the disruptive-aggressive behaviors of a third-grade class, the teacher sent home a "good behavior" letter if a child was not disruptive more than twice during one fifteen-minute period in class that day. The form letter expressed the teacher's pleasure at the student's good classroom behavior and reminded the parents to reward such behavior. Typical rewards given by parents included praise, special treats, weekend movies, extended television privileges, and money in the form of allowances. If a letter was not sent for a given day, the parents were to impose such sanctions as withholding allowances, taking away television or outdoor privileges, or imposing an earlier bedtime hour. This "good behavior" letter reduced classroom disturbances and ensured daily communication between school and parents.

Calpin, J. P., and Kornblith, S. J. "Training Aggressive Children in Conflict Resolution Skills." Mimeographed Report, 1979.

Four highly aggressive boys between the ages of eight and eleven received social skills training. The training involved teaching them to express affect in an appropriate way, such as "I don't like that" or "You've been teasing me a lot and that makes me feel bad." The boys were also instructed in how to request new behavior from others: "Why don't you quit swearing at me and maybe we can both play a game." "You can have it when I've finished looking at it." "After I've finished watching my show, you can watch yours." "Ask nicely." Training procedures involved instructions, modeling, videotape feedback, and behavior rehearsal. This assertiveness training program proved effective in reducing the hostility of the subjects.

Elardo, P. T., and Caldwell, B. M. "The Effects of an Experimental Social Development Program on Children in the Middle Childhood Period." *Psychology in the Schools,* 1979, *16,* 93-100.

Project Aware, a new social development program, was implemented with a group of nine- and ten-year-old children in an inner-city public school. The two main goals of the program were (1) to teach children to take the role of the other, that is, to be less egocentric and to develop the ability to put themselves in the other person's shoes, and (2) to encourage children to think up alternative solutions to problems so as to increase their flexibility in dealing with social problems. The results indicated that the children in the experimental group gained in respect for others, in patience, and in the ability to generate alternative solutions.

Henry, M. M., and Sharpe, D. F. "Some Influential Factors in the Determination of Aggressive Behavior in Preschool Children." *Child Development,* 1947, *18,* 11-28.

Between the ages of two and five, social interaction becomes more frequent and complex and seemingly opposite types of relations increase, such as aggressive-conflictive and friendly-sympathetic. Aggressiveness tends to increase as children in the preschool period grow older, and boys tend to be more aggressive than girls. The authors find that the nursery school environment influences both aggressive and sympathetic behaviors. In more controlled nursery schools, children make relatively fewer aggressive and sympathetic responses than do children of the same age in freer nursery schools. Controlled schools adhere to strict schedules, close adult supervision, and provide little opportunity or material for free play, outdoor play, or spontaneous social interchange.

Kirschner, N. M., and Levin, L. "A Direct School Intervention Program for the Modification of Aggressive Behavior." *Psychology in the Schools*, 1975, *12*, 202-208.

For about two months a school psychologist met with small groups (three to six participants) of children aged ten to thirteen) who had been identified as highly aggressive by their teachers. They engaged in such behaviors as fighting during class and lunch periods, threatening other students, frequently hitting other students in a playful manner, teasing, and name-calling. At an initial interview, the psychologist and students signed a formal agreement as to the behaviors to be changed (for example, fighting and threatening other children in the class) and the rewards (games, models, balls, "good" letter sent home) that weekly progress would earn for the child. The child's teacher would record twice a day if the specific aggressive behaviors were present or absent. The children could also earn points and privileges for behaving appropriately in the weekly group meetings. During the group meetings, each student was asked to bring up situations during the week in which he had had difficulty avoiding aggressive behaviors. The student and other group members would then role play the situation and rehearse several alternate ways of handling it. For example, if someone tapped a student on the back, he might respond by saying, "Hey, I don't want to get into trouble, so stop it" or "Hey, if you don't stop, I'm going to have to tell the teacher." This behavior rehearsal served to increase the social problem-solving skills of the students. The first half hour of the group meeting was devoted to these behavior rehearsals, to reviewing the frequency of misbehaviors for the week, to allowing students to "buy" reinforcers, and to discussing events of the week. The final half hour consisted of group athletic activities such as basketball or dodge ball. The athletic events increased the student's interest in the sessions and gave the group leader the chance to model ways of solving disagreements on the playground. The program proved effective in reducing the students' aggressive acts (fighting and threatening others).

McClain, W. A. "The Modification of Aggressive Classroom Behavior Through Reinforcement, Inhibition, and Relationship Therapy." *Training School Bulletin,* 1968, *65,* 122-125.

The author's basic premise is that many children display aggressiveness because they have not learned socially acceptable behavior due to insufficient reinforcement of social skills. The remedy is to reward (praise) the desired acts and ignore the others. This strategy was followed by a school psychologist who met with a ten-year-old boy in individual sessions over a six-month period and by the classroom teacher (the boy was in a special education class). Rather than punishing aggressiveness, the psychologist and the teacher tried to praise, encourage, and support prosocial behaviors. The stress was on establishing a relationship with the aggressive boy that would create positive motivation for future good behavior. Classroom rules were kept to a minimum of three: no walking around the room without permission, no fighting in class, and no speaking out without first raising one's hand. A reward (gold star) was given for daily adherence to all rules. Five consecutive stars earned a movie pass, and four consecutive weeks of gold stars entitled the boy to a model, such as a model race car. If any rule was broken more than three times during a day, a large black mark was placed on the chart for that day. The boy was also counseled by the psychologist twice a week to reinforce the teacher's efforts at behavior change. By the seventh week of this program the classroom behavior of the boy had been dramatically improved.

Pastor, D. L., and Swap, S. M. "An Ecological Study of Emotionally Disturbed Preschoolers in Special and Regular Classes." *Exceptional Children,* November 1978, Brief Reports.

Four emotionally disturbed preschool boys were found to exhibit more disruptive-aggressive behaviors in a regular nursery school than in a special therapeutic nursery school. A much lower pupil-teacher ratio was obtained in the special classes; teachers in the special class were present in the vicinity of the target children 80 percent of the time, while teachers in the regular class were present only 58 percent of the time. Consistent with the psychodynamic approach of their classes, the special class teachers more frequently explained to students the sequence of events that led to disturbances or interpreted to them the reasons for their behavior. Special class teachers deliberately tried to use both their relationships with the children and specific interventions as therapeutic tools. Even in the special class, however, the four boys became disruptive when there was relatively little teacher supervision, such as during outside activities.

Rashbaum-Selig, M. "Student Patrols Help a Disruptive Child." *Elementary School Guidance and Counseling,* October 1976, pp. 47-51.

Michael, a second grader, was referred to the school counselor because of aggressive and destructive behavior in school. Since the boy's parents were not willing to help with the problem, the counselor turned to the student patrols for assistance. The thirty-five student patrols directed younger children across streets and made sure safety and traffic rules were obeyed. The patrols agreed to try the following approach for managing Michael. First, they would ignore inappropriate behaviors such as crude remarks, unless Michael's actions could clearly hurt himself or others. Second, they would state clearly and specifically what they liked about Michael's behavior. Then they would try to find opportunities for praising Michael and say, for example, "I liked the way you walked your bike along the sidewalk, Mike." Third, after praising a specific behavior, they would reward Michael immediately with a "smiley face" token, a colored paper cutout that patrols could make and carry with them. Michael could then exchange these tokens for rewards from the counselor—ice cream (10 tokens), the opportunity to be an assistant patrol for a day (25 tokens), or a trip to a store to buy a model race car (100 tokens). Michael agreed to this plan for helping him get along better with others and visited the counselor once every two weeks during the four months that the plan was in effect. Within two weeks, a significant improvement was noted in Michael's behavior.

Schneider, M., and Dolnick, M. "The Turtle Technique: An Extended Case Study of Self-Control in the Classroom." *Psychology in the Schools,* 1976, *13,* 449-453.

The "turtle technique" is a promising procedure for helping children control their impulses toward aggressive behavior. The technique makes use of the image of the turtle, which withdraws into its shell when provoked by its external environment. Young children are taught to react to impulses to act aggressively by (1) imagining that they are turtles withdrawing into their shells, while pulling their arms close to their bodies, putting their heads down, and closing their eyes; (2) relaxing their muscles to relieve emotional tensions; and (3) using social problem-solving techniques to generate alternative, prosocial responses. The latter procedure involved teaching the children a number of alternative strategies for coping with their tendency toward aggressiveness and tantrums and for evaluating the consequences of each strategy. It was stressed to the children that they had *choices* other than to give in to an initial impulse. Two teachers of primary classes taught their students these three techniques. The approach was found to substantially reduce acts of physical aggression in the classroom.

Tidwell, R., and Bachus, V. A. "Group Counseling for Aggressive Schoolchildren." *Elementary School Guidance and Counseling,* 1977, October, pp. 2-7.

The authors conducted group counseling sessions with Afro-American males from grades four to six. The students were referred because of a high rate of physical fighting among themselves. The eight bimonthly counseling sessions were designed to instill in the boys the importance of helping others, of cooperation, and of empathy, along with respect for the feelings of others. Moreover, the boys were taught several decision-making skills, such as evaluating courses of action, deferring the consequences of various options, and analyzing the evidence to support or refute choices. Through this group experience the boys were given the opportunity to understand and change their nonproductive behavior.

Whitehurst, C., and Miller, E. "Behavior Modification of Aggressive Behavior on a Nursery School Bus: A Case Study." *Journal of School Psychology*, 1973, *11*, 123-127.

     · The aggressive behavior of two preschool boys on a nursery school bus was reduced by the introduction of a penalty for such behavior. The driver told the children just before the trip that anyone who misbehaved would not be allowed to get off the bus when it passed his home and would have to wait until the second pass of the bus to go home (delay of reinforcement). One warning was to be given by the driver if she observed the children acting aggressively during the trip. Appropriate behavior was praised by the driver, as was her normal practice. This procedure produced a dramatic decrease in the rate of aggression.

Wilson, C. C., Robertson, S. J., Herlong, L. H., and Haynes, S. N. "Vicarious Effects of Time-Out in the Modification of Aggression in the Classroom." *Behavior Modification*, 1979, *3*, 97-111.

     This study assessed the vicarious effects of a time-out penalty when it was applied to children's aggressive behaviors in the classroom. Whenever the kindergarten boys in this study behaved aggressively in class, they were immediately placed in the time-out area (a small open booth that blocked visual contact with other students) for five minutes. This procedure reduced not only the aggressive acts of the treated children but also the aggressive behavior of their untreated classmates.

Zahavi, S., and Asher, S. R. "The Effect of Verbal Instructions on Preschool Children's Aggressive Behaviors." *Journal of School Psychology*, 1978, *16*, 146-153.

     Aggressive preschool children were instructed by their teacher on the harm that results from aggression, its lack of effect as an interpersonal strategy, and the possibility that constructive alternatives, such as cooperating and sharing, would be more effective. The teachers met individually with each child for about ten minutes and engaged him in a conversation designed to teach three concepts: (1) aggression hurts another person and makes that person unhappy; (2) aggression does not solve problems and only brings about the resentment of the other person; and (3) positive ways to solve conflicts are sharing, taking turns, and playing together. Each concept was taught by describing typical classroom conflict situations, then asking the child leading questions and encouraging the desired response. The findings indicated that aggressive behavior decreased and cooperative behavior increased as a result of these instructions. So verbal discussion and providing rationales do seem to be effective ways to control aggression in children.

Prejudice

Prejudice refers to adverse judgments that individuals hand down on people who are of a different race, culture, religion, or sex. These judgments are without just grounds and are made without sufficient knowledge. Sociological surveys have found that racial and religious hatred is still rampant among today's teen-agers. Racial integration of schools, which began in the United States in the 1950s, has not always achieved the desired effects. At times, the consequences of desegregation have been fear, mistrust, and violence. Even where racial tensions are not present, cross-racial friendships tend to be rare. In recent years both researchers and educators have spent large amounts of time and money trying to develop approaches, programs, and/or materials that will be capable of reducing negative racial attitudes among the young. A variety of effective strategies are described in this section.

Modification of Racial Prejudice in White Children

AUTHORS: Phyllis A. Katz and Sue R. Zalk

PRECIS: Comparison of four short-term intervention techniques

INTRODUCTION: Racial prejudice in adults has been found to be relatively intransigent and difficult to change. With children, however, a variety of approaches have had some success in reducing negative racial attitudes. The authors designed a well-controlled study to evaluate the relative efficacy of four techniques with white and black children. The subjects were 160 white children (second and fifth graders) from two public schools in the New York City area. Both schools (one urban, one suburban) had been desegregated for some time. Children who were high in prejudice were randomly assigned to one of four experimental groups or to a control group.

METHODS: The first strategy—*group interaction technique*—involved increased contact and interaction between the two races. In the experimental group, teams composed of two black and two white children worked together for fifteen minutes to solve a jigsaw puzzle. The children were asked to give their team a name and were rewarded for successful work by verbal praise, having a Polaroid picture taken of their team, and receiving a prize for the fastest time. In the control group, all four members of the teams were white.

In the second technique—*vicarious contact*—groups of three children were asked to listen to a story that was accompanied by corresponding slides and then answer questions about it. The story slides for the experimental children contained black characters, while the control group viewed slides of white characters. The story itself described a child who overcomes adversity to help get a sick grandmother to the hospital.

There were two *stimulus predifferentiation* groups. The first experimental group was shown slides of black faces, and its members learned to associate a name with each face. The second experimental group was asked to view pictures of black faces and to count them. In this way the group received increased exposure to black faces. The control group viewed slides of white faces.

In the final technique, a *conditioning group* was reinforced (given models exchangeable for prizes) for selecting pictures of black rather than white animals. In this way they were being conditioned to associate the color black with something positive. The control group was reinforced for selecting the color orange over the color green.

An analysis of attitude and behavior measures revealed that children in the experimental groups showed a significant short-term reduction in prejudice. Vicarious contact and stimulus predifferentiation approaches were more effective than the other two. The long-term (four to six months) treatment effects were less substantial, but some gains were maintained.

COMMENTARY: The major finding of this well-designed investigation was that highly prejudiced white children who received short-term intervention procedures exhibited more tolerant racial attitudes on a two-week posttest than did control children. This is quite remarkable since each intervention lasted only about fifteen minutes. This study supports previous research in finding that young children's racial attitudes are quite malleable, particularly on a short-term basis. The authors conclude that schools could probably do much more to counteract racial prejudice than they are now doing.

SOURCE: Katz, P. A., and Zalk, S. R. "Modification of Children's Racial Attitudes." *Developmental Psychology*, 1978, *14*, 447-461.

Changing the Racial Attitudes of Children

AUTHORS: Thomas S. Parish and Robert S. Fleetwood

PRECIS: Effect of increasing the amount of conditioning

INTRODUCTION: Since racial attitudes are learned responses, they can be changed by systematic conditioning strategies. The present study sought to investigate the question: "Does increasing the number of conditioning trials that associate the color black with positively evaluated words serve to enhance the adoption of favorable attitudes to Afro-Americans by Euro-American kindergarten children?" The subjects were seventy-nine Euro-American children from a public school system in Oklahoma. The children were randomly assigned to one of three experimental groups or to a control group.

INTERVENTION: In groups of twenty, the experimental children viewed slides of four colors: black, orange, blue, and green. Only the color black was paired with the presentation of positively evaluated words, such as "good," "beautiful," and "nice." The children were asked to say aloud the colors and any words the experimenter used. A treatment session consisted of thirty-six presentations of the four colors. The children in the experimental groups received either one, four, or eight treatment sessions. Children in the control group did not receive any conditioning sessions. The results indicated that all the experimental groups adopted significantly more favorable attitudes to Afro-Americans than did the control subjects. It was also found that increasing the number of conditioning sessions yielded a greater increase in the positive attitudes of the experimental groups.

COMMENTARY: The present investigation indicates that a possible solution to reducing prejudices that are well entrenched and thus resistant to change is to increase the number of conditioning or learning sessions. The children's attitudes toward Afro-Americans became progressively more favorable as the number of learning sessions increased. This study did not investigate whether the change in racial attitudes held up over time or whether it generalized to situations outside the laboratory.

SOURCE: Parish, T. S., and Fleetwood, R. S. "Amount of Conditioning and Subsequent Change in Racial Attitudes of Children." *Perceptual and Motor Skills*, 1975, *40*, 79-86.

Integrating the Desegregated Classroom

AUTHOR: Robert E. Slavin

PRECIS: Using student learning teams to improve race relations

INTRODUCTION: The basic premise underlying the use of biracial cooperative groups to improve race relations is that when people must work together to achieve a common goal, they learn to like and help one another. People generally like those who help them receive rewards. This is the principle behind the Teams-Games-Tournaments (TGT) approach, in which students study academic material in four- or five-member biracial teams and then play simple academic games to display their knowledge. In a number of studies, researchers at Johns Hopkins University have demonstrated that the TGT technique increases cross-racial liking and helping. TGT has also been effective in raising student achievement in such basic skills as reading and mathematics.

METHOD: The author describes a method that simplifies TGT but retains its basic principles. This technique is called Student Teams-Achievement Divisions (STAD). This approach consists of two main elements: (1) biracial, ability-heterogeneous student teams and (2) achievement divisions. Achievement divisions involve a statistical technique that gives each student a good chance to earn the maximum number of points possible, regardless of the student's past performance.

Student Teams. The teacher assigns four or five students to each biracial learning team. Each team consists of a high achiever, a low achiever, and two or three average achievers and roughly reflects the racial and male-female composition of the class as a whole. Following an initial presentation by the teacher of the material to be studied, the teams receive worksheets on the subject. Team members work together to learn the academic material. They are then individually quizzed on the material they studied. This cycle (teaching-teamwork-quiz) takes two and a half forty-five-minute periods. The class has two of these cycles per week, usually for an interval of nine to ten weeks. Team scores are the total of individual scores as adjusted by the achievement division procedure described below. At the end of each week, successful teams are rewarded by recognition in a class newsletter prepared by the teacher.

Achievement Divisions. Apart from team membership, students are assigned to ability-homogeneous achievement divisions of about six members each. The students do not interact with others in their division; the division serves only as a reference group for computing student scores. Students earn eight points for their team if their quiz scores place them first in their divisions; six points if second; four points if third, and two points if they rank below third. This "level" system gives each student a roughly equal chance of earning a maximum number of points for hard work, regardless of past achievement. A "bumping" procedure changes division assignments from week to week to keep the level systems current.

The STAD system, then, is a cooperative reward and task structure in which students must help one another if they are to do well as a group and also one in which the contribution of each student has considerable value for the team. A study by the author of the effects of STAD in two seventh-grade English classes in the Baltimore public schools revealed that the procedure had positive effects both on cross-race friendship formation (blacks and whites) and on academic achievement.

COMMENTARY: The results of this and other studies indicate that the establishment of cooperative learning teams is an effective method for increasing cross-racial friendships and thus relieving racial tensions in integrated schools. This simple, enjoyable, and economical procedure has also proved effective in raising academic achievement. Clearly, the method warrants more widespread use in our elementary and secondary schools. A STAD manual for training teachers in the technique is available from the author.

SOURCE: Slavin, R. E. "How Student Learning Teams Can Integrate the Desegregated Classroom." *Integrated Education*, 1977, *15*, 56-58.

Effects of Cooperative Interethnic Contact

AUTHORS: Russell H. Weigel, Patricia L. Wiser, and Stuart W. Cook

PRECIS: Assessing the impact of cooperative learning experiences on ethnic relations

INTRODUCTION: The authors note that evaluation studies of programs designed to increase interethnic contacts are about equally divided in reporting favorable and unfavorable outcomes. It seems that increased contact does not in itself necessarily result in positive attitudes and behavior changes. The present study sought to further investigate the specific conditions under which school desegregation could reduce prejudice among students. Previous studies had suggested that cooperative contact seems to increase constructive interethnic relations, while competitive contact tends to inhibit them. Unfortunately, it seems that the classroom climate in American schools is heavily biased in favor of rewarding competitive rather than cooperative student behavior.

INTERVENTION: The study compared the effects of two types of interethnic contact, one involving student cooperation and the other not. Ten English teachers in Denver, Colorado (five from a junior high school and five from a senior high school) volunteered to teach one of their sections by the traditional method of lecturing to the whole class and another section by a small-group method in which the students would work in interethnic teams of four to six members and cooperate on assignments and classroom projects. Both the junior and senior high school samples were comprised of white, black, and Mexican-American students who, as a result of a school busing program, were attending integrated classes for the first time. The typical study group consisted of three white students, one black student, and one Mexican-American student.

The small study groups were encouraged to work toward common goals that required cooperation. For example, a film would be shown to the class, and then the study groups would meet to discuss and interpret the information. A group representative would then make a report to the rest of the class. Groups excelling on a task would be rewarded by being excused from additional assignments or by receiving bonus points on grades.

The study was conducted over an interval of four and one-half months in the senior high school and over a seven-month period in the junior high. The participating teachers received special training and guidance in implementing the two teaching strategies. An evaluation of this study revealed that the small study group method, compared to the traditional method of lecturing to a large class, resulted in more harmonious ethnic relations, as reflected in less cross-ethnic conflict and greater cross-ethnic helping. Participating teachers strongly favored the small-group technique and recommended it for use in newly desegregated schools.

COMMENTARY: The findings of this study support those of previous investigations in highlighting the positive effects of cooperative learning experiences on ethnic relations. Another important finding was that the more a small group was successful in competing with other groups to obtain rewards, the more the group members liked one another. The authors suggest, then, that absolute rather than relative standards of group success be employed in future studies, such as rewarding a small group for achieving five satisfactory grades on different assignments rather than receiving a higher mark than other groups. Since intergroup competition results in only a few winners, it may be counterproductive in this approach.

SOURCE: Weigel, R. H., Wiser, P. L., and Cook, S. W. "The Impact of Cooperative Learning Experiences on Cross-Ethnic Relations and Attitudes." *Journal of Social Issues*, 1975, *31*, 219-244.

Additional Readings

De Vries, D. L., Edwards, K. J., and Slavin, R. E. "Biracial Learning Teams and Race Relations in the Classroom: Four Field Experiments Using Teams-Games-Tournament." *Journal of Educational Psychology*, 1978, *70*, 356-362.

This study investigated the effects of Teams-Games-Tournament (TGT), an instructional strategy that employs biracial learning teams and instructional games, on cross-racial friendship in integrated classes (grades 7 to 12). The results indicated that TGT is an effective means of increasing cross-racial friendship in such classes.

Goldstein, C. G., Koopman, E. J., and Goldstein, H. H. "Racial Attitudes in Young Children as a Function of Interracial Contact in the Public Schools." *American Journal of Orthopsychiatry*, 1979, *49*, 89-99.

The relative effects of integrated and segregated schooling on racial attitudes were studied in a comparison of children aged five to six attending all-black, all-white, and integrated schools. Results of this photo-choice study suggest that segregated classes discourage realistic perceptions of the excluded race and promote a preference for whites among both whites and blacks, whereas interracial schooling contributes to acceptance of blacks by all students and has especially profound and complex effects on black children.

Houser, B. B. "An Examination of the Use of Audiovisual Media in Reducing Prejudice." *Psychology in the Schools,* 1978, *15,* 116-122.

This study evaluated the effectiveness of audiovisual media as instructional techniques for altering ethnic attitudes in children aged five through nine. The films used in the study were obtained from the Anti-Defamation League and ranged from ten to fifteen minutes. Their common theme was that appearance or color should not be considered important in relating to others. The films were found to reduce prejudiced responses among white, black, Oriental, and Mexican-American children. Two films were found to be no more effective than one film. The results demonstrate that audiovisual media are valuable aids in molding ethnic attitudes and that they can provide welcome help to teachers who feel ill at ease with that task.

Parish, T. S., Bryant, W. T., and Prawat, R. S. "Reversing Effects of Sexism in Elementary School Girls Through Counterconditioning." *Journal of Instructional Psychology,* 1978, *4,* 11-14.

Probably as a result of the American "socialization" process, females have tended to develop rather negative views of themselves. The premise that this negativism is part of a developmental indoctrination process is advanced in the present study by the finding that older girls demonstrated significantly less favorable evaluations of females than did younger girls. An attempt was made to improve these school-age girls' evaluations of females by showing them pictures of females along with positively evaluated words. Subsequently, the girls exposed to this counterconditioning procedure adopted significantly more positive attitudes toward females than did the girls in either the control or the placebo groups.

Shyness and Withdrawal

Shyness is defined as a tendency to avoid social interactions and to fail to participate appropriately in social situations. Shy, withdrawn children engage in a low number of social interactions and seldom initiate social contact. Social withdrawal in children is a problem in which males and females are equally represented. Surveys have indicated that a substantial number of elementary school children think of themselves as shy and that 40 percent of college students describe themselves as "shy persons." A teacher may not even be aware that a shy child has a problem because such children do not cause trouble or make noise. But shyness is a serious problem because it interferes with making friends, learning, developing self-esteem, and becoming psychologically adjusted. Shy people are often self-conscious, unassertive, lonely, and depressed. Since so many persons now regard shyness as a problem, various investigators have begun to develop remedies for social anxiety and social skills deficits.

459

Effects of Social Reinforcement
on a Withdrawn Preschooler

AUTHORS: K. Eileen Allen, Betty M. Hart, Joan S. Buell, Florence R. Harris, and Montrose M. Wolf

PRECIS: Controlling withdrawn behavior by teacher attention

INTRODUCTION: Reinforcement theory postulates that a child's behavior increases or decreases in strength depending upon its immediate consequences. Positive consequences, such as adult attention and approval, are likely to increase desired behaviors. The authors used this principle to increase the peer interaction of Ann, a four-year-old nursery school child. While Ann did not seem severely withdrawn or frightened of her classmates, she did not play freely or spontaneously with them. Although Ann displayed a variety of physical and intellectual abilities, she carried out most of her activities independently of other children. She rarely initiated conversation or cooperative play with her peers or responded to the social initiatives that other children directed toward her. Ann seemed overdependent upon adults and frequently sought teacher contact. Her teachers typically gave her attention on a one-to-one basis when Ann was apart from the group. It was decided, then, to reverse this process and to give her social reinforcement (attention and approval) contingent upon play with other children.

TREATMENT: After five days of observing her usual social interactions, Ann's teachers gave her no attention when she was alone and only minimal attention when she initiated contact with them. But any social interaction with another child or children was given immediate adult attention. Initially, Ann received adult attention whenever she was physically close to another child. The teacher would go to Ann and stay close to her as long as Ann was in close proximity to her classmates. The teacher would watch her and suggest to her ways of entering into play with those nearby.

Prior to this new strategy, Ann had been spending 50 percent of her morning time in solitary activities, 40 percent interacting with adults, and only 10 percent interacting with other children. The first day of the new procedure produced a dramatic change in her behavior. She now spent almost 60 percent of the morning playing with other children, while her teacher contacts dropped to less than 20 percent. These levels remained stable during the first six days of reinforcement for peer play. At this point, the teachers went back to their old system of paying attention to Ann when she was by herself. This reversal resulted in a deterioration of peer play to the previous low point. When Ann again received teacher attention contingent upon peer contact, her interaction with children again rose to a level of about 60 percent for the final nine days of treatment. Teacher attention for peer interaction was gradually given more intermittently during the final days of the program. Spot checks on Ann's peer interactions during the month after treatment revealed that these contacts continued to remain more frequent than the adult interactions.

COMMENTARY: This study supports a growing body of evidence that indicates that the systematic use of teacher attention can help withdrawn preschoolers relate more comfortably with their peers. The child in this case study not only increased the frequency of her peer contacts but was also observed to become more assertive with her peers, to speak in a louder and more fluid manner, and to reduce her concern over minor cuts and bruises. This study underscores the importance of early intervention for school behavior problems before the difficulties become chronic and highly resistant to change.

SOURCE: Allen, K. E., Hart, B. M., Buell, J. S., Harris, F. R., and Wolf, M. M. "Effects of Social Reinforcement on Isolate Behavior of a Nursery School Child." *Child Development,* 1964, *35,* 511-518.

Social Skills Training for Unassertive Children

AUTHORS: Mitchell R. Bornstein, Alan S. Bellack, and Michel Hersen

PRECIS: Increasing social assertiveness by providing instructions, feedback, behavior rehearsal, and modeling

INTRODUCTION: Certain children tend to passively withdraw in conflict situations with others. They are described as excessively cooperative, passive, shy, unassertive, and conforming by their teachers. Four such children, aged eight to eleven, were identified in an elementary school associated with the University of Pittsburgh. In addition to the aforementioned characteristics, the four children were also found to exhibit at least three of the following four unassertive behaviors: poor eye contact, short speech duration, inaudible responses, and inability to make requests.

TREATMENT: Each child received three weeks of social skills training in three sessions of fifteen to thirty minutes each week. Individual training was conducted in a videotape studio, with a male and a female college student providing the training. The college students were given directions by a psychologist in the control room. The college students and the child would pretend that they were in a variety of social situations requiring the child to be assertive. For example, pretending to cut in front of the child in a school lunch line, the college student would say, "Let me cut in front of you." The child was then asked to say what he or she would actually say if in that situation. The college student then trained the child to increase eye contact while speaking, to speak in an appropriately loud tone of voice, to increase speech duration (number of words spoken), and to request new behavior from the other person. For example, the child would have to ask the boy who cut in front of him or her to step to the end of the line. Or, in another situation he would have to request that his sister wait her turn to sit next to their mother at dinner.

In addition to giving the child feedback on his or her performance in the "pretend" social situation, the college student would discuss the feedback to be sure that the child understood it, model appropriate responses to the situation, give specific instructions concerning verbal and nonverbal assertiveness, ask the child to respond a second time, and rehearse the scene until the child displayed appropriately assertive behavior. Observations before and after treatment revealed that each of the four children showed considerable gains in overall assertiveness and in deficient components such as eye contact, loudness of speech, speech duration, and number of requests. These gains were being maintained at two- and four-week evaluations after treatment.

COMMENTARY: Training shy children in assertive behavior has become increasingly popular in recent years. The basic assumption of this approach is that shy children have never learned how to respond in an appropriately assertive way, so they tend to withdraw or give in when under stress. It is felt that they need specific instructions in how to stick up for their rights in a conflict situation and how to express negative feelings without becoming hostile. A major limitation of this study is that no data were collected as to whether the children acted more assertively in the natural environment. The authors point out this limitation and suggest further research to investigate this question.

SOURCE: Bornstein, M. R., Bellack, A. S. and Hersen, M. "Social Skills Training for Unassertive Children: A Multiple-Baseline Analysis." *Journal of Applied Behavior Analysis,* 1977, *10,* 183-195.

Modifying Social Withdrawal in Preschoolers

AUTHORS: Wendy Evers-Pasquale and Mark Sherman

PRECIS: Use of peer models to increase social interaction

INTRODUCTION: A previous study (R. D. O'Connor, "Modification of Social Withdrawal Through Symbolic Modeling," *Journal of Applied Behavior Analysis,* 1969, 2, 15-22) developed a twenty-three-minute film that depicted children interacting in a positive way with one another. O'Connor found that, after viewing this film, some isolated preschoolers seemed to imitate the behavior of the models in the film and to increase their own social behaviors. In the present study, the authors sought to investigate whether the film-modeling approach would be effective with children who are peer oriented. A test was constructed to measure the preference of children to do things by themselves, with adults, or with peers. Peer-oriented children were defined as those who consistently responded that they preferred to engage in play and other activities with peers rather than with adults or by themselves.

INTERVENTION: Teachers from three nursery school classes nominated nineteen of sixty-five children as the most socially withdrawn. Sixteen of these nineteen children were observed to spend less than 20 percent of their time interacting with their peers during free play time and were thus included in the study. The average age of the children was four years, four months. Nine of the sixteen children who were selected were found to be peer oriented from the test mentioned above. These nine children were assigned to the treatment group while the remaining seven children comprised the control group.

Each child in the treatment group was individually shown the modeling film developed by O'Connor. In each of eleven different film scenes that depicted preschoolers engaging in a variety of nursery school activities, a child (model) was shown interacting with a peer or a peer group after approaching the others and attentively viewing their behavior. In all the scenes, the model received positive reinforcement for joining the group.

The scenes were graduated with respect to the number of children in the peer group and the vigor of the play activity. An accompanying narration emphasized the benefits of playing with and helping other children and described ways to join an activity.

Children in the control group viewed a twenty-one-minute film about African wildlife. Observations of the children's social interactions two days and four weeks after the film showings revealed that the children in the treatment group engaged in significantly more social interactions than did those in the control group. Social interaction was defined as smiling at, touching, talking to, or playing with a peer, and receiving a reciprocal response. It was also found that, within the treatment group, the peer-oriented children exhibited more social interactions as a result of the film viewing than did the children who were not peer oriented.

COMMENTARY: The findings of this study suggest that for withdrawn children who wish to play with other children, learning how to initiate and enjoy playing with peers by watching films can be very effective. For other types of socially isolated children, such as the withdrawn child who likes only adult attention, teacher praise for interacting with peers may be the treatment of choice. The advantage of using filmed modeling is that it is simple, easy to administer by teachers, and economical. Moreover, several studies have now been conducted that indicate that a single viewing of a film demonstrating socially appropriate behavior by peers can produce a marked increase in social interaction by isolated children.

SOURCE: Evers-Pasquale, W., and Sherman, M. "The Reward Value of Peers: A Variable Influencing the Efficacy of Filmed Modeling in Modifying Social Isolation in Preschoolers." *Journal of Abnormal Child Psychology*, 1975, *3*, 179-189.

Use of Teacher Prompts and Attention to Increase a Child's Social Interaction

AUTHORS: Elizabeth M. Goetz, Carolyn L. Thomson, and Barbara C. Etzel

PRECIS: Comparison of various teacher approaches to reduce social withdrawal

INTRODUCTION: The authors compared three different approaches by teachers for increasing social interaction in children: (1) direct reinforcement; (2) direct and indirect reinforcement combined with direct and indirect primes; and (3) indirect reinforcement and indirect primes. Direct reinforcement refers to verbal or nonverbal behavior directed to a child while the child and at least one peer are interacting. For example, a teacher might say to a withdrawn child who is playing with a classmate, "Joan, you are certainly having a good time." Indirect social reinforcement is defined as teacher attention directed to the peer or group with which the withdrawn child is interacting; for example, "Lisa, you and Joan are building the biggest building yet." Notice that the comment was directed to the withdrawn child's peer. A direct prime or prompt is a suggestion, instruction, or directive to a withdrawn child to begin interacting with others; for example, "Bill, will you collect tickets for the show?" or "Look, Billy, Jim needs some help setting the table for dinner." When using an indirect prime, a teacher might approach a withdrawn child's peer and suggest to the peer that he or she play with the withdrawn child. For example, a teacher might say, "Jim, maybe Billy would help you carry those blocks for your house if you asked him." The indirect prime can be delivered in private to the peer, or it can be delivered publicly so that the withdrawn child hears it.

TREATMENT: The withdrawn child in this case study was four-year-old Vickie who was enrolled in a private preschool. Evidence of her low rate of interaction with her peers was found in the observation that she spent only 10 percent of the preschool day interacting with other children. The normal rate of peer interaction for girls in this school was between 25 to 40 percent of the school day. Vickie was highly verbal, especially with her teachers. Thus, she was a child who was withdrawn only with her peers—not with adults.

The treatment consisted of three different strategies by her teachers. First, they gave direct reinforcement when she interacted with her peers and they withheld attention when she was alone. If Vickie initiated conversation with her teachers, they kept this interaction to a minimum. This approach increased her peer interactions from a mean of 10 percent of total time observed during the first baseline period to 21 peicent. Next, Vickie was given a combination of direct and indirect reinforcement and direct and indirect primes. In other words, the teachers added primes to their reinforcement in an effort to increase her social interactions. This procedure increased her peer interactions to 24 percent. The final strategy involved only indirect reinforcement and indirect primes. This method resulted in an increase of social interactions to 37 percent of the time observed. Under this final method, Vickie's peer interactions for the first time surpassed her adult interactions.

COMMENTARY: The findings of this study clearly indicate that all three combinations of direct and indirect approaches were effective in increasing the child's social behavior over baseline conditions. Moreover the indirect reinforcement and indirect prompting procedure seemed to be the most effective. Since this study involved only one child, further research is needed to validate this finding.

SOURCE: Goetz, E. M., Thomson, C. L., and Etzel, B. C. "An Analysis of Direct and Indirect Teacher Attention and Primes in the Modification of Child Social Behavior: A Case Study." *Merrill-Palmer Quarterly*, 1975, *21*, 55-65.

Increasing Cooperative Play
of a Preschool Child

AUTHORS: Betty M. Hart, Nancy J. Reynolds, Donald M. Baer, Eleanor R. Brawley, and Florence R. Harris

PRECIS: Making teacher praise contingent upon socially appropriate behavior

INTRODUCTION: Martha, aged five, was enrolled in a preschool for normal children. Although she frequently interacted with other children, her contacts were typically brief and verbally aggressive in nature. Rather than playing when invited, she would taunt others ("I can do that better than you") or use foul language.

INTERVENTION: Two different strategies were employed by her teachers to promote cooperative social play. The first approach involved giving Martha a great deal more teacher attention than she normally had. She did not have to do anything to earn this attention. For seven days her teachers spent considerable time attending to Martha. This attention consisted of remaining near her and attending closely to her activities, sometimes supplying her with equipment or materials and sometimes smiling at her, conversing with her, and admiring her. This strategy did not change the rate of cooperative play exhibited by Martha, which averaged less than 5 percent of the day.

The second approach consisted of giving teacher attention only when Martha played cooperatively with other children. Since her cooperative play occurred so infrequently, it was initially necessary to use priming and shaping procedures. Priming involved prompting other children to speak to or play with Martha. (Martha never received such prompting herself). Shaping meant that Martha was at first given attention for responding to the verbalizations of others and that she subsequently received this social reinforcement only for cooperative play, such as pulling a child or being pulled by a child in a wagon, adding to a block construction of others, or sharing a toy with others. After twelve days of this procedure, Martha's rate of cooperative play increased dramatically from 5 percent to almost 40 percent. Often the teacher attention and approval were given to the entire cooperating group rather than just to Martha.

COMMENTARY: This study supports a number of previous investigations that have found that social reinforcement from teachers, when made contingent upon desired behaviors of a child, can successfully increase such behaviors. The lack of success of noncontingent attention indicates that Martha was not displaying hostility to her peers as a result of too little positive attention from the adults in her environment. So contingent rather than abundant adult attention was needed in this case.

SOURCE: Hart, B. M., Reynolds, N. J., Baer, D. M., Brawley, E. R., and Harris, F. R. "Effect of Contingent and Noncontingent Social Reinforcement on the Cooperative Play of a Preschool Child." *Journal of Applied Behavior Analysis,* 1968, *1,* 73-77.

===

The Teacher and the Withdrawn Child

AUTHOR: Orval G. Johnson

PRECIS: Commonsense advice for coping with the withdrawn child

INTRODUCTION: In the classroom, withdrawn children seldom or never volunteer for assignments or special activities. When left alone they tend to daydream, doodle, fidget, or engage in solitary, unconstructive activities. Unless helped, the withdrawn child tends to have less and less contact with other children. In the present study, a group of thirty-two first- and second-grade teachers from the public schools of Jackson, Michigan, described the methods they had found particularly effective in bringing the withdrawn child into the group.

FINDINGS: The recommendations of the teachers were classified according to certain subgoals that were important for the attainment of the ultimate goal of bringing the withdrawn child into closer contact with people in school. The seven subgoals are listed below in the order of frequency with which they were mentioned:

1. Enhance the child's self-esteem and self-confidence. Because 55 percent of the 137 suggestions fell into this category, it was broken down into the following subcategories:

(a) Take every opportunity to praise the child (even if it is just for "being such a good rester").

(b) Give the child recognition by talking "to" him during group sessions, that is, looking directly at him. from time to time. You might also call the group he is in by his name, for example, "Tom's group."

(c) Give the child responsibility by assigning her important tasks.

(d) Find areas or activities in which the child feels secure enough to participate. Some children can be drawn out by art activities, while others feel comfortable talking about their families or their pets.

(e) Ask the child for advice in areas where she is able to be helpful, such as teacher-pupil planning.

(f) Give the child an objective description of any progress he has made, such as the ability to do things he was not able to do before.

(g) Help the child when you feel she needs help so as to avoid traumatic failure experiences.

2. Arrange the environment to encourage the child's contact with his peers. Thirteen percent of the responses advocated some form of this approach, including placing the withdrawn child in group activities with friendly children, encouraging other children to play with the child, and seating the child near friendly, outgoing peers.

3. Gently move the child toward participation. Ten per-

cent of the responses suggested allowing the child to remain relatively anonymous at first and yet participate in the group. Later, when the child seems ready for individual participation, the teacher should encourage him to do so.

4. Discuss the child's need to participate and share with others. The most frequent recommendation under this category was to talk directly with the child, pointing out how much more fun she would have if she joined the others.

5. Help the child feel secure and "at home" in the classroom. Specific techniques included talking with the child about topics he is familiar with and directly assuring the child that he is needed and loved by the teacher and the rest of the class. One teacher took a withdrawn child home for dinner to help the child develop feelings of security.

6. Develop a climate of relaxed calmness in the classroom. Suggestions included moving at a moderate speed and talking in soft but clear voice tones.

7. Miscellaneous. Other methods included setting a good example of accepting and communicating with the withdrawn child.

COMMENTARY: The recommendations made by teachers in this study were based on years of teaching experience. Most of the suggestions fell into the ego-supportive or self-esteem category. In general, then, the teachers felt that the greatest need of the withdrawn child is to develop self-confidence, that is, a more favorable view of himself or herself. Many of the teachers felt that the child withdraws from social interaction to prevent failure and the consequent lowering of self-esteem. When children are drawn into a group and experience some success, they are usually able to continue in the group on their own.

SOURCE: Johnson, O. G. "The Teacher and the Withdrawn Child." *Mental Hygiene,* 1956, *40,* 529-534.

Promoting Cooperation in Preschoolers

AUTHORS: Ronald G. Slaby and Christy G. Crowly

PRECIS: Increasing teacher attention to cooperative speech

INTRODUCTION: The basic premise of this study was that teacher attention to cooperative speech would not only increase both verbal and physical cooperative behaviors in children but would serve to reduce incompatible aggressive behaviors in them. The subjects in the first experiment reported by the authors were twelve preschoolers enrolled in a private nursery school class.

INTERVENTION: For two weeks the teachers paid special attention to helpful or cooperative verbal interactions among the children while ignoring aggressive responses. The teachers were instructed to respond to helpful verbalizations by saying, in a friendly way, "[child's name], you said [the child's exact phrase]." The helpful phrases that the teachers were to attend to included (1) positive compliance (for example, "OK, I'll do it"); (2) offering help ("Can I help you?"); (3) bids for mutual interaction ("Let's build blocks" or "Let's do it together"); (4) bids for reciprocal interaction ("It's your turn" or "Now you be the baby"); (5) compliments ("That's very good"); and (6) expressions of friendship ("I like you"). Observations of the teachers revealed that because of other duties they were able to give the treatment response to only 16 percent of the children's cooperative talk during the first week of treatment and to only 12 percent during the second week of treatment.

The results indicated that there was a significant increase in verbal cooperation after the two weeks of treatment. Also noted was an increase in cooperative physical acts among the children, such as helping one another. In addition, the results disclosed a decrease in the aggressive behavior of the children after treatment. The results of a second experiment confirmed the positive effect of nonevaluative teacher attention on children's cooperative speech.

COMMENTARY: The findings of this study indicated that teacher reinforcement of helpful or cooperative speech in children was effective not only in decreasing aggressive behaviors but also in increasing the cooperative interactions of the children. The teachers did not praise the cooperative verbalizations of the children but simply gave a statement reflecting the child's own remarks. A number of other studies have similarly found that contingent attention from teachers is an effective reinforcer of children's social behaviors in the preschool classroom.

SOURCE: Slaby, R. G., and Crowly, C. G. "Modification of Cooperation and Aggression Through Teacher Attention to Children's Speech." *Journal of Experimental Child Psychology*, 1977, *23*, 442-458.

Additional Readings

Apolloni, T., and Cooke, T. P. "Socially Withdrawn Children: The Role of Mental Health Practitioners." *Social Behavior and Personality*, 1977, *5*, 337-343.

This article reviews the literature on the problems of social withdrawal in childhood. It concludes that sufficient behavior modification technology now exists to treat the problem of social withdrawal in regular classroom settings and that mental health workers should serve as resource people to classroom teachers to enhance the social development of withdrawn children.

Durlak, J. A., and Mannarino, A. P. "The Social Skills Development Program: Description of a School-Based Preventive Mental Health Program for High-Risk Children." *Journal of Clinical Child Psychology*, 1977, *6*, 48-52.

The Social Skills Development Program, a school-based and prevention-oriented mental health program for high-risk children, is described. Small-group activities, based on behavioral and relationship principles, are presented in detail. Shy-withdrawn and aggressive children can best be helped in small groups, where real-life opportunities exist for children to interact with one another under the direction of supervised group leaders. In this case, group leaders were undergraduate or graduate psychology students.

Gottman, J., Gonso, J., and Schuler, P. "Teaching Social Skills to Isolated Children." *Journal of Abnormal Child Psychology*, 1976, *4*, 179-197.

The effects of a social skill training program on two socially isolated children are reported. Each day for one week, two male coaches who were undergraduate psychology students worked individually with the third-grade students. The children were taught communication skills, how to make friends, and how to interact positively with peers. The program helped the children to gain in peer popularity.

Guerney, B. G., and Flumen, A. B. "Teachers as Psychotherapeutic Agents for Withdrawn Children." *Journal of School Psychology*, 1970, *8*, 107-113.

Eleven volunteer elementary school teachers, trained and supervised in client-centered play therapy by a psychologist and social worker, conducted weekly play sessions for fourteen weeks with nine of their most withdrawn pupils. A substitute teacher took over the classes of the teachers as they rotated in using the playroom. The result was that the children in the experimental group showed a significant increase in social assertiveness.

Jakibchuk, Z., and Smeriglio, V. L. "The Influence of Symbolic Modeling on the Social Behavior of Preschool Children with Low Levels of Social Responsiveness." *Child Development*, 1976, *47*, 838-841.

Preschool children with low levels of social responsiveness were given different treatments. Children in the self-speech training group improved the most in social interactions. The self-speech group watched videotapes of social interactions accompanied by a self-speech (first-person) sound track that described the thoughts and actions of a child model in moving from solitary play to active participation with peers. The following is a brief excerpt from one of the videotape sound tracks: "My name is Danny, and I go to nursery school. I'm sitting here all by myself looking at a book. . . . Those children over there are playing together. . . . I would like to play with them. But I'm afraid. I don't know what to do or say. . . . This is hard. But I'll try. . . . I'm close to them. I did it. Good for me. . . . I like playing with Johnny and Bobby. I'm really glad I decided to play with them. I'm having lots of fun."

Kirschenbaum, D. S. "Social Competence Intervention and Evaluation in the Inner City: Cincinnati's Social Skills Development Program." *Journal of Consulting and Clinical Psychology,* 1979, *47,* 778-780.

This article describes the first large-scale intervention program conducted in an inner city and based on a social competence conceptualization. Teachers identified elementary grade students with social problems, including moodiness, withdrawal, and excessive acting out. Intervention included therapy (group and individual) and consultations with parents and teachers designed to foster warm collaborative relationships and to produce specific plans for helping the children. Ratings by teachers indicated that interventions improved the children's social competencies but not their problem behaviors.

Oden, S., and Asher, S. R. "Coaching Children in Social Skills for Friendship Making." *Child Development,* 1977, *48,* 495-506.

Third- and fourth-grade socially isolated children were coached in social skills. The coaching method included three components. First, the children were verbally instructed by a psychologist in social skills. Next, they were provided with an opportunity to practice these social skills by playing with a peer. Finally, they had a postplay review session with the coach. The instruction included a discussion of social skills that were proposed as useful for making a game fun to play with another person: (1) participating in a game or activity (for example, getting started and paying attention); (2) cooperating (taking turns and sharing materials); (3) communication (talking with the other person, listening); and (4) validating or supporting (being friendly, giving a smile, looking at the other person, and offering help or encouragement). These social skills were selected since they have been found to be related to children's acceptance by their peers. The results indicated that the children in the coaching group improved significantly more on a peer popularity rating than did other groups. The gains were still evident on a follow-up a year later.

Weinrott, M. R., Corson, J. A., and Wilchesky, M. "Teacher-Mediated Treatment of Social Withdrawal." *Behavior Therapy*, 1979, *10*, 281-294.

Teachers of socially withdrawn children in grades 1 to 3 were trained to use the techniques of symbolic modeling, adult social reinforcement, individual contingencies, and a combination of individual and group consequences to increase the prosocial behaviors of these children. Treatment produced a significant increase in peer interaction.

Social Isolation

Shy children often want to interact more with others but lack the necessary social skills or confidence. The child who is extremely withdrawn, however, is generally quite fearful of social interactions and becomes very angry or agitated when forced to engage in them. This child will actively avoid the social initiatives of others. Among the causes of extreme social withdrawal are gross neglect or abuse from the child's parents, as well as hereditary and genetic factors.

Treating Extreme Social Withdrawal in Nursery School Children

AUTHORS: Henry J. Kandel, Teodoro Ayllon, and Michael S. Rosenbaum

PRECIS: Flooding or systematic exposure in the treatment of social isolation

INTRODUCTION: In some cases, social isolation appears to be a response to intense fear of interacting with peers. This fear or anxiety must be deconditioned if social interactions are to occur. The authors selected the flooding technique to eliminate fear in two nursery school boys.

CASE ONE: In nursery school, Paul, aged four, would frequently cling to the teacher, cry, talking to himself in a bizarre manner, and avoid interacting with other children. In fact, he would become violently angry when confronted with other children. He had been diagnosed as having minimal brain dysfunction and as being chronically anxious and hyperactive.

The treatment consisted of "flooding" Paul with children eager to interact with him. To motivate his classmates to play with Paul, the therapist brought a new toy truck into the classroom. When his classmates asked to play with the truck, they were told they first had to play with Paul for about two minutes. When the children asked who Paul was and how they were supposed to play with him, the therapist recommended that they ask Paul about his toy cars or wrestle with him in a playful way. This suggestion led a group of children to ask Paul questions and seek physical contact with him (wrestling with him and holding his hand). Paul tried to escape from these interactions during the first two sessions of treatment. After ten sessions, this flooding procedure was also initiated on the playground. The therapist told the children they could earn candy by interacting with Paul for about twenty minutes. Several children then called to him, asked him questions, and sought physical contact with him. It was difficult for Paul to avoid these social initiatives, even with two acres of land to run on. This strategy was effective in substantially increasing Paul's interaction with his classmates and in reducing his inappropriate self-talk. Even after the treatment was stopped, these gains were still evident at a five-month follow-up.

CASE TWO: A similar flooding procedure was employed with Bobby, aged eight, who was diagnosed as autistic or as having minimal brain dysfunction. Unable to attend public schools because of his withdrawn behavior and bizarre mannerisms, he had been attending a private school for emotionally disturbed children. At the school playground he would physically separate himself from other children by about twenty yards and talk to himself or pace back and forth.

Initially, the flooding procedure was used by telling the children they could earn candy by interacting with Bobby. This motivated about seven children to run after him and chase him from behind trees. Since Bobby became extremely upset and overwhelmed by this barrage, it was decided to reduce the number of children to two. Two children with the best social skills were told that they could earn candy by playing with Bobby and a toy of his that was brought to the playground. The therapist modeled appropriate play with Bobby for five minutes and then the two peers began playing with him. If Bobby tried to leave them, the two children were instructed to tell him to return or take his hand and lead him back. The two helping children received candy about once every three sessions. They also were given candy for playing with Bobby at juice time in the classroom. This procedure of systematically exposing Bobby to his peers resulted in his interacting with them about 50 percent of the time. Prior to this intervention there had been *no* interaction. A follow-up disclosed that the gains in social interaction evident during the twelve training sessions were still present on the playground after nine months.

COMMENTARY: This study illustrates that either flooding or systematic exposure can be effective in treating anxiety-related social problems in children in the school environment. Clearly, a socially isolated child's peers can be powerful change agents. Noteworthy is the fact that the increased social interaction persisted long after the classmates stopped receiving concrete rewards for relating to the withdrawn children. It is possible that the two children in this study learned how to respond to the social initiatives of others and found the social interactions reinforcing. Since the flooding procedure can sometimes trigger an extreme emotional upheaval in a withdrawn child, it seems advisable for the procedure to be carried out under the supervision of a skilled psychotherapist.

SOURCE: Kandel, H. J., Ayllon, T., and Rosenbaum, M. S. "Flooding or Systematic Exposure in the Treatment of Extreme Social Withdrawal in Children." *Journal of Behavior Therapy and Experimental Psychiatry*, 1977, *8*, 75-81.

Effect of Peer Interaction on the Withdrawn Behavior of Preschoolers

AUTHORS: Phillip S. Strain, Richard E. Shores, and Matthew A. Timm

PRECIS: Teaching peers to initiate contact with socially isolated classmates

INTRODUCTION: The goal of the present study was to investigate the effect of peer social initiatives on the social behavior of isolated preschoolers. The subjects were six boys who were enrolled in a treatment center for behaviorally handicapped children. The boys rarely engaged in positive interactions with their peers, they threw frequent tantrums, and they were delayed in language development.

TREATMENT: Each day three of the boys were brought from their classrooms to a playroom for a twenty-minute session. The accompanying teacher told the boys that this was a time to play together with friends. For each group of three withdrawn boys, a peer confederate was selected to play with the boys and show positive social behaviors toward them. The confederates were the most socially active children from a nearby daycare program.

Prior to playing with the isolated boys, each confederate had received four twenty-minute training sessions. During the training, the confederates were informed that they were to try their best to get the other children to play with them. The trainer also took the role of the withdrawn boys and encouraged the confederates to initiate social play. The confederates were advised that many of their attempts would be ignored at first but that it was necessary to keep asking the other children to play. They were taught specific ways to initiate play, such as saying, "Come play," "Let's play school," or "Let's play ball," while handing a ball or other play object to the other child. The confederates then spent a total of twenty sessions playing with the withdrawn children. At the end of each session the trainer praised the desirable behaviors exhibited by the confederates in the playroom. The efforts of the confederates immediately increased the positive social behavior of the withdrawn children. Moreover, five of the six isolated children showed an increase in the frequency of their social initiations.

COMMENTARY: The results of this study suggest that peers can be coached to increase the positive social behaviors of their isolated classmates. The data also indicated that the children gained in direct relationship to their initial social competence, that is, the children who were more socially responsive at the start improved the most. The practical implication of this study for teachers is that integrating socially outgoing children with isolated youngsters may enhance the social skills of the latter. However, careful instruction of the socially competent peers seems to be required.

SOURCE: Strain, P. S., Shores, R. E., and Timm, M. A. "Effects of Peer Social Initiation on the Behavior of Withdrawn Preschool Children." *Journal of Applied Behavior Analysis,* 1977, *10,* 289-298.

Additional Reading

O'Connor, R. D. "Modification of Social Withdrawal Through Symbolic Modeling," *Journal of Applied Behavior Analysis,* 1969, 2, 15-22.

Nursery school children who displayed marked social withdrawal were assigned to one of two conditions. One group observed a twenty-three-minute film that depicted increasingly active social interactions among children, with positive consequences ensuing in each scene, while a narrative sound track emphasized the appropriate behavior of the models. A control group observed a film that contained no social interaction. Control children displayed no change in withdrawal behavior, whereas those who had the benefit of symbolic modeling increased their level of social interaction to that of nonisolated nursery school children. The isolated children in this study displayed extreme social withdrawal, that is, they would actively and purposely retreat into corners, closets, and lockers to avoid interacting with their peers. The film for the experimental children portrays a sequence of eleven scenes in which children interact in a nursery school setting. In each of these episodes, a child is shown first observing the interactions of others and then joining in the social activities, with reinforcing consequences ensuing. The other children, for example, offer him play material, talk to him, smile and generally respond in a positive manner to his advances into the activity. The scenes are graduated on a dimension of threat in terms of the vigor of the social activity and the size of the group. The initial scenes involve calm activities such as two children sharing a book or toy while seated at a table. In the final scenes, as many as six children are shown gleefully tossing play equipment around the room.

6 ◎◎◎◎◎◎◎◎◎◎◎◎◎◎◎

Disturbed Relationships
with Teachers

◎◎◎◎◎◎◎◎◎◎◎◎◎◎◎

Over the past decade, "lack of discipline" has been the most serious problem in our schools, according to the Gallup poll responses of parents, teachers, and others involved in public education. In 1979, 24 percent of the national sample of adults said it was their greatest worry. "Use of drugs," generally considered part of the discipline problem, was mentioned second most often (13 percent of the sample).

Overt hostility to school authorities, as exhibited in violence, vandalism, disrespect, and defiance, is a particularly disturbing discipline problem. Recent societal changes have made adult authority and leadership less secure than in the past. This has resulted in increased disrespect toward school authorities and in more violent acts against them.

Student defiance and hostility toward teachers are quite disruptive to classroom learning and engender a great deal of anxiety in teachers. The effect of such behavior on the disrespectful child is also destructive. The dropout rate for hyper-aggressive teen-agers is two and one-half times higher than that for "normal" teen-agers, and a large number of the former turn up in mental health clinics.

Traditionally, the most common reaction of school authorities to student hostility has been a punitive one—corporal punishment, detention, suspension, or dismissal. But harsh punishments have usually not been effective. This chapter will present alternative ways of handling the problem—for example, by changing the educational system, counseling students at school, counseling families, training teachers to resolve conflicts, and using strategies to enhance student self-esteem and respect for others. For a difficult, complex problem such as this it is generally best for parents, teachers, and students to work together.

In addition to students who display hostility toward teachers, this chapter will discuss children with overdependent relationships with teachers and students who are shy and inhibited with teachers. At least three very different types of socially inhibited children have been identified. First, there is the "very shy" child who limits social interaction with all people—both children and adults. Then there is the child who readily interacts with peers but who avoids contact with adults. Finally, there is the child who seeks out adult contact but seldom plays with other children. This chapter will present ways of helping children who fall within the first two categories.

@@

Disrespect and Defiance

This section focuses on the student who openly refuses to comply with requests from a teacher. Achieving below grade level, some children get into trouble as a means of passing the time. The goal of these students needs to be changed from "get the teacher" to learning. Other students have emotional problems and are impulsive, self-centered, and prone to temper tantrums. Still other students have authority problems that are manifested by a rebellious, negativistic attitude toward teachers.

@@

Special Classes for Disruptive Children

AUTHOR: Thomas W. Allen

PRECIS: Effects of placing disruptive children in special classes

INTRODUCTION: It is often concluded that children who are aggressive and disruptive in class need psychiatric help because they are mentally ill. However, an alternative explanation is that the misbehavior is a response to the difficulty these children have in meeting the academic demands of the school. If the latter premise is true, then the school rather than a child guidance clinic should handle the problem. The author notes that a number of studies support the conclusion that a well-structured "special class" can have a positive impact on otherwise uneducable children. The present study investigated the effect of special class placement on a group of twenty-two aggressive and defiant elementary school children. The control group consisted of twenty-eight children with similar problems who were not sent to a special class program.

SPECIAL CLASSES: The experimental children were assigned to six classrooms with no more than eight children in each. The rooms were located in three regular elementary schools. Grouping was based on age, physical development, and individual needs as assessed by test batteries and psychiatric interviews. Mental health consultants prescribed specific goals and strategies to be implemented in the classroom.

Each classroom teacher was provided with an assistant—either a college undergraduate or a somewhat older person. The classes were carefully structured to help the children gain some control over their impulses. Remedial help directly related to the child's specific perceptual-motor or cognitive deficit was offered. To teach the relationship between behavior and its consequences, resource people were available to talk to a child when a problem occurred. Resource staff included teaching assistants, counselors, psychologists, and social workers. In order to keep classroom distractions to a minimum, some of the windows were covered or blocked, wall-to-wall carpeting was installed, and private, three-sided study booths were available. After a year of this new program, an evaluation of the educational progress of the students was conducted. The results indicated that the experimental students made significantly more progress on reading and arithmetic tests than did the control children.

COMMENTARY: The findings support the conclusion that special programs can educate and socialize disruptive children without recourse to long-term psychotherapy designed to deal with deep-seated emotional conflicts. The distinctive features of special education classes include small class size, close supervision, a high degree of structure, individual education plans based upon extensive assessment of each child and support personnel to conduct "life-space interviewing." The latter concept means an adult is immediately available to talk privately with a child to help him sort out his feelings, understand the consequences of behavior, and feel that somebody cares about him.

SOURCE: Allen, T. W. "The Evaluation of a Program of Special Classes for 'Disruptive Children' in an Urban School System." *Community Mental Health Journal*, 1970, *6*, 276-284.

Student Behavior in Alternate Schools

AUTHORS: Daniel L. Duke and Cheryl Perry

PRECIS: Effect of alternate high schools on student problem behaviors

INTRODUCTION: The authors interviewed students and teachers at eighteen alternate public high schools in California. Almost every "school-within-a-school" in the state was surveyed. A school-within-a-school exists under the administrative umbrella of a regular high school. However, these schools have an identity of their own, along with special staffs, curriculums, schedules, rules, and evaluation procedures. It was thought that the findings of this study were likely to hold true for alternate schools throughout the country.

The general finding was that the students and teachers in alternate schools reported fewer behavior problems in their schools than were present in neighboring public high schools. None of the respondents, for example, felt that disrespect to teachers or gang activity was a cause for concern at the alternate school. Problems that did exist in the alternate schools, such as drug use, cigarette smoking, and cutting classes, were believed to be less serious than at the regular high schools. Students in the alternate schools were predominantly white middle-class adolescents who were able to work well without supervision. The successful students in these schools were also able to assume responsibility for their behavior and were willing to participate in school activities.

FEWER BEHAVIOR PROBLEMS: Among the possible reasons identified by the authors for fewer discipline problems in the alternate schools were the following:

1. School Size—the average school enrolled only 111 students. Consequently, the classes were small (typically five to fifteen students), and the students received more individual attention from teachers than in regular high schools. Since the students had fewer teachers to deal with, there was less chance of conflicting expectations for student behavior or inconsistent rule enforcement among teachers. The fact that the alternate schools had fewer rules than regular high schools further reduced the likelihood of such inconsistency. The size of the schools also permitted flexible scheduling. Having fewer classes to schedule, the schools were able to offer a diversified program of elective courses that met at odd times, as well as off-campus learning experiences. Teachers also had time to act as advisers to students. Thus, when a student was upset or had a problem, the teacher usually could deal with it right away and prevent a minor upset from mushrooming into a major discipline problem.

2. Treatment of Students—in the alternate schools, the

students were treated as adults. Thus, they were expected to make their own decisions, beginning with the decision to attend the alternate school in the first place. The students enjoyed considerable freedom of choice as to what, when, and how they learned. Most of the schools featured independent study options. It seems that when students can choose and are not simply told what to do, they react less negatively toward teachers and academic requirements. Students were involved in establishing school rules, selecting teachers, allocating resources, and evaluating school effectiveness. When students encountered a problem at school, they were expected to assist in its resolution rather than passively wait until the teacher came up with an answer. Like adults, they were expected to think through a plan for dealing with a personal problem.

3. Teacher Attitudes Toward Student Behavior—the alternate school had few formal rules governing student behavior. Rules that seemed more for the convenience of the teachers than for the welfare of the students were often eliminated; for example, rules governing profanity, tardiness, gum chewing, talking during seatwork, and movement around the classroom. In this way, the alternate schools avoided the concern reported by students in regular high schools that their everyday behavior in school is controlled too much by rigid and seemingly arbitrary rules.

Teachers in the alternate schools tried to make punishments logically related to the misdeed. Thus, for inappropriate behavior, a student might be taken before a group of peers or a teacher-adviser. A discussion would ensue with the goal of developing some understanding of the problem and ways to solve it. In the event the student continually failed to complete assignments, he or she would probably receive no credit for graduation. Should the student accumulate a number of no-credit courses or steadfastly refuse to act responsibly, he or she would be told to return to the regular public high school. But ridicule, sarcasm, detentions, and suspensions were not used to punish the students. Behavior problems were viewed by the teachers as opportunities for student growth rather than as problems only. Instead of overnight cures, the teachers tried for gradual changes in the students' problem behaviors. They saw themselves as teacher-advisers first, then as disciplinarians. In contrast, many regular high school teachers complain about being policemen first and educators second.

4. Teacher Skills and Characteristics—the personality of the alternate school teachers seemed to be distinctive. Traits such as patience, sensitivity, sincere interest in others, and a sense of humor were prominent among them. The teachers did not seem to take themselves or their authority too seriously and valued student assertiveness. They confronted students about misbehaviors in a low-keyed, forthright manner that served to inform instead of incite. Thus, frictions between students and teachers were minimized. The students said they felt that the teachers cared about them as people, not just about what they learned in a particular course. Also noteworthy is the finding that the teachers took the time to really listen to the students without moralizing or making value judgments. In contrast, teachers in regular high schools often find that their time is tightly scheduled and that they are therefore less apt to be available when a student needs to talk.

COMMENTARY: The results of this study indicate that many factors combine to reduce behavior problems in alternate schools. Since teachers function more as advisers than as disciplinarians, there is little, if any, disrespect toward teachers reported in these schools. Students are expected to be responsible for their own behavior and to solve their own problems. Programs are individualized and the teachers try to develop a personal relationship with each student. Because of these factors, there tends to be a substantial increase in the proportion of a youth's successful—versus unsuccessful—experiences in the alternate school.

SOURCE: Duke, D. L., and Perry, C. "Can Alternate Schools Succeed Where Benjamin Spock, Spiro Agnew, and B. F. Skinner Have Failed?" *Adolescence*, 1978, *13*, 375-392.

Family Psychotherapy for a Disruptive Boy

AUTHOR: Stuart Kaplan

PRECIS: Teaching parents the use of behavior modification techniques

INTRODUCTION: Y, a ten-year-old male, was enrolled in a school for emotionally disturbed and learning-disabled children. Among the disruptive behaviors he exhibited in class were loud belching, somersaulting, running into the halls, and calling out irrelevant remarks. His teachers were unable to control him, and he defied their efforts to place him in a time-out room. At home his parents reported that he had been generally out of control since he was five years old. He ignored or defied his parents' requests to observe minimal rules, such as bedtime regulations and table manners. Previous unsuccessful efforts to change his behavior included four years of individual psychotherapy, three years of special school placement, and three years of medication (Ritalin). Y's father tended to deny that the boy had any problems, stating that much of his son's misbehavior was due to the influence of his classmates and the ineptitude of his teachers. The mother appeared depressed and had been suffering from insomnia for several years.

INTERVENTION: In the first session, the therapist met with the parents in an office on the grounds of the school. He confronted the parents with the magnitude of their son's misbehavior. The father attempted to blame others for the problem while the mother seemed in despair about controlling him at home. At this point, Y and two of his classroom teachers entered the room, and the teachers recounted that they had recorded 145 disruptive behaviors by the boy that week. The boy smiled mischievously when this list was read aloud. The mother began to sob loudly that she was no longer able to endure the temper tantrums that the boy threw when she tried to control him at home. The father declined the therapist's suggestion that he comfort his wife.

In the second session, the mother related that it was difficult for her to control her son's aggressiveness because she had been raised by an alcoholic father who had sexually and physically assaulted her. The son was then brought into the session, and the therapist reviewed his continued misbehavior in school over the past week. In a very authoritarian manner, the therapist stated that this behavior was unnecessary and could be controlled by the boy. The therapist then presented the following behavior modification system, which the parents agreed to implement at home: If Y exhibited more than three of the behaviors listed on his chart, he would receive a "poor" rating from the school; if he engaged in two or three misbehaviors he would receive an "OK"; and for one misbehavior or none, he would receive a "good." A "good" earned him a point toward a special treat; for an "OK," he received only his usual privileges; and for a "poor," he was to be confined to his room immediately after school and not allowed to watch television or have dessert. If the boy lost the daily behavior rating, which his teachers were to complete, he would be given a "poor" rating.

Y received a "poor" rating from school the next day, and his parents confined him to his room. His behavior in school then improved dramatically, and he had an average of only two disruptive behaviors per school week for the next sixteen weeks. In all, eighteen family therapy sessions were conducted with the parents and the boy. During these sessions it became obvious that the father had the greater difficulty in setting limits with the child. Allying himself with the mother, the therapist attempted to help her assume a more competent, equalitarian role in childrearing. The mother was able to become more decisive with the child and less dependent upon her husband. Toward the end of each session, the boy was invited in and praised for his good behavior the previous week. After fifteen sessions, the boy was promoted to a classroom for children who were judged to be able to return to a public school.

COMMENTARY: The author felt that the behavior modification program was the major reason for the sudden change in the boy's classroom behavior. Once it became evident that there was no way he could beat this system, the boy quickly stopped his disruptive behavior in school. The therapist was able to unite the parents and the teachers in making clear demands on the boy and in immediately reinforcing compliance or noncompliance. Family therapy made it possible for the parents to persevere at the system and to work at overcoming their marital conflicts.

SOURCE: Kaplan, S. L. "Behavior Modification as a Limit-Setting Task in the Family Psychotherapy of a Disruptive Boy." *Journal of Child Psychiatry*, 1979, *18*, 492-504.

Transactional Analysis for Classroom Management

AUTHORS: Konstantinos J. Kravas and Constance H. Kravas

PRECIS: Transactional Analysis as a new model for classroom management

INTRODUCTION: Transactional Analysis (TA) provides a theoretical framework for understanding a student's personality and social interactions in the classroom. It is an effective classroom management technique for both beginning and experienced teachers. The method was originally developed by Eric Berne, author of *Transactional Analysis in Psychotherapy* and *Games People Play*.

The basic premise of TA is that the human personality can be divided into three conceptually distinct ego states: the Parent, the Adult, and the Child. The Parent ego state reminds us of what we "should" and "ought" to be doing. These are the messages that we have learned from our parents. Sometimes these messages are judgmental, controlling, and critical; at other times they are nurturing and benevolent. The Adult ego state functions as our reality-testing agent and seeks to collect objective data for making decisions. Like a dispassionate computer, the Adult makes statements such as, "That alternative seems most probable," "I can understand what you are saying," or "I

am going to complete this task." Feelings and impulses control
the Child ego state. Sometimes the Child is creative, spontaneous, and uninhibited; at other times the Child becomes en-
raged, fearful, or sad.

Each person has these three ego states and moves in and
out of them frequently during a day. Each ego state is important, and none is superior to the others. However, certain ego
states are more appropriate than others for particular situations.
Solving arithmetic problems, for example, requires the rational-
objective Adult state to be dominant rather than the Child
state.

TA AS A MANAGEMENT TOOL: By closely observing a
child's behavior, the teacher can identify which ego state (that
is, Parent, Adult, or Child) the child is using to express himself
or herself at a given time. If a child too often displays actions
from one of these states, he or she can be helped to exhibit behavior from other ego states.

The child who "tests" a teacher by defiant actions or by
repetitively challenging what the teacher has said can be very
irritating. One way to handle this child is to respond by giving
controlling or judgmental messages from the Parent ego state
("Don't ever talk to me that way" or "What's the matter with
you?") that may unwittingly reinforce the student's childish behavior. An alternative response might involve an appeal by the
teacher to a more objective component of the student's personality, that is, his Adult ego state: "This is obviously very important to you. Let's talk about it in private."

The following example further illustrates how a teacher
may initiate adult interactions with students rather than always
speaking from the Parent state to the Child state of the students. After an emotionally arousing pregame assembly, Mrs.
Johnson's class has just returned to its room. When the teacher
enters several minutes later, she finds the class in an uproar. The
students are laughing, talking loudly, and chasing one another
around the room. The teacher resists her first impulse, which is
to respond from her Parent ego state by saying, "Quiet! Get
into your seats right this minute! You know better than to act
this way!" Rather, she comments, "Everyone still seems excited

after that assembly. I enjoyed it too and can understand why you are still so enthusiastic. Do you think it's possible for an assembly to have a positive effect on a team?" By using questions and statements, the teacher "hooks" the Adult state of the students into a rational discussion of issues. This interaction forms a transition for restoring the classroom to a better climate for learning. The children no longer behave exclusively from impulses and emotions that emanate from their Child ego state.

By teaching TA principles and terms to a class, a teacher can communicate about issues that previously were considered too threatening or dangerous. Thus, if a teacher made a hasty classroom decision in anger, she might open the door to other alternatives by observing to the class, "It appears that my Parent backed your Child into a corner."

COMMENTARY: Originally conceived of as a therapeutic technique, TA is now being applied in the classroom as well. One reason TA has become so popular of late is that it is readily understandable by adults and children alike. It is also a practical and comprehensive approach for understanding human personality and social interactions. The authors state that TA is particularly useful in those sensitive situations in which teachers and students view things differently and in which authoritarian directives by teachers appear to have harmful consequences.

SOURCE: Kravas, K. J. and Kravas, C. H. "Transactional Analysis for Classroom Management." *Phi Delta Kappan,* 1974, *56,* 194-197.

Treatment of Aggression
in a Sixteen-Year-Old Male

AUTHORS: James P. McCullough, Gwendolyn M. Huntsinger, and W. Robert Nay

PRECIS: Teaching self-control techniques to help a child avoid expulsion from school

INTRODUCTION: Larry, a high school sophomore, was brought by his parents for outpatient therapy because he was generally out of control at home. The therapist advised the parents to clearly spell out and enforce a few household rules. After five sessions, the school principal informed the therapist that Larry had just been suspended from school because he had had a violent verbal argument with his physical education teacher over being late for class. Larry verbally berated the teacher in front of the class and subsequently berated the principal and stormed out of his office. Larry had a long history of losing his temper at school. The therapist decided to deal with the present crisis by teaching Larry several self-control skills for avoiding future temper outbursts.

INTERVENTION: The first step in the treatment was to obtain Larry's cooperation. The goal of the therapy session was to have him admit that he was unable to control his temper. Whenever Larry attempted to justify his previous temper losses, the therapist asked, "And what did that get you?" Rather than condemning the outbursts, the therapist focused solely on the adverse consequences of such behavior. Larry eventually stated that he did not know how to control his temper and that this had been a problem for him all his life.

    The second phase of treatment—identifying antecedent components—involved having Larry describe the feelings, thoughts, and bodily sensations he had just before a temper outburst. With the therapist's help, he identified the following sequence of events that led up to an outburst: (1) he would curse to himself when confronted by another person in a stressful situation; (2) he found himself unable to comply with the requests of others at that moment; (3) a cool streak "ran up" his back-bone; (4) his body began to tense, beginning with his feet and gradually moving up his body; (5) his right arm muscles became tense; and (6) when he felt tension in his right arm, he either hit or verbally lashed out at others.

Role playing and videotape playback comprised the next step. Larry was videotaped acting out the conflicts that he had just had with the teacher and school principal. When the tape was replayed, he was somewhat shocked to see the aggressive body language and provocative attitude that he adopted in these situations.

Larry was then asked to role play incompatible behavior. Once again he played himself in conflict with school authorities, but this time he was instructed to avoid profanity, to talk calmly, and to tone down the aggressive posture he had observed on the video playback. But he was also encouraged to say what he wanted to say in these situations. The therapist played the role of school authorities and Larry observed, through video playback, the positive effect he had on others when he maintained control of himself.

The final phase of self-control training involved training Larry to stop the chain of events that preceded a temper outburst. The three antecedent events focused on were: (1) subvocal cursing, (2) progressive tensing of his body, and (3) tensing of his right arm followed by aggressive behavior. To control subvocal speech, Larry was taught the thought-stopping technique, that is, he was taught to say loudly to himself "Stop!" whenever he started cursing to himself. To counter body tension, he was instructed to relax and tense his entire torso in rapid succession. In the event his right arm became tense, he agreed to walk away from the interaction until he calmed down. When he had regained control of himself, he was advised to return and calmly resume the conversation. Larry practiced each of these strategies until he could produce it smoothly.

The therapist and Larry constructed a written contract that clearly spelled out each aspect of the treatment program. Larry agreed to follow the program and to report on his progress at each weekly therapy session. During the next two weeks, the therapist met individually with the principal, Larry's teachers, and his parents to describe the program. Everyone agreed that when Larry walked away to avoid a blowup, they would not pursue the conversation until he returned and calmly stated that he wished to talk again. All parties agreed to praise Larry whenever he walked away to regain control of himself or when he handled a stressful situation without losing his temper. The teachers gave him permission to walk out of the classroom to prevent an outburst, to stand in the hall by the door, and to reenter the room when he had calmed down. The school counselor collected daily reports from the teachers as to the number of temper episodes, as well as the number of stressful interactions that he handled successfully. These reports were mailed to the therapist each Friday afternoon after school. The therapist called the counselor on Monday to review these behavior observations. After about three months, the teachers no longer recorded his behavior, but the therapist continued to contact the school counselor about Larry's behavior.

This program proved successful in reducing Larry's temper outbursts during the semester it was in effect to three incidents. On numerous other occasions he handled stressful situations at school without losing control. The following year Larry lost his temper only twice at school.

COMMENTARY: Self-control training seemed to help Larry gain some control over his previously unmanageable temper. The school personnel played an active role in this program. The principal required Larry to have a plan for controlling his temper in order to be allowed back in school. His teachers agreed to record his classroom behavior, to allow him to walk away to avoid outbursts, and to praise him for self-control behaviors. In addition, the school counselor consented to act as liaison between the therapist and teachers. Another crucial aspect of this program was the use of role playing and video playback; these helped Larry see the effects of his behavior on others and thus motivate him to change.

SOURCE: McCullough, J. P., Huntsinger, G. M., and Nay, W. R. "Self-Control Treatment of Aggression in a Sixteen-Year-Old

Male." *Journal of Consulting and Clinical Psychology*, 1977, *45*, 322-331.

Additional Reading

Hamblin, R. L., Buckholdt, D., Bushnell, D., Ellis, D., and Ferritor, D. "Changing the Game from 'Get the Teacher' to 'Learn.' " *Transaction,* January, 1969, pp. 20-31.

The authors found that a token exchange system is an effective way to reduce aggressive-disruptive behavior in the preschool classroom. Children are given tokens (plastic discs) for completing work assignments or other appropriate behaviors. The tokens can be exchanged for rewards such as watching a movie or having a snack. Since aggressive behavior toward the teacher was ignored (the teacher simply turned her back on the child) and cooperative behaviors were reinforced with tokens, the only way for the child to gain teacher attention was by cooperative acts. This strategy discourages the game of getting the teacher's attention by misbehaving.

@@@@@@@@@@@@@@@@@@@@@@@@@@@@@@@@@@@@

Inhibition

*Children who are ill at ease with adults may have spent consid-
erable time with peers and siblings while growing up and thus
find these contacts more satisfying than adult contacts. The
child who is shy with adults will rarely initiate social interaction
with teachers and feels inhibited and anxious when speaking before the class. Quite sensitive to criticism and rejection, shy children often worry about saying the wrong thing or making fools
of themselves. Social skills training in which these students learn
and practice appropriate social responses has proved quite effective in reducing their social inhibitions.*

@@@@@@@@@@@@@@@@@@@@@@@@@@@@@@@@@@@@

Reinforcing Student Participation
in Class Discussions

AUTHOR: Ray E. Hosford

PRECIS: Training teachers in positive reinforcement procedures

INTRODUCTION: A school counselor taught four seventh-grade social studies teachers how to modify student behavior by systematic reinforcement procedures. The teachers then identified three students in each of their two classes who seldom participated in class discussions. One student in each class was randomly selected to receive the experimental reinforcement procedures while another was chosen to serve as a control.

METHOD: For three weeks the teachers gave immediate verbal reinforcement to the students in the experimental group when they asked a question, answered a question, or entered verbally into a classroom discussion. Other reinforcers, such as smiles and pats on the back, were also used. Even negative verbal comments were reinforced. Thus, if a student stated in class, "Mrs. Jones, you gave us too much homework last night," the teacher would respond with something like, "Thanks, Joe, for bringing that up. Teachers would never know just how much homework to assign if students didn't let them know from time to time whether the assignments are too long."

The school counselor met with every student in the experimental group during the third and fourth week of the study for the expressed purpose of discussing his or her program and career plans. However, all student responses related to "discussing in class" were reinforced by such remarks as "Gee, that's swell, tell me about it." The second interview was conducted in a similar manner, with the addition of a comment such as "One of your teachers happened to mention to me how pleased she was with the greater interest you have shown in class lately." The results of this project revealed that the experimental students increased the frequency with which they entered into class discussions significantly more than the control students.

COMMENTARY: The highly favorable findings of this study indicate that teachers can be trained to increase the classroom responsiveness of even their most inhibited students. Although the teachers in this study had initially requested individual counseling for students who never participate in class discussions, the school counselor was able to convince them that problems of this nature can often be best handled in the classroom where the behavior occurs.

SOURCE: Hosford, R. E. "Teaching Teachers to Reinforce Student Participation." In J. D. Krumboltz and C. E. Thoresen (Eds.), *Behavioral Counseling Cases and Techniques*. New York: Holt, Rinehart and Winston, 1969, pp. 152-154.

Testing a Severely Inhibited Child

AUTHOR: Edward G. Tava

PRECIS: Use of social reinforcement to increase verbal responsiveness

INTRODUCTION: Sally, aged six, was very inhibited with adults and appeared to be constantly afraid. For the first two months of school, she did not verbally respond to her teacher. She still talked quietly to adults and found it difficult to communicate with them even after eight months of school. The author, a psychologist, decided that the only way to get her to respond to testing was to give her a great deal of praise and attention for answering questions.

PROCEDURE: At first, every verbal response by Sally was reinforced by the examiner, and then every second or third response. Both verbal reinforcement ("good," "OK," and "good work") and nonverbal rewards (smile or head nod) were used.

Initially, Sally was reinforced for any verbal response she made, regardless of its correctness. In this way she was able to finish a complete psychological test battery that lasted over two hours. Without this social reinforcement, it is doubtful that she would have given enough responses to make it possible to evaluate her ability level.

COMMENTARY: This study suggests that the very inhibited child needs to receive positive reinforcement from adults for every verbal response he or she makes. Quite fearful, these children need consistent encouragement from adults if they are to leave their shell of reticence. At first, the questions one asks of such children should be quite simple and easily answered with a shake of the head or a simple yes or no. Only after the child has been repeatedly reinforced for simple answers should lengthier verbalizations be asked for.

SOURCE: Tava, E. G. "The Use of Social Reinforcement in Attaining Psychological Test Behavior from a Severely Inhibited Child." *School Applications of Learning Theory*, 1970, *1*, 31-33.

Helping a Child Speak Up in Class

AUTHOR: Barbara B. Varenhorst

PRECIS: Case study involving behavioral counseling for an inhibited child

INTRODUCTION: Cindy sought help from her school counselor in order to learn how to speak up in class. She said that she often had ideas that she wanted to express but that when called on she couldn't think of what to say or would say something "real dumb." Her particular goal was to able to speak well in art class, where the students were expected to criticize each other's work. Cindy admitted that she was worried about what people would think of her if she said something.

TREATMENT PLAN: Cindy's counselor suggested the following plan. They first made a chart of all her classes with the days of the week across the top. Whenever she said something in class, she would receive a check for that particular day. If she spoke up twice, she got two checks. Role-playing exercises were also conducted. The counselor played the role of the classroom teacher calling upon Cindy to discuss an assignment. Cindy was advised to try to remember only the main points of her talk, not the exact order of how to say it. This role-playing activity was repeated several times, and Cindy was coached to speak louder each time and to give her material in different ways. Finally the counselor told Cindy she was ready to speak up in social studies, which was a relatively easy class. Cindy's teacher was informed of the plan in advance, and Cindy received another rehearsal that day. Because Cindy performed well and spoke up twice in the class she was awarded two check marks. In a similar manner Cindy practiced with the counselor speaking out in other classes. Successes in other classes prepared Cindy to give a public critique in the art class. With support and encouragement from the counselor she was able to do this. Gradually the check marks and counseling sessions were faded out, and Cindy no longer needed outside guidance.

COMMENTARY: This case illustrates the use of behavioral techniques (charting, rewards, and behavioral rehearsal) to help a student with a specific problem. Rather than looking for underlying conflicts or problems, the counselor focused on Cindy's specific request to be able to speak up in class. In a systematic, step-by-step manner, Cindy learned to overcome her classroom inhibition.

SOURCE: Varenhorst, B. B. "Helping a Client to Speak up in Class." In J. D. Krumboltz and C. E. Thoresen (Eds.), *Behavioral Counseling Cases and Techniques*. New York: Holt, Rinehart and Winston, 1969.

Overdependency

The overdependent student shows such behaviors as seeking the teacher's attention frequently during the day, forgetting class assignments, losing papers, looking to see how others are doing an assignment before he or she does it, relying too much on the teacher for directions, having difficulty following instructions given in class, and finding it hard to decide what to do when given a choice between two or more possibilities. An overly close parent-child relationship is often the cause of these problems.

Effects of Teacher Social Reinforcement

AUTHORS: Florence R. Harris, Montrose M. Wolf, and Donald M. Baer

PRECIS: Differential application of teacher attention to children's behaviors

INTRODUCTION: The authors report the results of several cases in which they successfully trained nursery school teachers to reduce the behavior problems of their students. The basic procedure involved paying absolutely no attention to undesired behaviors (unless a child was in danger of being physically hurt). In the event the behavior occurred while the teacher was attending to the child, the teacher immediately turned to another child or task in a matter-of-face and nonrejecting way. At the same time, the teachers would immediately attend to desirable behaviors by the child. In this manner, the child received a great deal of teacher attention for avoiding "problem behavior."

CASE STUDY: A four-year-old boy cried and whined a lot in school following minor frustrations. Each school morning the boy averaged about eight crying episodes. In the past, this over-dependent behavior had consistently elicited solicitous concern from the teachers. Under the new approach, the teachers simply ignored his crying while immediately attending to and showing approval of all self-help behaviors. Within two weeks, this procedure virtually eliminated the crying response. When the teachers reversed the method and attended only to crying, this behavior rose to its previous high level. Another ten days of ignoring the outcries again resulted in a quick weakening of the response to a near-zero level.

COMMENTARY: The authors report that the procedure of systematically ignoring undesirable behaviors and paying attention to desirable behaviors was effective in reducing a number of problems in normal nursery school children, including over-dependence, isolated play, and excessive passivity. Since there was one teacher for every six children in the laboratory schools studied, it was possible to assign one teacher the role of principal "reinforcer teacher." This teacher gave a child immediate attention whenever he or she behaved in a specified way. In addition, observers were hired and trained to record the behavior of each child studied.

SOURCE: Harris, F. R., Wolf, M. M., and Baer, D. M. "Effects of Adult Social Reinforcement on Child Behavior." *Young Children,* 1964, *20,* 8-17.

Intensive Therapeutic Programs for Prepubertal Children

AUTHORS: Malcolm West, Myrna Carlin, Beverly Baserman, and Maxine Milstein

PRECIS: Case study of an overprotected child

INTRODUCTION: The authors note that learning-disabled children tend to fall into two types: (1) the child with a primary learning defect with secondary emotional problems (lowered self-esteem and feelings of discouragement), and (2) the child with primary emotional problems that interfere with learning. Since there is a close connection between learning capacity and personality, a remediation program often needs to bolster both of these. The following case reveals the need to change a child's personality traits in order to help him learn.

CASE STUDY: Robert, a plump, unkempt boy, was physically passive, demanding, and given to whining. The youngest of three boys, he had been overprotected by his mother. He was at least three years behind his classmates in both reading and spelling. Feigning helplessness, he would try to get others to do things for him by saying, "My pencil dropped, where's my pencil?" or "I lost my exercise book, find me another one." These ploys revealed an inability to work independently or to persevere in the face of even minor difficulty.

The boy was placed in a special learning clinic for one month during the summer with four other boys and three girls, ranging in age from eleven to thirteen years. The boy's nagging and pleas for help were systematically ignored by the teaching staff and then countered by a restatement of work orders. A careful record was kept of assignments completed and of time periods free of demanding attention or nagging and bossing others. Robert was given concrete rewards for progress in these areas, as well as for improvement in his physical appearance. Group discussions and role-playing situations relevant to his problems were used to teach him alternate responses. When Robert's work habits and attitudes improved, there was a corresponding improvement in his reading, spelling, and fine motor skills.

COMMENTARY: This article illustrates that, in helping children learn, the teacher often has to take on the role of a therapist in seeking to change such maladaptive personality traits as overdependency. The authors described a special education program that attempts to synthesize the roles of psychologist and teacher into one composite helping role. Children who attended this special summer program were described by their teachers the next year as much more self-confident, eager to learn, and persistent than they had been.

SOURCE: West, M., Carlin, M., Baserman, B., and Milstein, M. "An Intensive Therapeutic Program for Learning-Disabled Prepubertal Children." *Journal of Learning Disabilities,* 1978, *11,* 56-59.

Author Index

A

Adesso, V. J., 381
Alden, S. E., 373-375
Alexander, R. N., 195-196
Allen, J. I., 94
Allen, K. E., 219-220, 460-461
Allen, R., 287-289
Allen, R. P., 140
Allen, T. W., 486-487
Allgeier, A. R., 360
Allison, M. G., 277-279
Altman, K., 367-369
Altmann, H., 299
Ambuel, J. P., 353-354

Ammerman, M. S., 297
Anderson, S., 88-90
Anderson, W. H., 184
Apfel, C. H., 195-196
Apolloni, T., 473
Applegate, E., 216
Arnheim, D. D., 216
Arnold, C. R., 81-82
Ascare, D., 341-342
Asher, S. R., 447-448, 475-476
Atkinson, J. W., 351
Axelrod, S., 110-112, 341-342, 431-432
Ayllon, T., 90-91, 277-279, 441-442, 478-480

Azrin, N. H., 19-20, 54-56, 362, 370, 376-378, 394

B

Bachara, G. H., 216
Bachus, V. A., 446
Baer, D. M., 19, 468-469, 506-507
Bailey, J. S., 13-14, 105, 391
Balow, B., 1, 8
Barber, R. M., 29-32
Barden, R. C., 6, 7-8
Bardon, J. I., 425-427
Barkley, R. A., 161
Barrett, C. L., 275
Barrios, B. A., 379-381
Barton, E. S., 19
Baserman, B., 507-508
Basta, S. M., 88-90
Bauermeister, J. J., 321-322
Beck, A. T., 312-313
Becker, W. C., 78-79, 81-82
Beckman, G., 275
Beggs, V. E., 211-213
Bellack, A. S., 97-99, 462-463
Bennett, V. C., 425-427
Berg, I., 360-361
Bergland, B. W., 401-402
Berkovec, T. D., 379
Berne, E., 493
Bernstein, D. A., 379
Black, T., 216-217
Black, W. A. M., 57-58
Blackwood, R. O., 57
Blampied, N. M., 57-58
Blaylock, M., 367-369
Block, J., 347
Blom, G. E., 428-430
Bloom, R. B., 40-41
Bolen, D., 191-192, 293-295
Bond, F. T., 291-293
Boocock, S. S., 6, 7
Bornstein, M. R., 462-463
Bornstein, P. H., 122-124
Bower, E. M., 250-251
Brannigan, G. G., 176-179, 279-280, 336-338
Bratter, T. E., 61-63
Brawley, E. R., 468-469
Breckon, D., 414-415

Breitrose, H., 161
Brickman, P., 191-192, 293-295
Broden, M., 143-144, 345-347
Brooks, D. B., 25-27
Brooks, R. B., 17-18
Brown, J. A., 297-298
Brown, L., 386-388
Brown, R. A., 335-336
Brown, R. E., 339-340
Brown, S. D., 229-231
Bruce, C., 143-144
Bruchez, P. K., 425-427
Bryant, W. T., 458
Buckholdt, D., 499
Buckley, N. K., 156-158
Buell, J. S., 219-220, 460-461
Bullis, E., 347
Buntman, A. D., 253
Buntman, S. R., 253
Burgess, R. L., 188-189
Burns, R. C., 214
Busemeyer, M. K., 211-213
Bushnell, D., 499
Busk, P., 289-291

C

Caldwell, B. M., 442
Calpin, J. P., 442
Camp, B. W., 428-430
Campbell, R. A., 431-432
Carkhuff, R. R., 352-353
Carlin, M., 507-508
Carlson, C. S., 81-82
Carlson, P. M., 251
Carnine, D. W., 103
Carr, E. G., 281-282
Carrera, M. A., 416-417
Carter, J. L., 348
Carter, V., 143-144
Chadbourne, J., 198
Chal, A. H., 401-402
Chamberlain, P., 147-149
Chan, A., 72-74
Chess, S., 273
Chipman, J., 201-202
Chiu, A., 72-74
Clark, R. A., 351
Clark, R. N., 188-189
Clements, J. E., 161

Cleveland, J. C., 350-351
Cobb, J. A., 437-439
Cole, P. M., 184
Coleman, J., 356-358
Colligan, R. C., 319-321
Colligan, R. W., 319-321
Collins, B. E., 138
Cook, J. W., 367-369
Cook, S. W., 455-457
Cooke, T. P., 473
Coopersmith, S., 298
Copeland, R. E., 339-340
Corman, C., 406-407
Corson, J. A., 476
Couch, J. V., 104-105
Cowen, E. L., 3-4, 7
Cowen, R. J., 97-99
Cranston, S. S., 431-432
Cretekos, C. J. G., 256-258
Crowly, C. G., 472-473
Culbertson, F. M., 83-84
Cullinan, D., 43-44, 166-167, 168-170
Cunningham, C. E., 161
Cunningham, S. J., 137
Curtis, J., 299

D

Damico, S., 78
Darch, C. B., 103-104
Daudargas, R. W., 348-349
Davis, S. O., 251
Davison, G. C., 274-275
De Bruler, L., 38
de Vincentis, S., 209-211
Deal, T. E., 13-14
Deffenbacher, J. L., 124-125
DeGiovanni, I. S., 274
Deitz, S. M., 99-100, 114-115
Demsch, B., 34-35
Deputat, Z., 403-405
Devine, V. T., 145-147
DeVries, D. L., 349, 457
Dewey, J., 422
Diament, B., 3, 7
Dickens, H. O., 418-419
Dickinson, D. J., 132-133
Digate, G., 168-170
Digiuseppe, R., 232-233

Dillard, N. R., 397-399
Dilliard, M. K., 319-321
Dinkmeyer, D., 301
Dixon, D., 181-183
Doleys, D. M., 259-261
Dolnick, M., 446
Donahue, G. T., 361-362
Dougherty, A., 50-52
Dougherty, E. H., 50-52
Douglas, V. I., 163-164, 171-174
Doyal, G. T., 234-236, 310-312
Drabman, R. S., 74-75
Duer, W. F., 407
Duke, D. L., 487-490
Dunkleberger, G. E., 28-29
Durlak, J. A., 343-344, 473-474

E

Eastman, J., 216-217
Eaton, M. D., 59
Edwards, K. J., 457
Edwards, R. P., 105-106
Eimers, R. C., 58
Elardo, P. T., 442
Ellery, M. D., 57-58
Ellis, D., 499
Emery, J. R., 401
Epstein, J., 335-336
Epstein, M. H., 43-44, 166-167, 168-170
Epstein, R., 92-94
Erickson, M., 164
Erikson, E., 154, 155
Etzel, B. C., 466-467
Evans, T., 386-388
Evers-Pasquale, W., 464-465

F

Fairchild, T. N., 94-95
Farber, H., 200-201
Feingold, B. F., 130
Ferguson, L. N., 365-367
Ferritor, D., 499
Fixsen, D. L., 391
Fleetwood, R. S., 452-453
Flowers, J. V., 20-21
Flumen, A. B., 474
Fo, W. S. O., 35-36

Ford, M. E., 6, 7-8
Ford, R. C., 289-291
Forness, S. R., 239-241
Foulk, B., 198
Foundopoulos, M., 431-432
Foxx, R. M., 362, 370
Frankenpohl, H., 72
Franks, C. M., 273
Freeman, E., 418-419
Friedman, R. J., 234-236, 310-312, 317-318
Fryrear, J. L., 297

G

Garber, S. W., 277-279, 441-442
Garcia, C., 418-419
Garcia, E., 19
Garcia, K. A., 274
Gardner, D. C., 205, 331-332
Gardner, P. L., 205, 331-332
Garson, C., 171-174
Garth, J., 34-35
Gendelman, E. G., 392
George, T. W., 356-358
Gershman, L., 116
Giladi, D., 237-239
Gilchrist, L. D., 409-411, 412-413
Giles, D. K., 106
Gilmore, J. V., 142
Gittelman, M., 137-138, 142
Goetz, E. M., 466-467
Goldberg, C., 273-274
Goldstein, C. G., 457-458
Goldstein, H. H., 457-458
Gonso, J., 474
Goodwin, B., 351
Goss, C. M., 92-94
Gottman, J., 474
Grala, C., 32-34
Graubard, P., 147-149
Graves, A. W., 162
Graziano, A. M., 274
Greenberg, D. J., 85
Greenberg, J. S., 403-405
Greenwood, C. R., 349-350
Gresham, F. M., 37
Grieger, R. M., 430-431
Grieger, T., 430-431
Griffith, D. L., 224

Gruen, G. E., 266-268
Guerney, B. G., 474
Guess, D., 19
Gumaer, J., 67-68

H

Hall, R. V., 143-144, 205, 339-340, 345-347, 431-432
Hallahan, D. P., 162
Hamblin, R. L., 499
Hampe, E., 275
Haney, J. N., 322-324
Hanley, E. L., 106
Hansen, J. C., 5, 8
Harnett, A. L., 405-406
Haroldson, S., 389-390
Harris, F. R., 219-220, 460-461, 468-469, 506-507
Hart, B. M., 219-220, 460-461, 468-469
Hartley, D. G., 184
Harvey, J. R., 268-270
Hasazi, J. E., 271-272
Hash, V., 295-297
Hauserman, N., 291-293
Hawkins, R. P., 196-198
Hay, L. R., 104
Hay, W. M., 104
Haynes, S. N., 447
Hebert, F., 428-430
Hegerle, D. R., 104-105
Heider, J. P., 206
Helfen, C. S., 369-371
Hendee, J. C., 188-189
Hendel, D. D., 251
Hendrick, J., 433-435
Henker, B., 138, 140-141
Henry, M. M., 442-443
Herlong, L. H., 447
Herold, E. S., 418
Herr, E. L., 399-400
Hersen, M., 462-463
Hetherington, E. M., 186
Hewett, F. M., 154-156, 162
Hilliard, G., 114-115
Hollon, T. H., 198
Hong, K. M., 406-407
Hopkins, B. L., 63-65
Hops, H., 349-350

Hosford, R. E., 501-502
Houser, B. B., 458
Houser, J. E., 42-43
Hovell, M. F., 68-69
Huggins, G. R., 418-419
Humphrey, L. L., 332-334
Huntsinger, G. M., 496-499

I

Iwata, B. A., 105

J

Jackson, D., 205
Jackson, R. M., 350-351
Jaffe, P. G., 251
Jakibchuk, Z., 474-475
James, J. E., 392-393
Jemail, J. A., 321-322
Johnson, G., 37
Johnson, J., 181-183
Johnson, L., 209-211
Johnson, M. R., 112-113
Johnson, O. G., 469-471
Johnson, S. B., 274
Jones, F. H., 58, 95, 97-99
Josephs, E., 46
Jurgela, A. R., 271-272

K

Kagan, J., 186
Kagen, E., 141
Kagey, J. R., 29-32
Kahana, B., 179-181
Kandel, H. J., 478-480
Kanfer, F. H., 185
Kaplan, M. L., 393
Kaplan, N. R., 393
Kaplan, S., 491-493
Karagan, N., 317-318
Karoly, P., 332-334
Karpowitz, D. H., 68, 174-176
Karraker, R. J., 329-331
Kass, R. E., 74-75
Kassinove, H., 232-233, 252-253
Katz, P. A., 450-451
Kauffman, J. M., 4, 7, 162, 430-431
Kaufman, K. F., 74-75

Kaufman, S. H., 214
Kehl, D. G., 21
Kelly, F. D., 149-151
Kendall, P. C., 184-185
Kesecker, M. P., 104-105
Khatami, M., 312-313
King, L. A., 106
Kinsbourne, M., 185
Kipper, D. A., 237-239
Kirkwood, M., 59
Kirschenbaum, D. S., 332-334, 475
Kirschner, N. M., 443-444
Klein, S. A., 124-125
Knapp, T. J., 88-90
Knaus, W., 347
Knights, R. M., 137
Koch, K., 21
Koenig, G. R., 5, 7
Konarski, E. A., 112-113
Koopman, E. J., 457-458
Koppitz, E. M., 214
Kornblith, S. J., 442
Kosiewicz, M. M., 162
Krasnow, A., 299-300
Kratochwill, T. R., 189-191
Kravas, C. H., 493-495
Kravas, K. J., 493-495
Kravetz, R. J., 239-241
Kroth, R. L., 3, 7
Kubany, E. S., 47
Kuhl, P., 389-390
Kupst, M. J., 140

L

La Pray, A. J., 201-202
Lacey, H. M., 217
Lachowicz, J., 106
Lahey, B. B., 44-46, 211-213
Lambert, N. M., 121, 138
Lane, J., 300
Lazarus, A. A., 274-275
Leffingwell, R. J., 251-252
Lepper, M. R., 101-102
LeUnes, A., 261-263
Leventhal, T., 275
Levin, L., 443-444
Levine, B. A., 375-376
Levine, G. F., 355
Lewinsohn, P. M., 314

Lewis, B. L., 162
Lichty, E. C., 139
Lilly, M. S., 154
Linden, W., 241-243
Lindley, P., 283
Lloyd, J., 162
Logan, J. J., 418-419
Loney, J., 139
Losen, S. M., 3, 7
Lovaas, O. I., 305-307
Loveless, B. W., 88-90
Loveless, S. E., 88-90
Lovitt, A. O., 59
Lovitt, T. C., 59
Low, B., 305-307
Lowell, E. L., 351
Luiselli, J. K., 369-371
Lund, D., 205

M

McBrien, R. J., 139
McCauley, C., 32-34
McClain, W. A., 444
McClelland, D. C., 351
McCullough, J. P., 496-499
McDonald, J. E., 263-266
Macdougall, M. A., 297-298
McIntire, J. T., 406
McKay, G., 301
McKinlay, I. A., 217
McLaughlin, T. F., 203-204, 206, 351-352
McNees, M. C., 44-46
McNees, M. P., 44-46
Madsen, C. H., Jr., 78-79, 81-82, 243-245, 348-349
Malaby, J. E., 203-204, 206, 351-352
Maletzky, B. M., 79
Maly, J., 435-437
Manderscheid, R. W., 5, 7
Mann, J., 252
Mannarino, A. P., 473-474
Manning, W. H., 384-386
Margolis, H., 176-179, 336-338
Markle, A., 351
Marks, I., 283
Marlowe, M., 308
Martin, R. R., 389-390

Marton, P., 171-174
Masters, J. C., 6, 7-8
Matson, J. L., 220-222
Mayer, G. R., 200-201
Meichenbaum, P. H., 252
Meisels, L., 116-117
Merenda, P. F., 350-351
Merkert, F., 362
Meyers, J., 314-315
Miller, E., 447
Miller, J. S., 291-293
Miller, L. C., 275
Miller, N., 252-253
Miller, R. L., 191-192, 293-295
Miller, W. H., 95
Millman, H. L., 355
Milstein, M., 507-508
Minde, K., 140
Minuchin, S., 147-149
Mischel, W., 163
Mitchell, J. E., 406-407
Mitchell, M. A., 143-144
Mitts, B., 345-347
Mock, K. R., 185
Monohan, J., 21-22
Moos, B. S., 36-37
Moos, R. H., 36-37
Moreland, K. L., 184
Morgenstern, G., 163-164
Mosier, D., 47
Mudd, E. H., 418-419
Mueller, D. J., 72-74
Muhlfelder, C., 336-338
Muller, D., 300
Muller, S. D., 243-245
Munroe, R. L., 225
Myrick, R. D., 67-68, 149-151, 303-305

N

Nagle, R. J., 37
Nay, W. R., 496-499
Needels, M., 37-38
Neel, R. A., 38
Nelson, R. O., 104
Ness, E., 21
Newman, A., 185
Newsom, C. D., 281-282
Nixon, S. B., 161, 163

Noble, H., 275
Nunn, R. G., 376-378, 394

O

O'Connor, R. D., 464, 482
O'Donnell, C. R., 35-36
O'Donnell, W. J., 85
O'Hara, C., 211-213
O'Leary, K. D., 21-22, 74-75, 125-127
O'Malley, E., 347
Oden, S., 475-476
Ollendick, T. H., 220-222, 266-268

P

Page, D. P., 105-106
Palkes, H., 179-181
Parish, T. S., 253, 435-437, 452-453, 458
Parke, R. D., 186
Parry, P., 171-174
Pastor, D. L., 444-445
Patterson, C. J., 101-102, 163
Patterson, G. R., 437-439
Pease, G. A., 66-67
Pedrini, B. C., 362
Pedrini, D. T., 362
Pelham, W. E., 125-127
Pemberton, B. W., 369-371
Penny, H. A., 206
Perkins, J. A., 352-353
Perry, C., 487-490
Peterson, R. F., 88-90
Pettigrew, L. E., 373-375
Phillips, E. A., 391
Phillips, E. L., 192, 391
Philpott, R., 283
Pierce, L., 386-388
Pisor, K., 441-442
Pitcher-Baker, G., 213-215
Pitt, N. W., 314-315
Polefka, D. A., 274-275
Pollack, J. M., 283
Poston, M. A., 176-179
Powers, M. A., 54-56
Prawat, R. S., 458
Pressley, M., 185
Price, G. H., 125-127

Prout, H. T., 128-130, 268-270
Purkey, W., 78

Q

Quevillon, R. P., 122-124

R

Rashbaum-Selig, M., 445-446
Raskin, L. M., 213-215
Ray, R. S., 437-439
Redl, F., 4, 8
Reed, M., 216-217
Reimondi, R., 279-280
Reing, V. A., 361-362
Reisman, J., 369-371
Rekers, G. A., 305-307, 308, 365-367
Renshaw, K., 246-248
Repp, A. C., 43-44, 99-100
Reynolds, N. J., 468-469
Richards, C. S., 353
Rickard, H. C., 192
Rickels, K., 418-419
Ridberg, E. H., 186
Rie, E. D., 353-354
Rie, H. E., 353-354
Rincover, A., 281-282
Rinn, R. C., 351
Roberts, M. D., 90-91
Robertson, S. J., 447
Robinson, C. M., 253
Rose, S. E., 407
Rose, T. L., 130-131
Rosen, M., 283
Rosenbaum, E., 125-127
Rosenbaum, M. S., 478-480
Ross, J. A., 375-376
Rubin, R. A., 1, 8
Ruedi, J., 300-301
Runkel, P. J., 7, 8
Rush, A. J., 312-313
Rustin, L., 393-394
Rutherford, R. B., 3, 8

S

Sadler, O. W., 362, 397-399
Safer, D. J., 140

Sagotsky, G., 101-102
Saltz, E., 181-183
Salzberg, B. H., 63-65
Sanders, S. H., 322-324
Sanderson, R. A., 425-427
Sandoval, J., 121, 138
Sassone, D., 121, 138
Saunders, T. R., 192
Saxon, B., 419
Scales, P., 419-420
Schaefer, C. E., 355, 362-363
Schinke, S. P., 409-411, 412-413
Schmuck, P. A., 6-7, 8, 154
Schmuck, R. A., 6-7, 8, 154
Schneider, M. R., 85-86, 446
Schuler, P., 474
Schulman, J. L., 140, 289-291
Schumaker, J. B., 68-69
Schwarzmueller, E. B., 114-115
Scott, E. A., 322, 358-359
Scott, J. W., 348-349
Seiler, G., 246-248
Sewell, W. R., 322-324
Sharpe, D. F., 442-443
Shaw, C. K., 384-386
Shaw, J., 367-369
Sheats, D. W., 28-29
Shellman, J., 431-432
Sheperd, G., 263-266
Sherman, J. A., 68-69
Sherman, M., 464-465
Shirazi, A. M., 435-437
Shores, R. E., 480-481
Siegelman, E., 165
Siemglusz, S., 261-263
Silbergeld, S., 5, 7
Silver, L., 166-167
Silverman, J. S., 283-284, 298
Simmons, J. T., 152-154
Simpson, R. L., 3, 7
Sinclair, W. A., 216
Skiba, E. A., 373-375
Slaby, R. G., 472-473
Slack, D. J., 114-115
Slavin, R. E., 206-207, 349, 453-455, 457
Sloggett, B. B., 47
Small, R. W., 412-413
Smeriglio, V. L., 474-475
Smith, A. H., Jr., 22-23

Snow, D. L., 17-18
Snowden, J., 283
Sperling, K. A., 394-395
Sperling, M., 273
Stallings, J., 37-38
Stanton, H. E., 253
Steele, M., 117
Stevens, T. M., 140
Stewart, M., 179-181
Stewart, S., 353-354
Strain, P. S., 162, 480-481
Strathe, M., 295-297
Struble, J. B., 69-70
Sulzbacher, S. I., 42-43
Summerlin, M. L., 301
Suran, B. G., 140
Surratt, P. R., 196-198
Susskind, D. J., 273
Swanson, J. M., 185
Swanson, L., 52-54
Swap, S. M., 154-156, 444-445
Sweeney, D., 414-415
Swisher, J. D., 399-400
Switzer, E. B., 13-14
Switzky, H. N., 168-170
Sykes, D. H., 163-164

T

Tava, E. G., 502-503
Taylor, D. C., 217
Taylor, L., 63-65
Taylor, M. J., 189-191
Taylor, S. E., 72
Teel, S. K., 222-224
Teeter, N. C., 394-395
Thelen, H. A., 5, 8
Thomas, D. R., 78-79
Thomas, M. R., 394-395
Thompson, V. M., 248-250
Thomson, C. L., 466-467
Thorpe, H. W., 103-104
Tidwell, R., 446
Timbers, G. D., 391
Timm, M. A., 480-481
Tobias, S., 253-254
Tomlinson, J. R., 145-147
Tracy, D. B., 161
Trexler, L. K., 217
Truax, C. B., 352-353

Trutna, P. A., 384-386
Turner, P. F., 112-113
Tyler, V. O., Jr., 66-67

U

Ulrich, R. E., 196-198

V

Vaal, J. J., Jr., 47
van Doorninck, W. J., 428-430
Varenhorst, B. B., 503-504
Vargas, J. M., 381
Varni, J. W., 140-141
Vogelheim, R. M., 192-193
Voorhees, S. G., 207

W

Waber, C., 381-382
Wagner, M. K., 371
Wahler, R. G., 164, 394-395
Walker, H. M., 48, 156-158, 349-350
Ward, G. R., 301
Warner, R. W., Jr., 5, 8, 399-400
Warren, S., 23
Washington, K. R., 286-287
Wasik, B. H., 152-154
Wasserman, T. H., 108-110
Weatherly, T. J., 114-115
Webster, R. E., 439-441
Weigel, R. H., 455-457
Weinberger, G., 275
Weinrott, M. R., 476
Weiss, L. E., 47
Weissenburger, F. E., 139
Weithorn, C. J., 141
Wesolowski, M. D., 19-20
West, C. D., 300-301

West, M., 507-508
Whalen, C. K., 138
Wheeler, A. J., 63-65
White, D., 322-324
White, K., 287-289
Whitehurst, C., 447
Wicas, E. A., 352-353
Wilander, A. P., 114-115
Wilchesky, M., 476
Williams, P., 356-358
Williams, R. L., 354
Williams, S. C., 259-261
Williamson, D. A., 322-324
Wilson, C. C., 447
Wilson, S. H., 354
Wine, J. D., 254
Winston, A. S., 15-17
Wiser, P. L., 455-457
Wish, P. A., 271-272
Wolf, M. M., 106, 219-220, 391, 460-461, 506-507
Wolpe, J., 401
Woolfolk, A. E., 158-160
Woolfolk, R. L., 158-160
Woolson, R. F., 139
Workman, E. A., 132-133

Y

Yando, R. M., 186
Yawkey, T. D., 224
York, R., 386-388

Z

Zaba, J. N., 216
Zahavi, S., 447-448
Zalk, S. R., 450-451
Zentall, S. S., 134-137
Zimmerman, E. H., 76-77
Zimmerman, J., 76-77

Subject Index

A

Abbreviated Conners' Teacher Rating Scale, 126

Academic performance, poor: achievement motivation for, 351; behavior modification for, 341-342; biofeedback/relaxation for, 348; in college, 353; counseling for, 350-351, 352-353; described, 328; in elementary school, 329-331, 332-334, 339-342, 348-349, 350-352, 353-354; and feedback, 348-349; goal setting for, 331-332; helper therapy and, 343-344; individual and group contingency for, 341-342, 354; and parents, 329-331, 352-353; and positive grading practices, 335-336; and principal, 339-340; rational-emotive program for, 347; and reality therapy, 336-338; reinforcement for, 329-331, 351-352; response-cost for, 333-334, 351-352; and Ritalin, 353-354; in secondary school, 331-332, 335-338, 343-347, 351, 352-353; self-management for, 332-334, 345-347, 353; and skills training, 349-350; teacher training for, 350; Teams-Games-Tournaments for, 349

Activity schedules, for depression, 314

Adolescents. *See* Secondary school

Affect induction. *See* Rational-emotive therapy

Aggression: and classical conditioning, 435-437; and conflict resolution skills, 442; contingency contracts for, 438-439; described, 422-424; direct intervention and, 425-427, 437-439, 443-444; ecology of, 444-445; in elementary school, 425-432, 435-437, 440-442, 443-444, 445-447, 447; factors in, 442-443; group counseling for, 446; and home-school motivation, 441-442; medication for, 185; peer management of, 430-431, 445-446; in preschool, 433-435, 442-443, 444-445, 447-448; prevention of, 433-435; and punishment, 431-432, 447; and reinforcement, 430-431, 444; self-control for, 428-430, 446, 496-499; sex differences in, 424; and social development, 442; time-out for, 438, 439-441, 447; turtle technique for, 446; and verbal instructions, 428-430, 447-448; work box for, 437-438

Alcohol abuse, in elementary school, 406-407

Amphetamines, and hyperactivity, 138

Annoying others: described, 87; in elementary school, 88-95; and I-messages, 88-90; and jogging, 94; negative attention for, 95; and reinforcement, 90-91, 94-95; self-control for, 92-94

Anxiety: centrality of, 225-227; and impulsiveness, 177

Anxiety and tension: assertiveness for, 230-231; cognitive methods for, 252, 254; in college, 237-239, 251, 253; counseling for, 251, 253; counterconditioning for, 253; described, 228; desensitization for, 236, 237-241, 243-245, 252; diagnosis of, 234-235; in elementary school, 232-233, 235-236, 239-243, 252-253, 254; management of, 230, 248-251, 254; meditation for, 241-243; modeling for, 251; music for, 253; psychodrama for, 237-239; and psychogenic illness, 248-250; psychotherapy for, 234-236, 252; rational-emotive program for, 232-233, 252-253; reinforcement for, 231; relaxation for, 229-230, 236, 246-248; in secondary school, 232-233, 243-245, 250-251, 252, 253; self-control training for, 229-231; and self-image, 230; yoga for, 246-248

Articulation errors: described, 383; in elementary school, 391; peer management of, 391

Assertiveness: for anxiety and tension, 230-231; for shyness and withdrawal, 462-463

Attention, and impulsiveness, 178. *See also* Distractible and inattentive behavior

Attribution, and poor self-esteem, 293-295

Aversion therapy, for nail-biting, 381

B

Behavior modification: and academic performance, poor, 341-342; and cheating, 20-21; and compulsive-perfectionistic behavior, 277-279; and encopresis, 356-359; and masturbation, 365-367; and mutism, elective, 319-321, 322-323; and phobia, 274; and school phobia, 273; wide use of, 3

Behavior recording, and clowning, 79

Bender Motor Gestalt Test, 235

Bender Visual-Motor Gestalt, 173

Bereavement, teacher training for, 314-315

Biofeedback: for academic performance, poor, 348; for hyperactivity, 129. *See also* Feedback

Boisterous behavior: daily reports
on, 50-52; described, 49; in elementary school, 50-52, 53,
55-56, 57-58, 59; and group and
individual contingencies, 53-54,
57-58; and parents, 50-52; peer
management of, 59; and positive
practice, 54-56; punishment for,
52-54; in secondary school,
52-54, 57; and self-statements, 57
Borke's Empathy Test, 182
Bothering others. *See* Annoying others
Brain dysfunction, and immature behaviors, 120

C

Cheating: behavior modification for,
20-21; described, 12; praise and
punishment for, 15-17; and self-
instruction, 21-22
Children's Classroom Behavior
Scale, 152
Children's Embedded Figures Test,
242
Children's Manifest Anxiety Scale,
244
Children's Survey of Rational Beliefs, 233
Classroom management problems:
of cursing, 39-47; with destructive behavior, 107-117; of dishonest behavior, 12-23; of disturbances, 48-106; extent of,
9-10; therapies for, 9-117; of truancy, 24-38. *See also* Teacher
relationships, disturbed
Clowning: and behavior recording,
79; characteristics related to, 78;
described, 71; in elementary
school, 72-79; and praise and ignoring, 78-79; soft or loud reprimands for, 74-75; and systematic
attention, 76-77; and tutoring,
counseling, and reinforcement,
72-74
Cognitive methods: for anxiety and
tension, 252, 254; for sexual behavior, 412-413
Cognitive tempo. *See* Impulsiveness

College: academic performance in,
poor, 353; anxiety and tension in,
237-239, 251, 253; depression in,
312-313; nail-biting in, 376-381;
sex education in, 416-417
Community support: and destructive behavior, 117; and distractible and inattentive behavior, 164;
and truancy, 32-34, 35-36
Compulsive-perfectionistic behavior: approaches to, 283; anxiety
or guilt caused, 276, 283; behavioral approach to, 277-279; described, 276; in elementary
school, 277-282, 284; and operant conditioning, 283; psychoanalytic approach to, 284; self-
acceptance for, 279-280; sensory
extinction of, 281-282
Conditioning: and aggression,
435-437; and prejudice, 452-453
Confrontation, for stuttering, 392
Conners' Abbreviated Symptom
Questionnaire, 138
Conners' Rating Scale for Hyperactivity, 171
Conners' Rating Scales for Parents
and Teachers, 173
Contingencies. *See* Group contingency; Individual contingency
Contingency contracts: and aggression, 438-439; and truancy,
25-27, 35-36, 37
Contingency management: and destructive behavior, 116; and elective mutism, 323-324
Continuous Performance Task, 125,
163
Coopersmith Behavior Rating Form,
297
Coordination, poor: described, 208;
in elementary school, 209-217;
and kinetic family drawings,
213-215; and motor-sensory
training, 209-211, 216-217; reinforcement and feedback for,
211-213; and relaxation, 209-211
Counseling: for academic performance, poor, 350-351, 352-353;
for anxiety and tension, 251,
253; for clowning, 72-74; for in-

hibition, 503-504; for poor self-esteem, 286-289; for substance abuse, 399-400. *See also* Group counseling

Counterconditioning: for anxiety and tension, 253; for prejudice, 458; for school phobia, 269

Covert positive reinforcement (CPR), and hyperactivity, 132-133

Crying: described, 218; in elementary school, 222-224; overcorrection of, 220-222; Premack principle for, 224; by preschool children, 219-222; and reinforcement, 219-220; time-outs for, 222-224

Cursing: described, 39; in elementary school, 42-46; and group contingencies, 42-43; and reinforcement, 43-44, 46, 47; responses to, 40-41; time-out for, 44-46, 47

D

Daily reports: on boisterous behavior, 50-52; for hyperactivity, 125-127; and noncompliance, 68-69

Dawdling. *See* Procrastination and dawdling

Daydreaming: and depression, 198; described, 194; in elementary school, 195-198; and guided fantasy, 198; peer management of, 196-198; and reinforcement, 195-196; in secondary school, 198

Deconditioning, for phobia, 271-272

Depression: activity schedules for, 314; acute, 310; chronic, 310-311; cognitive-behavioral therapy for, 312-313; in college, 312-313; and daydreaming, 198; described, 309; in elementary school, 311-312; masked, 311; reinforcement for, 314; and school psychologist, 310-312; teacher training for, 314-315

Desensitization: for anxiety and tension, 236, 237-241, 243-245, 252; for elective mutism, 322; for phobia, 275; for school phobia, 262, 268-270; for substance abuse, 401-402

Destructive behavior: and community support, 117; contingency management for, 116; described, 107; in elementary school, 108-117; group and individual contingencies for, 110-112; negative reinforcement for, 108-110; and reinforcement, 112-115; and social competence training, 116-117

Detroit Tests of Learning Aptitude, 173

Developmental Test of Visual-Motor Integration, 214

Dextroamphetamine, and hyperactivity, 127

Differential reinforcement of low rates of responding (DRL): and cursing, 43-44; and destructive behavior, 114-115; and out-of-seat behavior, 99-100

Differential reinforcement of other behavior (DRO), 44

Differentiation training, and impulsiveness, 169, 178

Direct intervention, and aggression, 425-427, 437-439, 443-444

Dishonest behavior: cheating, 15-17, 20-22; described, 12; in elementary school, 13-18, 20-22; lying, 21, 23; stealing, 13-14, 17-20, 22-23

Disrespect and defiance: alternative classes and schools for, 486-490; described, 485; in elementary school, 486-487, 491-493; family psychotherapy for, 491-493; in preschool, 499; reinforcement and, 499; in secondary school, 487-490, 496-499; self-control for, 496-499; Transactional Analysis for, 493-495

Distractible and inattentive behavior: and classroom management, 152-156; and community sup-

port, 164; described, 142; ecological approach to, 154-156; in
elementary school, 143-154,
156-163; extent of, 142; group
counseling for, 149-151; and
hyperactivity, 142, 161, 163-
164; and peer management,
152-154; in preschool, 163; and
reinforcement, 145-147, 152-
154, 156-160, 161, 162, 163,
164; self-monitoring for, 162,
163; and teacher attention, 143-
144; and teaching learning skills,
147-149; and time-outs, 145-
147; workclock for, 145-147
Disturbance, classroom: by annoying others, 87-95; by boisterous-
ness, 49-59; by clowning, 71-79;
described, 48; by noncompliance,
60-70; by out-of-seat behavior,
96-106; by temper tantrums,
80-86; therapies for, 48-106
Drug abuse: in elementary school,
397-399; relaxation training for,
401-402; in secondary school,
399-402, 407
Durell Analysis of Reading Difficulty, 173

E

Ecology: of aggression, 444-445; of
distractible and inattentive behavior, 154-156; human, 4-7
Elective mutism. See Mutism, elective
Elementary school: academic performance in, poor, 329-331,
332-334, 339-342, 348-349,
350-352, 353-354; aggression in,
425-432, 435-437, 440-442,
443-444, 445-446, 447; annoying
others in, 88-95; anxiety and tension in, 232-233, 235-236,
239-243, 252-253, 254; articulation errors in, 391; boisterous behavior in, 50-52, 53, 55-56,
57-58, 59; clowning in, 72-79;
compulsive-perfectionistic behavior in, 277-282, 284; coordination in, poor, 209-217; crying in,

222-224; cursing in, 42-46; daydreaming in, 195-198; depression
in, 311-312; destructive behavior
in, 108-117; dishonest behavior
in, 13-18, 20-22; disrespect and
defiance in, 486-487, 491-493;
distractible and inattentive behavior in, 143-154, 156-163; drug
abuse in, 397-399; encopresis in,
356-359, 361-362; enuresis in,
360; gender disturbance in,
303-307; hyperactivity in, 124-
127, 130-133, 137-139, 141; impulsiveness in, 166-167, 171-
176, 178, 184-186; inhibition in,
502-503; masturbation in,
367-371; messy and sloppy behavior in, 191-193; mutism in,
elective, 319-324; noncompliance in, 63-68, 69-70; out-of-seat
behavior in, 97-106; overdependence in, 507-508; prejudice in,
450-453, 457-458; procrastination and dawdling in, 201-204,
205, 206, 207; school phobia in,
259-261, 266-268, 269, 270,
271-272, 273, 275; self-esteem
in, poor, 287-293, 294-295,
297-298, 299, 300, 301; sexism
in, 458; shyness and withdrawal
in, 462-463, 469-471, 474,
475-476; social isolation in,
479-480; stuttering in, 384, 386,
395; substance abuse in, 397-399,
406-407; temper tantrums in,
81-86; thumb-sucking in, 373-
376, 381-382; truancy from, 28-
32, 34-35, 37-38; venereal disease
prevention in, 414-415
Embedded Figures Test, 179
Emotionally disturbed children:
compulsive-perfectionistic behavior by, 279-282; disrespect and
defiance by, 491-493; encopresis
and, 361-362
Encopresis: approaches to, 362-363;
behavioral techniques for, 356-
359; described, 355; in elementary school, 356-359, 361-362;
lay volunteers and, 361-362; reinforcement for, 362

Enuresis: approaches to, 362-363; described, 355; diurnal, 360-361; in elementary school, 360; response-cost for, 360; scheduling method for, 362
Environmental manipulation, for hyperactivity, 129, 134-137
Exercise, for hyperactivity, 124-125
Eysenck Personality Inventory, 237

F

Fantasy: guided, and daydreaming, 198; training in, and impulsiveness, 181-183
Fantasy Judgment Test, 182
Feedback: and academic performance, poor, 348-349; and coordination, poor, 211-213; and hyperactivity, 140
Flooding, and social isolation, 478-480
Foundation for Child Development, 1, 7

G

Gender disturbance: described, 302; in elementary school, 303-307; modifying, 303-308; sex differences in, 302
Goal setting: and academic performance, poor, 331-332; and out-of-seat behavior, 101-102; and procrastination and dawdling, 205
Group contingency: for academic performance, poor, 341-342, 354; for boisterous behavior, 53-54, 57-58; for cursing, 42-43; for destructive behavior, 110-112; for obscene gestures, 42-43; for out-of-seat behaviors, 97-99, 103-106; for stealing, 13-14, 17-18; for temper tantrums, 85; for thumb-sucking, 375-376
Group counseling: and aggression, 446; and distractible and inattentive behavior, 149-151; and noncompliance, 67-68; and truancy, 37

Group interaction, importance of, 4-7

H

Habit, defined, 325
Habit disorders: enuresis and encopresis as, 355-363; interventions for, 326-327; masturbation as, 364-371; poor academic performance as, 328-354; sexual behavior as, 408-420; of speech, 383-395; substance abuse as, 396-407; therapies for, 325-420; thumb-sucking and nail-biting as, 372-382
Habit reversal, for nail-biting, 376-378
Harris County Department of Education, 407
Homework, daily reports on, 50-52
Hyperactivity: and artificial food colors, 130-131; and covert positive reinforcement, 132-133; daily reports and reinforcement for, 125-127; described, 121; and distractible and inattentive behavior, 142, 161, 163-164; in elementary school, 124-127, 130-133, 137-139, 141; and environmental stimulation, 134-137; exercise for, 124-125; extent of, 121; and feedback, 140; and impulsiveness, 171-174, 179-181, 185; interventions for, 128-130, 137-138, 139, 140; and medication, 121, 127, 137, 138, 139, 161, 163-164, 185; in preschool, 122-124; and punishment, 137; and reinforcement, 125-127, 136, 137, 140; relaxation for, 124-125, 139; self-instruction for, 122-124, 129, 140-141; sex differences in, 121

I

Idea Inventory, 233
I-messages, and annoying others, 88-90
Immature behavior: and brain dys-

function, 120; concept of, 119-120; and coordination, poor, 208-217; crying as, 218-224; daydreaming as, 194-198; distractible and inattentive, 142-164; hyperactivity as, 121-141; impulsiveness as, 165-186; messy and sloppy, 187-193; procrastination and dawdling as, 199-207; therapies for, 119-224

Implosive therapy: for bodily injury phobia, 266-268; for school phobia, 269

Impulsiveness: and anxiety, 177; and attention, 178; described, 165; and differentiation training, 169, 178; and direct instruction, 168-169; in elementary school, 166-167, 171-176, 178, 184-186; extent of, 165; and fantasy training, 181-183; and hyperactivity, 171-174, 179-181, 185; modeling for, 166-167, 169, 171-174, 177, 186; in preschool, 181-183; and reinforcement, 169-170, 171-172, 184, 185, 186; and reinstatement, 174-176; and required delay, 168; self-verbalization for, 166-167, 169, 171-174, 179-181, 184-185; and strategy training, 184; and teacher tempo, 186; and visual discrimination, 178

Inattentive behavior. See Distractible and inattentive behavior

Individual contingency: for academic performance, poor, 341-342, 354; for boisterous behavior, 57-58; for destructive behavior, 110-112; for temper tantrums, 85

Inhibition: behavioral counseling for, 503-504; described, 500; in elementary school, 502-503; reinforcement and, 501-503; in secondary school, 501-502; teacher training for, 501-502

Insecure behaviors: anxiety and tension as, 228-254; compulsive-perfectionistic, 276-284; depression as, 309-315; elective mutism as, 316-324; gender disturbance as, 302-308; phobias as, 255-275; and self-esteem, poor, 285-301; therapies for, 225-324

Instructed repetition, and cursing, 44-46

Intervention, direct, and aggression, 425-427, 437-439, 443-444

Isolation. See Social isolation

J

Jogging, and annoying others, 94

Johns Hopkins University, 453

Junior Eysenck Personality Inventory, 233

K

Kinetic family drawings, and poor coordination, 213-215

L

Low-intensity speech: described, 383; reinforcement for, 386-388; by retarded students, 386-388; in secondary school, 386-388

Lying: described, 12; reasons for, 23; teaching about, 21

M

Martin Screening Test for Motor Disabilities, 214

Masturbation: behavioral techniques for, 365-367; described, 364; in elementary school, 367-371; overcorrection for, 369-371; in preschool, 365-367; punishing, 367-369; and reinforcement, 371; by retarded students, 367-371

Matching Familiar Figures Test (MFFT), 125, 166-167, 168, 171, 173, 176, 177, 178, 179, 183, 185, 186

Medication: for aggression, 185; and hyperactivity, 121, 127, 137, 138, 139, 161, 163-164, 185; and withdrawal, 185

Meditation, for anxiety and tension, 241-243

Messy and sloppy behavior: and attribution or persuasion, 191-192; described, 187; in elementary school, 191-193; in preschool, 189-191; and reinforcement, 188-191, 192-193

Methylphenidate (Ritalin): and academic performance, poor, 353-354; and disrespect and defiance, 491; and hyperactivity, 127, 137, 138, 139, 161, 163-164, 185

Metropolitan Achievement Test, 242

Modeling: for anxiety and tension, 251; for impulsiveness, 166-167, 169, 171-174, 177, 186; for shyness and withdrawal, 464-465, 474-475; for social isolation, 482

Music, for anxiety and tension, 253

Mutism, elective: behavior modification for, 319-321, 322-323; contingency management for, 323-324; described, 316; desensitization for, 322; in elementary school, 319-324; management of, 317-318, 321-322

N

Nail-biting: aversion therapy for, 381; by college students, 376-381; described, 372; extent of, 372; habit reversal for, 376-378; relaxation for, 379-381

Name-calling, peer management of, 47

National Clearinghouse for Smoking and Health, 405

Negative attention, and annoying others, 95

Noncompliance: daily reports and parental reinforcement for, 68-69; delayed consequences for, 63-65; described, 60; in elementary school, 63-68, 69-70; group counseling for, 67-68; humanistic approach to, 61-63; and reinforcement, 69-70; and reinstatement, 68; responsibility-oriented process for, 61-63; in secondary school, 69; time-outs for, self-directed, 66-67

O

Obscene gestures, and group contingencies, 42-43

Obscenity. See Cursing

Operant conditioning: for compulsive-perfectionistic behavior, 283; for hyperactivity, 128-129; for procrastination and dawdling, 205; for thumb-sucking, 381-382

Out-of-seat behavior: described, 96; DRL schedule for, 99-100; in elementary school, 97-106; goal setting and self-monitoring for, 101-102; group contingencies for, 97-99, 103-106; on-task or academic contingencies for, 104; and reinforcement, 99-100, 104-105; and teacher presentation rates, 103; variable-interval contingencies for, 106

Overcorrection: for crying, 220-222; for masturbation, 369-371; for stealing, 19-20

Overdependency: described, 505; in elementary school, 507-508; in preschool, 506-507; reinforcement and, 506-507; teacher training and, 506-507; therapy for, 507-508

P

Parents: and academic performance, poor, 329-331, 352-353; and aggression, 441-442; and boisterous behavior, 50-52; and disrespect and defiance, 491-493; and noncompliance, 68-69; and school phobia, 256-258, 259-261, 275; and self-esteem, poor, 301; and stealing, 22-23; teacher cooperation with, 3; and truancy, 28-29

Peer counseling: for sexual behavior, 416-417; for substance abuse, 397-399

Peer management: of aggression,

430-431, 445-446; of articulation errors, 391; of boisterous behavior, 59; of daydreaming, 196-198; of distractible and inattentive behavior, 152-154; of name-calling, 47; of social isolation, 480-481

Peer pressure. *See* Group contingency

Peer relationships, disturbed: aggression as, 422-448; findings on, 421-422; prejudice as, 449-458; shyness and withdrawal as, 459-476; social isolation as, 477-482; therapies for, 421-482

Peers, influence of, 6

Pennsylvania, University of, School of Medicine Family Planning Service at, 418-419

Phobia: automated direct deconditioning for, 271-272; behavioral approach to, 274; bodily injury, implosive therapy for, 266-268; described, 255; desensitization for, 275; diagnostic groups of, 273; psychotherapy for, 275; sex differences in, 255. *See also* School phobia

Picture Test of Intelligence, 182

Placebo, for hyperactivity, 138

Porteus Maze Tests, 173, 179, 180

Practice, positive, and boisterous behavior, 54-56

Pregnancy prevention, in secondary school, 409-413, 418-420

Prejudice, racial: audiovisual media and, 458; and conditioning, 452-453; described, 449; in elementary school, 450-453, 457-458; modification of, 450-451, 457-458; in secondary school, 454, 456, 457; and student cooperation, 453-457

Prejudice, sexual, counterconditioning for, 458

Premack principle, for crying, 224

Preschool children: aggression by, 433-435, 442-443, 444-445, 447-448; crying by, 219-222; disrespect and defiance by, 499; distractible and inattentive behavior by, 163; hyperactivity among,

122-124; impulsiveness by, 181-183; masturbation by, 365-367; messy and sloppy behavior by, 189-191; overdependence by, 506-507; shyness and withdrawal by, 460-461, 464-469, 472-473, 474-475; social isolation of, 478-479, 480-482; stuttering by, 389-390

Principal: and academic performance, poor, 339-340; and out-of-seat behavior, 103-104; and truancy, 28-29

Procrastination and dawdling: described, 199; in elementary school, 201-204, 205, 206, 207; and goal setting, 205; and operant conditioning, 205; and reinforcement, 200-202, 203-204, 206-207; and retarded students, 207; in secondary school, 200-201, 205, 206-207; and structuring, 207; and teacher attention, 205

Psychologist, school, and depression, 310-312

Psychotherapy: for anxiety and tension, 234-236, 252; for compulsive-perfectionistic behavior, 284; for disrespect and defiance, 491-493; for hyperactivity, 128; for phobia, 275; for school phobia, 273-274

Public Law 94-142, x, 2

Punishment: and aggression, 431-432, 447; and boisterous behavior, 52-54; and cheating, 15-17; and clowning, 74-75; defined, 431-432; and hyperactivity, 137; and masturbation, 367-369

R

Racism. *See* Prejudice, racial

Rational-emotive therapy: for academic performance, poor, 347; for anxiety and tension, 232-233, 252-253; and learning, 6

Reality therapy, for academic performance, poor, 336-338

Reinforcement: and academic performance, poor, 329-331, 351-352; and aggression, 430-431, 444; and annoying others, 90-91, 94-95; and anxiety and tension, 231; and cheating, 15-17; and clowning, 72-74, 76-77, 78-79; and coordination, poor, 211-213; and crying, 219-220; and cursing, 43-44, 46, 47; and daydreaming, 195-196; and depression, 314; and destructive behavior, 108-110, 112-115; and disrespect and defiance, 499; and distractible and inattentive behavior, 143-144, 145-147, 152-154, 156-160, 161, 162, 163, 164; and encopresis, 362; and hyperactivity, 125-127, 136, 137, 140; and impulsiveness, 169-170, 171-174, 184, 185, 186; and inhibition, 501-503; and low-intensity speech, 386-388; and masturbation, 371; and messy and sloppy behavior, 188-191, 192-193; and noncompliance, 68-70; and out-of-seat behavior, 99-100, 104-105; and overdependence, 506-507; and procrastination and dawdling, 200-202, 203-204, 205, 206-207; and school phobia, 259-260, 269; and self-esteem, poor, 291-293; and shyness and withdrawal, 460-461, 466-469, 472-473; and stuttering, 384-386; and substance abuse, 399-400; and temper tantrums, 81-82, 83-84; and thumb-sucking, 373-375; and truancy, 29-32

Reinstatement: and impulsiveness, 174-176; and noncompliance, 68

Relaxation: for academic performance, poor, 348; for anxiety and tension, 229-230, 236, 246-248; for coordination, poor, 209-211; for drug abuse, 401-402; for hyperactivity, 124-125, 139; for nail-biting, 379-381; for stuttering, 394; for substance abuse, 401-402; for temper tantrums, 86

Response-cost strategies: for academic performance, poor, 333-334, 351-352; for enuresis, 360. See also Contingencies; Contingency contracts; Contingency management

Retarded students: and cursing, 42-43, 44-46; and destructive behavior, 110-112; and disturbed peer relationships, 432; encopresis and, 356-359; and impulsiveness, 178; and masturbation, 367-371; overcorrection for stealing by, 19-20; procrastination and dawdling by, 207; speech disorders and, 387-388

Ritalin. See Methylphenidate

Rowdy behavior. See Boisterous behavior

S

School behavior problems: in classroom management, 9-117; extent of, 1-2; of habit disorders, 325-420; of immature behavior, 119-224; of insecure behaviors, 225-324; in peer relationships, 421-482; recognizing and dealing with, 1-8; in teacher relationships, 483-508

School phobia: attendance contract for, 256-258; behavior modification for, 273; counterconditioning for, 269; described, 255; desensitization for, 262, 268-270; in elementary school, 259-261, 266-268, 269, 270, 271-272, 273, 275; extent of, 255, 268; implosive therapy for, 269; paraprofessional treatment for, 261-263; and parent involvement, 256-258, 259-261, 275; psychoanalytic approach to, 273-274; and rapid return, 256-258; and reinforcement, 259-260, 269; in secondary school, 256-258, 261-263, 269, 270, 273-274; and separation anxiety, 264; and successive approximations, 259-261; and test anxiety, 270; theories and approaches for, 263-266, 274-275; truancy distinct from, 24

Schools, human ecology in, 4-7. *See also* Elementary school; Preschool children; Secondary school

Secondary school: academic performance in, poor, 331-332, 335-338, 343-347, 351, 352-353; anxiety and tension in, 232-233, 243-245, 250-251, 252, 253; boisterous behavior in, 52-54, 57; daydreaming in, 198; disrespect and defiance in, 487-490, 496-499; drug abuse in, 399-402, 407; inhibition in, 501-502; low-intensity speech in, 386-388; noncompliance in, 69; pregnancy prevention in, 409-413, 418-420; prejudice in, 454, 456, 457; procrastination and dawdling in, 200-201, 205, 206-207; school phobia in, 256-258, 261-263, 269, 270, 273-274; self-esteem in, poor, 286-287, 296-297; sex education in, 416-417, 419-420; smoking in, 403-406; stuttering in, 392-394; substance abuse in, 396, 399-406, 407; truancy from, 25-27, 32-34, 35-37, 38; venereal disease prevention in, 414-415

Secretary, school, and truancy, 28-29

Self-control: for academic performance, poor, 332-334, 345-347, 353; for aggression, 428-430, 446, 496-499; for annoying others, 92-94; for anxiety and tension, 229-231; for boisterous behavior, 57; for cheating, 21-22; for disrespect and defiance, 496-499; for distractible and inattentive behavior, 162, 163; for hyperactivity, 122-124, 129, 140-141; for impulsiveness, 166-167, 169, 171-174, 179-181, 184-185; for noncompliance, 61-63; for out-of-seat behavior, 101-102; for truancy, 38

Self-esteem, poor: Adlerian ap-

proach to, 299-300; and alternative school, 295-297, 300-301; art counseling for, 287-289; and attribution, 293-295; and body image, 297; described, 285; in elementary school, 287-293, 294-295, 297-298, 299, 300, 301; and parents, 301; reinforcement for, 291-293; in secondary school, 286-287, 296-297; and self-description, 300; success counseling for, 286-287; and teacher skill training, 297-299; teaching for, 289-291

Self-Report Reading Scale, 244

Sensory extinction, of compulsive-perfectionistic behavior, 281-282

Sequential Memory of Stories, 182

Sex differences: in aggression, 424; in gender disturbance, 302; in hyperactivity, 121; in phobias, 255

Sex education: in college, 416-417; in secondary school, 416-417, 419-420

Sexism, in elementary school, 458

Sexual behavior: cognitive-behavioral approach to, 412-413; communication skills for, 409-412; decision making for, 413; extent of problem with, 408; peer counseling for, 416-417; and pregnancy prevention, 409-413, 418-420; values clarification for, 414-415; and venereal disease prevention, 414-415

Shyness and withdrawal: coping with, 469-471; described, 459; in elementary school, 462-463, 469-471, 474, 475-476; extent of, 459; literature on, 473; modeling for, 464-465, 474-475; in preschool, 460-461, 464-469, 472-473, 474-475; reinforcement and, 460-461, 466-469, 472-473; social skills training for, 462-463, 473-474, 475-476; teacher training for, 474, 476. *See also* Social isolation

Skills training: and academic performance, poor, 349-350; and aggression, 442; and coordination, poor, 209-211, 216-217; and destructive behavior, 116-117; and distractible and inattentive behavior, 147-419; and poor self-esteem, 289-291; and sexual behavior, 409-412; and shyness and withdrawal, 462-463, 473-474, 475-476

Sloppy behavior. See Messy and sloppy behavior

Smoking: prevention programs for, 403-406; in secondary school, 403-406

Social isolation: described, 477; in elementary school, 479-480; flooding and, 478-480; modeling for, 482; peer management of, 480-481; in preschool, 478-479, 480-482. See also Shyness and withdrawal

Special education students: and boisterous behavior, 59; and cursing, 43-44; and poor coordination, 209-213; and truancy, 37

Speech disorders, therapies for, 383-395

State-Trait Anxiety Inventory for Children, 233

Stealing: described, 12; and family system, 22-23; group contingencies for, 13-14, 17-18; overcorrection for, 19-20

Story Completion Test, 173

Story-Interpretation Test, 182

Strategies, choosing among, 10-11

Structuring, for procrastination and dawdling, 207

Stuttering: confrontation for, 392; described, 383; in elementary school, 384-386, 395; Gestalt approach to, 393; group program for, 393-394; modification of, 394-395; in preschool, 389-390; reinforcement for, 384-386; relaxation for, 394; in secondary school, 392-394; time-out for, 389-390, 392-393, 394

Substance abuse: of alcohol, 406-407; described, 396; of drugs, 397-402, 407; in elementary school, 397-399, 406-407; extent of, 396; peer counseling for, 397-399; relationship or reinforcement counseling for, 399-400; relaxation training for, 401-402; in secondary school, 396, 399-406, 407; systematic desensitization for, 401-402; of tobacco, 403-406; values clarification for, 397-399, 404, 407

Suinn Test Anxiety Behavior Scale, 237

Syracuse University, 420

T

Teacher relationships, disturbed: disrespect and defiance as, 485-499; inhibition as, 500-504; overdependency as, 505-508; therapies for, 483-508. See also Classroom management problems

Teachers, training of: and academic performance, poor, 350; and annoying others, 95; and bereavement, 314-315; and boisterous behavior, 58; as change agents, 2-4; and depression, 314-315; and inhibition, 501-502; and overdependence, 506-507; and poor self-esteem, 297-299; and shyness and withdrawal, 474, 476; tempo of, 103, 186

Teams-Games-Tournaments (TGT): and academic performance, poor, 349; and prejudice, 453-455, 457

Temper tantrums: described, 80; in elementary school, 81-86; group and individual contingencies for, 85; and reinforcement, 83-84; and relaxation training, 86; reward, punishment, and loss of attention for, 81-82; and turtle technique, 85-86

Tension. See Anxiety and tension

Test anxiety, 237-239, 241-243, 251-252, 253, 254, 270

Test Anxiety Scale for Children, 242

Thumb-sucking: described, 372; in elementary school, 373-376, 381-382; extent of, 372; group

contingency for, 375-376; operant conditioning for, 381-382;
reinforcement for, 373-375
Time-out: for aggression, 438,
439-441, 447; for crying,
222-224; for cursing, 44-46, 47;
for distractible and inattentive
behavior, 145-147; for noncompliance, 66-67; for stuttering,
389-390, 392-393, 394
Trail-Making Test, 180
Transactional Analysis, for disrespect and defiance, 493-495
Truancy: and classroom processes,
37-38; and community support,
32-34, 35-36; contingency contracting for, 25-27, 35-36, 37;
described, 24; from elementary
school, 28-32, 34-35, 37-38; and
group counseling, 37; home
contacts and, 28-29; multidisciplinary approach to, 34-35;
and reinforcement, 29-32; from
secondary school, 25-27, 32-34,
35-37, 38; and self-management, 38; and social climate,
36-37
Turtle technique: for aggression,
446; for temper tantrums, 85-
86

U

Underachiever. *See* Academic performance, poor

V

Values clarification: for sexual behavior, 414-415; for substance
abuse, 397-399, 404, 407
Vandalism, destructive behavior distinct from, 107
Venereal disease prevention: in elementary school, 414-415; programs for, 414-415; in secondary
school, 414-415

W

Walker School, 116-117
Wepman Auditory Discrimination
Test, 235
Wide-Range Achievement Test, 173
Withdrawal, medication for, 185.
See also Shyness and withdrawal

Y

Yoga, for anxiety and tension,
246-248